D0733929

TimeOut

Copenhagen

timeout.com/copenhagen

Published by Time Out Guides Ltd, a wholly owned subsidiary of Time Out Group Ltd.
Time Out and the Time Out logo are trademarks of Time Out Group Ltd.

© Time Out Group Ltd 2007
Previous editions 2001, 2003, 2005

10 9 8 7 6 5 4 3 2 1

This edition first published in Great Britain in 2007 by Ebury Publishing
Ebury Publishing is a division of The Random House Group Ltd,
20 Vauxhall Bridge Road, London SW1V 2SA

Random House Australia Pty Limited 20 Alfred Street, Milsons Point, Sydney, New South Wales 2061, Australia
Random House New Zealand Limited 18 Poland Road, Glenfield, Auckland 10, New Zealand
Random House South Africa (Pty) Limited Isle of Houghton, Corner Boundary
Road & Carse O'Gowrie, Houghton 2198, South Africa

Random House UK Limited Reg. No. 954009

Distributed in USA by Publishers Group West
1700 Fourth Street, Berkeley, California 94710

Distributed in Canada by Publishers Group Canada
250A Carlton Street, Toronto, Ontario M5A 2L1

For further distribution details, see www.timeout.com

ISBN 1-84670-002-7
ISBN 9781846700026

A CIP catalogue record for this book is available from the British Library

Colour reprographics by Wyndeham Icon, 3 & 4 Maverton Road, London E3 2JE

Printed and bound in Germany by Appl

Papers used by Ebury Publishing are natural, recyclable products made from wood grown in sustainable forests

Time Out Guides Limited
Universal House
251 Tottenham Court Road
London W1T 7AB
Tel + 44 (0)20 7813 3000
Fax + 44 (0)20 7813 6001
Email guides@timeout.com
www.timeout.com

Contributors

Introduction Dominic Earle. **History** Michael Booth. **Copenhagen Today** Michael Booth. **Architecture** Michael Booth.
Made in Denmark Michael Booth. **Where to Stay** Thomas Dalvang-Fleurquin, Jane Graham. **Sightseeing** Nikolaj Steen-Møller
(*My Copenhagen: Tim Rushton* Thomas Dalvang-Fleurquin). **Restaurants** Michael Booth. **Cafés & Bars** Michael Booth.
Shops & Services Julia Tierney. **Festivals & Events** Michael Booth. **Children** Michael Booth. **Film** Trudy Follwell, Diego Vega
(*My Copenhagen: Thomas Vinterberg* Thomas Dalvang-Fleurquin). **Galleries** Sebastian Schiorring (*My Copenhagen: Marco
Evaristti* Thomas Dalvang-Fleurquin). **Gay & Lesbian** Daniel Ayala. **Nightlife** Trudy Follwell, Thomas Dalvang-Fleurquin.
Performing Arts Trudy Follwell, Jane Graham (*My Copenhagen: Vivienne McKee* Thomas Dalvang-Fleurquin). **Sport & Fitness**
Nikolaj Steen-Møller. **Trips Out of Town** Michael Booth. **Directory** Cecilie Hahn-Petersen.

Maps john@jsgraphics.co.uk.
Map on p256 courtesy of DSB (www.dsb.dk).

Photography Héloïse Bergman, except: page 12 Bettmann/Corbis; page 15 akg-images; page 17 Getty Images;
pages 18, 21 Ted Fahn/Visit Denmark; page 19 AFP/Getty Images; page 26 Cees Van Roeden/Wonderful Copenhagen;
page 35 Bang & Olufsen; page 82 TopFoto.co.uk; page 207 Image Bank Sweden; page 210 Corbis; page 216 Dorte
Krogh/Visit Denmark; page 218 Klaus Bentzen/Visit Denmark; page 220 Christian Alsing/Wonderful Copenhagen.

The following image was provided by the featured establishment/artist: page 165.

The Editor would like to thank Scandinavian Airlines, the Square Hotel and all contributors to previous editions of
Time Out Copenhagen, whose work forms the basis for parts of this book.

Contents

Introduction

New York has the Empire State Building, Paris has the Eiffel Tower, London has Big Ben and Copenhagen has... um... well... ah, yes, the Little Mermaid. As city symbols go, this diminutive bronze fish perched on the windswept harbour front is a fairly reluctant stab at self-promotion. But then again, big has never been regarded as particularly beautiful in Copenhagen, a city where the tallest building is a restrained 106 metres (358 feet) off the ground. This is a community where modesty rules.

This modesty is born of self-assurance. In a recent survey, Denmark was ranked as the happiest country in the world, while the UK came 41st, and arriving in Copenhagen provides ample evidence to support the star rating. From the moment you step off the plane at Kastrup Airport and hop on the train for the 12-minute journey (FYI, Heathrow Express: £2.50 one-way) direct to the gates of the irrepressibly cute Tivoli pleasure park in the centre of town, you realise this is how cities should work. And once you've dropped your bags off at one of the burgeoning range of design-led hotels that now dot the city, you can enjoy life in one of Europe's most easy-going, hassle-free capitals. The shopping is superb, the restaurants are the best in Scandinavia, and the atmosphere is supremely cosy – or *hygge* as the Danes call it.

There are limitations, of course: traditional 'sights' are suited more to a leisurely long weekend than a week's intensive; and

Copenhagen currently ranks as the third most expensive city in Europe (don't worry, though, London is the most expensive). But somehow sipping a £5 pint in the sunshine on the waterfront at Nyhavn seems an entirely worthwhile proposition – and if you can afford to stay in Scandinavia a bit longer, then Malmö, one of Sweden's most vibrant cities, is just half an hour away across the impressive but underused 16-kilometre (ten-mile) Øresund Bridge that links Denmark with neighbouring Sweden.

Copenhagen is a compact place and all the sights are within half an hour's walk of the main pedestrian artery, Strøget. One of the things you'll notice as you wander around the charming centre, apart from the fact that everyone is extraordinarily good-looking (as Bill Bryson once commented, you could cast a Pepsi commercial here in 15 seconds), is that design is everywhere, from Bodum's five-floor flagship to the raft of stylish new buildings going up on the waterfront. And now even design king Sir Terence Conran is getting in on the action in a city he calls the 'Barcelona of the North'.

The twin town parallels might appear a little fuzzy on a dark, freezing cold day in January, but visit on a sunny June weekend and the combination of café culture, gorgeous palaces, striking modern buildings, waterfront living and designer boutiques gives the whole place a feeling of contentedness to rival any city on the Med.

ABOUT TIME OUT CITY GUIDES

This is the fourth edition of *Time Out Copenhagen*, one of an expanding series of Time Out guides produced by the people behind the successful listings magazines in London, New York and Chicago. Our guides are all written by resident experts who have striven to provide you with all the most up-to-date information you'll need to explore the city or read up on its background, whether you're a local or a first-time visitor.

THE LIE OF THE LAND

Copenhagen is an easy city to negotiate and most places listed in this guide are within half an hour's walk of Strøget, the city's main artery and the longest pedestrianised shopping street in Europe. To make the city even easier

to navigate, we've divided Copenhagen into areas and assigned each one its own chapter in our Sightseeing section. Some of these (such as Slotsholmen and Christianshavn) coincide with existing districts; others (such as Rosenborg & Around and Tivoli & Rådhuspladsen) are based on the area surrounding a key sight.

ESSENTIAL INFORMATION

For all the practical information you might need for visiting the area – including visa and customs information, details of local transport, a listing of emergency numbers, information on local weather and a selection of useful websites and books relating to the city – turn to the Directory at the back of this guide. It begins on page 222.

THE LOWDOWN ON THE LISTINGS

We have tried to make this book as easy to use as possible. Addresses, phone numbers, bus information, opening times and admission prices are all included in the listings. However, businesses can change their arrangements at any time. Before you go out of your way, we'd strongly advise you to phone ahead to check opening times and other particulars. While every effort and care has been made to ensure the accuracy of the information contained in this guide, the publishers cannot accept responsibility for any errors it may contain.

PRICES AND PAYMENT

We have noted where venues such as shops, hotels, restaurants and theatres accept the following credit cards: American Express (AmEx), Diners Club (DC), MasterCard (MC) and Visa (V).

The prices we've listed in this guide should be treated as guidelines, not gospel. If prices vary wildly from those we've quoted, ask whether there's a good reason. If not, go elsewhere. Then please let us know. We aim to give the best and most up-to-date advice, so we want to know if you've been badly treated or overcharged.

TELEPHONE NUMBERS

All telephone numbers in Copenhagen have eight digits. There are no area codes in the country. The international dialling code for Denmark is 45. For more on telephones and codes, *see p232*.

MAPS

The map section at the back of this book includes an overview map of the city, detailed street maps and a transport map showing all the local rail and Metro routes. The maps start on page 244, and now pinpoint the specific locations of hotels (❶), restaurants (❶), and cafés and bars (❶). There is also a Trips Out of Town map on page 206, and a street map of Malmö on page 209.

LET US KNOW WHAT YOU THINK

We hope you enjoy the *Time Out Copenhagen Guide*, and we'd like to know what you think of it. We welcome tips for places that you consider we should include in future editions and take note of your criticism of our choices. You can email us at guides@timeout.com.

There is an online version of this book, along with guides to over 100 international cities, at **www.timeout.com**.

Pedal power: a classic Christiania bike.

In Context

Features

Rosenborg Slot. *See p90*.

History

Copenhagen has come a long way in the last millennium, from humble fishing village to 'Barcelona of the north'.

Copenhagen has not always been the capital of Denmark. In fact, it didn't take over as the royal seat until the early 15th century and, up until that point, was a comparatively humble fishing village and defensive post from which the country tried to protect itself against marauding pirates and Swedes. However, it grew in strength throughout the Middle Ages to become one of the wealthiest cities in northern Europe, a political powerhouse and cultural centre of great importance. At the peak of its glory, Copenhagen was ruled by one of the most fascinating and reckless of Renaissance kings whose ambition and follies would eventually bring the country to its knees.

Evidence of human life in Denmark exists from 80,000 years ago in the form of discarded animal bones. But while the rest of Denmark busied itself with reindeer hunting, flint mining, the Bronze Age, the Viking Age, and the repelling of Charlemagne's advances on the southern border of Jylland (cAD 800), Havn (Harbour), as Copenhagen was known, was little more than an insignificant trading centre for the copious quantities of herring that inhabited the Øresund. It was said that this pungent, oily fish (still a staple of the Danish diet) was so common in these waters, which connect the Baltic with the North Sea, that fishermen could scoop them up into their boats with their bare hands.

THE FIRST DANISH STATE

The Vikings, who swept across northern Europe from southern Sweden around 800, established the first Danish state and rapidly augmented it with three of the four Anglo-Saxon kingdoms, as well as Norway.

The Vikings (meaning 'sea robbers') even took Seville in 844 and stormed Paris in the 880s. The subsequent retaking by the nascent Danes of Skåne (or Scania, now southern Sweden, directly opposite Copenhagen) was to be the catalyst for the voracious expansion of Copenhagen 300 years hence, but at the time the villagers probably remained oblivious to their strategic potential. It is likely too that they remained unruffled by the conversion of the unifying Viking king Harald I Bluetooth (and eventually the entire country) to Christianity by a German missionary named Poppo around 965, and played no part in the growing fad for regicide. Harald was mysteriously killed while relieving himself in the woods in 987, and many of his successors over the next 170 years met with similarly murky fates, so that by 1157 Valdemar I the Great was the only royal left standing.

GROWING PAINS

The gold mine of Denmark's medieval history (despite its preponderance of myth and legend) is the late 12th-century chronicle of Saxo Grammaticus, *Gesta Danorum* (Deeds of the Danes), in which, incidentally, the Hamlet legend arises. Grammaticus refers to Havn as *Mercatorum Portus*, meaning 'the Traders' Port' ('København' in Danish), and the name stuck.

Over the next century numerous churches blossomed on what was still an unappealing, boggy piece of coast, among them Vor Frue Kirke (later the site of Copenhagen's current cathedral), and Sankt Petri Kirke (also still a site of worship). In 1238 an abbey of Franciscan Grey Friars was founded; its church (Helligåndskirken) still sits on Strøget, modern-day Copenhagen's main shopping street.

In the late 12th and early 13th centuries King Valdemar and his sons Knud (Canute) VI and Valdemar II the Victorious reigned over a triumphant and expansionist Denmark, which not only conquered the Baltic Wends, but devoured Estonia and Holstein, and lorded it over Lübeck. This ended ignominiously with the loss of these Baltic territories in 1227.

'Under Christian IV, Copenhagen became a glittering jewel of the Renaissance.'

In 1250 a bout of regicide saw off Erik IV Ploughpenny who, in a biblical reversal, was killed by his brother Abel. Christoffer I fell foul of the classic poisoned chalice ruse in 1259; while the murder of Erik V Klipping when hunting in 1286 is unexplained to this day.

The second spurt of Copenhagen's growth occurred when Erik VII seized control of the town from the Church in 1417. Not only was the king now in charge, but he had become so fond of Copenhagen that he made it his home. This historic move ended the peripatetic tradition of Denmark's monarchy that had previously functioned on the basis that wherever it laid its crown was its home.

In 1438 the disaffected Swedes withdrew from the Kalmar Union, prompting the Danish nobility to depose the king. Bizarrely, Erik VII lived out the rest of his life with his mistress as a (by all accounts successful) pirate on the Baltic island of Gotland. In 1448 a distant relative, Christian I, the first of the Oldenburg dynasty, was crowned King of Denmark, Sweden and Norway in the first royal coronation to be held in Copenhagen. Inevitably, the city now became the economic, political and cultural focus for the nation.

By 1500 the town revelled in riches as its guilds dominated those of the Hanseatic League (whose influence was slowly waning), while the king too grew wealthy from the new tolls demanded of all who sailed from the North Sea through the narrow strait between Helsingør and southern Sweden on their way to the Baltic. There was no doubt that this was now Denmark's capital, and its leading citizens ruled via the Rigsråd (National Assembly), made up of clergy, prominent estate owners and the king.

A more apt seat of power the Machiavellian Christian II could not have hoped to inherit. Though politically astute enough to marry a sister of Holy Roman Emperor Charles V, Christian had a tendency to recklessness that saw him keep his Dutch mistress, Dyveke, close at hand in a house around the corner from the palace. She died suddenly in 1517 and, believing her to have been poisoned by the governor of Copenhagen Castle, Christian vented his grief on his courtiers with an indiscriminate purge. This merely enhanced his reputation as a schemer not to be crossed. He was later reported to have said, 'If the hat on my head knew what I was thinking, I would pull it off and throw it away'.

This did little for Christian's reputation abroad or at home, where his stringent taxation added to his unpopularity, eventually forcing him to flee Denmark for poverty in Holland. He was replaced, in 1522, by his uncle, who reigned as Frederik I. On his uppers, Christian took up an offer from allies in Norway to assume their country's crown but as he attempted to lay siege to Oslo he was captured by the Danish fleet. Meanwhile the ever awkward Copenhagen remained loyal to the old king, prompting Frederik to lay siege to the town for a month, with eventual success.

CIVIL WAR AND REFORMATION

The birth of the 16th century was a tense, troubled time throughout Europe as the Catholic Church's increasingly poor public relations began to turn large sections of the continent against it. Out of this discontent in 1517, in the German town of Wittenberg, the

Lutheran Church emerged. Martin Luther's church door antics were to have an almost immediate domino effect on Denmark.

During Frederik's rule, several popular uprisings – with Copenhagen as a particular hotbed – had unsuccessfully tried to unseat the monarch and replace him with the exiled, pro-Lutheran Christian II. But when Christian finally returned as a prisoner to a Denmark now ruled entirely by Frederik I in 1532, it was to spend the rest of his life imprisoned in Sønderborg Castle. Christian may have had the last, hollow laugh, however, as he outlived his next two successors.

Upon Frederik's death in 1533 the Catholic prelates intervened to postpone the accession of his son Christian III, whose Lutheran tendencies they were having none of. Unforeseen by the prelates, the Danish people were as keen on reformation (and the consequent redistribution of clerical property) as the rest of northern Europe and they wanted Christian II back. His supporters in Copenhagen, both peasants and more prosperous townspeople, continued their belligerent stance by seizing control of the town. The mercantile character of Copenhagen and its people had determined that they'd rather take their chances by joining the Hanseatic League, and the mayor of Lübeck, always happy to help stir up trouble in Copenhagen.

The involvement of the Lübeckers was to provoke one of the most damaging tiffs in Copenhagen's history: the Grevens Fejde (Counts' Feud) of 1534-6, Denmark's last civil war. The Germans' meddling and the accompanying peasant revolt so concerned the bishops that they finally relented and allowed Christian III to take the throne and suppress Copenhagen. He was crowned in Vor Frue Kirke in 1534. His coronation charter did, however, include the handing over of ultimate power to the aristocracy of the Rigsråd from the Crown.

As things turned out, the bishops were to lose power anyway as, in order to pay his own German mercenaries (without whom he would never have retaken Copenhagen), Christian III was forced to liquidate many of the Church's assets. As the final stroke of a brilliant coup that heralded the Danish Reformation of 1536, Christian III imprisoned the bishops.

In a display of the consensual diplomacy that still typifies Denmark's political machinations, Christian III offered the bishops the 'get-out' of conversion to Lutheranism, with the added sweetener that under the new doctrine they could marry and have children. Nearly all accepted, with two consequences: most of Denmark's priests remained with their flocks; and those flocks increased substantially.

(In fact, in several churches from that era you can find epitaphs to wives who died young, often during childbirth, attesting to the priests' newfound reproductive zeal.)

Lutheranism was now the official state religion of Denmark; Copenhagen celebrated with extravagant festivities. The nobility benefited hugely from the transfer of money from the Church into their all-too-eager hands, not to mention exemption from taxes. Across Denmark, and especially in Copenhagen, this wealth was made manifest in the grandest Renaissance mansions. In fact, most of Danish society basked in a period of unprecedented economic prosperity.

THE SUN KING

Into this brave new world of wealth, expansion and optimism was born one of the great figures of Danish history. To this day, he is a man with whom Danes enjoy a paradoxical relationship that blends scorn with admiration, gratitude and sympathy. Copenhagen was to be his grandest epitaph, and into its modern-day skyline is still written his vision, bravura and conceit. Denmark's 'Sun King', Christian IV (photo p15) was a man possessed of heroic appetites, who never let the tedious demands of reality get in the way of a heroic scheme. He ruled for 60 years, and is probably Denmark's best-remembered monarch. It is hard to know where to begin in detailing the transformation that Copenhagen underwent during Christian IV's reign. You could equate it to London under Elizabeth I, or the arrival of the Mafia in Vegas.

'After being defeated by the Swedes in 1645, Denmark ceded large areas of land.'

The city grew in all directions (literally, thanks to reclaimed land) in the grandest of styles, with new buildings; a remodelling of its coastal access; improved defences and housing; the construction of entire new districts, bridges, churches, palaces, towers, observatories and theatres; and all the glittering hallmarks of the Renaissance. Upon his death, however, Copenhagen and Denmark would be a spent force, bankrupt, defeated, humiliated and seemingly doomed to an existence of debt and suppression by its enemies.

Christian IV was a complex, highly educated man with widespread interests in music, architecture and foreign affairs. He married Anna Catherine of Brandenburg; after she died in 1612 he went on to father 24 children, half of them out of wedlock by a variety of mistresses.

Christian IV. *See p14.*

In 1617 Christian married one of them, Kirsten Munk, morganatically (she was considered to be far below him socially so had no right to his possessions or title). Much to the king's fury she gave birth to a child that clearly wasn't his (he'd been away at war when the child was conceived) and she was banished in 1630. Christian, in his misery, turned to her chambermaid for comfort. (This episode in Christian's life is enjoyably romanticised in Rose Tremain's 2000 Whitbread Prize-nominated novel *Music and Silence*.)

The problem was that the many ambitious construction projects undertaken during his rule, not to mention Christian's longstanding, simmering rivalry with his close contemporary King Gustavus Adolphus of Sweden during the Thirty Years War (1618-48), were becoming a constant burden on the country's finances. When Christian came to the throne Copenhagen had little industry to speak of, and most of his subjects made their living through agriculture. But, though he tried his best to establish industry in the capital, its wheeler-dealer trading heritage always somehow seemed to undermine the fruitful work ethic that had developed. Copenhagen's products could never match the quality of those made by the best European craftsmen, which was a source of constant frustration and embarrassment to the king.

Christian's first priority was to cement Copenhagen's position as the major harbour of the region and, with this in mind, the channel between Sjælland and the small nearby island of Slotsholmen was straightened, narrowed and reinforced with wharfs. Slotsholmen was extended and, as the century closed, a new armoury (Tøjhuset) and a new supply depot (Provianthuset) were constructed to maintain the fighting readiness of the navy. These buildings still stand and several of the huge iron mooring rings where the king's fleet was tethered can also still be seen on the walls of the old Royal Library's garden.

Further symbols of Christian's reign are found in the much expanded palaces, prime among them the richly decorated Rosenborg Slot (Rosenborg Castle; home today to the crown jewels). But the most extraordinary of his creations is the Rundetårn (Round Tower), an ambitious observatory graced by a radical, stepless spiral ramp, completed in 1642. This Renaissance beacon is another of the period's architectural treasures that have survived to enrich the Copenhagen skyline.

Another new district, Nyboder ('Navy Booths'; next to Kastellet, on the north side of the centre), grew up to house Christian's naval personnel. The sailors were billeted in very low, single-storey, ochre-painted terraced cottages.

Copenhagen-based international trading companies attempted to establish colonies in Africa and Asia, but they were as fleas on the shoulders of comparable Dutch and British enterprises. Instead, to try and raise money, Christian attempted to turn Copenhagen into the financial capital of Europe by ordering the construction of Børsen (Stock Exchange – still standing, but not open to the public), but despite the building's unquestionable architectural and decorative splendour (this wedding cake of an edifice can hold its own against any of the more startling modernist works of the city today, the highlight being a fabulous spire of four intertwined dragon tails) that too was a damp squib. Increasingly desperate for cash, Christian made a fateful attempt to establish a silver mining venture in Norway, and failed.

In 1523 Gustavus I of Sweden finally dissolved the Kalmar Union (though the union of Denmark and Norway lasted until 1814). During Christian's reign the increeasing strength and confidence of Denmark's northerly neighbour were to threaten the very existence of the Danish state. At stake was control of access to the Baltic, which usually meant control of the region itself. In 1611, in a bid to protect his vital income from the Sound tolls (extorted at Helsingør Castle, the model for Shakespeare's Elsinore, north of Copenhagen), and to restore

The great escape

The Danes don't have an awful lot to be proud of regarding their involvement in World War II – at least not the first half of it – so they tend to cling to a few noble incidents from that dark period of occupation. Of them all, the most cherished incident of Danish heroism in the face of the Nazis was the mass covert evacuation of almost the entire Jewish population of Denmark, in October 1943.

At the time there were around 8,000 Jews living in Denmark. As with elsewhere in northern Europe, the Danish Jewish community had been well established and integrated into Danish society for centuries. For the first half of the war Danish Jews were allowed to live relatively unbothered by the attentions of the Gestapo as Denmark, essentially, continued to govern itself as a German 'protectorate'. But as Germany's fortunes changed elsewhere in Europe, and Denmark at last began to oppose the occupiers with national strikes and an emerging underground resistance movement, Berlin soon began to impose its will and direct rule followed.

In September 1943, to curry favour with Berlin, the German plenipotentiary in Denmark, Werner Best, sent out a telegram asking what was to be done with Denmark's Jews – though he later claimed to have regretted this and tried to stop the telegram. The news was leaked to the Danish resistance who in turn told the leaders of the Jewish community. The vast majority of Denmark's Jews (most of them Copenhagen residents) immediately went into hiding; only around 450 were arrested on 1 October (mainly the elderly who didn't want to leave their homes – they were sent to a concentration camp in what is now the Czech Republic), by a special unit that was brought in from Norway.

In some cases the refugees hid for weeks in the homes of friends until slowly, under the cover of darkness and in all manner of craft, nearly 7,000 of them, the majority of the Jewish population, were spirited away across the Sound to Sweden – and safety – by their fellow Danes. They travelled in everything from large fishing boats to kayaks and, though several perished during the ten-mile journey from Denmark to Sweden, most made it.

Probably the two best-known Danes of Jewish extraction had already left Denmark, though. Borge Rosenbaum left in 1940 to forge a career in comedy as Victor Borge, famously returning in secret a few months later to visit his dying mother. 'Mama, I'm going to Hollywood to get into the movies, and when I do, I'll send for you, and we'll live in California in a big house with a swimming pool,' he said. 'Borge, don't let it go to your head,' she replied. Meanwhile atomic physicist Niels Bohr, who left just a month before the mass evacuation, would later play a significant role in the ending of the war; his work was crucial to the development of the atomic bomb.

the Kalmar Union, Christian declared war on Sweden. The Kalmar War raged, with Denmark generally dominant, until 1613, when a peace accord brokered by the British concluded with a large ransom being paid by the Swedes to Denmark.

Danish triumphalism was short-lived, however, as Christian and his forces soon became embroiled in the Thirty Years War, in an effort to protect Danish interests on the north coast of Germany from Swedish expansion. The Danes' involvement in the war ended with a devastating defeat by the Swedes at the Battle of Lutter-am-Barenburg in 1626. The Danes got off more lightly than they deserved in the final peace settlement at Lübeck in 1629, in which Christian had to promise to take no further part in the war.

Christian's reign was to be marked by a third fateful conflict, Torstensson's War (1643-5), named after the Swedish general Lennart Torstensson, who marched on Jylland after Christian had raised the Sound tolls to try to recover the costs of past military failures. It was during this war, while in the thick of the action on his flagship Trefoldigheden during the Battle of Kolberger Heide in July 1644, that the 67-year-old Christian lost his right eye and received 23 shrapnel wounds (his blood-stained clothes are displayed in Rosenborg Slot). A much heftier defeat by united Dutch and Swedish forces in October ended the war and a peace treaty, signed in 1645, saw Denmark cede large areas of territory (chiefly, central parts of Norway, Halland and the islands of Gotland and Osel) to Sweden, and waive future Sound tolls. This was a dramatic and humiliating moment in Danish history, for which you sometimes suspect the Danes have yet to forgive their northern neighbours. Thirty years followed in which Denmark barely survived as an independent state.

'In 1711, Copenhagen was ravaged by a plague in which 23,000 people died.'

Christian didn't live to see his nation's darkest moment, however. He'd already been dead ten years when his successor Frederik III, Prince Bishop of Bremen (who'd taken the throne after his elder brother drank himself to death, doubtless at the prospect of having to inherit such a shambles), started another Swedish-Danish war in 1658. The Swedes then forced the Danes to accept the humiliating Treaty of Roskilde by which Denmark ceded Scania (the southern tip of Sweden). Not content, Karl Gustav decided he wanted to take the whole of Denmark and besieged Copenhagen in the winter of 1658-9. He led his German troops (camouflaged in white hooded cloaks) across the frozen sea surrounding Slotsholmen but, in a last gasp of defiance, Frederik himself is said to have led the fight against Karl Gustav's army. As the enemy propped their ladders against the castle walls, all able-bodied citizens of Copenhagen assembled above them to rain down anything that wasn't nailed to the ground. This spirited defence with cannon shot, bullets, pistols, logs and boiling tar and water to melt the ice, gave time for a Dutch army to arrive and save the capital (not to mention Holland's interests in a free-access Baltic).

The fortuitous sudden death of Karl Gustav at the start of 1660 ended Sweden's ambitions to conquer Denmark, but the price of Denmark's salvation was steep, and Frederik was forced to capitulate control of the Sound (and its tolls), as well as all of Denmark's provinces to the east (though the island of Bornholm pluckily fought back to Danish rule). Two attempts to win back southern Sweden in 1675 and 1709 resulted in no permanent gains for the Danes, despite several victories in battle. Europe would never again allow Denmark, now a third of its former size, to hold power in the region.

PEACE WITH SWEDEN
The support given by the people of Copenhagen to the king left him with little choice but to concede more trading and tax advantages to the town. But, in an impressive and bloodless coup against the still powerful nobility, Frederik made himself 'king by God's grace'; in other words, the

absolute monarch. The new regime was formalised in the 1665 Kongeloven (Royal Act). Though this document conferred total power over all of Denmark upon the king, making him and his male heirs the highest authority on earth and above all laws, no one was allowed to see it for 50 years and no copies were made.

Once again Copenhagen picked itself up to rebuild and refortify, with the construction of a new rampart to protect Slotsholmen. Out of this came the new quarter of Frederiksholm, which sprang up on reclaimed land between the Frederiksholm Canal and modern-day Vester Volgade. The impressive Kongens Nytorv square was laid out in 1670 and was soon surrounded with imposing baroque houses and abutted by Nyhavn Canal – today one of the city's major tourist draws. An improved water supply, a company of watchmen and new street lighting complemented a fast-growing, modern capital whose population had doubled within 100 years to 60,000 by the early 18th century. Many would have gained employment in the forerunner of the civil service, established by Frederik to run the foreign service, the military and commercial affairs.

The next few decades saw a limited return to prosperity and a restrengthening of the navy, which was all the encouragement several successive, though largely ineffective, Danish kings needed to try to recapture their lost empire. Frederik III's son Christian V was

Hans Christian Andersen. *See p19.*

Queen Margrethe II. *See p23.*

the first to attempt to avenge defeat by their neighbours in the Skåne Conquest (in the south of Sweden, 1675-9). He gained little from the war other than the restoration of national pride, as the rest of Europe preferred that no one country dominate access to the Baltic.

A final, conclusive peace treaty with Sweden, signed in 1720, at last gave everyone breathing space to concentrate on domestic affairs, while the following pan-European boom increased demand for agricultural produce, which Denmark was happy to meet.

FIRE AND RENEWAL

In 1711, during the reign of Christian's successor, Frederik IV, Copenhagen was ravaged by a plague in which 23,000 people died. It was also razed to the ground by fire twice during the century (in 1728 and 1795). The first fire broke out in a candle-maker's in Nørreport, and strong winds, negligible water supplies and general chaos ensured it travelled swiftly across town, destroying 1,700 houses, the town hall and the university, and leaving 12,000 people homeless. The situation was made worse by the fact that the firemen happened to be drunk that night (they had spent the money they'd earned for fire drills on booze) and that a local brewer, in a rush to help, left a lamp burning in his stable, igniting another, separate blaze. Similar slapstickery

helped the 1795 fire along when firemen couldn't find the keys to the pump house beside Sankt Nicolaj Kirke, and its burning spire collapsed into the surrounding neighbourhood.

Happily, the building of the new five- and six-storey townhouses, taller than any before them, and the grand public buildings that replaced the combustible wooden, low-rise constructions of the 17th century, were strictly monitored by the building codes of the time, with the result that the capital was reborn more splendidly than ever before. The castle too was completely demolished (even though Frederik IV had had it rebuilt at great expense a few years earlier) and vast amounts of money were spent replacing it with the baroque Christiansborg Slot, only for the second fire to return it to the ground.

To celebrate the 300th anniversary of the House of Oldenburg, headed since 1746 by Frederik V, work began in 1749 on a grand new quarter, Frederiksstaden. It was designed by the architect Nicolai Eigtved with wide, straight streets fronted by elegant, light rococo palaces. At the heart of the new area was Amalienborg Plads, circled by four palaces that were financed by the noblemen of the town. When another fire at Christiansborg levelled a large part of the palace, the royal family found themselves homeless. They commandeered the four Amalienborg palaces, employing CF Harsdorff to connect them with an elegant colonnade, and have lived there ever since.

The second, larger fire of the century broke out on Gammelholm in 1795 and was even more destructive than the first, but again this only gave the city's architects and builders a chance to keep up with the fashion for the neo-classical. For the very highest echelons of Danish society in the Age of Prosperity nothing less than columns would do, and if you go to No.14 Ved Stranden or the headquarters of Handelsbanksen on Kongens Nytorv (built as the private home for leading ship owner Erikh Erikhsen), you can see for yourself the excesses of the age. The fire also destroyed buildings in the centre of town, making Nytorv and Gammeltorv into one large square.

In 1771 Kongens Have (King's Gardens) opened. This new attraction was a huge success with the flourishing bourgeoisie, whose voracious appetite for the pursuit of nature was a symptom of the new Age of Enlightenment. One of those less likely to participate fully in the educational revolution was the new king, Christian VII (1766-1808), who managed to rule for 42 years despite frequent and prolonged bouts of insanity.

In 1784 the 16-year-old crown prince Frederik (later Frederik VI) took power and acted as regent until his father's death in 1808. By 1801 he probably wished he hadn't, as the first of two terrible bombardments by the British navy took place; Denmark, against its better nature, soon became drawn into the Napoleonic Wars and painful losses of territory and power.

During the 18th century Denmark's neutrality proved increasingly irksome to the British, particularly as the Danish merchant fleet was an enthusiastic supplier to the enemies of Britain. To protect itself from increased interference by the Royal Navy, the Danes entered into an armed neutrality pact with Russia and the old foe Sweden.

'The Danes sided with Napoleon, not Britain.'

As a result, in April 1801, a British fleet under Admirals Nelson and Parker sailed into the Øresund and commenced bombardment of the Danish navy. The Danes only survived thanks to a change in the direction of the wind, which left some of the English fleet at risk of being driven ashore. Nelson was instructed by his commanders to withdraw but, though he had been impressed by the Danes' courage, he merely put his telescope up to his blind eye and ignored them. Instead, he sent an envoy to threaten King Frederik with the destruction of his entire fleet, including the burning alive of its crews, unless he surrendered and withdrew from the pact. This Frederik did, but not before the clash had cost the Danes 1,000 men.

However, Denmark continued to profit from the trade that had so angered the British, and anti-British fervour swept Copenhagen. That anger would be fuelled six years later when the British, under the Duke of Wellington, returned with a show of force that made the 1801 battle seem a mere fireworks display. Napoleon was on the move across Europe and, with his fleet already destroyed by Nelson at Trafalgar, there were strong rumours in 1807 that the French were about to commandeer the Danish navy as a replacement. In fact, Frederik was preparing to defend his country from attack by the French in the south when he was visited by a British envoy who offered him this ultimatum: surrender the Danish fleet to Britain, or the Royal Navy will come and take it. The Danes refused and so the British sailed again on still neutral Copenhagen and bombarded it for three days.

Understandably, the Danes now baulked at an alliance with the British, siding instead with Napoleon. This was a decision they were to rue in the painful years hence when the British blockaded Denmark and Norway. Much of

Norway starved, while Denmark fared little better, enduring great hardship until the defeat of Napoleon. The Treaty of Kiel (1814) saw Sweden (now in alliance with Britain) take control of Norway, which had been for 450 years as much a part of Denmark as Sjælland. The loss of the consistently problematic duchies of Schleswig and Holstein to Germany in 1864, following a brief attack by Otto von Bismarck, would further diminish a Danish empire that had once dominated the Baltic.

A period of introspection, from which many say Denmark has never really emerged, followed, typified by the slogan: 'We will gain internally what was lost externally.' In fact, despite a nationwide drive to grow new oak trees with which to rebuild the navy (many of which still flourish in the countryside), Denmark would not officially go to war again until its troops took part in a UN peacekeeping exercise in Bosnia in April 1994.

DANISH IDENTITY TO THE FORE

Fortunately, this was to be a period of cultural growth for a country struggling to come to terms with a new identity based on little more than a shared language and religion. With all hope of playing a role on the international stage gone, and with little financial power to wield either (Denmark as a state was declared bankrupt in 1813 and sold its colonies in Africa and India), the country instead began to extend itself in the arts and sciences. The storyteller Hans Christian Andersen (born in Odense, but

PM Anders Fogh Rasmussen. *See p23.*

a longtime Copenhagener; **photo** *p17*),
existentialist Søren Kierkegaard (the archetypal
Copenhagener) and the theologian Nikolai
Frederik Severin Grundtvig each contributed
to the emergence of a defined Danish identity
during the 19th century.

This was also to be a golden age for Danish
art. Many painters learned their craft elsewhere
in Europe before returning to Denmark to
depict the unique ethereal light and colours
of the Danish landscape. Among the most
notable were Christen Købke, his mentor
and founder of the Danish School of Art
Christoffer Wilhelm Eckersberg, JT Lundbye
and Wilhelm Marstrand. Denmark's greatest
sculptor, the neo-classicist Bertel Thorvaldsen,
also returned to a hero's welcome after 40
years in Rome, while August Bournonville
revitalised the Danish ballet at Det Kongelige
Teater (Royal Theatre). Denmark also looked
to its past to restore its sense of national pride,
with the romantic poet Adam Oehlenschläger's
mythologising of the country's history in his
epic poems, and the historical novels of BS
Ingemann. As a counterbalance, the Dagmar
Theatre (1883) and Det Ny Teater (1908)
became known for their adventurous,
modern programming.

In contrast to the aftermath of past wars,
Copenhagen rebuilt only modestly following
the British attack. The town hall was
eventually reconstructed on the eastern side
of Nytorv, while Christiansborg and Vor Frue
Kirke were also repaired (Thorvaldsen's
sculptures gracing the latter's interior). The
'corn boom' of the 1830s revitalised growth and
the industrial revolution consolidated the city's
revival, with a prosperous shipyard, Burmeister
& Wain, starting up on Christianshavn in 1843.
Tivoli gardens opened in the same year, using
part of the old city moat as its lake, but the
less well-off would have preferred Bakken's
beer garden in Dyrehaven. Frederiksberg
also became an entertainment mecca with
its numerous skittle alleys, variety halls and
dance venues. To help keep the revellers well
oiled, the Carlsberg brewery expanded, moving
to the suburb of Valby. Carlsberg's owner,
Carl Jacobsen, would later use his profits
to create a marvellous art collection, which
he opened to the public at what is now the
Ny Carlsberg Glyptotek in 1897 (and whose
Etruscan exhibits and collection of paintings
by Paul Gauguin are one of the highlights of
Copenhagen's art treasures today). Visitors
would doubtless have used Denmark's first
railway line to travel to the capital's many
new attractions; it was built from Copenhagen
to Roskilde by a crew of English navvies, and
opened in 1847.

DEMOCRACY AND GROWTH

With such potent augurs of the approaching
modern age, Frederik VII knew that the days
of absolute power were waning, and when in
March 1848 a demonstration culminated with
a loud (but relatively peaceful) protest outside
his palace, the king capitulated immediately
saying: 'I am happy to be able to tell you
that I have already complied with what you
are demanding.' Denmark's first written
constitution followed in 1849, without a drop
of blood being spilled, establishing two elected
chambers, Folketinget and Landstinget
(the latter abolished in the 1950s), as well as
an independent judiciary.

Copenhagen's political and artistic life may
have been moving with the times during the
mid 1800s, but the standard of living for most
of its 130,000 inhabitants, crowded tightly in
cellars and ever higher tenements, had not kept
pace with the higher echelons of society.

In 1853 a cholera outbreak killed 5,000
people, finally prompting the new City Council
(founded in 1840) to do something about
the water supply and hospital provision.
Housing remained a dire problem, despite
the progressive new terraces in Østerbro, and
in 1852 the ban on construction outside the
city's defences was lifted. In the latter part of
the century a huge building boom saw swathes
of land filled with inhospitable blocks of small
so-called 'corridor' flats (one-room properties
arranged like the rooms of a hotel along one
long corridor). Blågårdsgade, Nørrebro and
Vesterbro became notorious for the prevalence
of such slum housing. Similar squalor festered
behind the majestic façades of Kongens Nytorv.

Yet as soon as new housing popped up, the
population expanded to fill it. By 1900 more
than 400,000 people had moved to Copenhagen
to escape the grinding poverty of rural areas.
(To indicate some idea of the capital's
disproportionate growth, the next largest towns
in Denmark had around 20,000 inhabitants.)
The council granted permission for the creation
of a new open space, Ørsteds Parken, where
the city's levelled ramparts once stood, together
with the building of the Botanisk Have
(Botanical Gardens), Statens Museum For
Kunst (National Gallery) and a brand new
observatory. In 1888 Denmark held its version
of London's Great Exhibition on Rådhuspladsen.
The agricultural, industrial and art displays
attracted more than 1.3 million people from
Denmark and the surrounding countries. Strøget,
the city's main shopping street, flourished with
the arrival of the major department stores Illum
and Magasin du Nord and their radical new
window displays, complemented by the new
gas lighting. Electricity came to the capital in

1892 (electric trams followed in 1897), as did flushing toilets and a vastly improved sewerage system that made full use of the Øresund. The prostitutes who operated in the slums behind Kongens Nytorv were forced to move to Vesterbro when the area was redeveloped, but they may have found some consolation in the founding of the Rudolph Berg Hospital, which specialised in the treatment of sexually transmitted diseases.

In 1913 Copenhagen gained its international emblem, HC Andersen's Den Lille Havfrue (Little Mermaid), a diminutive statue planted on some rocks in Langelinie, south of Frihavn. Ever since, visitors who have flocked to see the statue have been united in their sense of anticlimax (occasionally someone vents his disappointment by cutting her head off.

OCCUPATION AND FREEDOM

Despite its neutrality, Denmark was very much in Germany's pocket during World War I. It still, however, made provision for an outright attack by Germany, calling up 60,000 men to form a defence force, most of whom were stationed on the fortifications of Copenhagen. Fortunately, they weren't needed, and Denmark survived the Great War intact.

Between the wars the great figure to emerge in Danish politics was the Social Democrat

One nation under the Dannebrog

Though the Danes are always quick to pour scorn on what they see as America's schmaltzy love of the Stars and Stripes, they actually have a very similar relationship to their own national flag, the Dannebrog. Few nations respect and use their flag as much as Denmark. Dannebrogs are hauled up to mark everything from coronations to the cat's birthday. Virtually every garden, be it a Strandvejen mansion or suburban semi, has a flagpole for this very purpose – they even have them in the gardens of their summer houses just in case – and will run up the Dannebrog on al birthdays and anniversaries. Flags fly from public buildings and even buses in Copenhagen on every royal birthday. And during corporate buffets or kindergarten parties no piece of cheese or cake will remain unadorned by a small paper version.

The Dane's love of myth is put to good use in explaining the origin of the Dannebrog. The red banner with a white cross is said to have fallen from the sky on 15 June 1219, as a holy inspiration to the Danish troops, led by King Valdemar II the Victorious against the pagan Estonians at Lyndanise, with an accompanying celestial voice to explain its importance. In fact the flag is more likely to have been given to the nation by the Pope to mark the crusade. It was first used on the seal of the Kalmar Union in 1397, but appeared long before that in the coat of arms of the Estonian city of Tallinn.

Ask any Dane and he or she will tell you that the Dannebrog is the oldest national flag in the world, and most will be well versed in its protocol: flags must be taken down at dusk and raised only during daylight (although a pennant version can be left up overnight by the lazy); a Dannebrog must never be allowed to touch the ground, and so on. These days the Dannebrog is the standard rectangle of most national flags, but the royal family, the State and the navy are permitted to fly a swallow-tailed version.

And of course, once you realise how dearly they treasure their flag, you can understand how deeply the Danes were affected by seeing it burned in the streets of the Muslim world during the Mohammed cartoon crisis of late 2005.

Thorvald Stauning, who achieved the feat of transforming his party from near revolutionaries to true social democrats. A champion of inclusive politics and a tactical magician, Stauning appointed the first woman government minister and helped revive the shaky Danish economy with the famous Kanslergarde Agreement in 1933 between his government and the liberals – a typically Danish exercise in discussion and compromise (standing in stark contrast to how Germany was reacting to economic depression at the same time). The agreement allowed for the devaluing of the krone against the British pound and the subsequent resuscitation of Danish agriculture.

When World War II broke out on September 1 1939, Denmark braced itself to hold tight and sit out the conflict in peaceable neutrality, just as it had 25 years earlier. It was soon disabused of that notion, when at 4am on 9 April 1940 Hitler's troops landed at Kastellet, fired a few shots on Amalienborg Slot (killing 16 Danes) and issued an ultimatum: allow Germany to take control of Denmark's defences or watch Copenhagen be bombed from the sky. After an hour-and-a-half of deliberation the Danish government and king agreed, and entered into a unique deal whereby the country remained a sovereign state but Germany gained access to Norway, the Atlantic and Sweden. Denmark's Aryan genes ensured it was welcomed into the bosom of the Third Reich and, as a rich agricultural provider, it was spared much of the brutality and suppression endured by neighbouring occupied states.

Most Danes took a while to recover from the shock of this supposedly friendly occupation by 200,000 German soldiers and its resistance movement was slow in forming. It wasn't really galvanised into action until the banning of the Danish Communist Party in 1941. Indeed, many in the government, including foreign minister Erik Scavenius, openly opposed any resistance, endorsing instead full co-operation with the occupation forces.

By the end of the war, the Danish Resistance numbered around 60,000. They were never called upon to fight, however, and documents unearthed after the war revealed that the German army had expected them to be far more troublesome than they actually were. But, perhaps as a result, compared with most of Europe's capitals Copenhagen survived the war with little damage. Liberation was anxiously awaited, but would it be the Russians or the British who arrived first? In the end it was Field Marshall Montgomery who accepted the surrender of occupying forces on 4 May 1945, which was something of a close shave for Denmark.

POST-WAR DENMARK

After the war Denmark, governed by an endless series of coalitions dominated by the Social Democrats, faced several immediate domestic problems, which the founding of its welfare state would address. Culminating in the Social Security Act of 1976, the provision by the government of a safety blanket for the sick, the unemployed and the elderly has been one of Denmark's most widely admired achievements. Critics, however, point out that it was initially largely funded by foreign loans and has seen modern Denmark burdened by a vast public sector workforce and the crippling income tax levied to pay for it.

'Denmark was the first state to legalise pornography.'

With its capital more densely crowded than ever, the government sought to decentralise industry and intensify urban planning. A somewhat idealistic 'Finger Plan', in which the city's expansion would incorporate open spaces, was drawn up in 1947, but this was soon discarded to make way for more sprawling suburbs. Copenhagen's first tower blocks were built in 1950 at Bellahøj, but a public outcry curbed the extent to which they could be used to solve the perennial housing shortage. Instead, an urban renewal programme saw Adelgade and Borgergade, among other areas, refurbished. Much of Nørrebro and Vesterbro were also developed during the 1960s, and the latter would benefit from a second renewal programme at the end of the 20th century.

The use of cars increased exponentially in Copenhagen during this time and, as a result, Strøget, for centuries the city's main shopping street, was pedestrianised in 1962. During the 1960s Denmark (along with the rest of the West) was forced to confront the sexual revolution. But while America and Britain looked on in Victorian-style disgust, or were nudge-nudge, wink-winking about those free-loving Scandinavians, Denmark, in June 1967, became notorious as the first state in the world to legalise pornography, when restrictions on the sale of pornographic literature were abolished.

Meanwhile, in 1968, Copenhagen's students, like those across the rest of the continent, grew restless. This being Copenhagen, though, their protest was hardly cataclysmic. Aside from storming the office of Copenhagen University's vice-chancellor and smoking all his cigars, the students caused little trouble. Nevertheless, the spineless university still went ahead and abolished professorial powers.

Copenhagen's youth unrest lasted well into the 1970s, and its ultimate trophy still draws tourists from around the world. In 1971 a group of squatters occupied Bådsmandsstræde Barracks, 41 hectares (101 acres) of former military accommodation, on the eastern side of Christianshavn. In protest against what they saw as oppressive social norms, the squatters announced the founding of the Free State of Christiania. The police moved in, but underestimated the commune, whose numbers had been swollen by many like-minded hippies from across the country. Eventually the government gave in and allowed Christiania to continue as a 'social experiment' and its 1,000 or so inhabitants quickly began creating their own schools, housing, businesses and recycling programmes. The commune became well known across Europe for its tolerance of drugs but the current government has cracked down heavily on Christiania (*see p93* **Christiania is dead, long live Christiania**).

Though Copenhagen's pre-eminence as a port came to an end with the advent of the superships (too big for the Øresund, they made instead for Gothenburg and Hamburg), in the 1970s the city nevertheless enjoyed full employment. That, in turn, led to a shortage of workers and efforts were made to attract foreigners from southern Europe, Turkey and Pakistan, who tended to settle in Nørrebro and Vesterbro. Like London's docks, Copenhagen's waterside was to be

redeveloped with expensive housing, exclusive restaurants and new businesses.

In 1973 Denmark joined the European Common Market (as it was then), mainly to secure continuation of lucrative bacon and butter exports to the UK, but even after 20 years its membership was still the subject of a heated national debate. In June 1992 Europe would twice more turn its attention to Denmark, which emerged from the margins of the European Union to stick a spanner in the works of the progression towards federalism. Denmark has never been a wholehearted member of the EU, and 51 per cent of Danish voters went a step further in June 1992, rejecting the pivotal Maastricht Treaty and causing a mighty kerfuffle in the process. There were protests, some violent, on the streets of Copenhagen. In the end, after a re-vote in 1993 the Danes finally ratified the Treaty (by a majority in favour of just 51.05 per cent), but only after they had been promised the right to abstain from common defence and currency commitments. Never mind that the Danes have received more from agricultural subsidies than they ever put in (due in part to a loophole that saw them receive subsidies for mountainous areas, despite there being no mountains in the country), the Danes have always had a fear of being swallowed by the European machine.

Meanwhile the Danish national football team, brought in to replace war-torn Yugoslavia in the 1992 European Championships, promptly won the trophy, beating Germany in the final. Naturally, the team returned to a heroes' welcome in Copenhagen.

Copenhagen celebrated its tenure as Cultural Capital of Europe in 1996 with several new arts projects, including Arken Museum for Moderne Kunst (*see p107*) and saw major celebrations in 1997 on the occasion of the 25th anniversary of the reign of Queen Margrethe (**photo** *p18*). In July 2000 the eyes of the world were on Copenhagen for the opening of the historic and very expensive Øresund Bridge to Sweden and again in 2004 for the royal wedding of Crown Prince Frederik to the Australian commoner Mary Donaldson (or 'Queen Sheila' as she has been nicknamed).

Early 2005 saw the re-election of Prime Minister Anders Fogh Rasmussen (**photo** *p19*) at the head of a Liberal-Conservative coalition in which the rather unsavoury power brokers remain the right-wing Danske Folkepartie (Danish People's Party). Later that year Denmark became the focus of a political-religious crisis when a Jutland newspaper published cartoons depicting the prophet Mohammed, and Muslims around the world rose up in often violent condemnation of Denmark and its people.

Christiania, a drug haven no more.

Copenhagen Today

Crippling taxes, dark winters, rising house prices. Welcome to the happiest place in the world.

Copenhagen is at the very heart of Denmark. Not literally, you understand. In fact it couldn't be further from the centre of the country, lying as it does on the far eastern coast of Sjælland, closer to Sweden than most of Denmark (of course, once upon a time this was the centre of the Danish empire, which then included southern Sweden, Norway and Iceland). But with over a quarter of the country's population living in the city, and many of the rest dreaming of moving there (if they are under 20) or having retired from there (if they are over 60), Copenhagen can justly lay claim to being, if not the soul, then at least the political, cultural and economic nerve centre of the country.

Only 600,000 live in the city centre proper, but Copenhagen claims a total population of 1.7 million, including the surrounding 26

communes (the country as a whole has 5.3m inhabitants). But its compact size is a large part of the city's appeal for visitors. You can amble across the city centre in an afternoon; take in most of its main sights in a long weekend; and really get to know your way around in under a week. This is an accessible city, in all senses: English is spoken to a high level wherever you go; the transport system is peerless; the tourist board is efficient and slick; and these days, following a massive hotel boom over the last few years, there is plenty of accommodation of all descriptions.

About the only thing that isn't so easy to get to know about Copenhagen is its people. The Danes are a close-knit tribe. You may be familiar with the concept of 'six degrees of separation'; with the Danes it is generally three degrees or fewer – if two strangers meet, within a minute they will be able to find a common acquaintance. The Danes have enough in themselves. They are neither welcoming nor unwelcoming towards strangers; they might be slightly bemused as to why you have come to Copenhagen instead of, say, Berlin or Stockholm, but they are basically glad you bothered and will help you, within reason, if you ask for it.

'Denmark has the smallest gap between rich and poor of any country in the world.'

The Danish are a trusting and trustworthy bunch (except when it comes to bicycle theft). Though their obsessive obedience to rules can make them seem sheep-like from time to time (you will notice that they never, ever cross the road unless the green man tells them it is safe to do so – cross on a red and you will be 'tutted' at), they are far more relaxed than the Swedes or Norwegians when it comes to the sale of alcohol and the use of soft drugs. And though the Danes are extremely wealthy in global terms, they consider it deeply vulgar to make any kind of display of the fact. Denmark has the smallest gap between rich and poor of any country in the world. Essentially, the Danes are one giant middle class, with all that implies for the national character and exchequer both good and bad.

BUILDING BOOM

Perhaps the only exception to this pervasive modesty are the many major construction projects that have been completed in and around Copenhagen in recent years, like the Øresund Bridge from Amager to Malmö in southern Sweden; the ever-expanding Metro; and the various snazzy concrete and glass buildings overlooking the harbour (*see p31* **On the waterfront**). The building is continuing apace, particularly on the island of Amager where the new town of Ørestad continues to expand close to the airport. While weekend visitors rarely get to see the exclusive apartment buildings that have shot up beside the harbour to the north and south of the city, they can't miss the mammoth opera house (which opened in 2005), or the new National Theatre, due to open in 2008 just across the water from it.

In recent years several former slum areas and red light districts have emerged as 'hot' new shopping and nightlife areas. Vesterbro, behind Central Station, is one. Its red light district (around Halmtorvet) is now a cool café

area, and the once infamous 'sex street', Istedgade, is packed with boho cafés and trendy clothing boutiques (the sex shops, hookers and junkies remain, however). It is also a great place to find exotic foodstuffs.

Nørrebro is another buzzing part of town. Its café scene is centred on Sankt Hans Torv and Elmegade, with one of the city's best nightclubs, Rust, and cosiest cinemas, Empire Bio, both just around the corner. Meanwhile the latest street to draw the artsy crowd is Nansensgade, just north of HC Ørsteds Park, where there are now several cool boutiques, cafés, restaurants and bars.

DEATH AND TAXES

There are downsides to life in Copenhagen, of course. The weather is the most obvious one. Bluntly put, it sucks for most of the year. You would expect this not to bother the stoic, hardy locals but it does, and many enter a kind of hibernation during the winter, emerging for the brief Christmas festivities (which Copenhagen does very well, incidentally). The weather must be held at least partly responsible for the country's disproportionately high suicide rate, and the fact that the Danes drink, smoke and eat to a more unhealthy degree than virtually anyone else in Europe.

Consequently, they have a shorter life expectancy than most of their European neighbours, attributable at least in part to their stubborn denial of the consequences of smoking (one in five deaths are smoking related). A ban on smoking in public places has been mooted, but the smallprint reveals it is limited in scope. For visitors to Copenhagen the smell of cigarette smoke – in the air, on their clothes, in their hair – is a Proustian memory jogger that remains long after they have returned home.

They are drinkers too. Alcohol-related deaths are doubling every five years and 350,000 Danes are said to be technically obese due to an addiction to sweets and chocolates that rivals even the Scots.

Other factors which contribute to the Danes' existential angst (invented, of course, by Copenhagener Søren Kierkegaard) are the punitive tax rates and generally high cost of everything. The *Economist* recently ranked Denmark as the third most expensive country in the world in which to live. Most Danes can expect to say goodbye to as much as 60 per cent of their income at source; cars cost around three times the price they do in the UK; while visitors will wince at 25 per cent VAT and the often exorbitant cost of dining out. House prices are not far off London's, and there is a shortage in Copenhagen, which looks set to stoke them further still.

Smile, you're in Scandinavia

The people of Denmark have grown used to making headlines around the world in the last few years, what with the fairytale marriage of their Crown Prince to an Australian in 2004 and the outrage provoked throughout the Muslim world by the publication of cartoons of the prophet Mohammed by the Danish newspaper *Jyllands-Posten* in 2005. Nevertheless, many of them reacted with some bewilderment when they awoke on the morning of 28 July 2006 to discover they had been named the happiest people in the world. ('Why did no one tell us?' pondered one newspaper columnist.)

The world's media clamoured to discover their secret, following the publication of a study by analytical social psychologists at the University of Leicester which placed Danes just ahead of the Swiss, the Austrians and Icelanders in terms of all-round contentment.

Visitors might be foxed by all this, as the Danes are not the most conspicuously joyous of people – self-satisfied, perhaps, but gay in the old-fashioned sense of the word? No. True, they have a carnival once a year, and they certainly like a drink but, at heart, they remain a dour, often depressive Nordic race in the true Viking tradition. Yes, this is the country that gave us Aqua's 'Barbie Girl', but don't forget it is also the birthplace of Existentialism. Swedes and Danes will argue the night away about which of them lays claim to having the world's highest suicide rate.

So why are they – supposedly – so happy? It doesn't hurt that this is a small country with a small capital, and small countries – particularly small European countries – always do well in life satisfaction surveys due to their inherent sense of collectivism which breeds a greater sense of personal responsibility, civic pride and social support. Money has a great deal to do with it as well, of course. In the last decade the Danish economy has boomed thanks to an unexpected North Sea oil bonanza, and world-class technology and pharmaceutical

sectors. Though not quite as wealthy as their neighbours the Norwegians (which is a constant source of irritation to the Danes), Denmark has one of the lowest rates of unemployment in Europe and some of the highest wages. Social and economic stability ensures the Danes are well looked after by the state in terms of healthcare, education, childcare and social benefits. The streets of Copenhagen are clean, safe and buzzing with confidence and creativity. Transport is efficient and reasonably priced (the Metro, which commenced operating in 2002, has to be the ultimate transport infrastructure overkill in a city that already had excellent local train and bus services).

But aside from the comfort of hard cash, the Danes seem to have mastered several other fundamental prerequisites of contentment. They work a little less than the rest of us ('Why work longer, you only have to pay more tax?' they reason), spend more time with their families, read more, don't complain nearly as much as you might expect about their taxes, embrace their horrid climate and spend as much of their lives as possible outdoors. Above all, they try to keep things *hygglige* – which is the Danish name for their unique brand of amiable cosiness and, we believe, the true secret of their happiness.

As for temperament and political outlook, to the outside world the Danes are liberal, open-minded and tolerant. They were pornography pioneers in the 1960s; this was one of the first nations to permit gay marriage; and they give more per capita in overseas aid than any other nation on earth.

CARTOON CRISIS
The Danes are less sceptical about Europe than they were when they rejected the euro four years ago, though they, like many, have still not ratified the EU Treaty. In fact, Europe as an issue is one hot potato that seems to have been put on the political back burner in recent years. During the last general election in February 2005, race and social welfare were deemed far more pressing by the political leaders, the latter issue continuing to play to the advantage of the odious far right Dansk Folkepartie (Danish People's Party) with its sinister 'mother' figure, Pia Kiersgaard, at its head. The DF increased its share of the vote, though the Liberal-Conservative coalition, led by the continuing prime minister Anders Fogh Rasmussen, remains strong. Rasmussen's popularity ratings seemed largely unaffected by his government's support of the US invasion/liberation of Iraq, despite the vocal protestations of Copenhagen's intellectual liberal elite. The left, meanwhile, continues its inexorable decline. This was the Social Democrats' worst election since 1973 and, in general, Denmark's left wing has struggled to keep up with the times.

> **'The Danes' beloved Dannebrog flag was burned from Tehran to Cairo.'**

And then, of course, there was the Mohammed Cartoon Scandal which erupted some months after the Danish newspaper *Jyllands-Posten* (the Jutland Post) published a series of 12 cartoons featuring Mohammed in September 2005. The cartoons were considered blasphemous by Muslims, and embarrassingly unfunny by the rest of the world. Several Muslim countries imposed boycotts on Danish products; the Danes' beloved Dannebrog flag (*see p21* **One nation under the Dannebrog**) was burned from Tehran to Cairo; and there were riots as far away as Afghanistan. Fogh Rasmussen baulked at offering an official apology, but claimed this was a global crisis. It did more to taint the image of Denmark abroad than anything in its history.

While visitors to Copenhagen are highly unlikely to experience overt racism, even liberal, well-educated Danes still, for example,

The city's sparkling new **Metro**.

talk of 'second generation Danes', referring to peope who, though they have been born in Denmark, have lived in Denmark, speak Danish and pay Danish taxes, are still not, well, you know, white. If one Dane tells of a crime he has heard about, the first question asked will be the colour of the perpetrator's skin.

It is a familiar story throughout Europe, of course, and smaller nations like Denmark and Holland are hypersensitive to issues of race and immigration. Copenhageners will tend to accuse their compatriots in Jutland of being the racist right-wingers, and there is some truth in that, but the continuing growth of racial ghettos in the capital suggests this is an issue that even this cosmopolitan capital can't ignore forever.

Børsen. *See p29.*

Architecture

A wonderful triumph of form, function and free thinking.

Although little survives of pre-17th century Copenhagen (a series of fires saw to that, *see p18*), a closer look reveals a city of great historical substance. There are Christian IV's 17th-century monuments; Danish rococo in Frederiksstaden; Golden Age classicism's geometric, grandiose constructions; and 20th-century functionalism's sleek lines all marry an international sensibility with a Danish lightness of touch. In a city whose historic buildings are so well preserved, you might expect Copenhageners to be a conservative bunch when it comes to new buildings, but far from it. They have embraced modern architecture in all its extremes.

BIRTH OF THE CITY 1167-1588
Slotsholmen, the small island in the centre of the city, is where Copenhagen was born. There was said to be a fishing village on the site for hundreds of years before King Valdemar I the Great gave the district to his blood brother Bishop Absalon, but it was Absalon's construction of a fortress on the island in the mid 12th century that is traditionally regarded as the foundation of the city. The ruins of Absalon's castle were uncovered underneath

the Christiansborg Slot and can be visited in the **Ruinerne Under Christiansborg** (Ruins under Christiansborg).

During the Middle Ages the town spread out from Slotsholmen towards present-day Rådhuspladsen. The oldest standing building in Copenhagen is **Helligåndskirken** (Church of the Holy Spirit) on Strøget. The city's only surviving medieval building, the church complex includes the remains of a late 13th-century convent and the late Gothic **Helligåndhus** (House of the Holy Spirit), dating from the 15th century.

CHRISTIAN IV 1588-1648
Christian IV was the first king to play a major role in the planning of the city. Before his reign, the Copenhagen borders were Vester Voldgade, Nørdre Voldgade and Gothersgade, three roads that encircle the old centre today. Christian's grand scheme was to expand the city to twice its previous size. Rosenborg Slot, built at the northern corner of the old city, and **Kastellet** (the Castle; 1662-4), along the coast to the north, would be the two main edifices of this new area. Christian's new Copenhagen included the building of the **Nyboder** district (between

Sølvgade and Østerport), a residential area of cottages for the military; it was ground-breaking aesthetically and socially.

The earliest substantial work of Christian's reign was the transformation (1599-1605) of Slotsholmen; he built a naval yard, supply depot (**Provianthuset**), brewery (**Kongens Bryghus**, supplying the navy's beer) and arsenal (**Tøjhus**; now Tøjhusmuseet). The 160-metre (520-foot) long arsenal and the distinctive eight-storey hip-roofed brewery still stand. To house the new naval yard workers, the king embarked on another major construction project (starting in 1617): **Christianshavn**. The king employed Dutch engineers to lay out the new quarter, partially on reclaimed land. A number of residences in this Amsterdam-like district survive, notably on Sankt Annæ Gade (Nos. 28, 30 and 32, dating from around 1640).

This most ambitious of Denmark's kings was also responsible for a number of Copenhagen's most distinctive individual buildings. The long, low **Børsen** (Old Stock Exchange; 1619-24; **photo** *p28*) is one of Copenhagen's most beautiful buildings, topped by the intertwining tails of the famous Dragon Spire (1625).

'Christian transformed Rosenborg Slot from a small summer house to a palace worthy of the Sun King.'

The king indulged himself most fully in the building of the **Rosenborg Slot** (Rosenborg Palace; 1606-34). With the help of the Dutch architect Hans van Steenwinckel the Younger, Christian transformed Rosenborg from a small summer house into a lavish palace worthy of Denmark's 'Sun King'. Today its treasure-filled rooms offer a fascinating glimpse into the domestic lives of the Danish kings.

Christian's last project was the extraordinary **Rundetårn** (Round Tower; 1637-42), Europe's oldest functioning observatory, distinguished by its cool inner spiral ramp, wide enough for a coach and horses to make the climb to the top.

The disastrous fires of the 18th century meant that little domestic architecture survives from Christian's reign, apart from the modest houses at Magstræde 17-19.

BAROQUE & ROCOCO 1648-1759

Christian IV's successor, Christian V, completed the fortifications at **Kastellet** in 1660. The most striking of the building within its five-pronged bastions is the yellow-stuccoed church.

Christian V also laid out **Kongens Nytorv** in the 1680s. **Charlottenborg** palace (1672-83) faces this most grand square on the corner of

Nyhavn. The huge, sober baroque building marks a decisive break with the previously popular decorated-gable style.

An even better example of Danish baroque architecture is **Vor Frelsers Kirke** (Church of Our Saviour; 1682-96) in Christianshavn. It was built by **Lambert van Haven**, an expert in European baroque, and boasts a playful spire with external spiral staircase (added in 1749).

French rococo ornamentation became popular in the mid 18th century. The aesthetic was used in the city's most ambitious building project of the time: **Christiansborg Slot** (Christiansborg Palace; 1733-45; burned to the ground in 1794). A combination of massive, pompous Italian baroque buildings with French rococo touches, it came to define Danish rococo style – seen at its best around Frederiksstaden.

Named after King Frederik V (reigned 1746-66), **Frederiksstaden** was the first major urban building project undertaken since Christian IV. Court architect **Nicolai Eigtved** masterminded an ambitious grid-plan quarter, the centrepiece of which were the four palaces that today make up **Amalienborg Slot** (Amalienborg Palace; 1750-60), home of the Danish royal family.

CLASSICISM 1759-1848

Christian Frederik Hansen was the central figure in Danish architecture during Denmark's so-called Golden Age (1800-50) and during his lifetime became an architect of international renown. The destruction caused by the fire of 1795 and the 1807 bombardment by the English provided a blank canvas for Hansen's ascetic, disciplined romantic classicism. Fine examples include **Domhuset** (1805-15) on Nytorv, the severe radicalism of **Vor Frue Kirke** (Church of Our Lady; 1811-29) and the minimalist **Christiansborg Slotskirke** (Christiansborg Palace Church; 1811-28) with its modest Ionic portico and coffered dome.

In contrast, **MGB Bindesbøll**'s decorative design for **Thorvaldsens Museum** (1839-48) is an important late example of neo-classicism, with its Etruscan-style frescoes along its exterior walls and lavish use of colour.

CIVIC PRIDE & ART NOUVEAU 1848-1914

Following 1848, the year of continent-wide revolutions, the new Danish king Frederik VII accepted the end of absolute monarchy, ushering in a period of major civic building. Among the largest projects were **Vilhelm Dahlerup** and **Ove Petersen**'s magnificent Italian Renaissance-style **Det Kongelige Theater** (Royal Theatre; 1872-4). Dahlerup was also responsible (along with Georg EV

Bellevue Teatret.

Møller) for the stodgy **Statens Museum For Kunst** (National Gallery; 1889-96) and the more impressive, richly decorated **Ny Carlsberg Glyptotek** (New Carlsberg Sculpture Museum; 1892-7). Other significant public works built in the stately red-brick National Romantic style included **Martin Nyrop**'s **Rådhuset** (Town Hall; 1892-1905) and **Heinrich Wenck**'s **Hovedbanegården** (Central Station; 1904-11).

> **'After World War I, romantic themes were replaced by brutal, ascetic classicism.'**

When CF Hansen's Christiansborg Slot burned to the ground in 1884 (only the Slotskirke and the stables survived), **Thorvald Jørgensen** designed its replacement, with its neo-rococo façade clad with 750 different types of granite.

The first efforts to improve the housing of the poor were MGB Bindesbøll's simple, small terraced cottages (Østerbrogade 57/Øster Allé 34; 1853), influenced by Nyboder and a model for future social housing.

NORDIC CLASSICISM 1914-28

Neutral Denmark had emerged from World War I in relative prosperity and turned its back on the romantic, nationalistic, ornate themes of the previous decades to develop a brutally ascetic version of classicism entirely its own.

Public housing projects, such as the massive **Hornebækhus** block (Ågade/Skotterupsgade/ Borups Allé/Hornebækgade 5; 1922-3) by **Kay Fisker**, show Nordic classicism at its most uncompromising. Belonging to the same period is the sinister-looking **Politigården** (Police Headquarters; 1918-24). Quite why a modern social democratic state like Denmark would choose to build such a severe edifice – a chilling precursor of later fascist architecture – remains something of a paradox.

FUNCTIONALISM/INTERNATIONAL MODERNISM 1928-60

Functionalism was first conceptualised by the Swedish architect Gunnar Asplund in an exhibition in Stockholm in 1930, inspiring architects across Scandinavia to adopt the tenets of international modernism. The first project to create a major impact was **Arne Jacobsen**'s **Bellavista** housing development (1934) and **Bellevue Teatret** (1937). Taking inspiration from the German modernists, Denmark's master builder created in Bellavista an uncompromisingly modern development, with white surfaces and large windows (all apartments have sea views), in a posh coastal suburb north of Copenhagen.

Arne Jacobsen went on to design buildings all over Denmark, including the ultimate expression of 'total design', the **Radisson SAS Royal Hotel** (*see p39*). Jacobsen's last architectural project was the transatlantic-style 'slab on a podium' **Nationalbanken** (1965-78); it was finished after his death in 1971 by Dissing+Weitling.

SOCIAL DEVELOPMENT 1960-94

During the 1960s, the type of tower blocks that were to blight much of Europe were erected in Copenhagen; in fact, much of Nørrebro remains brutalised by these 'panel buildings' today. But the five **Høje Gladsaxe** blocks are an exception (Gladsaxevej, Søborg; 1963-8); they boast a silvery gleam following a revamp in the '90s.

The state Lutheran Church funded a lavish post-World War II programme of ecclesiastical building. Notable products of this include the rectilinear-without, curvy-within **Bagsværd Kirke** (1974-6) on Taxvej in Bagsværd by **Jørn Utzon** (of Sydney Opera House fame), and the courtyard-centred, pitched-roofed **Egedal Kirke** (Egedalsvej 3, Kokkedal; 1990) by the **Fogh & Følner** practice.

BUILDING FOR THE FUTURE
1994-TODAY

The designation of Copenhagen as the European City of Culture in 1996 prompted a period of intense development, which has continued over the past decade. Two major architectural works to come out of the event were **Henning Larsen**'s Impressionists gallery in the Ny Carlsberg Glyptotek (1996) and **Søren Robert Lund**'s ship-like **Arken Museum for Moderne Kunst** (Arken Museum of Modern Art; 1994-6).

Neither was as spectacular as the **Øresund Fixed Link** tunnel and bridge which joins Copenhagen and Malmö in Sweden, and opened in 2000. Although not as popular as expected, the bridge is still an incredible engineering feat.

But indigenous architects are under threat from an invasion of global superstars. **Daniel Libeskind**, architect of the new building for the Twin Towers site in New York, drew the **Jewish Museum** (2004) – housed in a converted 17th century royal boathouse beside the National Library; **Jean Nouvel** has drawn the astonishing, long-delayed blue cube **Copenhagen Concert Hall** for Danmarks Radio, in central Amager (expected to open in 2008); even **Lord Norman Foster** has been in town working on, of all things, a new elephant house for **Copenhagen Zoo** (2007).

Today Danish architects seem to be wrestling with two opposing approaches. On one side is the desire to continue with the development of Nordic tradition (simple lines, functional designs, local materials); on the other is the influence of international fashions that tend towards the more flamboyant. It is likely that if a distinctive Danish style is to emerge in the future, it will spring from a compromise between these two contradictory tendencies.

On the waterfront

Until around a decade ago Copenhagen was in denial of its seaside location. You would hardly have known the Øresund Sea and harbour bordered half of the city. But in recent years the city and its people have embraced the surrounding seas with radical new buildings overlooking the water, the ambitious lagoon development on Amager Strand (Amager Beach), and the construction of open-air swimming pools in the harbour itself. The water is so clean here now that even the locals happily swim in it.

In terms of public buildings, you can date the city's harbour renaissance to the 1999 opening of the Black Diamond extension to the National Library, by the architect firm Schmidt Hammer and Lassen. This dramatic parallelogram is made from Zimbabwean granite and paved the way for several large-scale, modernist leviathans overlooking the water, including the Nordea Bank building beside Langebro, the windswept apartment blocks in Tuborg Havn and the gigantic £232m Opera House by Henning Larsen.

The latest arrivals include the new Norway ferry terminal in Nordhavn by architects 3 x Nielsen (pictured), which resembles a giant lightbox, and the Theatre building opposite the new Opera House on the site of the old ferry terminal on Langelinie (currently under construction; the curtain is due to rise there sometime in 2008). Even Sir Terence Conran is getting in on the act with a new restaurant complex in the former Customs House, scheduled to open in late 2006.

In fact, these days virtually every stretch of Copenhagen's waterfront is being developed; Holmen, Amager Strand and Sydhaven (the South Harbour) are all filled with large-scale building sites from which are erupting cool, modern apartment blocks. Of particular note is the extraordinary Gemini Residence: two massive, converted grain silos by Dutch architects MVRDV, each boasting that all-important sea view – essential to any self-respecting 21st-century Danish yuppie.

Made in Denmark

Are you sitting functionally? Then let's begin…

Danish design is renowned around the world, beyond all proportion to the size of the nation that fostered it. Collectors and designers flock to Copenhagen to find that original Jacobsen Egg chair or Henningsen lamp in the shops and showrooms of Bredgade and Ravnsborggade, or to seek inspiration in the capital's excellent museums. But why is Danish design so revered? Why is this the place *Wallpaper** magazine comes to first to furnish its fashion shoots and dip its litmus paper in the test tube of fashion?

In the first half of the 20th century a wave of Danish designers emerged on the world stage, influenced in part by the radicalism of Bauhaus, to change contemporary interiors for ever. They looked anew at the style and function of everyday objects, as well as the materials used to make them, and created icons. Danish design has had a reputation to live up to ever since, and by and large it continues to surpass all expectations.

Architect **Kaare Klint** gave a succinct expression of the new Danish design philosophy when he said, 'The form of an object follows its function'. In the 1930s Klint (influenced by his father PV Jensen Klint) wrote again and again in his notes that architecture and interior design should be unified in what he called 'the living life'. Design should be intrinsic to function, and styling should exist only to enhance practicality. Allying this idea with the traditional hallmarks of the best Danish work – industrial quality, outstanding craftsmanship and artistic flair – Klint produced a series of ground-breaking designs, and passed on his theories as a teacher at Copenhagen's Royal Academy of Architecture. Klint's students were advised that if, for example, they were making a chair, then its function (ie comfort) should be the starting point – studying human proportions and posture then applying this scientific rationale to the construction of the furniture should always be the primary objective. **Børge Mogensen**, **Mogens Koch** and **Hans J Wegner** were among his students and their production of simple, practical furniture swept across the country in the 1950s and their designs can be seen in homes all across Denmark to this day.

Arne Jacobsen took this notion of functional and stylistic unity to its extreme when he designed one of Copenhagen's most famous buildings: the **Radisson SAS Royal Hotel** (*see p39*). With this still controversial building (which turned out to be the first and last proper skyscraper to be constructed in the centre of the city), Jacobsen embraced the principle of 'total design' with characteristically obsessive attention to detail, designing not only the building but its lighting, furnishings and interior, right down to the cutlery in the restaurant (which is awkward to use but looked futuristic enough for Stanley Kubrick to have all of his characters use it in *2001: A Space Odyssey*). Today everything in the hotel's room 606 – the lamps, fabrics, cutlery, glasses, furniture and door handles – is Jacobsen-designed and has been left untouched as a tribute to his genius.

Denmark is still reaping the benefits of this design explosion. The furniture of that era has been (and still is) hugely influential and remains in great demand, but there were a number of Danish pioneers who influenced concepts of modern functionalism before this.

'It doesn't cost money to light a room correctly, but it does require culture.'

The silverware created by **Georg Jensen**, for example, was revolutionary in its field. Jensen trained as a sculptor and silversmith who opened his first silverworks in Copenhagen in 1904. From then until his death in 1935 he constantly challenged the conventions of silver design with creations that were both aesthetically pleasing and user-friendly. The cutlery, bowls and jewellery he created with the painter **Johan Rohde** were at the vanguard of modern design back then and today the Georg Jensen brand remains as desirable as ever.

LIGHTING THE WAY
At the same time that Jensen was challenging cutlery conventions, fellow Copenhagener **Poul Henningsen** was innovating in the field of home lighting. 'From the top of a tram car, you look into all the homes and you shudder at how dismal they are,' he wrote. 'It doesn't cost money to light a room correctly, but it does

Arne Jacobsen's **Bellavista** housing complex. *See p34.*

require culture. My aim is to beautify the home and those who live there. I am searching for harmony.' So, in 1924, Henningsen designed a multi-shade lamp based on scientific analysis of its function. The size, shape and position of the shade determine the distribution of the light and the amount of glare. The 'PH' lamp, which featured several shades to help correct the colour and shadow effect of the light, won a competition at the Paris World Fair, and Henningsen became a star. His lamps continue to light many Danish households, particularly the classic PH-Contrast (1962).

Other design trailblazers included silversmith **Kay Bojesen**, whose 'Grand Prix' silver service (1938) was the template for aspiring cutlery designers, and the artist **Ebbe Sadolin**, with his plain white tableware, which was considered quite radical at the time.

'Classic Danish furniture still looks fresh despite the fact its designs are 50 years old.'

Two major talents to emerge in the field of furniture design in the 1950s were **Nanna Ditzel** (who is still working and winning prizes for her revolutionary designs today) and Jacobsen's contemporary **Poul Kjærholm** (whose PK22 chair was influenced by Mies van der Rohe's designs). In the 1960s **Verner Panton**, another of Jacobsen's former colleagues, addressed the frequent criticism levelled at designers – that their work was far too expensive and exclusive – and took on the challenge of pushing the boundaries of design aesthetics even further. Panton trained at the Royal Danish Academy of Fine Arts in Copenhagen, and initially worked in Arne Jacobsen's architectural practice. International attention soon centred on Panton's designs, based on geometric forms, and constructed from cheap, tough plastics that had previously only been used for industrial purposes. Combined with a use of vivid colours and outlandish shapes, Panton's inspirational style helped define the 'pop' aesthetic of the 1960s, with design icons like the 'Flowerpot' lamp, the 'Cone' chair and the Panton chair. Although some contemporary critics dismissed Panton's work as a fad, before his death in 1998 it was reassessed and a new generation of designers saw it as being way ahead of its time.

PRODUCT PLACEMENT

Starting with Verner Panton, the best place to see his work is in the funky Panton Lounge in the **Langelinie Pavillion**. These rooms are upstairs and only open for functions, but if you

ask at the bar someone might well show you them. Another café dedicated to the work of a single designer is **Café PH**, on Halmtorvet in Vesterbro, which is a shrine to the work of Poul Henningsen. As well as the SAS Royal Hotel, the **Jacobsen Restaurant** (*see p124*) is another shrine worth visiting for design fans of Arne Jacobsen, as it is furnished exclusively with his designs, including his cutlery. It is housed in one of Jacobsen's pioneering housing complexes, **Bellavista** (*photo p33*), close to Klampenborg Station.

You find classic Danish furniture everywhere in Copenhagen, from the chair you sit on in the library, to cool bars and restaurants. **Stereo Bar** (*see p186*) illustrates the point perfectly. This hip DJ bar is kitted out with streamlined Danish modern furnishings, though few of its trendy habitués probably ever think twice about the Panton motif painted on the walls, the Søren Østergaard and Arne Jacobsen chairs, or the 'PH' lamps; it still looks fresh despite the fact that the designs are 50 years old.

For accommodation, the SAS Royal is an obvious choice, but best of all for design fans is the **Alexandra Hotel** on HC Andersens Boulevard. Several of the rooms are furnished with design classics by Jacobsen, Wegner, Ole Wanscher and Finn Juhl.

If you are looking to buy, head for the cool second-hand and antiques shops on Ravnsborggade in Nørrebro or the more exclusive dealers on Bredgade. A good one-stop shop for both contemporary and classic Danish design is the design temple **Illums Bolighus** on Amagertorv (*see p157*), and the neighbouring **Royal Copenhagen** stores, selling contemporary and classic porcelain, glassware and silverware (*see p139*). Even if you can't afford a major purchase, it's well worth wandering through the gallery/museum-style halls to be tempted by a Jensen stainless steel watch, the perfect porcelain of Bing & Grøndhal, or the crystal creations of contemporary Danish craftsmen like Michael Bang, Torben Jørgensen and Allan Scharf. Even the area outside the store has designer pedigree; the geometric patterns of the marble-paved fountain square were designed by Bjørn Nørgaard in 1996.

Further up Strøget towards Kongens Nytorv is the five-storey glass-fronted **Bodum** (*see p158*) kitchenware shop, while on the square itself is **Bang & Olufsen**'s new flagship store (*see p35* **Sound engineers**). Heading in the opposite direction towards Rådhuspladsen you will pass two **Rosendahl** glass and kitchenware stores – the first on the corner of Bernikowsgade, the second flagship store closer to Rådhuspladsen.

Sound engineers

While their neighbours to the south in Germany aspire to owning a Mercedes and the Swedes keep up with the Jensens by buying a yacht, the Danes are a more modest bunch, preferring cheap French cars and perhaps a kayak. But there is one luxury status symbol they all yearn for, one treasure every Dane must own before they reach 30: a Bang and Olufsen stereo.

Visit any Danish home and the odds are there will be a BeoSound Beolink system or a Beosound Ouverture with slick flush surfaces, automatic sliding glass doors and still futuristic design, in pride of place in the living room. Older B&O products were built like battleships, so the unit could easily be 25 years old and still working like a dream.

The company was founded in Western Jutland in 1925 by two engineers, Peter Bang and Svend Olufsen, in the attic of Olufsen's family manor house. They were the first to produce a radio that plugged directly into the mains instead of using batteries, and by the 1930s they had made a name for themselves with other firsts, like a push-button radio and a radiogram. The Germans destroyed the factory in 1945, but the pair rebuilt the business after the war.

Between launching their first TV in the

1950s and their first fully transistorised radio, the Beomaster 900, in the late 1960s, they made a global name for themselves through their radical yet simple designs – initially heavily influenced by Mies van der Rohe – and superior quality.

'Bang and Olufsen is for those who discuss design and quality before price,' went the company's advertising campaigns and, accordingly, several B&O products made their way into the Museum of Modern Art in New York. The company has also managed to attract some of the world's top designers, including Vesterbro-born Jacob Jensen, and usually features in the top five of any 'coolest brands' list.

The Bang and Olufsen families continue to be involved in the running of the company which, though it now has manufacturing plants all over the world, is still based in their home town of Struer. Bang and Olufsen's flagship store (*see p157*) is definitely worth a visit, even if you haven't the slightest intention of spending a couple of grand on a wireless. Alternatively, there is a thriving collector's market if you'd prefer something a bit more old school.

For those interested in learning more about Danish design, **Kunstindustrimuseet** (Museum of Decorative and Applied Art; *see p86*) houses a collection of Danish design for you to immerse yourself in. And since early 2000 Danish design has had the purpose-built showcase it has always been crying out for: the five-storey **Dansk Design Centre**, built by the prolific architect Henning Larsen. Behind the smoked-glass exterior there are interactive installations, interesting exhibitions, a shop that sells design-related artefacts and a café. The centre's aim is to act as a 'window to the world' for Danish design, as well as being a meeting place for designers, industry figures and innovators from across the planet.

The best guides to enjoying London lif

(but don't just take our word for it)

'More than 700 places where you can eat out for less than £20 a head... a mass of useful information in a geuinely pocket–sized guide'

Mail on Sunday

'Armed with a tube map and this guide there is no excuse to find yourself in a duff bar again'

Evening Standard

'I'm always asked ho up to date with shopp and services in a city as London. This guide the answer'

Red Magazine

'Get the inside track on the capital's neighbourhoods'

Independent on Sunday

'A treasure trove of treats that lists the best the capital has to offer'

The People

Rated
'Best Restaurant Gui

Sunday Times

Where to Stay

Ibsens. *See p46.*

Where to Stay

Beds in the capital are still not cheap, but at least they're getting more cheerful.

The hotel landscape has exploded of late, improving massively over the last couple of years. The rates still hurt, but at least now you might feel like you are staying in one of Europe's style capitals. Thanks to this boom, the hotels now have to work harder to fill their rooms, especially in the low season, which means bargaining is on the side of the guests. The capital can now also lay claim to 'the fanciest youth hostel in the world', which opened in 2004.

RESERVATIONS, RATINGS AND RATES

Booking in advance is always a good idea, but if you arrive in the city without a reservation, the **Wonderful Copenhagen Tourist Information Bureau** (70 22 24 42/www. visitcopenhagen.com) can make same-night reservations for hotels at reduced rates. The service is also available from the tourist information desk in Copenhagen Airport's arrivals hall.

Denmark has a one- to five-star ranking system for hotels, comparable with those of most other European countries. As a rough guide, a double room in a one-star hotel should be around 550kr per night; 900kr in a two-star; 1,100kr in a three-star; 1,900kr in a four-star; and 2,500kr in a five-star. Breakfast is almost always included in the price.

Most low- and mid-range Copenhagen hotels are situated in the trendy Vesterbro neighbourhood, just west of Central Station,

where hip designer shops and bars rub shoulders with sex shops. Meanwhile the more prestigious hotels (except the Radisson SAS Royal) tend to be on the other side of the city centre, near Kongens Nytorv and Amalienborg Slot. For accommodation catering primarily to a gay clientele, see p183.

Tivoli & Rådhuspladsen

Deluxe

Copenhagen Marriott Hotel

Kalvebod Brygge 5, 1560 Copenhagen V (88 33 99 00/fax 88 33 99 99/www.marriott.com/cphdk).
Bus 5A, 48. **Rates** 1,295kr-1,395kr single; 1,295kr-1,795kr double; 1,695kr-2,795kr suite. **Credit** AmEx, DC, MC, V.
This relatively new five-star block of luxury is the place to go if you want to be pampered in proper American fashion. Standards are high and there are a million extras on offer, but aside from the harbour view this hotel suffers from a problem that is common in chains: you could be in any Marriott hotel anywhere in the world. Be sure to ask for a room on one of the upper floors on the water side of the building; you could sit there all day, sipping champagne and watching the aquatic goings-on down below from behind the wall of glass.
Bar. Business services. Concierge. Disabled: adapted rooms (4). Internet (broadband/wireless). Gym. Non-smoking rooms. Parking (150kr-180kr/night). Restaurant. Room service (24hrs). TV: pay movies.

Palace Hotel

Rådhuspladsen 57, 1550 Copenhagen K (33 14 40 50/fax 33 14 52 79/www.palacehotel.dk). **Rates** 1,795kr single; 1,995kr double; 2,195kr-2,700kr Ambassador Room. **Credit** AmEx, DC, MC, V.
Map p250 O12 ❶
This large luxury hotel stands adjacent to Rådhuset (the Town Hall) at the western end of Strøget, and is one of Copenhagen's landmark buildings. The Palace was built in 1907-1910 by architect Anton Rosen, in order to provide prestigious accommodation for visiting officials on business at the then-new Town Hall. The Ambassador Rooms have balconies overlooking Rådhuspladsen. While the reception and bars have kept their old-fashioned brown and

The best **Hotels**

For sleeping on the cheap
Hotel Sct Thomas. *See p47.*

For a room with a view
The Square. *See p41.*

For star treatment
Hotel d'Angleterre. *See p42.*

For designer decadence
Hotel Front. *See p45.*

For seaside chic
Skovshoved Hotel. *See p47.*

---

❶ Green numbers given in this chapter correspond to the location of each hotel as marked on the street maps. See pp244-253.

Kong Arthur. See p46.

dark-red Chesterfield style, the rooms have been smartened up and modernised, and the hotel is upgrading to a five-star instead of a four-star, after its acquisition by Le Meridien hotel group.
Bar. Concierge. Internet (dataport). Non-smoking rooms. Parking (150kr/night). Restaurant. Room service (24hrs). TV: pay movies.

Radisson SAS Royal Hotel

Hammerichsgade 1, 1611 Copenhagen V (33 42 60 00/fax 33 42 61 00/reservations 38 15 65 00/www. radissonsas.com). **Rates** 1,195kr single; 1,445kr double; 2,345kr-4,900kr suite. **Credit** AmEx, DC, MC, V. **Map** p250 O11 ❷

Arne Jacobsen's modernist masterpiece was Copenhagen's only designer hotel for many years, designed from top to bottom (and from door handles to forks) in 1960 by the legendary architect-designer. Though the rooms were recently revamped, just entering the lounge and street-level café, with Jacobsen's 'Egg' and 'Swan' chairs and the Scandinavian Airlines desk, you're swept into a magical 1970s era when airport terminals and avant-garde design were romantic and exclusive. Room 606 has legendary status: the original 1960s design has been preserved, and the hotel prints a special postcard of the room, available only to those who stay in it. The hotel's central location is another boon – Tivoli, Central Station and Rådhuspladsen are just across the street. Copenhagen's skyline is so devoid of towers this high that any room on one of the upper floors gives a superb view. For a spot of haute, haute cuisine, the SAS Royal boasts one of Copenhagen's finest (yet priciest) restaurants, Alberto K, on the top floor (*see p115*).
Bar. Business services. Concierge. Internet (dataport/ LAN/WiFi). Disabled: adapted rooms. Gym. Non-smoking floors. Parking (190kr/day). Restaurants (2). Room service (24hrs). TV: pay movies.

Sofitel Plaza Copenhagen

Bernstorffsgade 4, 1577 Copenhagen V (33 14 92 62/ fax 33 93 93 62/www.sofitel.com). **Rates** 1,950kr single; 2,150kr double; 3,199kr-6,999kr suite. **Credit** AmEx, DC, MC, V. **Map** p250 P11 ❸

The Plaza, commissioned by King Frederik VIII in 1913, has recently been transformed from an old English-style hotel into something a little more 'Scandinavian'. The rooms are airy and pleasant with big beds. The lobby retains a distinctive early 20th-century atmosphere, fitted out with leather and wood, and with a very cool glass elevator. The Library Bar (*see p127*) was named 'one of the five best bars in the world' by *Forbes* magazine, and a central pillar in the lounge carries plaques naming the hundreds of famous personalities who have stayed here over the years. The Plaza enjoys a good view over Tivoli across the street, but its location next to Central Station also means windows opening out on to either heavy traffic or railway noise.
Bar. Business centre. Concierge. Internet (broadband). Non-smoking floors. Parking (165kr/day). Restaurants (2). Room service (7am-midnight). TV: cable/pay movies.

Expensive

Imperial Hotel

Vester Farimagsgade 9, 1606 Copenhagen V (33 12 80 00/fax 33 12 80 03/www.imperialhotel.dk). **Rates** 1,020kr-2,015kr single; 1,285kr-2,315kr double; 2,200kr-5,455kr suite. **Credit** AmEx, DC, MC, V. **Map** p250 O10 ❹

This 1956 hotel has been renovated and modernised to good effect, with a major focus given to the indoor 'garden' restaurant and the bedrooms. About half of the 163 rooms are decorated in fine Danish contemporary style and the suites are even better – students at the Danish Design School equip each one as part of their final exam. For those with designer allergy, the rest of the rooms are all far more traditional. The hotel is centrally located near the lakes and the planetarium, in the middle of the movie theatre district, and a short stroll from Tivoli.
Bar. Business services. Concierge. Disabled: adapted rooms (2). Non-smoking floors (2). Parking (135kr/day). Restaurants (2). Room service (6.30am-10.30pm). TV: cable/pay movies.

Kong Frederik

Vester Voldgade 25, 1552 Copenhagen V (33 12 59 02/fax 33 93 59 01/www.remmen.dk). **Rates** 1,040kr-1,440kr single; 1,240kr-1,840kr double; 3,240kr-4,540kr suite. **Credit** AmEx, DC, MC, V. **Map** p250 N12 ❺

The Kong Frederik goes full tilt for the traditional English style, with wood panelling, Chesterfields and a blazing fireplace. In the lobby hang portraits of all Denmark's (many) King Frederiks and the restaurant (called, well, what do you expect, Frederiks) is accessible straight from the street – it's worth visiting both for its decor (imported piece by piece from a London pub) and its haute cuisine. The rooms are comfortable with appealing, unobtrusive decor, although the bathrooms are a bit small. Guests prepared to make the trek get free use of the upmarket spa and pool at Kong Frederik's sister Hotel d'Angleterre (*see p42*).
Bar. Internet (dataport/broadband). Non-smoking rooms. Parking (200kr/day). Restaurant. Room service (7am-9.45pm). TV: pay movies.

The Square

Rådhuspladsen 14, 1550 Copenhagen V (33 38 12 00/fax 33 38 12 01/www.thesquarecopenhagen.com). **Rates** 915kr-2,345kr single; 1,325kr-2,325kr double; 2,050kr-3,255kr suite. **Credit** AmEx, DC, MC, V. **Map** p250 O12 ❻

The Square is a moderately priced temple to elegant, modern Scandinavian decor. The entrance area is impressive, being part-lobby, part light-flooded art installation, and the hotel is located right in the heart of the action on Rådhuspladsen. Up the elevators, you'll find 192 uniformly smart and bright rooms, the higher ones (and the sixth-floor breakfast room) commanding great views down on to the square.
Internet (broadband). Non-smoking rooms. Room service. TV: movie channels/pay TV.

Where to Stay

Moderate

Copenhagen Hotel 27

Løngangstræde 27, 1468 Copenhagen K (70 27 56 27/fax 70 27 96 27/www.hotel27.dk). **Rates** 795kr single; 950kr double. **Credit** AmEx, DC, MC, V. **Map** p251 O13 **7**

What used to be the Mermaid Hotel is undergoing a massive transformation to turn it into 'the coolest place in town'. This three-star designer hotel is on a side street off Rådhuspladsen and will have all 202 of its rooms completely refurbished by autumn 2007. Until then, the hotel remains open to guests as the renovation process takes place.
Non-smoking hotel. TV.

DGI-Byens Hotel

Tietgensgade 65, 1704 Copenhagen V (33 29 80 50/ fax 33 29 80 59/www.dgi-byen.dk). **Rates** 825kr-1,295kr single; 925kr-1,495kr double. **Credit** AmEx, DC, MC, V. **Map** p250 Q11 **8**

Just around the corner from the main railway station and part of the DGI sports and cultural centre (*see p201*), this hotel makes up for its rather desolate location among meat markets, warehouses and railroad tracks with its interior style, comfort and facilities. The ultra-cool *Vandkulturhuset* ('Water Culture House'), Copenhagen's state-of-the-art swimming pool and spa, occupies one wing of the building and guests are admitted free. The spacious rooms are distinguished by excellent, modern, minimalist Scandinavian design (lots of light – natural and artificial – and plenty of wood). There are some good weekend deals.
Disabled: adapted rooms. Gym. Internet (broadband). Non-smoking rooms. Parking (90kr/day). Restaurant. Spa. Swimming pool (indoor). TV: cable/pay movies.

Hotel Tiffany

Halmtorvet 1, 1652 Copenhagen V (33 21 80 50/ fax 33 21 87 50/www.hoteltiffany.dk). **Rates** 745kr-995kr single; 955kr-1,195kr double. **Credit** DC, MC, V. **Map** p250 Q11 **9**

Tiffany bills itself as 'a sweet hotel', and it is. Each spacious, modern bedroom is well equipped with the essentials and a small kitchen. Add in a friendly atmosphere (fresh rolls are placed outside your door each morning) and it's easy to see why neighbourhood locals often use the hotel to put up overnight guests, and the guests thank them for it too. It's only a five-minute walk from Central Station, in one of the most attractive squares in Vesterbro.
Non-smoking rooms. TV.

Savoy Hotel

Vesterbrogade 34, 1620 Copenhagen V (33 26 75 00/fax 33 26 75 01/www.savoyhotel.dk). **Rates** 540kr-1,075kr single; 640kr-1,375kr double; 915kr-1,695kr family. **Credit** AmEx, DC, MC, V. **Map** p250 P10 **10**

A recently renovated three-star hotel in a wonderful building, with a green- and gold-decorated façade designed by Anton Rosen (who also designed the

Palace Hotel). The carvings of lions in the lobby refer to the building's original name, 'Lovenborg', or 'Castle of the Lions', while those with a fondness for history should check out the original lift and staircase. The large, bright rooms are set back from the street, making them quiet and peaceful. The hotel has its own restaurant with courtyard terrace open in the summer months.
Business services. Internet (lobby). Restaurant. TV.

Budget

The **Cab-Inn** chain has three hotels in the city and is a reasonable option for budget travellers. If you can, book into the Cab-Inn City, just behind Tivoli, which opened in mid 2004. The other two are slightly less well located, though still only a 15-minute walk from the centre. The sleeper-train/'cabin'-style rooms are almost identical in all three locations, although you can upgrade to a slightly larger format with double (rather than single bunk-style) beds. All rooms have kettle and TV, and there's free lobby internet access in all three hotels, as well as in the rooms at Cab-Inn City.

Cab-Inn City (*Mitchellsgade 14, 33 46 16 16, www.cabinn.com*). **Map** p251 Q13 **11**

Cab-Inn Scandinavia (*Vodroffsvej 55, Frederiksberg, 35 36 11 11, www.cabinn.com*). **Map** p245 M9 **12**

Cab-Inn Copenhagen Express (*Danasvej 32-34, 33 21 04 00, www.cabinn.com*). **Map** p245 N8 **13**

A two-bed room costs 630kr; a single 510kr. An upgrade to the larger 'Commodore' class, available at Cab-inn City and Scandinavia, costs an extra 100kr per person. Breakfast costs an extra 50kr per person.

Hotel Selandia

Helgolandsgade 12, 1653 Copenhagen K (33 31 46 10/fax 33 31 46 09/www.hotel-selandia.dk). **Rates** 455kr-995kr single; 570kr-1,195kr double. **Credit** AmEx, DC, MC, V. **Map** p250 P10 **14**

The Selandia is located just behind Central Station and is very popular due to its relatively cheap rates and cheerful, friendly service. The 84 rooms are simple and functional, but note that the 25 'economy' rooms do not come with en suite bath.
Internet (lobby access). TV.

Nyhavn & around

Deluxe

Hotel d'Angleterre

Kongens Nytorv 34, 1021 Copenhagen K (33 12 00 95/fax 33 12 11 18/www.remmen.dk). **Rates** 2,280kr-3,330kr single; 2,600kr-3,650kr double; 4,700kr-17,720kr suite. **Credit** AmEx, DC, MC, V. **Map** p251 M15 **15**

Unique in its class, Copenhagen's grand old five-star Hotel d'Angleterre is traditional to its very core. The massive 18th-century building with its 123

All form, little function

Copenhagen's 'chic metropolis' boom, which started with the building of the new airport terminal in the late 1990s and continues today with the massive waterfront regeneration, reached its 'cool' zenith in April 2005 with Project Fox: a unique, multi-million-Euro event designed to celebrate the worldwide launch of Volkswagen's new Fox car.

The launch took place simultaneously in three locations around the city: Club Fox held a 21-day, non-stop party with the hottest DJs from the European club scene (Whitey, Hot Chip, A Guy Called Gerald); Fox Studio was a huge work-in-progress art gallery; and, last but not least, the Hotel Fox provided all the journalists with somewhere to rest their heads, with rooms designed by Europe's top graphic designers, illustrators and graffiti artists. German company Event Lab took over an existing three-star hotel and then let loose the 21 creatives for a couple of days to decorate the 61 bedrooms in their own style. The results, as you can imagine, were more funky than functional.

Now all the journalists have gone and the DJs have stopped, the Fox has been handed back to its owners as a going concern. The problem is that while it looks great on paper, if you are not a creative street artist you will probably feel a lot more relaxed sleeping in a regular hotel. In short, the Fox's best attributes in the real world are its website and restaurant (which is super, by the way).

Hotel Fox
Jarmers Plads 3, Vesterbro (33 95 77 55/ fax 33 14 30 33/www.hotelfox.dk). **Rates** 945Kr small; 1,120kr medium; 1,320kr large; 1,620kr x-large. **Credit** AmEx, DC, MC, V. **Map** p250 N11 **③**

bedrooms is located at the upmarket eastern end of Strøget right on Kongens Nytorv, facing café-lined Nyhavn. From Robbie Williams and Ricky Martin to guests of the Royal Family (Amalienborg Slot, the Queen's residence, is just around the corner), this is where the rich and famous stay (and for a cool 17,720kr you can feel like one of them, with a night in the Royal Suite). The spa and swimming pool (10x12m) are a treat. Afternoon tea, served at 2.30pm, is a luxurious way to enjoy the art of Danish cakes and pastries.
Bar. Business services. Concierge. Gym. Internet (broadband). Non-smoking rooms. Parking (205kr/night). Restaurant. Spa. Swimming pool (indoor). Room service (24hrs). TV.

Phoenix Copenhagen
Bredgade 37, 1260 Copenhagen K (33 95 95 00/ fax 33 33 98 33/www.phoenixcopenhagen.dk). **Rates** 990kr-2,150kr single; 1,290kr-2,550kr double; 2,190kr-6,700kr suite. **Credit** AmEx, DC, MC, V. **Map** p249 L16 **⑯**
Housed in a massive building dating from 1780, the Phoenix is one of Copenhagen's most extravagant hotels: the flashy foyer has tall mirrors, a fountain, huge candelabras and paintings. Its chic location, tucked between Kongens Nytorv and Amalienborg Palace, means the hotel is surrounded by some of Copenhagen's hottest art galleries. The hotel has elegant bedrooms, decorated in Louis XVI style, and the owner, who is passionate about art, indulges that

taste by displaying only originals on his walls. The Phoenix was a fashionable favourite for rock bands and fashionistas for a couple of decades, until the new generation of designer hotels like the Skt Petri and brand new Hotel Front put the glamour back into Copenhagen hotel living.

Bar. Business services. Internet (broadband). Non-smoking rooms. Parking (145kr/day). Restaurant. Room service (24hrs). TV: pay movies.

Expensive

Copenhagen Admiral Hotel

Toldbodgade 24-28, 1253 Copenhagen K (33 74 14 14/fax 33 74 14 16/www.admiralhotel.dk). **Rates** 1,210kr single; 1,540kr double; 1,625kr-2,500kr suite. **Credit** AmEx, DC, MC, V. **Map** p252 M17 ⓱

You could be forgiven for thinking you're sailing in the hold of some massive Roman galley inside the Admiral. The tree-trunk-thick beams criss-crossing the huge lobby area and most of the rooms add to the already existing maritime atmosphere of this waterside hotel. A 2003 refurbishment has created appealing, cosy rooms, well appointed with solid teak furniture. About half of the bedrooms have sea views. At SALT, the bar and restaurant downstairs, you can finger the shrapnel scars on the beams from 19th-century bombardments by the British Royal Navy, or agonise over which of the three different types of salt to pinch over your brasserie-style fare.

Bars (2). Business centre. Disabled: adapted rooms. Non-smoking floors. Internet (web TV/Wi-Fi). Parking (free). Restaurant. Room service (24hrs). TV: pay movies.

Hotel Front

Skt Annæ Plads 21, 1022 Copenhagen K (33 37 06 56/fax 33 37 06 30/www.front.dk). **Rates** 1,390kr 'small', 1,590kr 'medium', 1,890kr 'large', 2,190kr 'x-large'. **Credit** AmEx, DC, MC, V. **Map** p252 M17 ⓲

While there is now an abundance of designer-chic hotels in Copenhagen, few capture a sense of decadence and fashion as sharply as the brand new Hotel Front, which opened in 2006. Owned, surprisingly, by the most traditional hotel family in Copenhagen, it seems the Remmens (who also own the Hotel d'Angleterre) went for a radical and modern twist with the revamp of the Front: new name, new design, new rooms, new everything. There are mp3 players to borrow for the gym, free wireless internet, even personal yoga trainers. The design is all 'hot pink and cosy grey' and the rooms, with giant flatscreen TVs and the finest designer furniture, combine cosy and extravagant. Unlike the Hotel Fox (*see p43* **All form, little function**), Front is not all about the look; here, comfort and service follow. The surrounding neighbourhood is also in the midst of a revival, thanks to the regeneration of the whole waterfront area.

Bar. Business centre. Non-smoking rooms. Internet (Wi-Fi). Restaurant. Room service (24hrs). TV: cable/pay movies.

71 Nyhavn

Nyhavn 71, 1051 Copenhagen K (33 43 62 00/ fax 33 43 62 01/www.71nyhavnhotel.com). **Rates** 1,585kr-1,785kr single; 1,885kr-2,455kr double; 3,135kr-5,535kr suite. **Credit** AmEx, DC, MC, V. **Map** p252 N17 ⓳

Perched at the end of Nyhavn within a splendid early 19th-century warehouse, this relaxed and well-regarded hotel enjoys a prime location. Thoroughly refurbished in 2001, the small, modern bedrooms have managed to keep their character, thanks in part to their wood-beamed ceilings. When you check in, be sure to ask for a view over the water or you could find yourself facing the neighbouring building at the rear. Good breakfasts.

Bar. Business services. Concierge. Internet (ISDN/ broadband). Non-smoking floor. Parking (free). Restaurant. Room service (noon-midnight). TV: movie channels/pay TV/VCR.

Moderate

Comfort Hotel Esplanaden

Bredgade 78, 1260 Copenhagen K (33 48 10 00/ fax 33 48 10 66/www.choicehotels.dk/hotels/dk007). **Rates** 958kr-1,146kr single; 1,046kr-2,125kr double. **Credit** AmEx, DC, MC, V. **Map** p249 K17 ⓴

This central three-star hotel looks out on to the attractive Kastellet park on the corner of Esplanaden and Bredgade. The building dates from 1891 and has been 'gently renovated', which means it has kept its old-fashioned feel. This is a good bet for solo travellers: about a third of its 117 rooms are singles. Esplanaden was the first hotel in Denmark to become completely non-smoking.

Bar. Internet (broadband/wireless). Non-smoking throughout.

Hotel Opera

Tordenskjoldsgade 15, 1055 Copenhagen K (33 47 83 00/fax 33 47 83 01/www.hotelopera.dk). **Rates** 815kr-1,740kr single; 1,025kr-1,840kr double; 2,055kr-3,080kr suite. **Credit** MC, V. **Map** p252 Q16 ㉑

An old-fashioned, cosy three-star hotel with 91 small but very charming rooms named after the old Opera House, not the new one; the hotel is located right next to the Royal Theatre, under the arches. There's a special cheap weekend rate as well as lots of winter offers; check the website.

Bar. Internet (broadband). TV.

Budget

Sømandshjemmet Bethel

Nyhavn 22, 1056 Copenhagen K (33 13 03 70/fax 33 15 85 70/www.hotel-bethel.dk). **Rates** 595kr-795kr single; 795kr-895kr double. **Credit** MC, V. **Map** p252 M16 ㉒

The Sømandshjemmet Bethel is perfectly located on Nyhavn and has charming premises in a former seaman's hostel. The bright, pleasant rooms are all equipped with bath, telephone and TV. When you book in it's worth requesting a quayside view, so long as you're not too sensitive to noise, which can come drifting across from the canal-side bars. Alternatively, you could go and visit one of them, because alcohol is not sold or allowed inside the hotel. *Non-smoking rooms. TV.*

Nørreport & around

Deluxe

Hotel Skt Petri
Krystalgade 22, 1172 Copenhagen K (33 45 91 00/ fax 33 45 91 10/www.hotelsktpetri.com). **Rates** single from 1,795kr; double from 1,995kr. **Credit** AmEx, DC, MC, V. **Map** p251 M13
Occupying a former department store in the 'Latin Quarter', Copenhagen's number one designer hotel is the most central for sights and shopping. All 270 rooms are hugely welcoming, with every feature you'd expect, including large, comfortable beds spread with soft, cool linen and a bold, bright (but not overwhelming) use of colour throughout. It's well worth trying to get one of the 55 rooms with balconies or terraces on the higher floors. The large atrium contains Bar Rouge, a swanky cocktail bar, while the street level Café Blanc is a popular stop for power-shoppers on a break. Finally, Brasserie Bleu is a luxury restaurant in an impressive setting. *Bar. Business Centre. Concierge. Internet (broadband/wireless). Non-smoking rooms. Parking (150kr/day). Restaurant. TV: pay channels.*

Expensive

Kong Arthur
Nørre Søgade 11, 1370 Copenhagen K (33 11 12 12/fax 33 32 61 30/booking 33 95 77 22/www.kong arthur.dk). **Rates** 1,265kr-1,365kr single; 1,520kr-1,720kr double; 2,120kr-3,500kr suite. **Credit** AmEx, DC, MC, V. **Map** p246 L11
Given a royal inauguration by King Christian IX in 1882, the Kong Arthur stands alone in its class: a charming, family-run hotel that offers quality accommodation at a competitive price. This beautiful, 107-room mansion, filled with antique furniture, is conveniently located, with the lakes on one side and hip Nansensgade on the other. **Photo** *p39.* *Bar. Business services. Concierge. Internet (broadband/wireless). Non-smoking floors. Parking (free). Restaurants (3). Room service (24hrs). TV.*

Moderate

Hotel Nora
Nørrebrogade 18C, 2200 Copenhagen N (35 37 20 21/fax 35 37 26 21/www.hotelnora.dk). **Rates** 750kr-1,150kr single; 850kr-1,300kr double; 1,800kr-3,000kr family suite. **Credit** DC, MC, V. **Map** p248 J10
This two-star hotel at the bottom of Nørrebrogade opened around 2002 in an old apartment block and has retained much of the old interior, meaning that

Old-school charm at **Ibsens**.

the large rooms feel more like those in a flat than a hotel. To find the reception, turn into the courtyard, buzz the door immediately on your left and walk up to the first floor where the bustle of Nørrebrogade seems hardly noticeable. The design is modern yet unobtrusive, and includes flat-screen TVs in all rooms. The hotel prides itself on its 'one price' philosophy, meaning that wireless internet access is available from all rooms and complimentary welcome drinks can be found in the refrigerators; visitors can also use the office on the third floor, complete with fax machine and scanner. *Parking. Internet (broadband/wireless). TV.*

Ibsens
Vendersgade 23, 1363 Copenhagen K (33 13 19 13/ fax 33 13 19 16/booking 33 95 77 44/www.ibsens hotel.dk). **Rates** 1,045kr-1,145kr single; 1,220kr-1,420kr double; 2,200kr suite. **Credit** AmEx, DC, MC, V. **Map** p246 L11
Ibsens is a lovely three-star hotel with an appealing reception, breakfast room and bar. It's a romantic place, with flowery curtains and flowers on the balconies of what is a typical Danish 19th-century building. The location (near Nørreport Station) is about as central as you can get in Copenhagen. *Bar. Disabled: adapted rooms. Internet (broadband). Babysitting service. Non-smoking floor. TV.*

Budget

Hotel Jørgensen
*Rømersgade 11, 1362 Copenhagen K (33 13 81 86/
fax 33 15 51 05/www.hoteljoergensen.dk).* **Rates**
575kr single; 700kr double. *Shared bath* 475kr single;
575kr double. **Credit** MC, V. **Map** p246 L12 ⓲
This appealing, spotless budget hotel offers
scrubbed wooden floors, a relaxed atmosphere and
small, basic rooms with cable TV. It's an easy walk
from the city centre, close to Nørreport Station.
Bar. Restaurant. TV: cable.

Vesterbro & Frederiksberg

Moderate

Avenue Hotel
*Åboulevard 29, 1960 Frederiksberg C (35 37 31 11/
fax 35 37 31 33/www.avenuehotel.dk). Bus 250S, 12,
66, 68, 69.* **Rates** 825kr single; 1,025kr double;
1,425kr family. **Credit** AmEx, DC, V.
This three-star hotel is slightly out of town in
Frederiksberg, but the location offers both the handsome Frederiksberg neighbourhood and the wilder
Nørrebro within easy reach, as well as a very high
standard for the price. The Avenue was completely
renovated in 2005, and now all 68 rooms include free
internet access, cable TV and fridge.
Bar. Internet (broadband). Parking (free). TV.

Budget

Hotel Sct Thomas
*Frederiksberg Allé 7, 1621 Copenhagen V (33 21
64 64/fax 33 25 64 60/www.hotelsctthomas.dk).
Bus 6A, 26.* **Rates** 395kr-595kr single; 595kr-795kr
double. **Credit** V. **Map** p245 P8 ⓳
This small hotel is one of our favourites: low rates,
a welcoming atmosphere and a great location on
Frederiksberg Allé, one of the most sought-after
residential areas in town. There are 44 rooms (26
come with en suite) and, though the services offered
are limited, the free internet access (in the TV room)
and breakfast are much appreciated.
*Internet (free lobby access). Parking (50kr/day).
Non-smoking rooms. TV.*

Further afield

Deluxe

Radisson SAS Scandinavia Hotel
*Amager Boulevard 70, 2300 Copenhagen S
(33 96 50 00/fax 33 96 55 55/www.radisson
sas.com). Metro Islands Brygge/bus 5A, 250S.*
Rates 1,145kr single; 1,295kr double; 3,495kr-
16,000kr suite. **Credit** AmEx, DC, MC, V.
The biggest hotel in Copenhagen houses the
Copenhagen Casino, four restaurants, a large lounge
bar, a conference centre for 1,200 people and a total
of 545 bedrooms. Although it's only a 15-minute
walk from Rådhuspladsen, the SAS Scandinavia is
not as centrally located as most other Copenhagen
hotels. There are some non-smoking floors and
'theme floors' featuring different design styles, such
as 'oriental', 'hi-tech' and 'Scandinavian'. The well-
regarded 25th-floor Dining Room (*see p121*) serves
up Franco-Danish cuisine and superb views out over
the city and beyond.
*Bars (2). Business services. Concierge. Internet
(broadband/wireless). Disabled: adapted rooms. Gym.
Non-smoking floors. Parking (free). Restaurants (4).
Room service (6.30am-11.30pm). Swimming pool
(indoor). TV: pay movies.*

Skovshoved Hotel
*Strandvejen 267, 2920 Charlottenlund (39 64 00
28/fax 39 64 06 72/www.skovshovedhotel.dk). Bus
14.* **Rates** 1,200kr-1,400kr single; 1,400kr-1,600kr
double; 2,800kr suite. **Credit** AmEx, DC, MC, V
(4.75% transaction fee).
Among the cutesy thatched cottages and grand
ambassadorial residences in the charming former
fishing village of Skovshoved (about 10km/six miles
north of Copenhagen along the Danish Riviera; *see
p215*) you'll discover the Skovshoved Hotel.
Skovshoved is one of the more romantic accommodation options out of town, skilfully blending moder-
nity with tradition and style with homeliness. It has
20 double rooms in an airy Scandinavian style. Each
room is equipped with wireless internet connection
and flatscreen TV; some have sea-facing balconies.
There's a popular restaurant with an Italian and
French-inspired menu and a cosy living room. The
owners – Mr and Mrs Nadelmann – only took over
Skovshoved in the spring of 2003 but have already
established it as one of the best hotels in the country. *Condé Nast Traveller* magazine voted it one of
the world's 50 coolest and we'd be inclined to agree.
*Bar. Business services. Internet (Wi-Fi). Parking
(free). Restaurants (2). Room service (7am-7pm). TV.*

Hostels

Other than the DanHostel Copenhagen City,
Copenhagen has two hostels that are part of the
International Youth Hostel Association, one
north and one south of the city, and both about
20 minutes away by bus. There are other 'sleep-
ins' which serve just the same purpose, but are
not part of the official hostel network. Prices
start from around 100kr per person per night
without breakfast. **Use It** (Rådhusstræde 13,
33 73 06 49, www.ui.dk) can provide help and
information to young travellers on a budget.

DanHostel Copenhagen Amager
*Vejlands Allé 200, 2300 Copenhagen S (32 52 29
08/fax 32 52 27 08/www.danhostel.dk/copenhagen).
Metro Bella Center or Sundby/bus 30, 100S.* **Rates**
110kr dorm; 340kr-425kr double; 430kr-500kr triple;
490kr-600kr 4-person room; 550kr-600kr 5-person
room. **Credit** AmEx, MC, V.

DanHostel Copenhagen City. *See p49.*

This modern hostel on the island of Amager, just south-east of the centre, is 15 minutes by bus from the city centre and offers private rooms as well as dorms, with or without bathroom. Breakfast is included in the price and there's an internet café. A Youth Hostel membership card is required to stay here (60kr), but you can buy a temporary card for 30kr per night. Closed for the last half of December. *Internet (lobby access).*

DanHostel Copenhagen City
H.C. Andersens Boulevard 50, Vesterbro (33 11 85 85/bookings 33 18 83 32/fax 33 11 85 88/www. danhostel.dk); **Rates** 130kr-150kr per person; buffet breakfast 50kr. **Credit** MC, V (2.75% transaction fee). **Map** p251 Q14 ㉙
Tagged as 'the largest designer hostel in Europe', the five-star DanHostel Copenhagen City opened in 2004 with designer Scandinavian furniture all over and a sharp, modern look. It is just five minutes' walk from landmark attractions like Tivoli and the Royal Library, with a fantastic view over Langebro Bridge. You can rent a whole room for yourself by paying for empty beds. This gives you a fine room for 600kr (520kr in the low season) in a lively hostel right in the centre for less than a room in a two- or three-star hotel. This is definitely one of the best ways to stay in Copenhagen on a budget. **Photo** *p48.*
Internet (lobby access).

Mick & Blodwyn's Backpackers Inn
Herluf Trolles Gade 9 (33 93 23 00/http:// mickandblodwyns.homepage.dk/). **Rates** 180kr per person. **No credit cards. Map** p252 N16 ㉚
With space for just 20 people in three bunk-bed dorm rooms and shared facilities, things are cramped in this converted inn, which was transformed into a backpackers' crash pad back in 2004. It's worth considering, however, for its proximity to Nyhavn, the friendly owners, the small but convivial bar serving cheap beer and the inclusion of lots of extras in rates such as breakfast, bedding, use of the owner's kitchen facilities and free internet access. The only extra cost is a 100kr deposit for the front door key. *Internet (free lobby access).*

Sleep-In Green
Ravnsborggade 18, 2200 Copenhagen N (35 37 77 77/fax 35 35 56 40/www.sleep-in-green.dk). Bus 5A. **Rates** 100kr per person, blanket and pillow extra 30kr. **No credit cards. Map** p246 J11 ㉛
This sleep-in has a total of 66 beds (in three rooms: eight, 20, 38 beds) and tries to be as ecologically minded as possible, serving up organic breakfasts (40kr), solar-powered lights, etc. It is closed from November until June.

Apartments

Adina Apartments
Amerikaplads 7, Østerbro (39 69 10 00/www. adina.dk). **Rates** 1,150-2,050kr 1-2 person apartment; 2,400kr-3,200kr 2-4 person apartment. **Credit** AmEx, DC, MC, V.

Located in a smart residential area, this brand new hotel/apartment building opened in 2006. A stay here offers a feeling of independence for those who like having their own set of keys and their own kitchen; but there are a wide range of hotel service options and a swimming pool to boot.

Citilet Apartments
Fortunstræde 4, 1065 Copenhagen K (70 22 21 29/fax 33 91 30 77/www.citilet.dk). **Rates** 950kr-2,300kr double. **Credit** AmEx, DC, MC, V.
Map p251 N14.
The first hotel/apartment chain in Copenhagen is still the best, but the chain recently went down from running 27 flats to five, which means getting a booking for a short stay is now a miracle. The first-rate serviced flats (25-115 sq m), fully furnished with luxury bathrooms, are all located close to Strøget. Breakfast is restocked in the kitchen each day, there is a daily maid service, low telephone charges and free wireless internet. Apartments are comparable with a large suite in a hotel, for the price of a room in a three-star hotel.

Bed & breakfast

Check with **Bed & Breakfast in Denmark** (39 61 04 05, fax 39 61 05 25, www.bbdk.dk). Prices are usually 250kr-300kr for a single room, 300kr-450kr for a double, with extra beds about 175kr-200kr and breakfast at 30kr-50kr.

Bed & Breakfast Bonvie
Frederiksberggade 25C, 2nd floor, 1459 Copenhagen K (33 93 63 73/www.bbbonvie.dk). **Rates** bunk bedroom 400kr; double 500kr-600kr. **Credit** MC, V.
Map p250 O12 ㉜
You can't get more central than this tiny (four guest rooms) B&B right among the shopping action of Strøget. There's a family feel (so be prepared to share communal space – and washing machine – with your friendly hosts), and a courtyard to sit in while reading and relaxing, weather permitting. *Internet access.*

Camping

Denmark's unreliable climate makes camping risky. Danes are good at comfort, though: sites are well kept and have plenty of facilities.

Camping Charlottenlund Fort
Strandvejen 144B, 2920 Charlottenlund (39 62 36 88/fax 39 61 08 16/www.campingcopenhagen.dk). Train to Charlottenlund, then 10min walk/bus 14, 169. **Open** early May-mid Sept. **Rates** tents 25kr-35kr plus 80kr per person; 35kr under-12s. **Credit** MC, V.
The best campsite around Copenhagen is located 8km (5 miles) north of the centre (accessible by bus every 20 minutes or train in under half an hour) around an old seafront fort, complete with (drained and grassy) moat. The beach is just 50 metres away.

SPECIAL EXHIBITIONS AND LARGE COLLECTION OF FRENCH AND DANISH ART IN ORIGINAL ARCHITECTURE

Ordrupgaard is situated in a spacious park, just north of Copenhagen.

A visit to the museum offers worldclass art as well as classic and modern architecture. The museum's permanent collection comprises French and Danish art from the 19th and the early 20th century.

Today the exquisite collection is still kept in the collectors home and gallery built in 1918. During the summer of 2005, Ordrupgaard inaugurated a new extension to the museum designed by the Iraqi star architect Zaha Hadid. Special exhibition are exhibited in the new extension.

CEZANNE
COROT
COURBET
DAUMIER
DEGAS
DELACROIX
GAUGUIN
HAMMERSHØ
MONET
MANET
MATISSE
MORISOT
PISSARRO

ORDRUP GAARD
MUSEUM
of FRENCH
IMPRESSI
ONISM

VILVORDEVEJ 110
CHARLOTTENLUND
COPENHAGEN
PHONE: +45 39 64 11 83
ORDRUPGAARD.dk
TUE>THUR>FRI 13-17
WEDNESDAY 10-18
SAT>SUN 11-17

Nykredit
MAINSPONSOR

New extension by Zaha Hadid, 2005

Sightseeing

Features

Rådhuspladsen. *See p61.*

Introduction

Copenhagen is small but perfectly formed.

'West of Valby Bakke' is not simply a location, it's a definition. Any Copenhagener worth his salt will tell you that anything beyond this hill, which looks down on the suburbs to the west and the city to the east, is absolutely nowhere.

It's tough but fair. Indeed, Copenhagen's medieval centre probably has everything the casual visitor could want. It has the great museums and the royal palaces, it offers ample shopping and fine dining, and you can get anywhere within its beautiful, atmospheric streets in minutes, by foot. You probably won't even have cars bothering you – watch out for the bicycles, though.

However, Copenhagen's real city living goes on outside the centre's canals and cobbled streets, whether it's in charming, bohemian Vesterbro; confidently graceful Frederiksberg; or in the melting pot that is Nørrebro. This is where you'll see the locals shop, club and drink, and eat out at restaurants and cafés like it's going out of style.

Note: the guide provides public transport directions for all sights that are located outside the city centre.

COPENHAGEN CARD

If you're planning on doing some intensive sightseeing, then you may save money by investing in a **Copenhagen Card**. The card (valid for 24 or 72 hours) offers free travel by public transport (though most attractions are within easy walking distance of the centre) and free entry to more than 60 museums and sights in the greater Copenhagen area, plus discounts to many others. Prices for 2006 were: 24hrs – 199kr, 129kr children (10-15yrs); 72hrs – 429kr, 249kr children. The cards are available from travel agents, hotels, main railway stations and the **Wonderful Copenhagen Tourist Office** (70 22 24 42, www.visitcopenhagen.com).

It's worth noting that many museums are free on Wednesdays.

The best Places to go

For a walk in the park
Wander through the **Botanisk Have** – Copenhagen's answer to Kew. *See p90.*

To get closer to heaven
Vor Frelsers Kirke – climb up Christianshavn's dominant spire for wonderful views of the city. *See p93.*

With the kids
Tivoli – get all misty-eyed at the magical pleasure gardens. *See p54.*

For a history lesson
Nationalmuseet – chart Denmark's turbulent past, from the Vikings onwards. *See p61.*

For a touch of titillation
Porn uncovered at **Museum Erotica** – naughty, but nice. *See p66.*

To get a glimpse of the royals
Amalienborg Slot – the home of Queen Margrethe II. *See p82.*

Ways to see the city

By bike

City Safari Bike Tours
33 23 94 90/www.citysafari.dk. Depart from Reventlowsgade, by Central Station. **Tours** *Apr-Sept* 1.30pm, 8pm daily. *Oct-Mar* by appointment. **Duration** 2.5hrs (day trips also available). **Price** from 150kr. **No credit cards.**
City Safari offers a range of bike tours. Themes include historical, Danish design and night sights.

Copenhagen Rickshaw
34 53 01 22/www.rickshaw.dk. Depart from city centre. **Tours** all year. **Duration** varies. **Price** from 35kr; sightseeing tours from 125kr for 30mins. **No credit cards.**
Copenhagen Rickshaw operates 50 rickshaw taxis. Hail them in the street; they're particularly prevalent in Rådhuspladsen. Worth haggling over the fare.

By boat

DFDS Canal Tours
33 42 33 20/www.canal-tours.dk. Depart from Nyhavn & Gammel Strand. **Tours** *Late Mar/early Apr-late Oct* half-hourly daily (Gammel Strand). *Mid June-late Aug* half-hourly daily (Nyhavn). **Duration** 50mins. **Price** 60kr; 25kr concessions. **Credit** AmEx, DC, MC, V.

Cruise on down to **Christianshavn**. *See p91.*

See p91.

Runs tours around the harbour, including the Opera House, the Little Mermaid and Christianshavn. Dinner tours are also available.

Kajak-Ole
40 50 40 06/www.kajakole.dk. Depart from Gammel Strand. **Tours** May-Sept. **Duration** 1.5-3hrs. **Price** 165kr-210kr. **No credit cards**.
Guided kayak tours. Stops at a Christianshavn café.

Netto-Bådene
32 54 41 02/www.havnerundfart.dk. Depart from Holmens Kirke. **Tours** Apr-June, Sept-late Oct 10am-5pm. *July, Aug* 10am-7pm, 2-5 times per hr daily. **Duration** 1hr. **Price** 30kr; 15kr concessions. **No credit cards**.

By bus

Frequent hour-long tours leave from Rådhuspladsen daily, 9.15am-5.45pm (Apr-Sept) and 9.45am-4.15pm (Oct-Mar). Tickets cost 120kr-140kr (60kr-70kr concessions). Call 32 66 00 00 or visit www.sightseeing.dk.

On foot

For details of personal guided tours, visit **www.guides.dk**.

Christiania Tours
32 57 96 70/www.christiania.org. Depart from Prinsessegade entrance. **Tours** *late June-8 Aug* 3pm daily. **Duration** 1.5hrs. **Price** 30kr. **No credit cards**.
Get the inside story on the Free State.

Copenhagen Walking Tours
Skydebanegade 38, 1 (40 81 12 17/www.copenhagen-walkingtours.dk). Depart from various points. **Tours** Sat, Sun; *1 June-1 Sept* Thur-Sun. **Duration** 2 hrs. **Price** 100kr. **No credit cards**.
This well-known operator offers English language walking tours on a variety of specialised and general themes including, of course, Hans Christian Andersen, historic Copenhagen and the city's Jewish heritage. Dressed in red, the guides are hard to lose and they walk all year, in sun or snow. Private tours also available.

Ghosttour.dk
51 92 55 51/www.ghosttour.dk. Departs from Nyhavn 22, next to Café ship Liva. **Tours** 8.30pm Thur-Sat. **Duration** 90 mins. **Price** 85kr; 60kr concessions. **No credit cards**.
With its old architecture and romantic atmosphere, Copenhagen is ideal for a ghost tour. This guided (English) walk explores some of the spookier sites.

Guided walks of the city in English
32 84 74 35/booking 39 64 48 94/www.woco.dk. **Price** 60kr-100kr. **No credit cards**.
A variety of walking tours of the city given, as the name suggests, in English. They include the Night Watchman Tour (booking advised), a general walking tour and the History Tour.

Jazz Guides
33 45 43 19/www.jazzguides.dk. **No credit cards**.
A variety of tours of the city's many jazz venues. Every Thursday there's a tour costing 900kr per person, including club entrance fees, meal and drinks.

Tivoli & Rådhuspladsen

Welcome to the land of make-believe.

Tivoli

Whenever plans are introduced to change Tivoli's appearance, usually to include a fierce new ride, protests erupt immediately. And not just from touchy neighbours who have come to dread half a year of all-day shrieking. The old ladies with season tickets, the visitors from abroad, all the Danes who remember their first visit like it was yesterday – everyone wants the 'Old Garden' to stay more or less the same.

In many ways, a visit to **Tivoli** is the definitive Danish experience. It is the ultimate expression of 'hygge', the unique type of cosiness that the Danes strive to create in all aspects of their lives: there are thrill rides, but none is too extreme (apart, perhaps, from the Demon rollercoaster); there are hot dogs and candy floss and ice-cream and beer; and a host of family entertainments, from jugglers to orchestras, to parades, to Sting.

The fact that year after year Tivoli attracts major international artists, albeit those with severe MOR tendencies – people like Tony Bennett, the Beach Boys and Phil Collins – to its open-air stage is a testament to its pulling power. Michael Jackson tried to buy the whole place after he played there in the early 1990s, as did Disney a few years back. But the very idea of their beloved Tivoli falling into the hands of Americans, especially Disney, horrified the nation and there was an outcry. The park's long-time owners, Carlsberg, had no qualms, however, about selling a 43.4 per cent stake to Scandinavian Tobacco in 2000 (the rest is owned by Danish banks and small investors).

Tivoli's glitzy blend of escapist, fairytale gaiety and defiant traditionalism may not be to all tastes, but even the most cynical of visitors

usually find themselves won over by its relentless, wide-eyed schmaltz. This is Denmark's number one tourist attraction (beating even Legoland on Jylland) and an incredible 4.5 million visitors (a figure close to the national population) pass through the gates each summer. In all, over 300 million people have visited in over a century.

So what is so special about this relatively small, 80,000-square-metre (20-acre) plot of land, sandwiched between Central Station and Rådhuspladsen? By day Tivoli is undoubtedly charming, with its picturesque lake, wide range of rides, over-priced but cosy restaurants and magnificent flowerbeds. It has a unique atmosphere – part traditional beer garden, part Victorian pleasure park, part (whisper it) Disneyland. But it isn't really until night falls, when the 100,000 specially made soft-glow light bulbs and over a million standard bulbs are switched on, and the scenery becomes a kaleidoscope of diffused colour (there is no neon here, and the place is a mecca for lighting technicians from all over the world) that the magical transformation from amusement park to dreamland takes place. Passers-by can only glimpse through the trees the beguiling world within and hear distant squeals from the rollercoasters, as Tivoli enters its nightly childhood Twilight Zone. Something genuinely special happens when night falls: Tivoli seems to expand and transform into something really rather, dare we say, magical.

But you might like to OK a visit with your bank manager beforehand. Tivoli is expensive, with a steep entrance fee (75kr) that verges on the ridiculous once you get in and discover that you have to pay extra (typically 20kr) for the rides. And brace yourself for the bill if you dine: Tivoli's many restaurants are among the dearest in the city.

History

Like most of Copenhagen's landmarks, Tivoli has royal roots. In 1841 King Christian VIII was much vexed by the burgeoning civil unrest in his country and his increasingly untenable position as absolute monarch, and, so the story goes, he allowed the Danish architect Georg Carstensen to build the park as a distraction. 'When people amuse themselves they forget politics,' the king is reputed to have said. Carstensen, a self-made publishing magnate and son of a diplomat, was born in Algiers in 1812. Tivoli grew out of a carnival he arranged for his readers in Kongens Nytorv. Its success is thought to have swayed the king in favour of a permanent site for public pleasure. His new park would blend three main ingredients: light, fairytales and music, the king's only condition being that the park would not contain 'anything ignoble and degrading'. The original Tivoli, little changed today, was based on similar gardens then extant in Paris and London and named after the little Italian town near Rome known for its fountains.

The park opened on 15 August 1843 and welcomed 16,000 visitors in its first day, Hans Christian Andersen among them. However, for Carstensen, the park's success was bittersweet. Buoyed by its popularity, he attempted to repeat the formula abroad, but failed abjectly. The board of directors at Tivoli became increasingly concerned about his outlandish and expensive projects until, finally, after one argument too many, Carstensen left in high dudgeon for America. Legend has it that upon his return years later, the guard at the turnstiles failed to recognise him and he had to pay to get in. Carstensen died a bankrupt, aged 45.

Unlike many other amusement parks, Tivoli is now right in the centre of the city. But it wasn't always so. When it was built the park stood in the countryside among fields dotted with cattle and crops, on land that was once part of Copenhagen's old fortifications, donated by the government. Today, Tivoli Lake is the model of picturesque charm, boasting flower borders, weeping willows and, at night, illuminated dragonflies, but it used to be part of the city's defensive moat (the remains of which can be seen in the lakes of Botanisk Have Ørstedsparken and Østre Anlæg park).

In 1944 Tivoli's peace was shattered by the occupying forces of Nazi Germany who were quick to recognise the significance of the park to the Danish people. They used it as a target for retaliatory attacks following the increased activity of the Danish Resistance. The main victim was the original Concert Hall. Within a week the resilient Danes had erected a tent in the grounds to replace it. A permanent, new hall (still standing) was built in 1956.

Many of the buildings constructed in Tivoli in the post-war era were seen by Denmark's architects as an opportunity to let their creative hair down and so the park is packed with boisterous structures. Elsewhere many might have been outlawed on grounds of taste, but in Tivoli they somehow seem appropriate.

A tour of Tivoli

There are three entrances to Tivoli: one is located opposite the main entrance to Hovedbanegården (Central Station), another lies across the road from the Ny Carlsberg Glyptotek, but by far the grandest is the main gate (on Vesterbrogade), a Renaissance-inspired

Tivoli's main gate.

Impeccable taste abounds at the **Dansk Design Center**. *See p61.*

confection decorated with Corinthian columns and a dome, dating from 1889. On the right as you enter is a statue to the garden's architect, Georg Carstensen. In front of you, beside the extraordinary Moorish façade of Restaurant Nimb (breathtaking at night), is a perspex fountain, with bubbling tubes, like a gigantic lava lamp. It was designed by the Nobel Prize-winning Danish physicist Niels Bohr. On your left is the Peacock Theatre, while before you is Plænen (the Lawn), the open-air concert venue. Beyond that is the 1956 Tivolis Koncertsal, a camp orgy of pastel colours.

There are over 30 rides to choose from in Tivoli, from tame roundabouts decorated with winsome HC Andersen characters, to the new Star Flyer carousel (*see p57* **Life is a carousel**) and the mad exhilaration of Det Gyldne Tårn (the Golden Tower) vertical drop. The tower was likened by one sniffy critic to a high tension pylon, but few rides unleash the butterflies with quite the force of this terrifying 63-metre (207-foot) vertical drop. At night you can see Sweden twinkling in the distance from the top. Predictably, the tower, which, like much of Tivoli, is designed in a faux-Arabian style, has prompted accusations of blatant Disneyfication from the older generation of Tivoleans. They would prefer that time had stood still with the tepid wooden rollercoaster, constructed in 1914 and still running.

All the traditional fun of the fair is here too, including shooting alleys, electronic arcade games, a hall of mirrors, bumper cars, a test-your-strength machine, an execrable chamber of horrors, the unintentionally creepy HC Andersen fairytale ride, and Det Muntre Køkken (the Crazy Kitchen), where you can

vent pent-up frustration by hurling tennis balls at crockery targets. The hot air balloon Ferris wheel, dating from 1943, is a traditional focus for courting couples.

Many visitors, particularly the elderly, who flock here in their thousands, come simply to enjoy the flora. Tivoli boasts hundreds of trees (predominantly lime, chestnut, weeping willow and elm) and many more flowers within its perimeter fence. The flowers help to keep the park visually fresh throughout the season – if you visit during spring the tulips will be out, followed by the rhododendrons, then come the roses, lilacs and laburnum with the summer and, by the time the park closes for winter, the chrysanthemums are in bloom.

Slightly contrary to its fairytale image, Tivoli has its own nightclub, open Thursday to Saturday. Although it can hardly be said to push the envelope of contemporary club culture, Mantra Nightclub is still fun for teens, and for many Danes it's their first taste of clubbing.

In late 1994 a new tradition was inaugurated at Tivoli: the Christmas Market. The market has since become a fixture on Copenhagen's calendar, with hundreds of thousands of visitors a year braving sub-zero temperatures. Though many of the rides don't run at this time of year, there's lots to do, including cabarets, shows and concerts, and many of Tivoli's food outlets serve seasonal fare, such as traditional roast pork, rice pudding and *æbleskiver* (a kind of mini doughnut), all washed down with *glögg* (mulled red wine). The gardens also play host to a large market, selling decorations and gifts, and Father and Mother Christmas administer seasonal cheer. If you think Tivoli is saccharine in summer, wait till you get a load of this.

Performance venues

Tivoli is a riotous collage of architectural styles, from Moorish palaces to Chinese towers, with everything in between. The oldest building in the park is the remarkable outdoor Chinese-style **Peacock Theatre**, designed by Vilhelm Dahlerup (also responsible for Det Kongelige Teater) in 1874. It stages classical pantomime in the tradition of commedia dell'arte. The performances are complex, hard-to-follow shows, starring Pierrot, Harlequin and Columbine, but are worth a look if only to see this extraordinary theatre, operated only by cords and pulleys. The theatre's 'curtain' is a peacock's tail feathers, which fold back to reveal the stage. The oriental theme is echoed elsewhere in the park – a legacy of Georg Carstensen's peripatetic childhood, which fuelled a love of exotic cultures – in the **Chinese Pagoda**.

Plænen (*see p197*) is Tivoli's largest venue. Most of its (capacity) 50,000-strong audience stand in the open air before the circus-like stage. This is where returning Danish heroes (rare, but it does happen occasionally), such as the 2000 Eurovision Song Contest winners the Olsen Brothers, are fêted by the crowds, and where big events are celebrated. Performances – musical and otherwise – are twice nightly (international acrobats are a speciality). A recent, popular innovation has been the Friday Rock Concerts. Danish bands usually headline, but each year an international star or two is booked as a treat, free of charge to park visitors. Naturally, these acts draw huge crowds so arrive early to bag a good view and bring provisions so that you don't have to leave your spot for too long.

Every Wednesday and Saturday at 11.45pm visitors are treated to a fireworks display. After over a hundred years with the Barfod family, the new fireworks choreographer is Michael Wulff Pedersen, only the eighth powder supremo in Tivoli's history. The bombshells are no longer handmade in Denmark, mostly for financial reasons, but still look (and sound) spectacular in or around the gardens.

Throughout the summer you can also catch parades and performances by the Tivoli Garden Guard, a children's marching band, founded in 1844, and made up of a 100 or so local boys aged between nine and 16. The Guard is on holiday for two weeks in mid July.

The renowned **Tivolis Koncertsal** (*see p191*), which seats 1,900, is home to the Sjælland Symphony Orchestra and visiting orchestras, ballet companies, ensembles and soloists of world repute also play here. You'll recognise the hall by the row of Danish flags along the front of its roof.

Tivoli

Vesterbrogade 3 (33 15 10 01/ticket centre 33 15 10 12/www.tivoli.dk). **Open** *Mid Apr-mid June, mid Aug-mid Sept* 11am-11pm Mon-Wed, Sun; 11am-midnight Thur, Sat; 11am-1am Fri. *Mid June-mid Aug* 11am-midnight Mon-Thur, Sun; 11am-1am Fri, Sat. *Halloween* Dates & times vary. *Christmas Market* (late Nov-30 Dec 11am-10pm Sun-Thur; 11am-midnight Fri, Sat. Closed 24 & 25 Dec. *Ticket Centre* 11am-8pm daily. **Admission** 75kr; 35kr concessions. **Credit** AmEx, DC, MC, V. **Map** p250 P12.

Life is a carousel

Here's the problem: you're respected and loved, but you're getting on a bit and the kids are starting to find you just a bit... well... boring. It's a problem in all walks of life, but when you're Tivoli – the biggest tourist attraction in Denmark – and you're approaching your 150th birthday with falling attendances, it's a definite cause for alarm.

Unfortunately, the fairytale trappings and gorgeous lighting displays of Copenhagen's legendary pleasure gardens just weren't paying the bills. The solution? To risk annoying the hell out of the loyal pensioner market with weekly rock concerts and noisy thrill rides.

Next to the brutal vertical drop of the Golden Tower and the short, sharp shock of the Demon, the latest addition to Tivoli's line-up of thrill rides is certainly a more subtle breed of white-knuckle attraction. But don't be fooled – the Star Flyer is neither for the faint of heart nor those with a trace of vertigo. That's because it is an 80-metre (260-foot) high tower with a carousel attached to it. Riders find themselves lifted, feet dangling freely in the fresh air, to a height that easily matches the top of Arne Jacobsen's high-rise Radisson SAS Royal Hotel across the street. At the top you get spun round slowly enough to take in the sights of the city and, on clear days, some way beyond it. Soon after the ride opened in 2006, the thing got stuck for 45 minutes on a windy spring afternoon – probably too much of a good thing, but for a minute or so the unforgettable view is well worth the inevitable queasiness.

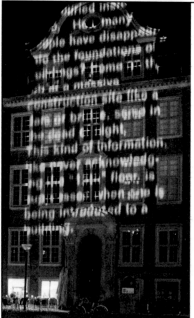 

Around Tivoli

From Tivoli's main gates (and, in fact, from just about anywhere in Copenhagen) you can see Arne Jacobsen's world-famous, 22-storey **Radisson SAS Royal Hotel** (*see p41*). It dates from 1960, though that's hard to believe given its uncompromising functionalist lines. With his customary all-encompassing attention to detail, Jacobsen designed not only the exterior but the interior too, right down to the cutlery still used in the restaurant.

Across the road from the hotel you'll find the **Wonderful Copenhagen Tourist Information Bureau, Copenhagen Right Now** (which offers plenty of material in English; *see p233*). A little further down the street stands **Hovedbanegården** (Central Station), from where you can catch trains to the airport, the rest of the country and beyond. The station, which dates from 1911, has a well-equipped centre for Interrailers, complete with showers and lockers, not to mention several food outlets, a bank, a police station, newspaper kiosks and a bookshop.

Close by is the **Sofitel Plaza Copenhagen** (*see p41*) with its wood-panelled **Library Bar** (*see p127*), redolent of a London St James's gentlemen's club (though, this being Denmark, women are, of course, also admitted).

Immediately north of the main entrance to Tivoli is Copenhagen's cinema district. Here you'll find several cinemas, all within a few minutes' walk (*see p176*). To the south-east of Tivoli is the **Ny Carlsberg Glyptotek** (*see p61*). As a member of Sjælland's quartet of world-class art collections (the others are Arken, *see p106*; Louisiana, *see p216*; and Statens Museum for Kunst, *see p90*), the Ny Carlsberg Glyptotek has much to live up to. But with a breathtaking line-up of ancient sculptures, the largest collection of Etruscan art outside of Italy, as well as an exceptional array of more recent Danish and French paintings and sculpture, it more than holds its own in such vaunted company. And with the opening in 1996 of a well-received extension by the Danish architect Henning Larsen, the Glyptotek boasts a thoroughly modern, yet intimate, space for its impressive collection of French Impressionist paintings.

The original *glyptotek* (sculpture collection) was donated to the city in 1888 by the brewer/philanthropist Carl Jacobsen (son of the founder of the Carlsberg brewery, IC Jacobsen) and his wife Ottilia. He intended the museum to have 'a beauty all its own, to which the people of the city would feel themselves irresistibly drawn', and pretty much got his way. His vision has been financed, run and much expanded by the Ny Carlsberg Foundation for more than 100 years and is housed in a building rich in architectural delights that was specially designed for the original collection by Vilhelm Dahlerup and Hack Kampmann. During the summer of 2006, three years of renovation and expansion was completed. The results were impressive. There is better access for disabled visitors; the entire cellar level was revamped to host exhibitions, and the whole collection is now displayed in brighter surroundings. All this, and a shiny, clean façade to lure visitors.

The highlight of the old building is the glorious, glass-domed **Winter Garden** – a steamy palm house bursting with monster subtropical plants and graced by Kai Nielsen's beautiful fountain piece *Water Mother with Children*. The Winter Garden's excellent café (open 10am-4pm daily except on Mondays, and great for cakes) is a popular meeting place for art-loving Copenhageners and is an excellent spot in which to thaw out during winter.

The Glyptotek's thousands of pieces can be roughly divided into two groups: ancient Mediterranean, and 18th- and 19th-century French and Danish. The first four rooms are dedicated to the oldest pieces, some dating back 5,000 years (the Egyptian hippopotamus is a crowd favourite). The exhibits proceed to trace the history of sculpture from the Sumerians, Assyrians, Persians and Phoenicians, through to a collection of ancient Greek pieces (one of the best in Europe) and some highly entertaining, privately commissioned (and therefore far more lifelike than officially commissioned) Roman busts. Jacobsen's unrivalled Etruscan collection – including bronzes, vases, and stone and terracotta sculptures – is another highlight of the old building.

The French painting collection, housed in Larsen's intriguing extension, is impressive. It includes 35 works by the Impressionist Paul Gauguin (*see p60* **Gauguin's Danish period**), who lived for a brief, thoroughly cold, time in Copenhagen. As well as this unique collection (donated by Jacobsen's son Helge in 1927), the Glyptotek is home to one of only three complete sets of Degas bronzes in the world (including an insouciant ballerina in an original, evocative tulle costume). There is also an array of paintings by the Impressionist movement's leading lights, including Corot, Manet, Renoir, Monet, Pissarro and a remarkable self-portrait by Cézanne. The rest of the post-Impressionist movement is similarly stellar, represented by the likes of Van Gogh, Toulouse-Lautrec, Bonnard and Signac.

Sightseeing

Over 30 works by Auguste Rodin dominate the French sculpture rooms, but the pieces by his contemporaries are equally fascinating. Another surprise awaits in the collection of Danish sculpture: for those who think that Danish sculpture began and ended with Bertel Thorvaldsen, other leading lights (Dahl, Købke and Eckersberg) are also represented, though the collection of the Danish Golden Age (1815-50) is surpassed by those of Statens Museum For Kunst and **Den Hirschsprungske Samling** (see p89).

On Sundays from October to March the Glyptotek hosts a variety of music events; for details contact the museum.

A little further up HC Andersens Boulevard is the **Dansk Design Center** (Danish Design Centre; see p61; **photo** p56). This beautiful five-storey, 86-million kroner complex is a centre for education, research and exhibitions. Like the Glyptotek extension, it was designed by Henning Larsen and opened in January 2000. The basement of the Design Center is usually given over to classics from the past, as well as international design icons, while the ground and first floor house temporary exhibitions, both of Danish and international designs. These might focus on one particular designer, a huge corporate manufacturer or a theme such as recycling. The centre has a café and a small shop that sells books and Danish design items.

Head east from HC Andersens Boulevard and you come to **Nationalmuseet** (National Museum; **photo** p61). Housed in a sumptuous former royal palace, boasting some of the finest rooms in the city, and extensively modernised in recent years, Denmark's National Museum is the country's oldest historical collection, with its origins as Frederik II's Royal Cabinet of Curiosities (c1650). It focuses, naturally, on Danish culture and history, but there are also world-class Egyptian, Greek, Roman and ethnographic departments. All exhibits have excellent English captions.

The museum's main home is in Prinsens Palæ (Prince's Palace). Visitors enter via a large, airy main hall, once a courtyard, but now enclosed with a glass roof, which also acts occasionally as a venue for concerts. To the right, on the ground floor, you enter the Prehistoric Wing, showing Danish history from the reindeer hunters of the Ice Age to the Vikings. Here you can marvel at archaeological finds from the Early Bronze Age unearthed in Denmark's bogs – the most impressive of which is the collection of large bronze horns, or *lurs* (some still playable), used to appease the sun god.

Upstairs, the glorious Medieval and Renaissance department covers the pre- and post-Reformation periods, and majors on ecclesiastical and decorative art. It is the era of the great Renaissance kings: Christian III, Frederik II and Christian IV. The surviving example of Frederik's tapestries of kings, made for the Great Hall of Kronborg Slot (see p267), is a marvel.

The Royal Collection of Coins and Medals, though one of the more specialist sections in the museum, is intriguing. The room itself (Room 146) is worth a visit. It is said to be one of the most beautiful in the city, and has views over Marmorbroen (Marble Bridge) and Christiansborg Slot.

Gauguin's Danish period

If you are wondering why the Ny Carlsberg Glyptotek has such an impressive collection of paintings by Paul Gauguin (born 1848), it is because he actually lived in Copenhagen for one winter, at Gammel Kongevej 105 (long since demolished), in Frederiksberg.

Gauguin had married a Danish woman, Mette Sofie Gad (1850-1920), whom he met in Paris in 1873. The painter, who had variously been a stockbroker and a sailor before finding his artistic calling, soon found himself broke and out of work, hence the move to his wife's home. As with many foreigners, Gauguin never got to grips with the Danish weather, the coldness of the Danes or the suffocating ways of the Copenhagen bourgeoisie, although he did stay long enough to hold his first ever exhibition at the **Kunstforeningen** (Arts Society, see p178). Gauguin also fathered five children with Mette during their nine-year marriage (the rest of which they spent in France), and today has over 50 descendants living in Denmark (including well-known musicians, painters and TV personalities).

By all accounts Paul and Mette had a tempestuous relationship, each being strong, passionate personalities and, for a while, deeply in love with the other. Eventually, though, the call of the Pacific lured Gauguin away and he moved to French Polynesia where he was to paint some of his most famous pieces. He died on Hiva-Oa in the Marquesas Islands in 1903.

Danish culture and history uncovered at **Nationalmuseet**.

On the top floor is the museum's Collection of Antiquities, a mini British Museum, with pieces from Egypt, Greece and Italy. On the same floor is a charming toy museum, which begins with a mention of a rattle in Saxo Grammaticus's *Gesta Danorum* and continues through early 16th-century German toys, a spectacular array of doll's houses, Lego (of course) and toy soldiers. Though the main museum is excellent for kids, in the basement is a Children's Museum, which attempts to condense all the rest of the museum into an exhibition suitable for four- to 12-year-olds.

Dansk Design Center

HC Andersens Boulevard 27 (33 69 33 69/www. ddc.dk). **Open** 10am-5pm Mon, Tue, Thur, Fri; 10am-9pm Wed; 11am-4pm Sat, Sun. **Admission** 40kr; 20kr-25kr concessions; free under-12s. **Credit** AmEx, DC, MC, V. **Map** p251 P13.

Nationalmuseet

Frederiksholms Kanal 12 (33 13 44 11/ www.natmus.dk). **Open** 10am-5pm Tue-Sun. **Admission** 25kr; free under-16s. Free to all Wed. **Credit** AmEx, DC, V. **Map** p251 O13.

Ny Carlsberg Glyptotek

Dantes Plads 7 (33 41 81 41/www.glyptoteket.dk). **Open** 10am-4pm Tue-Sun. **Admission** 50kr; 20kr concessions; free under-18s. Free to all Sun. **Credit** MC, V. **Map** p251 P13.

Rådhuspladsen

Tivoli's neighbour to the east is the usually frenetic **Rådhuspladsen** (Town Hall Square; **photo** *p62*). Though the square is less architecturally appealing than Kongens Nytorv at the other end of Strøget, Denmark's answer to Times Square and Piccadilly Circus is more friendly to pedestrians and, at night, when the neon adverts on the surrounding offices are lit up, quite spectacular. This square, stretching out from **Rådhuset** (Town Hall; *see p63;* **photo** *p63*), bustles constantly with a mixture of commuters (the city's bus terminus is here), shoppers, sightseers, *pølse* (Danish hot dog) sellers and, on weekends and holidays, street performers, gatherings and protests. The square is an important focal point for Copenhageners and Danes as a whole (Denmark's matches are shown here on a big screen during World Cups, for instance). It is also the prime gathering point for New Year's Eve celebrations. And, in the holiday season, a gigantic Christmas tree is lit up in the square on the first Sunday of Advent.

Rådhuspladsen is part of the original site of Havn, the small fishing village that stretched to Gammeltorv and down to the sea before Bishop Absalon set it on its course to regional

Rådhuspladsen: Copenhagen's main square is a byword for bustle. *See p61.*

domination. By the 13th century the city rampart, protected by a moat, stretched from Vester Voldgade on the eastern side of the square, along Nørre Voldgade and down Gothersgade to what is now Kongens Nytorv, in a defensive arc that marks the boundaries of medieval Copenhagen. All that remains of those medieval fortifications today is Jarmers Tårn, a small ruin located on a roundabout in Jarmers Plads (at the north end of Vester Voldgade). The square itself lay outside the ramparts as it was used (up until 1850) as a haymarket and there was a risk of fire. The layout of the streets within the medieval ramparts also remains pretty much intact from that period – a blind Copenhagener from the 14th century could probably still find his way from Rådhuspladsen to Købmagergade (if he didn't become disorientated by the smell from kebab vendors).

Rådhuspladsen is also where the last western city gate stood until the middle of the 19th century. In 1888 the square hosted a million visitors at a huge exhibition of industry, agriculture and art. At that time the square was designed in a shell shape, like the famous main piazza in Siena, Italy, but the pressures of the internal combustion engine soon saw its corners squared off.

There's lots to see in and around this area. On HC Andersens Boulevard is a large statue of, appropriately enough, Hans Christian Andersen. In front of that stands the striking Dragon Fountain, by Joachim Skovgaard. Nearby is a small carved stone pillar that marks the centre or 'zero point' of Copenhagen. And high on the corner of the Unibank building on HC Andersens Boulevard and Vesterbrogade

is one of the city's quirkiest talking points: a barometer erected in 1936 and designed by Danish artist E Utzon-Frank, featuring a girl on a bicycle (if it's fair) or under an umbrella (if it's not).

Also on the Tivoli side of the square is **Louis Tussaud's Wax Museum** (*see p63*), founded by Marie Tussaud's great-grandson. Slavishly following the model of Madame Tussaud's tourist honey pot in London, this smaller collection of celebrity wax effigies (200 in total) opened in 1974. As with the original museum, the likenesses are erratic but at least an effort has been made to incorporate figures from Danish history into the collection.

Towering over the opposite side of Rådhuset is a pillar crowned by a bronze statue of two Vikings blowing lurs (S-shaped bronze horns). These are similar to the ones you can see in Nationalmuseet. The statue, by Siegfried Wagner, was erected in 1914. Next to the pillar is the elegant façade of the Anton Rosen-designed **Palace Hotel** (*see p38*).

Next door is **Ripley's Believe It or Not Museum** (*see p63*), part of a worldwide chain of freak shows based on an idea by the American showman Robert Ripley. The grotesque bric-a-brac on display here includes two-headed animals, voodoo dolls and Papua New Guinean penis sheaths. Housed (or rather crammed) within the same complex is a new and, sadly, pitiful **Hans Christian Andersen** exhibition, cobbled together to coincide with the 200th anniversary of his birth in 2005, and featuring fibreglass reconstructions of 'olde worlde' Odense streets and a few factoids about the great man's life. And little else. Bearing in mind that Copenhagen was Andersen's home from the age of 14 onwards, it is sad bordering on outrageous that it is the only permanent exhibition about the writer in the city.

Rådhuset (*see below*), situated on the southern side of Rådhuspladsen, is the city's administrative and political heart, as well as a venue for exhibitions and concerts. Denmark's second tallest tower (105.6 metres/346 feet; the tallest, just, is part of Christiansborg Slot), located on its eastern side, is almost incidental to the decorative splendour of this, the sixth town hall in Copenhagen's history. Completed in 1905, Rådhuset has been the site of numerous elections (polling takes place in its central hall); home to as many city administrations; endured occupation by the Germans during World War II; and welcomed the returning football heroes from the 1992 European Championships, when Schmeichel, Laudrup and company famously brought the city to a standstill during their appearance on the balcony overlooking Rådhuspladsen.

At first glance Rådhuset, inspired, like the square, by its Sienese counterpart, looks imposing, monolithic and a little bit dull, but at close quarters this national romantic masterpiece by architect Professor Martin Nyrop reveals its witty, sometimes gruesome, but invariably exuberant architectural detail. The balcony is above the front door and above that is a golden statue by HW Bissen of Bishop Absalon. Higher up, lining the front of the roof, stand six watchmen, separated by the city flagpole (watch for a swallow-tailed flag on special occasions, such as the Queen's

birthday). This rises from the city's coat of arms, presented in 1661 by King Frederik III in thanks for the people's support during a city siege. Across the façade are countless gargoyles, reliefs and individually crafted stone and iron figures (check out the hilarious walruses guarding the back door), while by the right-hand side of the entrance are three grotesque bronze dragon-gargoyles, hunched as if ready to spring into action.

Inside, Rådhuset's endless corridors, halls, council chambers and meeting rooms offer a decorative feast to inquisitive visitors who can roam with surprising freedom. Highlights include busts of HC Andersen, the physicist Niels Bohr, Professor Nyrop and sculptor Bertel Thorvaldsen (in the central hall), the library, the banqueting hall, various mosaic floors, chandeliers, reliefs, intricate brickwork and painted ceilings.

Rådhuset is also home to an horological masterpiece, **Jens Olsens Verdensur** (Jens Olsen's World Clock). The clock cost one million kroner to build (and 27 years to make; it was first set in 1955) and is very accurate, losing only milliseconds each century. It displays the local time, sidereal time (gauged by the motion of the earth relative to the fixed background of distant stars, rather than the sun), firmament and celestial pole movement, the movement of the planets, and sunrises and sunsets. The clock is in a room on the right by Rådhuset's main door. An information office, where you can also buy tickets to the clock and the tower, is on the left.

Louis Tussaud's Wax Museum

HC Andersens Boulevard 22 (33 11 89 00/www.tussaud.dk). **Open** *Apr-mid Sept* 10am-11pm (last entry 10pm) daily. *Mid Sept-Mar* 10am-6pm (last entry 5pm) daily. **Admission** 80kr; 35kr-59kr concessions. **Credit** MC, V. **Map** p250 O12.

Rådhuset

Rådhuspladsen (33 66 25 82/83/www.kk.dk). **Open** 7.45am-5pm Mon-Fri; 9.30am-1pm Sat; closed Sun. *Guided tour* June-Sept 1pm (3pm in English) Mon-Fri; 10am, 11am Sat. Oct-May 10am, 1pm, 2pm (3pm in English). *Rådhuset Tower tour* June-Sept 10am, noon, 2pm Mon-Fri; noon Sat. Oct-May noon Mon-Sat. *Jens Olsens Verdensur* 10am-4pm Mon-Fri; 10am-1pm Sat. **Admission** *Rådhuset guided tour* 30kr. *Rådhuset Tower tour* 20kr. *Jens Olsens Verdensur* 10kr; 5kr concessions. **No credit cards**. **Map** p250 O12.

Ripley's Believe It or Not Museum

Rådhuspladsen 57 (33 91 89 91/www.ripleys.dk). **Open** *10-31 May, 1-12 Sept* 10am-8pm daily. *June-Aug* 9.30am-10pm daily. *13 Sept-9 May* 10am-6pm Mon-Thur, Sun; 10am-8pm Fri, Sat. **Admission** 88kr; 42kr-66kr concessions. Credit DC, MC, V. **Map** p250 O12.

Rådhuset,

Strøget & Around

From Bang & Olufsen flatscreens to Little Mermaid mugs, Strøget wants your kroner.

Strøget might be the best-known street in Copenhagen, but you won't find its name on any maps (apart from in this guide). In fact, Strøget (meaning 'stripe' and often referred to as 'the walking street') is actually made up of five streets – Østergade, Amagertorv, Nygade, Vimmelskaftet and Frederiksberggade – running from Kongens Nytorv at its eastern end, more than a kilometre (0.6 of a mile) to the west. Formerly called Routen, the streets had become so congested with traffic by the early 1960s that extreme measures were taken: the whole thing was temporarily turned into a pedestrian zone in 1962. It was so successful, two years later the arrangement was made permanent. These days it's hard to imagine it filled with cars.

Broadly speaking, Strøget becomes more downmarket as you approach Rådhuspladsen, with the very posh shops, like Louis Vuitton, Prada and Birger Christensen, clustered at the eastern end towards Kongens Nytorv. The 'posh watershed' is Amagertorv, where you will find the magnificent Royal Copenhagen stores. The middle section of Strøget from Amagertorv to Gammeltorv and Nytorv is middlebrow, dotted with familiar chains such as H&M and Zara, while beyond there is a touristy mix of kebab vendors and souvenir shops. Keep in mind, though, that 'downmarket' in Copenhagen terms is still very presentable.

Despite its cosmopolitan feel and stylish shopfronts, Strøget's medieval origins have ensured that it has retained an intimate charm. In fact, it makes Oxford Street or the Champs-Elysées look like motorways in comparison. And it helps make Copenhagen one of the most user-friendly shopping cities in the world.

Eastern Strøget & Købmagergade

As well as shops and cafés, Strøget has several museums. From Kongens Nytorv the first you arrive at is the **Guinness World Records Museum** (*see p66*). Part of a chain, the Guinness museum unaccountably lures in the passing crowds. Kids like it, though, and the fact that the **Mystic Exploratorie** (a bizarre mix of science and the supernatural; *see p66*) has recently moved here is a bonus.

Further down Strøget, you come to Sankt Nikolaj Kirke in historic Nikolaj Plads. The church is no longer used for services, but is now home to the **Nikolaj – Copenhagen Contemporary Art Center** (*see p179*), which holds six different shows a year. The church dates from the 13th century, but the fire of 1795 destroyed all but the tower; it was rebuilt in 1917. The beautiful square is a main venue for the Copenhagen Jazz Festival.

Back on Strøget, among the designer stores, is **Illum** department store (*see p139*), which stretches to the corner of Købmagergade.

A third of the way from Kongens Nytorv Strøget meets its pedestrian tributary, Købmagergade. Walk up Købmagergade and you'll come to Copenhagen's most infamous attraction, **Museum Erotica** (*see p66*), founded by Ole Ege (son of a chief of police). Though not for the faint-hearted, it offers a fascinating trawl through the history of pornography – from Roman and oriental decorative erotic art to *Playboy* and rather more extreme genres (animal lovers should stay away!). Like the highest shelf in a newsagent's, the museum doesn't get really sleazy until you reach the top, where an entire wall of TVs screening non-stop hardcore porn videos awaits. The museum has excellent English captions, best employed in the salacious room dedicated to the sex lives of the famous (where visitors discover the secret of Toulouse-Lautrec's success with the ladies and that Rousseau waited in dark alleys with his trousers round his ankles in the hope that passing women might spank him). The Gay and 'Shock Room' sections add further variety.

Kronprinsensgade, the fashion epicentre, is off Købmagergade, with numerous top label clothing and shoe stores, plus two cafés and a great chocolate shop. Most of the streets north of Østergade (the first leg of Strøget) – Pilestræde, Grønnegade, Ny Adelgade and Ny Østergade – are eminently wanderable.

Back on Købmagergade is the **Post & Tele Museum** (*see p66*), a surprisingly well-presented museum dedicated to the 400-year history of Denmark's communications services. All the state-of-the-art museum know-how in the world can't, however, make stamps that interesting to non-philatelists. Do, though, visit the rooftop café with views of old Copenhagen to rival the Rundetårn's (only here there's a lift). It's open afternoons, and late on Wednesdays, when it serves a menu of Danish and international cuisine.

A little further up is Købmagergade's other main draw: the **Rundetårn** (Round Tower; *see p66*). Completed in 1642 at the behest of Christian IV (it was his last major building project), the red-brick Rundetårn was originally intended as an observatory for the nearby university, and is still the oldest functioning observatory in Europe. Christian is commemorated on the front in a red and gold wrought iron lattice; the letters RFP stand for the famously lecherous king's unlikely motto: *Regna Firmat Pietas* – 'Piety Strengthens the Realm'. The Rundetårn is unique in European architecture for its cobbled spiral walkway that winds seven-and-a-half times round its core for 209 metres (686 feet) almost to the top of the tower, 34.8 metres (114 feet) above the city. There are only a few stairs at the very top, from where the view, as you'd expect, is superb. Tsar Peter the Great rode all the way to the top in 1716 (the Tsarina followed in a carriage); while a car is said to have driven up in 1902. Halfway up is an exhibition space (formerly the university library hall) that hosts a changing programme of artistic, scientific and historical

Strøget.

The bare facts, brazenly displayed at **Museum Erotica**.

displays. The observatory at the top is sometimes open, with an astronomer on hand to explain what you can see through the telescope. The Rundetårn was deemed such a significant building that during the 18th century the Royal Danish Academy of Sciences used it as the main reference point for the surveying of Denmark.

The tower stands beside **Trinitatiskirke** (Trinity Church; *see p67*), which was erected in 1637, and boasts a baroque altar by Friedrich Ehbisch as well as a three-faced rococo clock from 1757. Opposite the Rundetårn you'll find **Regensen**, built in 1616 as a student hall of residence for the nearby University, and still in use as such today. Around the corner, on Krystalgade, is the city's **Synagoge** (synagogue), dating from 1833.

Towards the northern end of Købmagergade is **Kultorvet**, a large square that becomes gridlocked in summer with café tables, fruit and veg stalls and beer stands. Continue on over Nørre Voldgade (the northern boundary of the old city ramparts) and you arrive at **Israels Plads**. The square was named in honour of the the Danes who helped 7,000 Jews escape during World War II. Israels Plads hosts a large fruit and veg market daily and, on Saturdays in the summer, a small antiques and flea market.

Guinness World Records Museum & Mystic Exploratorie

Østergade 16 (33 32 31 31/www.guinness.dk). **Open** *Mid June-Aug* 9.30am-10.30pm (last entry 9.30pm) daily. *Sept-mid June* 10am-6pm Mon-Thur, Sun; 10am-8pm Fri, Sat. **Admission** 83kr; 42kr-66kr concessions; free under-5s. **Credit** DC, MC, V. **Map** p251 M15.

Museum Erotica

Købmagergade 24 (33 12 03 11/www.museum erotica.dk). **Open** *Oct-Apr* 11am-8pm Mon-Thur, Sun; 10am-10pm Fri, Sat. **Admission** 109kr, incl catalogue; 79kr-89kr concessions. **Credit** AmEx, DC, MC, V. **Map** p251 M14.

Post & Tele Museum

Købmagergade 37 (33 41 09 00/www.ptt-museum.dk). **Open** 10am-5pm Tue, Thur-Sat; 10am-8pm Wed; noon-4pm Sun. **Admission** 30kr; 15kr concessions; free to all Wed. **Credit** MC, V. **Map** p251 M14.

Rundetårn

Købmagergade 52A (33 73 03 73/www.runde taarn.dk). **Open** *Tower* June-Aug 10am-8pm Mon-Sat; noon-8pm Sun. Sept-May 10am-5pm Mon-Sat; noon-5pm Sun. *Observatory* 1 Oct-25 Mar 10pm Tue, Wed. 26 Mar-30 Sept closed. **Admission** 25kr; 5kr concessions; free under-5s. **Credit** AmEx, DC, MC, V. **Map** p251 M13.

Trinitatiskirke
Landemærket 2 (33 32 09 04/www.trinitatiskirke.dk).
Open 9.30am-4.30pm Mon-Sat; times of services Sun.
Admission free. **Map** p251 M13.

The 'Latin Quarter'

North of the middle part of Strøget lies what's
ambitiously termed Copenhagen's 'Latin
Quarter' (on account of its narrow alleyways,
cobbled café squares and bustling student life).
At its heart is **Gråbrødretorv**, a delightful
restaurant square, like Nyhavn without a canal.
It comes alive in summer as tables and parasols
from its (good but costly) restaurants spill out
on to the cobbles. The square was created in
1664 after Corfitz Ulfeldt, the secretary of war
and husband of Eleonore Christine (daughter
of Christian IV), had his mansion torn down
as punishment for high treason. After a fire in
1728 many houses here were rebuilt with
triangular gable-ends, typical of the period.

West of here, on Nørregade, is Copenhagen's
modest cathedral, **Vor Frue Kirke** (Church
of Our Lady; *see below*), where Crown Prince
Frederik married his Australian wife Mary
Donaldson. Six churches have stood on this site
since 1191, the first five suffering from a variety
of misfortunes. The destruction of Vor Frue
Kirke's art treasures by the Lutherans during
the Reformation in the 16th century stands as
one of their more barbaric acts.

The current structure by CF Hansen was
consecrated in 1829 and replaced the church
destroyed by the British bombardment of
1807 (they used its 100-metre/328-foot spire
as a target). The interior's spartan whitewash
is relieved by several figures by **Thorvaldsen**
(*see p78*), including his famous depiction of
Christ. The church often hosts musical events.

Next to Vor Frue Kirke is a large cobbled
square, **Frue Plads**. The rather grimy
building opposite the church is part of
Universitet, founded by Christian I in 1479.
The present building stands on the same site
as the original (itself built over the Bishop's
Palace), and was designed by Peter Malling
and inaugurated by Frederik VI in 1836. The
ornate great hall is worth a look and, if you
have time, pop into the University Library
round the corner in Fiolstræde. Halfway up
the stairs is a small glass cabinet containing
some fragments of a cannon ball and the book
in which they were found embedded after the
British bombardment. The title of the book, by
Marsilius of Padua, is *Defender of Peace*.

Vor Frue Kirke
Nørregade 8 (www.koebenhavnsdomkirke.dk).
Open 8am-5pm Mon-Sat. **Admission** free.
Map p251 N13.

Central Strøget & Gammel Strand

In 1985 three venerable Strøget institutions
on Amagertorv amalgamated to form **Royal
Copenhagen**, the pride of the city's retail
portfolio and an absolute must for visitors
even if you find the prices a touch steep.

Amagertorv dates from the 14th century. In
the 17th century a law was passed that meant
all the produce grown on Amager island (where
the airport is now located) had to be sold at the
market here and soon shops grew up around
the stalls. This has always been one of
Copenhagen's main markets and meeting
places and, though the stalls have long gone,
the fountain is still much used as a rendezvous.
Adjoining Amagertorv, towards Slotsholmen,
is another busy square, **Højbro Plads**. Its
main feature is a 1902 equestrian statue of
Bishop Absalon (*see p28; photo p70*), the
founder of Copenhagen, by HW Bissen, with an
inscription that reads: 'He was courageous, wise
and far-sighted, a friend of scholarship, in the
intensity of his striving a true son of Denmark.'

South of Strøget is **Gammel Strand**
(Old Beach), home to some pricey restaurants
(**Thorvaldsens Hus** – *see p112* – is one of
the best). In the time of Bishop Absalon, and
for centuries afterwards, Gammel Strand was
where fish was sold (and therefore the city's
commercial centre). It was here that the
Øresund herring were landed before being
transported throughout Catholic Europe – fish
being vital for a population that often abstained
from meat. Gammel Strand remained part of
Copenhagen's seafront, which stretched from
what is today Fortunstræde, along Gammel
Strand to Snaregade, Magstræde and
Løngangstræde until well into the Middle Ages.
By the bridge from Højbro Plads to Slotsholmen
is a stout stone statue (dating from 1940) of a
foul-mouthed and quarrelsome fishwife
grasping a huge flounder by the gills, in
memory of a trade that continued into the 20th
century. There is still a fishmonger's nearby
on Højbro Plads (it does a swift trade in sushi).
Cross to the other side of the bridge and look
into the water and you'll see the sculpture of
the Merman with his Sons (it's illuminated at
night). All of Gammel Strand, except for
No.48, burned to the ground in 1795. During
the summer, take a canal tour or harbour trip
to the Little Mermaid from Gammel Strand.
Or try the excellent kayak tour (for both, *see
p52* **Ways to see the city**).

The next major sight as you continue west
along Strøget is **Helligåndskirken** (Church
of the Holy Spirit; *see p70*), dating from 1400.

Walk From capitalism to Christiania

Start: Kongens Nytorv.
Finish: Christianshavn metro station.
Length: 6km (4 miles) approximately.
Time: 2.5 hours (not including sightseeing and refreshment stops).

This walk gives you a really good feel for the city, ancient and modern, and takes in many of its major sights, from Europe's longest pedestrianised shopping street and its most magical theme park, to Copenhagen's political heart and its 'alternative' mini-state.

Begin at Kongens Nytorv, the city's grandest square, fronted by **Det Kongelige Teater** *(see p193)*, the French Embassy, the new **Bang & Olufsen** flagship store *(see p157)* and **Magasin** *(see p139)*, Scandinavia's largest department store. If you face the famous **Hotel d'Angleterre** *(see p42)*, the pedestrianised street to the left of the hotel is Strøget, the backbone of Copenhagen and its main shopping area. Walk down what is Strøget's 'posh' end, past the flagship **Bodum** store *(see p157)* and the **Illum** department store *(see p139)* on your right, and you soon arrive at Amagertorv, and the elegant Storkespringvandet (the Stork Fountain). The square has some of the most exclusive shops in the city.

From Amagertorv, head north along Købmagergade past the mildly titillating **Museum Erotica** *(see p66)* on your right. After a few minutes the extraordinary **Rundetårn** observatory tower *(see p66)* looms on your right. Climb the cobbled spiral walkway to the top for superb views over the city. Take Store Kannikestræde (opposite the tower's entrance) and walk through what is known as Copenhagen's 'Latin Quarter', where the oldest part of the city's university is located. At the end of the street you come to Vor Frue Plads, a large cobbled square with, on the right, the red-brick university buildings and, in its centre to your left, **Vor Frue Kirke** *(see p67)*, Copenhagen's austere neo-classical cathedral. Turn left down Nørregade at the far end of the square and walk down to Gammeltorv and Nytorv, two more ancient squares.

Frederiksberggade brings you to crowded **Rådhuspladsen** *(see p61)* and **Rådhuset** (the Town Hall; *see p63*). Cross the square and turn left on to HC Andersens Boulevard.

Heading south-east from Rådhuspladsen along the side of **Tivoli** *(see p54)* brings you to the **Danish Design Center** *(see p61)*, on the left, and, a little further down on the right, the **Ny Carlsberg Glyptotek** *(see p61)*, one of the city's finest art collections and a great place to stop for coffee and cake in the handsome winter gardens. From here turn left on to Ny Kongensgade, then Tøjhusgade, which takes you through the middle of Slotsholmen, the island on which the city was founded 1,000 years ago. Today the area has several draws, including **Christiansborg Slot** (containing the Danish parliament; *see p79*), **Tøjhusmuseet** (the Royal Arsenal Museum; *see p79*), **Thorvaldsens Museum** (dedicated to Denmark's greatest sculptor, Bertel Thorvaldsen; *see p79*) and Copenhagen's most striking modern building, the new waterside extension to the national library, the **Black Diamond** *(see p79)*.

At the end of Tøjhusgade, turn right on to Børsgade and walk past **Børsen** (the former stock exchange, with its famous dragons' tails spire – not open to the public). When you reach the harbour it is a short hop across Knippelsbro bridge to Christianshavn. Carry on along the main Torvegade, cross over the cutesy Christianshavns Canal, and turn left on to Dronningensgade. At the end of the street, turn right on to Bådsmandsstræde and head into the Free Town of **Christiania** *(see p93)*, where flower power is still stumbling along in the face of development, its laid-back vibe making it a great place to unwind. Head across the Free Town to **Morgenstedet** *(see p121)* for a mean vegetable curry at an even meaner price. Once you've finished unwinding, pass back under the sign at the entrance saying 'You are now entering the EU', turn left and walk along Prinsessegade. Another of the city's most recognisable landmarks, **Vor Frelsers Kirke** *(see p93)*, soon looms into view. If you have a head for heights and a bit of energy, climb the 400-odd steps to the top of the fab 90-metre (295-foot) high copper and gold spire; it offers one of the best views of the city. Back at ground level, continue along Prinsessegade. At Torvegade, turn right and it's only a few steps to the gleaming Christianshavn metro station, from where it's one stop back to Kongens Nytorv.

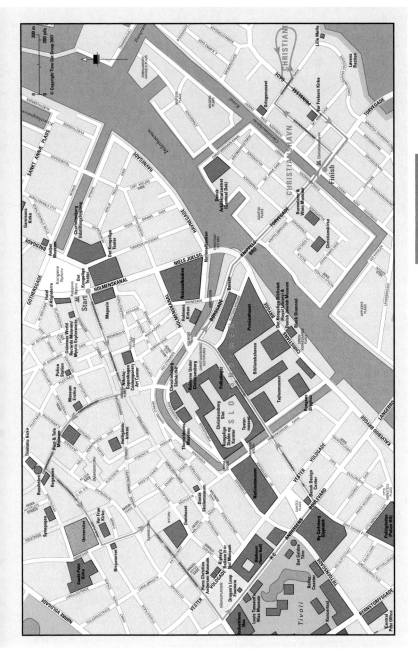

It was originally part of the Grey Friars monastery, the oldest religious site in the city, founded in 1238. The early monks were hardy, ascetic souls and their devoted piety earned them much respect, but when they relaxed their standards during the 16th century they were expelled from the city by the Protestant reformers. The current neo-Renaissance structure dates from 1880. In the churchyard is a memorial to the Danish victims of Nazi concentration camps.

Helligåndskirken

Nils Hemmingsensgade 5, Amagertorv (33 15 41 44/www.helligaandskirken.dk). **Open** noon-4pm Mon-Fri; times of services Sun. **Admission** free. **Map** p251 N14.

Western Strøget

West from Helligåndskirken, Strøget starts downmarket, with various cheap eateries serving pizzas, kebabs, ice-cream and waffles. The watershed comes at Gammeltorv and Nytorv, two picturesque cobbled squares, beyond which things start to get very touristy. During the 14th century Gammeltorv, the oldest square in the city, was the hub of Copenhagen, a busy market, meeting place and (occasional) jousting site for the 5,000 residents of what was the largest settlement in northern Europe. The two squares became one (though they are bisected by Strøget) after the fire of 1795 destroyed the town hall that separated them.

When visitors arrive in Gammeltorv, one of the first things they notice is the extraordinary **Caritas Springvandet** (the Charity Fountain; **photo** *p71*). Dating from 1608, this Renaissance masterpiece is made from copper and depicts a pregnant woman and two children with fishy gargoyles at their feet. On royal birthdays golden apples dance on the water jets.

Of interest chiefly because of its grand neo-classical façade, featuring six Ionic columns, Copenhagen's imposing and elegant **Domhuset** (Court House) on Nytorv was built in 1805-15 (work was suspended for a while in 1807 due to the bombardment by the British). The dusky pink building was designed by CF Hansen, who was also responsible for Vor Frue Kirke (*see p67*), just a short walk away up Nørregade. Domhuset was built on the site of the former town hall and, up until 1905, it served as both courthouse and town hall. Today it houses court rooms, conference rooms and chambers. The nearby Slutterigade (Prison Street) annexe was built as a prison in 1816 and converted to court rooms and chambers in 1944. It is attached to Domhuset via two recently restored arches, one of which joins the many crossings around the world known as the Bridge of Sighs (prisoners, bemoaning their fate, are led across it when going to and from the court rooms).

In 1848 Nytorv was the starting point for the relatively peaceful march by 10,000 Copenhageners on Christiansborg Slot, demanding the end of absolute monarchy. Frederik VII had conceded defeat before they even arrived. Søren Kierkegaard (*see p104* **Dead famous**) lived for a while in Nytorv in a house on a site now occupied by Den Danske Bank. Look out too for the outline of Copenhagen's first town hall (before it moved to Rådhuspladsen) traced in the paving of Nytorv beneath the fruit and veg sellers who usually pitch here. Incidentally, Mozart's widow Constanze lived with her second husband (Georg Nikolaus Nissen, a Danish diplomat) at Lavendelstræde 1. The street runs from Nytorv's southern corner towards Rådhuspladsen.

In Rådhusstræde, south of Nytorv, is the **Dansk Skolemuseum** (*see below*), dedicated to the history of Danish education. Only really for those with a special interest, the museum includes old classrooms and exhibitions divided by subject. Its pride and joy are 12,000 period educational illustrations from the first half of the 20th century, many of which are on show.

The final stretch of Strøget is along Frederiksberggade, which opened up between Nytorv and Rådhuspladsen when the fire of 1728 razed the buildings here. On the right as you approach Rådhuspladsen is the rough and ready Club Absalon, built on the site of the city's first church, Sankt Clemens Kirke. The church was probably built by Absalon in the 1160s, but was demolished in the early 16th century. Rather ignominiously, some of its foundations can be seen in the bar's toilets. In a city that usually cares for its heritage this seems something of a dereliction of duty.

South of Strøget is a network of narrow medieval streets (including Farvergade, Magstræde, Snaregade, Kompagnistræde and Læderstræde), packed with a range of excellent independent shops, as well as some of the best cafés in the city. It's yet another place that the medieval city planners appear to have designed with 21st-century window shoppers in mind.

To the north of Frederiksberggade, in an area bookended by Nørregade and Vester Voldgade, lies the liveliest area around Strøget, known as Pisserenden. 'Piss' means the same in Danish as it does in English, and this district was thus named due to its notoriety as an odoriferous dwelling for prostitutes and criminals, until it was purged by the first great fire of 1728. Today Pisserenden is one of the youngest and most vibrant shopping and café areas of Copenhagen, full of the coolest (but relatively cheap) clothes, skateboarding, book and record shops. Most of the streets (which include Kattesundet, Vestergade, Larsbjørnsstræde and Teglgårdstræde) are also blessed with great restaurants, cafés and bars.

Dansk Skolemuseum

Rådhusstræde 6 (33 15 58 10/www.skolemuseum. dk). **Open** 10am-4pm Mon-Fri; noon-4pm Sun. **Admission** 30kr; 20kr-25kr concessions. **No credit cards. Map** p251 O13.

Renaissance relaxation at **Caritas Springvandet**. *See p70.*

Nyhavn & Kongens Nytorv

Cameras at the ready, Nyhavn is cute Copenhagen at its best.

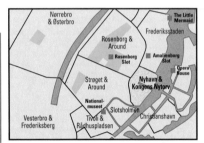

Nyhavn

King Christian V opened the canal of **Nyhavn** in 1670 to allow ships access to central Copenhagen, but these days water traffic consists mostly of canal tour boats and a couple of floating cafés. The real traffic now is found on the sunny canalside pavements – whenever a hint of spring appears, the place is teeming with locals and tourists out for a stroll, a drink or both, sitting at an expensive café or perching on the cobblestones with a shopping bag full of *høkerbajere* (beers from the off-licence).

After the British bombardment of 1807, Nyhavn's so-called 'Palmy Days' of prosperity were brought to a rude end and the wealthy merchants moved out. By coincidence, **Hans Christian Andersen** moved in shortly after, and lived at three different addresses on the canal during his lifetime. During this time Nyhavn's quayside saw service as one of the city's red light districts and was notorious for its crime rate and confidence tricksters. As recently as the 1950s this was a disreputable place, lined with drinkers' bars, knocking shops and tattoo parlours, and in fact one strip club and the famous Ole's tattoo parlour remain. Together with the historic ships moored here as part of Nationalmuseet's collection, they are an evocative reminder of the past.

These days Denmark's greatest writer would hardly recognise the place. If the sun so much as peeps from behind the clouds, hundreds of tables from Nyhavn's ever popular restaurants and cafés (plus, in the autumn months, the

all-important umbrella heaters) pour out on to the quayside. It has to be said that the restaurants along Nyhavn vary from decent to dreadful and few represent good value (Cap Horn at 21 and Salt, around the corner on the harbour front, are exceptions – *see p116*), but the quayside is always a great place for a beer or two before going on elsewhere.

Two charming shopping streets, **Store Strandstræde** and **Lille Strandstræde**, are good for antiques, women's clothes, art and ceramics, and lead off Nyhavn on the north side. On the quieter south side, the main draw is the 17th-century Dutch baroque palace of Charlottenborg, home to Det Kongelige Kunstakademi (the Royal Academy of Fine Arts) since 1754. Charlottenborg offers a constantly changing programme of exhibitions of contemporary art in the **Charlottenborg Udstillingsbygning** (Charlottenborg Exhibition; *see p177*).

Kongens Nytorv

Windswept and stately, **Kongens Nytorv** (1680) always had the potential to become Copenhagen's grandest square and the planting of beech trees (the national tree) and a face-lift have improved things, though the traffic still encircles it 24/7. But the square is graced by some of the city's finest buildings; in its centre is a faintly absurd statue (by Abraham-César Lamoureux; 1687) of its patron, Christian V, depicting him as a Roman general astride his horse. The weight of the gilded lead statue eventually proved too much for the horse's legs and it had to be recast in bronze in 1946.

Kongens Nytorv was built on the site of former ramparts that ringed the city in an arc all the way from Rådhuspladsen. It is an excellent starting point for a tour of the city, as Bredgade, Nyhavn and Strøget all radiate from it and most of the other main sights are within a few minutes' walk. Around Christmas time its artificial ice rink is a major draw.

The square is dominated to the south-east by **Det Kongelige Teater** (the Royal Theatre; *see p194; photo p74*). Prior to the opening of

Hans Christian Andersen's Copenhagen

He may have been born in the Fyn town of Odense but Denmark's greatest writer, **Hans Christian Andersen**, couldn't wait to leave and seek his fortune in Copenhagen. Andersen arrived on Monday, 6 September 1819 (he had to walk the last few miles into town because he couldn't afford the full fare), a day so momentous that he marked it as his 'second birthday' every year thereafter.

'The whole city was in commotion,' he wrote of that day when, unknown to him, Copenhagen was in the grip of its last pogrom, 'and the noise and tumult far exceeded any idea which my imagination had formed of this, to me at that time, great city.'

He arrived virtually penniless and alone – but for a few names he thought worth contacting. Yet he possessed an almost supernatural amount of self-confidence. Andersen believed he was something special from an early age and immediately set about making something of his talents at the Royal Theatre. On his first visit, the night he arrived in the city, he was so naïve that he accepted a ticket from a tout as if it were a gift.

Andersen's confidence was shaken by the rejection of his ballet dancing, singing and acting skills, but slowly he built up contacts among Copenhagen's cultured bourgeoisie who would sponsor his education and finance his early attempts at writing. These were not instantly successful, but his first published piece of any significance, a fantasy based on a walk on New Year's Eve across the city to Amager, was a moderate hit. It was all the encouragement his pathological need for recognition required. Poetry, plays and novels followed, few of which hold up to scrutiny today. But in 1835, almost as an afterthought, he published a small book of stories for children. Little did he know it, but these would be the works for which Andersen would be remembered. Over 150 stories followed, many becoming world famous. Tales like *The Little Mermaid, The Emperor's New Clothes, The Snow Queen, Thumbelina, The Princess and the Pea, The Red Shoes* and *The Little Match Girl* remain widely read and translated, their messages and morals as universal today as when they were written. Copenhagen features often in these stories, both its places and people.

Andersen was a nomad. He travelled more widely in Europe than any other Dane of his time, and that nomadic instinct extended to his domestic living arrangements. He never owned his own home (he didn't even buy a piece of furniture until he was 60, and that was a bed), instead living at various addresses in Copenhagen and, in his later infirmity, at the homes of aristocratic friends (he was an accomplished social climber).

From the inn on Vestergade where he stayed for his first nights in the city, Andersen moved to a windowless room in a house in the brothel street of Ulkegade behind Kongens Nytorv. And though he moved often, it was never far from the Royal Theatre, the centre of his life. He stayed, variously, in the attic of Copenhagen's oldest house, **Vingårdstræde 6** (today you'll find Kong Hans Restaurant in the basement – *see p115*), rooms in the **Hotel d'Angleterre** (*see p42*) and its neighbour **Hotel du Nord** (now Magasin – *see p139*), where he lodged from 1838 to 1847. But it was **Nyhavn** that he returned to again and again, lured by its whiff of travel. He lived there initially at No.20, where he wrote his first fairytales, then from 1848 to 1865 at No.67, and finally from 1873 to 1875 at No.18.

When Tivoli Gardens opened in 1843 Andersen was among the first through the gate and he visited often; in fact, he was inspired to write one of his most famous stories, *The Nightingale*, after a visit (Tivoli marks this association with a dated Hans Christian Andersen fairytale ride). Andersen is commemorated nearby with the boulevard that bears his name, featuring a large statue of him on the corner of Rådhuspladsen. Another statue stands in **Kongens Have** (*see p89*). And of course, the city's famous symbol, the **Little Mermaid** (*see p83*), is inspired by one of his darkest fairy tales. There is a poor Hans Christian Andersen Museum, as part of the **Ripley's Believe It or Not** (*see p63*) freak show, but real fans will do better to head to **Odense** where there are two museums dedicated to Andersen, housed in his former childhood homes.

Hans Christian Andersen died, aged 70, in 1875 and is buried in **Assistens Kirkegård** (*see p104* **Dead famous**).

Not just for pleasure: the grand and imposing **Kongelige Teater**. *See p72.*

the new opera house, Denmark's national theatre was unique in that it produced opera, ballet and theatre together in two auditoria – Gamle (old) Scene, and Nye (new) Scene – seating 2,550 people. Now that a new venue for staging plays is being built at Kvæsthusbroen (due to open in 2008), the theatre will eventually be used exclusively for ballet.

The main neo-Renaissance building (the fourth on this site), by Vilhelm Dahlerup and Ove Petersen, dates from 1872, but the theatre was founded in 1748. The Nye Scene was added in 1931, connected via an archway to the other side of Tordenskjoldsgade. The inscription '*Ei blot til lyst*' outside is taken from the original building designed by Nicolai Eigtved and translates as 'Not just for pleasure'. This may suggest that Royal Theatre productions are rather worthy affairs, and they can be; but that doesn't stop most selling out way in advance, hence the theatre's need for other venues such as the Turbinehallerne at Adelgade 10 and Baron Bolten in Boltens Gård.

The theatre's most famous former boss was Auguste Bournonville, director of the Danish Ballet from 1830 to 1877. Outside stand statues of two other significant figures from the theatre's history, the playwright Ludvig Holberg (the father of modern Danish

theatre) and Adam Oehlenschläger, the poet. Its most famous former employee was Hans Christian Andersen, who made it his first stop when he arrived from Odense as a 14-year-old in 1819 with hopes of being a ballet dancer.

Working clockwise round the square from the theatre you come to Denmark's first department store, the grand **Magasin** (*see p139*), which replaced the Hotel du Nord in 1894 and now has a stylish new Metro station outside its main entrance; Hviids Vinstue, a venerable drinking den dating from 1723; the eastern end of Strøget; and **Hotel d'Angleterre** (*see p41*).

On a corner of the square opposite the hotel is an ornate kiosk decorated by a gold relief depicting Denmark's early aviators. At No.4 is another of the square's finest buildings, the Dutch Palladian-style **Thotts Palais** (1685), named after a previous owner, Count Otto Thott. Today the pink stucco palace houses the French Embassy. On the other side of Bredgade is the **Amber Museum** (*see below*).

Amber Museum

Ravhuset, Kongens Nytorv 2 (33 11 67 00/www. houseofamber.com). **Open** *mid May-mid Sept* 10am-7.30pm daily; *mid Sept-mid May* 10am-5.30pm daily. **Admission** 25kr; 10kr concessions. Free under-12s. **Credit** AmEx, DC, MC, V. **Map** p252 M16.

Slotsholmen

The heart of Copenhagen's power for more than 800 years.

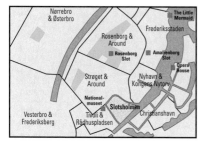

This is where it all began. Bishop Absalon, the founding father of Copenhagen, built his fortress here in the 12th century, and a city was born. The island, surrounded by harbours and canals, is a more accessible place these days, with its museums, the great Børsen stock exchange and the futuristic Black Diamond royal library. Hang around long enough, and you might even spot a government minister swanning about, still with few security concerns compared with most countries.

The largest building on Slotsholmen is **Christiansborg Slot** (Christiansborg Castle; *see p80;* **photo** *p76*), the modern day parliament building. For many centuries the previous castles that stood on this site effectively were Copenhagen, so central were they to the lives and prosperity of the townsfolk and so important were they as a power base for the region.

Its development can be divided into three stages: Absalon's fortress dating from 1167; the 17th century; and the current palace. The warrior-bishop Absalon built the original fortress on what was then the small islet of Strandholmen, in the channel separating the island of Amager from Sjælland. The fortress was ringed by a strong, thick wall of limestone blocks, with its internal buildings made from brick and timber – the first time bricks had been used in Denmark.

Bishop Absalon's fortress was badly damaged in 1259 by the avenging Wends and then burned to the ground in 1369 by an alliance of forces led by the Lübeckers against King Valdemar Atterdag. It was replaced by the first Copenhagen Castle. From 1416, when Erik of Pomerania moved in, the castle became the permanent home of the royal family (until they moved to Amalienborg Slot in 1794).

As was his way, the architect king Christian IV had the place demolished in the early 17th century, replacing it with a typically over the top baroque building, with its own chapel and very grand stables. During Frederik II's reign the castle nearly fell to the Swedes who, following a two-year siege, in February 1659 advanced towards it across the frozen sea, dressed in white cloaks to camouflage themselves. But the boiling oil, tar and water that the Danes rained down drove the Swedes away. They gave up and went home when their king, Karl Gustav X, died at the beginning of 1660. Soon after, Frederik III instructed the Dutch military engineer Henrik Ruse to build a new rampart where the Swedes had advanced. This became known as Vestervold (Western Rampart) and between it and Slotsholmen a new quarter, Frederiksholm, grew up.

Frederik IV extensively modernised the castle between 1710 and 1729 but, in 1732, Christian VI tore it all down on aesthetic grounds (the place was a mess of styles), and because its foundations were weak. The baroque replacement was one of the biggest palaces in Europe; its foundations alone cost three million *rigsdalers*, then equivalent to the entire value of Sjælland's arable land.

On the night of 26 February 1794 the whole lot burned down (bar the stables, which are still in use today). The royal family finally gave up on Slotsholmen and, like monarchical magpies, bought **Amalienborg Slot** (*see p82*). Work on the next Christiansborg Slot didn't start until 1803, due to the national bankruptcy under Frederik VI, and the building, a neo-classical masterpiece, was completed in 1828. That too was badly damaged by a fire in October 1884.

Over the years the various castles/palaces on Slotsholmen have come in for a bit of stick. In 1588 a French traveller commented, 'It is remarkable more for its age than its magnificence'. A German visitor of 1600 said that 'It resembles the dwelling of a little prince rather than a great king'. Englishman William Bromley, writing in 1699, agreed: 'The King's palace is one of the meanest that I ever saw, with a foul stinking ditch about it'.

The original castle is long gone but you can still see remnants of its foundations in the enjoyable **Ruinerne under Christiansborg** (Ruins under Christiansborg, *see p80*), a

Sightseeing

Christiansborg Slot. *See p80.*

museum dedicated to the 800-year history of the current castle site. Housed in three large underground rooms are excavations of the older castles' foundations, including stonework from Absalon's fortress, the foundations of Denmark's most famous prison, the Blåtårn (Blue Tower), and what is called Absalon's Well (though it probably dates from the 19th century). The Blåtårn was used for several centuries to house prisoners of note – most famously Leonora Christina, the daughter of Christian IV. She wrote what was probably the most important piece of 17th-century Danish prose, *Jammersminde*, while imprisoned here on suspicion of being involved in her husband's treason plot. Viewing this jumble of ancient masonry is like trying to put together the discarded pieces from several jigsaw puzzles, but the exhibition works hard to help you decipher the rubble (with English captions).

The current palace is built directly above and houses the Danish parliament, **Folketinget** (*see p80*), where 179 members sit in a semi-circle in their party groups (of which Denmark has many), facing the speaker. Government ministers sit on the right-hand side of the chamber with the prime minister closest to the platform. Folketinget is opened annually in a ceremony attended by members of the royal family on the first Tuesday in October. A public gallery is open when parliament is in session, and there are English-language tours during the parliamentary recess from July to September (2pm Mon-Fri, Sun). Christiansborg also houses the High Court, several ministries, the prime minister's department, the Royal Reception Chambers (De Kongelige Repræsentationslokaler) and the Queen's Reference Library.

You would hardly term the present-day Christiansborg a castle. Nor is it especially graceful. But it is big. Its neo-baroque granite and concrete façade was designed by Thorvald Jørgensen and was the first Christiansborg to have been built by the people's representatives. They were apparently still touchy about the monarchy as, during its design, they demanded to have at least the same number of windows overlooking the palace square as the king. Its central tower is the tallest (by 40 centimetres) in Denmark at 106 metres (358 feet). Frederik VIII laid the foundation stone for the current castle in 1907, and the Ruinerne museum displays several amazing photographs from that time.

Near the Ruinerne museum is the equestrian arena with entrances to two particularly enchanting royal attractions: the **Kongelige Stalde og Kareter** (Royal Stables and Coaches) and **Teatermuseet** (Theatre Museum; for both, *see p80*). If you can endure the equine odours the stables with their vaulted ceilings and marble columns, offer a glimpse into an extravagant royal past. The Queen's horses and coaches are still kept in grand style here and are often used for state occasions (as is a rather dusty Bentley convertible from 1969). Teatermuseet, which opened in 1922, is housed in the old Royal Court Theatre, designed by the French architect Nicolas Henri Jardin. It dates from 1766 and was modernised in 1842 – HC Andersen once performed in a ballet here in his youth. The exhibits include costumes, set designs and artworks. There is also a special cabinet of objects connected with the Royal Ballet choreographer Auguste Bournonville.

Continue across the equestrian arena to the archway beyond and you come to Frederiksholms Kanal, which is forded by

My Copenhagen Tim Rushton

Tim Rushton has been the artistic director of Danish Dance Theatre since 2001, and has shaped the company into a dynamic force on the international scene. Born in Birmingham, he came to Denmark as a dancer with the Royal Danish Ballet and left during the mid 1990s to concentrate on choreography. Since he took over the helm at DDT, the company has developed into a remarkable institution, producing fascinating pieces both nationally and internationally.

'The best part of Copenhagen is **Christianshavn**. There's a great mix of old and new, and the canals are pleasant to wander around. The cafés here are not as hyped as those in the city centre, and then of course there's my favourite restaurant, **Bastionen og Løven** (*see p135*), just behind Christiania – it's housed in an old windmill. It's got a very relaxed atmosphere and they do a superb brunch.

'One of the most magical places in the city is over the bridge in **Slotsholmen**, in the back yard of Parliament. On the left-hand side there's an old garden, **Bibliotekshaven** (*see p80*) – the Gardens of the old Royal Library. It's a very peaceful place and rarely visited by tourists. Before they moved it to the Black Diamond, the Royal Library used to be one of my favourite places to do a bit of thinking on a rainy day; you could go into the large reading rooms and look at all the sheet music.

'Copenhagen is a great shopping city and one of the best streets for a spot of retail therapy is **Stræget**, which runs parallel to Strøget. It used to be open to traffic, but now it's been pedestrianised and there's a really cosy feel to it.

'One of my favourite places to go in the early evening is **Kulturhuset** on Islands Brygge (Islands Brygge 18, 32 95 13 94, www.k-i-b.dk). I'm a sun lover, and you can enjoy the sun here on the terrace longer than anywhere else in Copenhagen. It's not sophisticated, but they serve great, cheap food. The walk here from Tivoli, past the Copenhagen Police Headquarters where Danish Dance perform the Summerdance show and over the bridge, is beautiful.'

Bibliotekshaven.

Marmorbroen (the Marble Bridge). Quite a fuss is made over this bridge, designed by Nicolai Eigtved for Christian IV and completed in 1745, but, frankly, aside from some decorative sandstone portraits, it isn't all that special (and it isn't even all marble).

Slotsholmen museums and sights are generally tucked away behind doors or in unlikely corners, which somehow makes them all the more rewarding when you do manage to track them down – that's a polite way of saying that it's a bit of a labyrinth and its main attractions are, in typical Danish fashion, poorly signposted. (It's a good idea to come on a Sunday afternoon when all the attractions are open at the same time.)

There is, however, no missing the classical stuccoed mausoleum (by Gottlieb Bindesbøll) that houses the definitive collection of works by Denmark's master sculptor, Bertel Thorvaldsen. **Thorvaldsens Museum** (*see p80*) is a must, not only for sculpture fans but for all art lovers. Denmark's greatest sculptor was born in Copenhagen on 19 November 1768. He studied at the Academy of Art, where he won the Gold Medal, and then, in 1797, a scholarship saw him off to Rome, where he lived for nearly 40 years, developing a style that was heavily influenced by Graeco-Roman mythology and creating works of a majestic, classical beauty, frequently on an epic scale.

His breakthrough, which catapulted him into the highest echelons of the neo-classical sculpture fraternity, came with the piece *Jason*, completed in 1803, and now housed in the museum. His figure of Christ, which can be seen in **Vor Frue Kirke** (*see p80*), became the model for statues of Christ the world over and remains a religious icon to this day.

Thorvaldsen returned to Copenhagen towards the end of his life and his return, as well as a general artistic revival, helped boost morale and contributed to the emergence of a cultural and social essence that is still recognisably Danish today. In 1833 he was appointed director of the Danish Academy of Fine Arts. Before his death in March 1844, Thorvaldsen bequeathed his works (plaster moulds, sketches and finished works in marble) and a collection of ancient Mediterranean art to the city, and the royal family built Thorvaldsens Museum. The sculptor is buried at its centre.

The museum is the oldest art gallery in Denmark and is a charming blend of celestial blue ceilings (painted in part by Christen Købke), elegant colonnades and mosaic floors. Although the monumental scale of Thorvaldsen's work and his prolific output are often hard to take in, it is worth persevering. His subjects include not only figures from mythology, his epic studies of Christ and numerous self-portraits, but busts of contemporaries such as Byron, Walter Scott and the Danish poet Adam Oehlenschläger. Also featured are Thorvaldsen's collections of Egyptian and Roman artefacts, contemporary Danish art, sketches and personal belongings. Outside, a fresco depicts the return of the sculptor and his works from Rome. Some English information is available.

Immediately behind Thorvaldsens Museum is **Christiansborg Slotskirke** (Christiansborg Palace Church; *see p80*), one of CF Hansen's neo-classical masterpieces, with a columned façade and a beautiful white stucco interior and dome. It was completed in 1829 and survived a fire in 1884, but the roof was destroyed by another fire that started during the Whitsun carnival in 1992. Restoration was completed just in time for the 25th anniversary of Queen Margrethe's coronation in 1997.

Børsen (the Old Stock Exchange), on the other side of Christiansborg Slotsplads, is the oldest stock exchange in Europe, built between 1619 and 1640. It still serves as a business centre and home to Copenhagen's Chamber of Commerce and, as such, is not open to the public. However, the exterior of this Renaissance wedding cake is a riot of

Christiansborg Slotskirke. *See p80.*

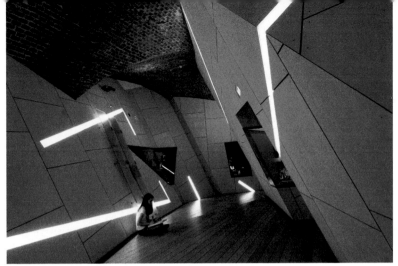

The Danish Jewish Museum, designed by Daniel Libeskind. *See p80.*

stonework, embellished gables and green copper. Above it towers one of Copenhagen's most recognisable landmarks – a fantastical 54-metre (177-foot) copper spire made of four intertwined dragons' tails, built in 1625 to a design by Ludvig Heidtrider. The three gold crowns topping the spire represent the three Nordic nations: Denmark, Sweden and Norway. Børsen (which translates as 'the covered market') was built at the behest of Christian IV, who desperately wanted Copenhagen to become the financial capital of Europe (it didn't). When it was first built, ships could moor at its doors to unload cargo into the downstairs trading hall, while upstairs were shops and businesses.

In 1634 the French diplomat Charles Ogier wrote: 'Everything decorative and practical for all male and female purposes is for sale here. It is a new and splendid building much visited by people of quality, as many women as men.'

An unusually ostentatious (for a Lutheran church) altarpiece is the main draw of **Holmens Kirke** (*see p80*), a church dedicated to sailors. Denmark's tallest pulpit (it extends right to the roof, and has recently been restored) is worth a look too. Converted, aptly, from an anchor smithy in 1619 under the orders of Christian IV, the church's rather bland exterior was augmented by the main portal (on the east side), originally from Roskilde Cathedral. Holmens Kirke is often used for royal occasions – in 1967 Queen Margrethe and Prince Henrik married here. Walk through the side door on the left of the altar and you enter a room dedicated to Denmark's naval heroes and graced by numerous ornate sarcophagi.

Across the street is a forbidding concrete building housing **Nationalbanken** (the National Bank), the work of Arne Jacobsen. Sadly, its wonderful interior and inner courtyard are not open to the public.

Another treat is **Tøjhusmuseet** (the Royal Arsenal Museum; *see p80*). Comprising an endless vaulted Renaissance cannon hall (the longest in Europe, modelled on the one in Venice), and a mind-boggling number of arms and armour in an upstairs display, this is probably the finest museum of its kind in the world. On the ground floor of what was Christian IV's original arsenal building (dating from 1589 to 1604), within walls four metres (13 feet) thick, are a vast number of gun carriages, cannons, a V-1 flying bomb from World War II and the teeniest tank you ever saw (from 1933). Upstairs, the glass cases, containing everything from 15th-century swords and pikes to modern machine guns, seem to go on forever. Many items, such as the beautiful ivory inlaid pistols and muskets, are works of art, and the royal suits of armour are equally stunning. The small arms section of the museum is housed in **Kongens Bryghus** (the King's Brewery), erected during Christian IV's reign (probably to quench the king's Herculean thirst, as well as that of his navy) which was never actually used for brewing beer but merely to store it.

Copenhagen's most beautiful 'hidden' garden, **Bibliotekshaven** (the Library Garden; *see p80;* **photo** *p77*), lies behind the old ivy-covered **Det Kongelige Bibliotek** (the Royal Library; *see p80*), through a gateway on Rigdagsgården, opposite the entrance to Folketinget. Arranged in a square around a fountain and duck pond, the garden blooms beautifully in summer, when even the bronze statue of Søren Kierkegaard looks cheerful. You can see some of the old ships' mooring rings from Christian IV's time on the walls surrounding it.

The Danes love nothing more than to juxtapose old and new, but when the designs for the new extension to the Royal Library, by architects Schmidt, Hammer and Lassen, were unveiled, few were prepared for something this radical. There are several ways to approach Denmark's national library extension, which had already earned the nickname the **Black Diamond** before it opened in autumn 1999. Perhaps the best is to walk through the old library's garden so that you are suddenly confronted with the vastness of the new structure close up.

This malevolent parallelogram, made from glass, black Zimbabwean granite (cut in Portugal and polished in Italy), Portuguese sandstone, silk concrete and Canadian maple, abuts the old building with little consideration for the clash of styles that then ensues. Its reflective surfaces interact constantly with the sky and water, altering the building's colour by the second. The 500-million-kroner library houses 200,000 books, an exhibition space, a shop, a concert hall, the **National Photography Museum** (with regular temporary exhibitions in the basement), a restaurant (**Søren K**; *see p116*), a café and conference rooms. The basement also hosts occasional exhibitions from the Book Museum. The old library, the largest in Scandinavia, with its glorious reading room (open to non-members) is accessed through a glass walkway from the first floor. Since it opened, the Black Diamond has been a huge success.

The Kongelige Bibliotek is also home to Copenhagen's newest museum, the **Danish Jewish Museum** (*see below;* **photo** *p79*). This striking adaptation of the Royal Boat House was designed by Daniel Libeskind, responsible for the new development on Ground Zero in New York. The museum is inspired by the Hebrew word 'Mitzvah', which loosely means 'compassion' and 'good deeds' – referring in part to the good deed done by the Danes towards the Jewish community during World War II (*see p16* **The great escape***).* Danish-Jewish art, history and culture are well represented.

Bibliotekshaven

Rigsdagsgården (33 92 63 00/www.ses.dk). **Open** 6am-10pm daily. **Admission** free. **Map** p251 O14.

Christiansborg Slot

Slotsholmen (33 92 64 94/www.ses.dk/ christiansborg). **Tours** (in English) *May-Sept* 11am, 1pm, 3pm daily. *Oct-Apr* 3pm Tue-Sun. Tickets 60kr; 50kr-25kr concessions. **No credit cards. Map** p251 O14.

Christiansborg Slotskirke

Christiansborg Slotsplads (33 92 64 51/www.ses.dk). **Open** *Aug-June* noon-4pm Sun. *Easter, July, 1wk mid Aug* noon-4pm daily. **Admission** free. **Map** p251 N14.

Danish Jewish Museum

Kongelige Bibliotek, entrance via garden (33 11 22 18/www.jewmus.dk). **Open** *Sept-May* 1-4pm Tue-Fri; 10am-5pm Sun; *June-Aug* 10am-5pm Tue-Sun. **Admission** 40kr; 30kr concessions; free under-16s. **Credit** AmEx, DC, MC, V. **Map** p251 P15.

Folketinget

Rigsdagsgården (33 37 55 00/www.folketinget.dk). **Tours** *July-14 Aug* 10am, 11am, 1pm, 3pm (2pm in English) Mon-Fri, Sun; *15 Aug-Sept* 3pm (2pm in English) Mon-Fri, Sun. **Admission** free. **Map** p251 O14.

Holmens Kirke

Holmens Kanal (33 13 61 78/www.holmenskirke.dk). **Open** 9am-2pm Mon-Fri; 9am-noon Sat; times of services Sun. **Admission** free. **Map** p251 O15.

Det Kongelige Bibliotek

Søren Kierkegaards Plads 1 (33 47 47 47/ www.kb.dk). **Open** *Main building* 9am-9pm Mon-Fri; 9am-4pm Sat. *Library* 10am-5pm Mon-Fri; 10am-2pm Sat. *Exhibitions* 10am-7pm Mon-Fri; 10am-5pm Sat. **Admission** *Main building & library* free. *Exhibitions* 35kr; 25kr concessions; free under-16s. *Concerts* prices vary. **Credit** V. **Map** p251 P15.

Kongelige Stalde og Kareter

Christiansborg Ridebane 12 (33 40 26 77/ www.ses.dk). **Open** *Jan-Apr* 2-4pm Sat, Sun. *May-Sept* 2-4pm Fri-Sun. *Oct-Apr* closed. **Admission** 20kr; 10kr concessions. **No credit cards. Map** p251 O14.

Ruinerne under Christiansborg

Christiansborg Slot (33 92 64 94/www.oplevslot sholmen.dk). **Open** *May-Sept* 10am-4pm daily. *Oct-Apr* 10am-4pm Tue-Sun. **Admission** 40kr; 20kr-30kr concessions. **No credit cards. Map** p251 O14.

Teatermuseet

Christiansborg Ridebane 18, southern wing of Christiansborg Slot (33 11 51 76/www.teater museet.dk). **Open** 11am-3pm Tue, Thur; 11am-5pm Wed; 1-5pm Sat, Sun. **Admission** 30kr; 20kr-25kr concessions; free under-18s. **No credit cards. Map** p251 O14.

Thorvaldsens Museum

Bertel Thorvaldsens Plads 2 (33 32 15 32/ www.thorvaldsensmuseum.dk). **Open** 10am-5pm Tue-Sun. **Admission** 20kr; 10kr concessions; free under-18s; free to all Wed. **Credit** MC, V. **Map** p251 O14.

Tøjhusmuseet

Tøjhusgade 3 (33 11 60 37/www.thm.dk). **Open** noon-4pm Tue-Sun. **Admission** 40kr; 25kr concessions; free under-17s. **No credit cards. Map** p251 P14.

Frederiksstaden

Home to three of Denmark's most powerful institutions – the Queen,
the head office of Maersk and a little bronze mermaid.

Rich on elegance, if not on atmosphere,
Frederiksstaden has a regal ambience
about it. There's old money here, and the
restaurants around Bredgade and Store
Kongensgade are a favourite lunch spot for
lawyers and stockbrokers. Along the water,
museums, galleries, cruise ships and yachts
dominate. Oh, and the area is also home to
Copenhagen's reluctant city symbol, the
Little Mermaid, sitting slumped on a rock.
Frederiksstaden's other famous residents, the
Queen and her family, live at the low-key
Amalienborg palaces right in the centre.

You come to Frederiksstaden by heading
north from the tourist hubbub of Nyhavn into
Bredgade. Here the architecture changes
dramatically, from quaint, multicoloured gabled
houses to the straight, wide, French-influenced

streets laid out in the 18th century for
Copenhagen's nobility and nouveaux riches.
Frederiksstaden was the vision of Frederik V,
who wished to celebrate the 300th anniversary
of the House of Oldenburg in 1749 with a grand
new building project. The king didn't, however,
fancy paying for it so, instead, he donated the
land on the condition that selected members of
Copenhagen's nobility commission the rococo
architect Nicolai Eigtved to build a stylistically
uniform quarter. Today Bredgade (meaning
'wide street') is itself packed with treasures,
some more obvious than others.

The main auction houses are based here, as
are numerous art and antiques dealers from
the higher end of the market, which make for
good window-shopping. A short way down
Bredgade on the right is Sankt Annæ Plads,
a quiet tree-lined square, with a statue of King
Christian X at its head and a dull, red-brick
church, **Garnisonskirken**, to the right.

Another, far more impressive, church,
Frederikskirken, better known as
Marmorkirken (the Marble Church; *see p86*),
awaits a short walk away. Although today it is
one of Copenhagen's most breathtaking sights,
the circular, domed Marmorkirken very nearly
didn't get built. Work on the church, designed
by Nicolai Eigtved as the focal point of the new
quarter, began in 1749 with the laying of the
foundation stone by the king, but was halted in

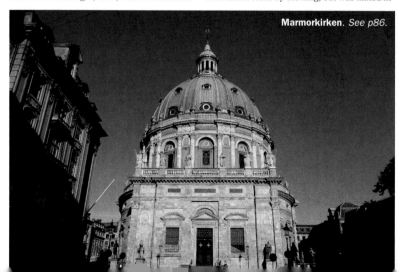

Marmorkirken. *See p86.*

1770 due to its exorbitant cost, with the walls only ten to 15 metres (33-49 feet) high. It wasn't until the deep-pocketed industrialist CF Tietgen intervened in the late 1800s that the church (by then a grass-covered ruin) was completed in cheaper Danish Faxe marble, instead of the original Norwegian marble. It was topped with a 46-metre (151-foot) dome by the architect Ferdinand Meldahl – inspired by St Peter's in Rome, it remains one of the largest of its kind in Europe (from the top you can see Sweden).

Down Frederiksgade are the four rococo palaces surrounding a grand cobbled square that together make up **Amalienborg Slot** (Amalienborg Palace). Home to the royal family since 1794, the palaces were originally built by four wealthy traders as part of Frederik V's scheme for the area. The royal family commandeered the buildings after a fire destroyed their previous home, Christiansborg. As you enter the square along Frederiksgade from Marmorkirken, the palaces are (clockwise from the left) Levetzau Palace, Brockdorff Palace, Moltke Palace and Schack Palace (originally Løvenskjold Palace). The current, much loved Dronning (Queen) **Margrethe II** lives in Schack Palace (formerly Christian IX's palace). The Danes' unstinting love for their Dronning is one of the great paradoxes of the national psyche. Bearing in mind their determined egalitarianism in other areas of life, plus a very healthy tradition of democratic equality, this royalism can seem downright peculiar to foreigners. Literally every Dane you meet, while perhaps not wholeheartedly endorsing the abstract notion of a monarchy, won't have a bad thing to say about their Queen. And the explanation is simple: Margrethe is a charming, modern, talented, conscientious and hard-working royal. And she smokes like a laboratory beagle, which is always likely to endear her to the Danes.

What a performance

The new Copenhagen Opera has caused quite a stir since it was initially commissioned by AP Møller, head of (arguably) the most important company in Denmark, Maersk. While it might seem petty to squabble over a 'gift' worth more than two billion kroner, critics of the building may have a point this time. Firstly, running the place costs an absolute fortune. Secondly, the Maersk chief is used to getting his way and insisted on some odd changes to architect Henning Larsen's blueprint, most notably the addition of gaudy metal bars across the façade that make the building resemble a car grille.

Still, the Opera is a spectacular sight in the evening, especially when the lights come on. The hulking surrounding office blocks and the clumsy roof structure disappear from view, and through the bars you can see the glorious foyer with its three huge chandeliers, all of which produce an awesome reflection in the water.

These same chandeliers also cast a golden hue on to the foyer's red background – and bear an uncanny resemblance to Christiania's flag (*pictured below*). As urban legend has it, the lights were placed there on purpose by the interior designer in support of the beleaguered hippy state. It's pure speculation, of course, but the thought of Christiania's flag glowing towards the royal family in Amalienborg Castle from the face of such a bourgeois institution can't help but raise a smile or two.

Margrethe Alexandrine Thorhildur Ingrid was born during the dark days of Denmark's occupation by Germany in 1940, the daughter of King Frederik IX and Queen Ingrid. During the 1960s Margrethe went to universities in Copenhagen, Cambridge, Århus, London and the Sorbonne, her main subject being political science. She also spent time in the Women's Flying Corp and the WAAF in England. In 1967 she married a French diplomat, Henri, Comte de Laborde de Monpezat (now Prince Henrik, fondly if irreverently regarded by Danes). They have two sons, Frederik (the crown prince, born 1968, genial, handsome and wildly popular, who has a son with his equally adored Australian wife Mary) and Joachim (born 1969, aloof and somewhat feudal, whose public stock sank further in 2004 following separation from his wife Alexandra).

Margrethe became queen only after the Danes voted in a referendum in 1953 to overturn the laws of succession to allow a female to take the throne and, upon the death of her father in 1972, she did just that. It has proved to be a wise decision. When Margrethe is in residence a flag flies from the roof.

A major photo op for tourists visiting Amalienborg is the changing of the guards featuring the ever present Royal Life Guards, whose duty it is to protect Queen Margrethe in the highly unlikely event of an attack. The guards stand in their blue, red and white uniforms beside their pretty red boxes day and night. The daily ritual actually begins at the barracks beside **Rosenborg Slot** (*see p89*) at 11.30am, from where the soldiers process through the streets of Copenhagen, with the military band of the Royal Life Guards playing a few tunes as they go. The route takes them south-west to Kultorvet, down Købmagergade, left on to Østergade (part of Strøget), around Kongens Nytorv and up Bredgade, before taking a right into Frederiksgade and Amalienborg Slotsplads at noon. The Queen's birthday, on 16 April, is the cause for some even more impressive pageantry and crowds.

The **Amalienborg Museum** (within Levetzau Palace; see *p86*) features several private rooms and studies belonging to the Royal Glücksborg family, from 1863 to 1947, starting with Christian IX. Note Frederik IX's pipe collection, Queen Louise's rococo drawing room and a number of quite abysmal pieces of art created by members of the family over the years (in contrast to the works by the current, more gifted queen).

In the middle of the square stands French sculptor Jacques Saly's 12-metre (39-foot) statue of Frederik V, modelled on the equestrian statue of Marcus Aurelius on the Capitol in Rome.

It took 20 years to complete due to a financial wrangle over payment from its backers, the East Asiatic Company, but remains an important piece of European sculpture.

Behind the mighty statue of Frederik V is **Amaliehaven**, a small harbour-side park donated by the industrialist AP Møller in 1983. In the summer the walk from the vast cruise ships that dock here, past the Royal Cast Collection, the spectacular, newly restored Gefion Fountain and on to the Little Mermaid, is extremely popular among Copenhagen's perambulators, dog walkers and joggers. You may even bump into Queen Margrethe or Prince Henrik, who walk their dachshunds here.

South of Amaliehaven, down along the harbourfront, lies a row of classic warehouses facing the Kvæsthusbroen dock. This was a busy transport hub for hundreds of years, and the daily ships for Oslo and Bornholm departed from here until recently, but now it's a recreational area and an occasional landing site for visiting jetsetters in ferry-sized yachts. Behind Kvæsthusbroen, by the corner of Nyhavn, is where the new playhouse is being built halfway into the actual harbour, with walkways above the water to surround the venue when work finishes in 2008.

A short distance north along the waterside from Amaliehaven is **Den Kongelige Afstøbningssamling** (the Royal Cast Collection; *see p86*), the exterior of which is marked by an incongruous bronze replica of Michelangelo's *David*. Inside, 2,000 plaster casts of the world's most famous and outstanding sculptures cover a period of 4,000 years.

A walk along the old harbour brings you to Copenhagen's most eye-catching piece of public statuary, **Gefionspringvandet** (the Gefion Fountain). Built in 1908 by sculptor Anders Bundgaard and financed by the Carlsberg Foundation to celebrate the brewer's 50th anniversary, the statue of the goddess Gefion commanding four ploughing bulls is inspired by the ancient Norse saga about the birth of Sjælland. Gefion was told by the King of Sweden that she could keep as much land as she could plough in a night, and that hard night's labour, with the help of her sons who were transformed into bulls for the purpose, earned her Sjælland. (If you don't believe the myth, check out Lake Vänern in southern Sweden, where she ploughed – it is a very similar size and shape to the Danish island.)

Finally, after passing the ramparts of **Kastellet** along Langelinie, you arrive at **Den Lille Havfrue** (the Little Mermaid). Sculptor Edvard Eriksen's statue, inspired by the Hans Christian Andersen story, was erected in 1913 and funded by the brewer

Sightseeing

Walk Parks & palaces

Start: Kongens Nytorv.
Finish: Nørreport station.
Length: 6km (4 miles) approximately.
Time: 2.5 hours (not including sightseeing and refreshment stops).

Begin at Kongens Nytorv. With the Hotel d'Angleterre behind you, cross over the square to the historic canal of **Nyhavn** (*see p72*), where Hans Christian Andersen lived at three different addresses. Walk down the north side of the canal (which will be on your right), past **Charlottenborg** (*see p177*), a former royal palace, now an art space. You will pass Nyhavn's bustling cafés, restaurants and bars, as well as the ships from Nationalmuseet's collection. When you come to the harbour, turn left and walk north along the harbour front until you come to the waterside **Amaliehaven** gardens (*see p83*).

If you head inland from here, you come to the residence of Denmark's much-loved Queen Margrethe II, **Amalienborg Slot** (*see p82*), which also offers a great view of the **Opera House** (*see p192*).

Back on the waterfront you come to a replica of Michelangelo's *David* outside **Den Kongelige Afstøbningssamlingen** (the Royal Cast Collection; *see p86*). A few minutes further on is the stunning **Gefionspringvandet** (the Gefion Fountain; *see p83*). Walk inland, past **Frihedsmuseet** (the Museum of the

Danish Resistance; *see p86*), and enter **Kastellet** (*see p86*), former home of the Danish army. Climb the ramparts to the east and walk north. At the north-east corner of the fortress you can see **Den Lille Havfrue** (the Little Mermaid; *see p83*).

Head back across Kastellet and walk south along Bredgade. On your left you pass the elegant **Kunstindustrimuseet** (Museum of Decorative and Applied Art; *see p86*), the **Medicinsk-Historisk Museum** (Medical History Museum; *see p86*) and **Skt Ansgars Kirke** (*see p86*), the Roman Catholic cathedral. A little further up Bredgade are the golden minarets of the Russian Orthodox **Alexander Nevsky Kirke** (*see p86*). Turn right at Frederiksgade and you arrive at Copenhagen's most impressive church, **Frederikskirken** (better known as Marmorkirken, the Marble Church; *see p86*).

Continue west and you come to the junction with Store Kongensgade; turn left. Take the first right on to Dronningens Tværgade, then at the end, cross over Kronprinsessegade and enter Kongens Have (the King's Gardens), home to **Rosenborg Slot** (*see p90*). Walk across the gardens and exit at the northern gate. Opposite is the peaceful **Botanisk Have** (Botanical Garden; *see p90*). After tea in the café, exit by the south-eastern gate and hop on the wonderfully efficient Metro at Nørreport for a one-stop return to Kongens Nytorv.

Carlsberg. Since 1964 it has been the victim of vandalism on eight occasions. She has been painted red twice, had her head hacked off three times, an arm lopped off once and been blown from her rocky perch on the windswept Langelinie harbour front by a bomb. The winsome work was based on the prima ballerina Ellen Price, with the sculptor's wife sitting for the body to avoid any 'artist caught with celebrity nude' scandals, and, together with the urinating toddler in Brussels, it must rank as one of the most overexposed and overrated pieces of sculpture in the world.

Opposite the Mermaid is the island of **Holmen**, home to the Danish navy for several hundred years. A good walk further along the harbour takes you to Copenhagen's main cruise liner port, busy from spring to late summer.

Back on Bredgade a few of those hidden treasures await. Just around the corner from Marmorkirken is another smaller, but equally

fascinating church, **Alexander Nevsky Kirke** (*see p86*). The only Russian Orthodox church in Denmark is easily identified by its three incongruous gold onion domes; to step inside is to travel back into pre-Revolutionary Russia, as your eyes adjust to the Byzantine gloom, and begin to take in the gold icons that glimmer on the walls. The church was built in 1881-4 at the behest of Princess Dagmar, daughter of Christian IX, who married Grand Duke Alexander, later Emperor Alexander III, and converted to Orthodoxy. She apparently needed somewhere to worship when she visited Copenhagen (and the fact that Nevsky, Prince of Novgorod, once famously defeated a Swedish army in the 13th century can only have helped get the project through). On the right-hand side of the church an icon of the Holy Virgin, painted in a monastery on Mount Athos in Greece in 1912, and mounted on its own stand, is said, occasionally during spring, to weep real tears.

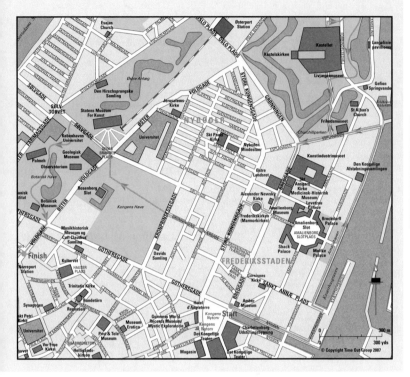

If you doubt it, you can see for yourself where water has run from her eyes and tarnished the paint. The nearby icon of St Nicholas is said to have been the only item to have survived the wreck of a Russian warship.

It's easy to miss the **Medicinsk-Historisk Museum** (Medical History Museum; *see p86*), but well worth taking one of its guided tours – the only way to see the fascinating medical exhibits. Copenhagen's small but beautiful neo-Romanesque Catholic cathedral, **Sankt Ansgar Kirke** (*see p86*), built in 1841, is next door.

Immediately north of the church is **Kunstindustrimuseet** (the Museum of Decorative and Applied Art; *see p86*). Housed around a grand courtyard in the old Frederiks Hospital designed by Nicolai Eigtved (where Søren Kierkegaard breathed his last breath in 1855), the 300,000 items here are focused around living rooms from the Middle Ages to the present day, with the emphasis on Danish

design and craft. As you'd expect, chairs dominate, but there are also textiles, carpets, clothing, ceramics, cutlery, silverware, glassware, art and other furniture on display. The exhibits from Asia are particularly good. The strength of the museum is its blending of the old with the contemporary in a pleasant, soothing rococo setting. This is yet another of Copenhagen's museums funded by the Ny Carlsberg Foundation. There are English captions throughout.

Bredgade ends at a small park, **Churchillparken**, located in front of Kastellet, and named after Britain's wartime leader (there's a small, curmudgeonly bust of him here). Maintaining the British theme, you'll also find **St Alban's Church** (*see p86*), a perfect English Gothic flint church (bizarrely, part of the Anglican Diocese of Gibraltar), which looks like it's been lifted straight from the Sussex countryside.

The entrance to **Frihedsmuseet** (the Museum of Danish Resistance; *see below*) is marked by a battered armoured car, once used by the plucky minority that constituted the Danish Resistance during World War II. Inside this purpose-built wooden hall, arranged around an open courtyard, are numerous moving testimonies to the endeavours of the Danish Resistance and the suffering of their country under occupation. The museum is divided into four areas: 1940-1 Adaptation; 1942-3 Resistance; 1943-4 Terror; and 1944-5 Liberation. The letters (translated into English), from Resistance fighters to their mothers before their execution, and indeed the very execution stakes they stood against to face the firing squads, are here, as are the various home-made weapons and sabotage equipment used by the Resistance. There are biographies of the movement's leaders and displays about the boys' groups who were the first to rebel. Nearby in the park is an underground air raid shelter, open on Sundays during the summer.

Denmark was something of a military backwater during World War II, of use chiefly as Germany's larder and, as such, it was in the occupier's interest to allow life to continue as normally as possible. However, when in 1942 Hitler took offence at King Christian X's terse response to his birthday greeting, the German leader sent Werner Best, one of the architects of the Gestapo, to run the country. That year saw numerous uprisings, the largest of which came in August. In the same year around 7,000 Danish Jews were spirited away to neutral Sweden before they could be deported (*see p16* **The great escape**).

Frihedsmuseet is overlooked by **Kastellet** (the Citadel; *see below*). Built by Frederik III in 1662 after the Swedish siege of 1658, this vast star-shaped fortress with its five bastions was the base for the Danish army for many years and still houses troops in pretty red terraces inside the ramparts. Ironically, it was right in front of Kastellet that the Germans landed many centuries later in 1940. Its prison (1725) housed the treasonous Count von Struensee, who for a brief time (around 1770) virtually took over the throne of Denmark in the mental absence of King Christian VII, before he met his grisly end (his right hand was cut off, then he was beheaded and quartered).

These days the path around the ramparts makes a good jogging track. From the north-east you get a good view of the Little Mermaid and the Swedish coast. Turn around and there's Marmorkirken's dome and the windmill on Kongens Bastion. There is a museum of army regalia, **Livjægermuseet** (the Life Guards Museum; *see below*), at the southern gate.

Alexander Nevsky Kirke

Bredgade 53 (33 13 60 46/tours 20 76 16 47). **Open** 11.30am-1.30pm Tue-Thur; times of services Sat, Sun. **Admission** free. Tours by arrangement only, 25kr; 20kr concessions. **No credit cards.** **Map** p249 K16.

Amalienborg Museum

Christian VIII's Palace, Amalienborg Plads (33 12 08 08/www.ses.dk). **Open** *May, Sept-Oct* 10am-4pm daily. *June-Aug* 10am-5pm daily. *Nov-Dec* 11am-2pm Tue-Sun. *Jan-Mar* closed. **Admission** 65kr; 50kr concessions; free under-18s. **Credit** MC, V. **Map** p249 L16.

Frihedsmuseet

Churchillparken (33 13 77 14/www.frihedsmuseet.dk). **Open** *May-Sept* 10am-4pm Tue-Sat; 10am-5pm Sun. *Oct-Apr* 10am-3pm Tue-Sat; 10am-4pm Sun. *Air raid shelter* May-Sept 11am-1pm Sun. **Admission** free. **Map** p249 J17.

Kastellet

Langelinie (33 47 95 00/www.vejpark.kk.dk). **Open** 6am-10pm daily. **Admission** free. **Map** p249 H17.

Den Kongelige Afstøbningssamling

Vestindisk Pakhus, Toldbodgade 40 (33 74 85 85/www.smk.dk/kas). **Open** 2-8pm Wed; 2-5pm Sun. **Admission** free. **Map** p249 K18.

Kunstindustrimuseet

Bredgade 68 (33 18 56 56/www.kunstindustrimuseet.dk). **Open** *Temporary exhibitions, café & library* 10am-4pm Tue, Thur-Fri; noon-6pm Wed; noon-4pm Sat, Sun. *Permanent exhibitions* noon-4pm Tue, Thur-Sun; noon-6pm Sun. **Admission** 40kr; 25kr concessions; free under-18s. **Credit** MC, V. **Map** p249 K17.

Livjægermuseet

Kastellet (33 47 95 00). **Open** *May-Sept* noon-4pm Sun. *Oct-Apr* closed. **Admission** free. **Map** p249 H17.

Marmorkirken

Frederiksgade 4 (33 15 01 44/www.marmorkirken.dk). **Open** 10am-5pm Thur; noon-5pm Fri-Sun. *Dome* Sept-14 June 1pm, 3pm Sat, Sun. 15 June-Aug 1pm, 3pm daily. **Admission** free. *Dome* 20kr; 10kr under-12s. **No credit cards.** **Map** p249 L16. **Photo** *p81.*

St Alban's Church

Churchillparken (tours 39 62 77 36/www.st-albans.dk). **Open** *May-Sept* 10am-4pm daily. *Oct-Apr* for services only, 10.30am Wed; 9am, 10.30am Sun. **Admission** free; tour prices vary (ring a week in advance to book). **Map** p249 J18.

Sankt Ansgar Kirke

Bredgade 64 (33 13 37 62/www.sanktansgar kirke.dk). **Open** 8am-6pm Mon-Sat; times of services Sun. Mass 8am, 4.30pm Mon-Fri; 5pm Sat; 8am, 10am Sun. **Admission** free. **Map** p249 K17.

Rosenborg & Around

Grand parks, fairytale palaces and Denmark's national gallery.

King Christian IV, the architecturally minded 17th-century monarch, may have helped to bankrupt Denmark with his inept meddling in Nordic politics, but he is still one of the country's most admired rulers, not least for the great buildings that were constructed in Copenhagen during his reign. **Rosenborg Slot** (Rosenborg Palace) is arguably his greatest achievement; an excellent Renaissance palace built over the best part of 30 years and a royal residence for over a century.

West is **Østre Anlæg** park, the lakes of which follow the line of the city's old defensive moat. Within the park are two fine museums. **Statens Museum For Kunst** (*see p90*) is Denmark's national gallery and largest art museum, a position that it consolidated in 1998 with the opening of an extension by architect Anna Maria Indrio. As with Nationalmuseet, the world-class collection of Statens Museum For Kunst, though founded in 1824, has its origins in royal collections from centuries earlier. During the 19th century the collection was based in Christiansborg Slot, until a fire meant it had to move to the current building specially designed by Vilhelm Dahlerup (also responsible for Ny Carlsberg Glyptotek and Det Kongelige Teater) in 1896.

Unlike Henning Larsen's acclaimed extension to the Ny Carlsberg Glyptotek, Indrio's glass and stone addition has proved to be a controversial space for the museum's collection of Danish and European art from the 20th century onwards. Some say the new gallery fails to provide appropriate rooms in which to exhibit the paintings, others find its mixture of vast glass windows (overlooking Østre Anlæg park) and unrelenting stone offers a pleasing spatial puzzle. It's true that every window

offers a perfectly framed vista but it is not quite the neutral backdrop the museum claims, more a grand piece of 'event' architecture against which the art sometimes struggles to be heard.

The museum's main focus is, of course, Danish art, and, as you'd expect, the artists from the so-called Golden Age of the early 19th century figure prominently. These rooms are dedicated to Danish masters, such as CW Eckersburg and his pupils Christen Købke and Constantin Hansen. The landscapes of JT Lundbye, the stark portraits of Vilhelm Hammershøi, the powerful portraits by LA Ring and the symbolist pieces by PC Skovgaard (whose mighty canvas, *Christ in the Kingdom of Death*, a milestone in Danish art, has now been restored), and their forerunners from the 18th century, like Nicolai Abildgaard and Jens Juel, are among the best treats in the museum. The Skagen artists (Michael and Anna Ancher and PS Krøyer), who were specialists in everyday scenes and light, summery landscapes, and the Fyn painters (Peter Hansen and Frits Syberg) are also well represented. Though the works are sometimes sentimental, no one before or since has quite captured the unmistakable, crisp Danish light as these artists did, and their paintings often also depict brutal, beautiful and compelling stories concerning 'real' people's lives, be they butchers, maids, schoolchildren, farmers or fishermen. If you haven't seen them before, allow as much time as you can in these rooms.

In the new wing, the astounding collection of 25 paintings by Henri Matisse, as well as works by Braque, Munch and Picasso, are highlights, as is the Danish modernist collection featuring the painters Giersing and Isakson, and sculptors Kai Nielsen and Astrid Noack. In the old wing the Italians are well represented by Titian, Tintoretto, Filippino Lippi, Mantegna and Guardi. Dutch and Flemish 15th- to 17th-century masters here include Rubens, Bruegel, Rembrandt, Van Dyck and Van Goyen. French 18th-century works are by Fragonard, Poussin and Lorrain, among others. Statens Museum also has one of the world's oldest collections of European prints and drawings (some 300,000), by artists such as Degas, Toulouse-Lautrec, Picasso, Giacometti, Rembrandt and Piranesi. On the ground floor is a children's art museum (not always open) with hands-on displays

Kongens Have.

(compensation perhaps for the loss of the great toboggan hill – one of the few in Copenhagen – that the new extension now covers), and the museum also has a large bookshop and an excellent café serving fine cakes, and boasting an interior also by Indrio.

Nearby is **Den Hirschsprungske Samling** (Hirschsprung Collection; *see p90*), a collection of art from the 19th and early 20th centuries that is particularly strong on the Danish Golden Age (1800-50). It was created by tobacco manufacturer Heinrich Hirschsprung (1836-1908), who crammed the paintings and sculptures into his home on Højbro Plads. Before he died Hirschsprung donated the collection to the Municipality of Copenhagen on condition that they be displayed in similarly intimate surroundings, hence the series of small rooms around three larger halls that make up the building. The museum opened in 1911 and has continued to purchase works ever since.

Across Sølvgade is **Geologisk Museum** (Geological Museum; *see p90*), with displays of fossils, dinosaurs, and Denmark's and Greenland's geography. There are several English-language leaflets, but the museum is showing its age, and is really only for those with a special interest.

Adjoining is **Botanisk Have** (Botanical Garden; *see p90*), providing Elysian relief from the city's streets in summer, while its balmy Palmehus (Palm House), modelled after the one at Kew, can provide refuge from the arctic frost of winter. There is also a **Botanisk Museum** here, open only in summer. The garden was laid out in 1871 to designs by HA Flindt, with a lake that was once part of the city moat as its centrepiece. You'll find examples of most of Denmark's flora, as well as those exotic plants that could be persuaded to grow this far north.

Just south of Botanisk Have is **Arbejdermuseet** (Workers' Museum; *see p90*). The museum's entrance was once guarded by a statue of Lenin that looks like it's come straight from a provincial Soviet town square, but the current right-wing government turned this into a political issue and the statue has been moved round the back of the museum. In fact, the statue is here because the Danish co-operative, the Workers' Fuel Suppliers, helped pay for Lenin's passage from exile in Switzerland home to Russia. Arbejdermuseet recently reopened following a nine-month refurbishment but it remains a rather dry, worthy place and is a fairly unlikely choice for the average tourist. It is housed in an atmospheric building, formerly the headquarters of the Social Democratic Party with a wonderful period basement café and ølhal (beer hall). While the museum's aim – to show how Danish workers' lives have changed over the century – is admirable, its political bias gets a little oppressive, though it does offer glimpses into how Danes used to live. The most interesting exhibit is an entire apartment that remained unaltered through the course of the last century, and was donated to the museum in 1990. The various rooms tell the moving story of the real-life Sørensen family, who occupied them for two generations. The rooms chart the progress of the family's escape from rural poverty, the father's work at a brewery, the parents' deaths, and how one of their eight children, their daughter Yrsa, took over the home in 1964. Be warned, it swarms with school trips on weekdays.

Diagonally across from Statens Museum is the entrance to the oldest park in Copenhagen, **Kongens Have** (King's Garden), and **Rosenborg Slot** (*see p90*). A glimpse of this fairytale, Dutch Renaissance castle in the heart of Copenhagen never fails to surprise and more pleasures await, not least the crown jewels.

Though it was built at the same time as Frederiksberg Slot, Rosenborg was Christian IV's favourite residence and pet project. Towards the end of his life, Christian, aged 70, was taken by sleigh through the snow from Frederiksborg to Rosenborg to die. He literally pulled up the palace drawbridge to escape the harsh economic realities of Denmark's ruin and contemplate a bitter death.

The castle started as a small summer house. Christian extended it between 1606 and 1634, finishing off with the octagonal staircase tower designed by the fantastically named Hans van Steenwinckel the Younger. Rosenborg is still jammed full of the king's fancies: toys, architectural tricks, inventions, art objects and jewellery, which he gathered from around Europe like a regal Mr Toad. A source of great pride was the castle basement, where his orchestra would perform, its music travelling up through a complex system of pipes connected to his living quarters. (Rose Tremain's novel *Music and Silence* gives an imaginative account of the strange world of the palace musicians.) These days the basement houses the Treasury, the stronghold of the crown jewels. It is a collection in which quality, not quantity, is the watchword. The star is the Golden Crown of the Absolute Monarchy, decorated with sapphires, diamonds and rubies, made by Poul Kurtz in 1670, and used by Denmark's kings for 170 years. Christian IV's gold, pearl and jewel-encrusted saddle and crown (1595) are, as you'd expect, jaw-dropping.

Rosenborg was a royal residence until 1838, when these collections were opened to the public, along with the many rooms that had remained intact from the time of Christian IV (1588-1648) to Frederik IV (1699-1730); later rooms were recreated. The decision to arrange the rooms chronologically was, at the time, radical and, consequently, Rosenborg claims to be the first museum of contemporary culture in Europe. The 24 rooms currently on show offer an insight into the lives of Renaissance kings that is perhaps unparalleled in Europe for its atmosphere and intimacy. Christian IV's toilet, covered in beautiful blue Dutch tiles, for example, is as fascinating a treasure as the jewels in the basement.

Other must-sees include Christian's study with his elegant writing desk; Frederik III's marble room; the breathtaking Mirror, Porcelain and Venetian Glass Cabinets; and the last room to be completed (in 1624), the Long Hall, with an amazing throne made from narwhal horns, and guarded by three solid silver lions from 1670

(they somehow escaped being melted down to fill the bottomless pit of Denmark's finances in the late 17th century).

Despite existing happily for more than a century without it, Rosenborg has now installed electricity. That's a great shame, because the palace's Stygian gloom was a major part of its appeal. But at least the special torch-lit, night-time tour still takes place here once a year on **Kulturnatten** (*see p166* **For one night only**).

Just south of Rosenborg is the **Musikhistorisk Museum og Carl Claudius' Samling** (Musical History Museum and Carl Claudius' Collection; *see p90*), another of Copenhagen's specialist curio museums, founded in 1898. Here, in three 18th-century houses, you'll find just about every musical instrument from Europe, Asia and Africa that you can imagine. Oddities abound in this collection, and include King Frederik IX's zither, Prime Minister HC Hansen's mandolin and a life mask of Beethoven, as well as many other fantastically ornate 17th- and 18th-century instruments. Carl Nielsen's piano, or one of them at any rate, is another star among the 2,000 or so exhibits.

On Gothersgade is **Filmhuset** (Film House; *see p175*), a world-class complex devoted to Danish and international cinema, while on Kronprinsessegade is yet another hidden treasure house of a museum, Davids Samling,

Den Hirschsprungske Samling. See p90.

although the gorgeous collection of Danish, Islamic and European art will be closed to the public for renovation until 2008.

At the north end of Store Kongensgade is **Nyboder**. While Kastellet was for centuries home to the army, the Royal Navy lived in the Lilliputian, ochre terraces of Nyboder, built during Christian IV's time, to house over 2,200 naval staff (a purpose it still serves). There's a small museum, **Nyboders Mindestuer** (Nyboder Memorial Rooms).

Arbejdermuseet

Rømersgade 22 (33 93 25 75/www.arbejder museet.dk). **Open** 10am-4pm daily. **Admission** 50kr; 40kr concessions; free under-18s. **Credit** MC, V. **Map** p246 L12.

Botanisk Have & Museum

Gothersgade 128 (35 32 22 40/www.botanic-garden.ku.dk). **Open** *Garden* May-Sept 8.30am-6pm daily. Oct-Apr 8.30am-4pm Tue-Sun. *Palm house* 10am-3pm daily. *Insectivorous greenhouse* 10am-3pm daily. *Cactus greenhouse* 1-2pm Wed, Sat, Sun. *Orchid greenhouse* 2-3pm Wed, Sat, Sun. *Endangered species* 1-3pm Wed, Sat, Sun. *Museum* June-Aug noon-4pm daily; times vary, phone to check (35 32 22 00). Sept-May closed. **Admission** free. **Map** p247 K13.

Geologisk Museum

Øster Voldgade 5-7 (35 32 23 45/www.geologisk-museum.dk). **Open** 1-4pm Tue-Sun. **Admission** 25kr; 10kr-15kr concessions; free under-6s; free to all Wed. **Credit** MC, V. **Map** p247 K13.

Den Hirschsprungske Samling

Stockholmsgade 20 (35 42 03 36/www. hirschsprung.dk). **Open** 11am-4pm Mon, Wed-Sun; phone to check. **Admission** 35kr; 25kr-30kr concessions; free under-18s; free to all Wed. **Credit** AmEx, DC, MC, V. **Map** p247 J14. **Photo** *p89.*

Musikhistorisk Museum og Carl Claudius' Samling

Åbenrå 30 (33 11 27 26/www.natmus.dk). **Open** May-Sept 1-3.50pm Mon-Wed, Fri-Sun. Oct-Apr 1-3.50pm Mon, Wed, Sat, Sun. **Admission** free. **Map** p247 L13.

Nyboders Mindestuer

Sankt Pauls Gade 24 (33 32 10 05/www. orlogsmuseet.dk/nybod22). **Open** 11am-2pm Wed; 11am-4pm Sun. **Admission** 10kr; 5kr concessions. Guided tour 200kr. **No credit cards.** **Map** p249 K16.

Rosenborg Slot

Øster Voldgade 4A (33 15 32 86/www.rosenborg slot.dk). **Open** *Jan-Apr, Nov-mid Dec* 11am-4pm Tue-Sun. *May, Sept, Oct* 10am-4pm daily. *June-Aug* 10am-5pm daily. *Mid Dec-26 Dec* closed; *27-30 Dec* 11am-4pm. **Admission** 65kr; 50kr-40kr concessions; free under-18s. **Credit** AmEx, DC, MC, V. **Map** p247 K14.

Statens Museum For Kunst

Sølvgade 48-50 (33 74 84 94/www.smk.dk). **Open** 10am-5pm Tue, Thur-Sun; 10am-8pm Wed. **Admission** 70kr; 50kr concessions; free under-18s. **Credit** AmEx, MC, V. **Map** p247 J14.

Dog day afternoons at Denmark's national gallery, **Statens Museum For Kunst**.

Christianshavn

From laid-back to seriously chilled.

Nørrebro
& Østerbro

The Little
Mermaid

Rosenborg &
Around

Frederiksstaden

Rosenborg
Slot

Amalienborg
Slot

Opera
House

Strøget &
Around

Nyhavn &
Kongens Nytorv

National-
museet

Slotsholmen

Vesterbro &
Frederiksberg

Tivoli &
Rådhuspladsen

Christianshavn

The people of Christianshavn will wince if you suggest that they're part of the island of Amager. The neighbourhood does indeed have a charm and a character that are utterly unique, but there are only a few bridges separating Christianshavn from the rest of Copenhagen. The surrounding streets have a laid-back feel to them, as does the central canal that cuts through the middle of the area. Of course, laid-back soon becomes seriously chilled when you come to Christiania, even though events of the past few years have made the mood of the place a little more tense these days.

Christianshavn was built to the east of Slotsholmen in the early 17th century to protect Christian IV's burgeoning city from attack, and to ease overcrowding within the city walls. The king's complex plan, inspired by Amsterdam's grid of canals, was eventually simplified for reasons of cost, but remains pretty much intact today following sympathetic renovation in the 1980s and '90s. Christianshavn's charming houses and courtyards also escaped most of the fires that ravaged Copenhagen over the centuries, though developers are now doing their utmost to spoil the historic ambience.

To the north of Christianshavn is Holmen, the old dockland area that was built on reclaimed land in the 17th century. Holmen still has its naval base, but the area has changed and now throngs with students who head off on summer evenings to the numerous seasonal 'beach' bars in the area. And the new **opera house** (*see p192*) has put this area at the forefront of Denmark's cultural life. Holmen is a fascinating place, best explored by bicycle.

Christianshavn's dominant landmark is **Vor Frelsers Kirke** (Church of Our Saviour; *see p93*), whose fabulous 90-metre (295-foot) high copper and gold spire can be seen from most parts of the city centre. Sadly, the church is closed for restoration at the moment, but is due to reopen in autumn 2008. The church, on Sankt Annægade, was built by architect Lambert van Haven for Christian V in 1682 in the Palladian Dutch baroque style, from red brick and sandstone. Don't be taken in by Danes who tell you that the spire's architect, Laurids de Thurah, threw himself off the top because it wound the wrong way – he actually died in poverty seven years after its completion. The spire was inspired by the lanterns on the Church of Sant'Ivo alla Sapienza in Rome and was completed in pine with copper cladding and gilt decoration in 1752. On the day of its dedication King Frederik V climbed to the top to receive a 27-gun salute as crowds cheered below. This extraordinary spire is open to any visitors who feel they can conquer their vertigo and its 400 or so steps, which spiral ever narrower to the summit. Inside, the church is spacious but prosaic in the typical Lutheran manner, though its immense three-storey organ, which was completed in 1698, is stupefying.

Christianshavn's other significant church is **Christians Kirke** (*see p92*). It is notable for its unique interior, laid out in the style of a theatre. The rococo structure, with its neo-classical spire, was designed by Nicolai Eigtved

Vor Frelsers Kirke. *See p93.*

Worth the climb: the incredible view from the top of **Vor Frelsers Kirke**. *See p93*.

in 1755 for the German population of Christianshavn. Financed by a lottery, it was known for a long time as the Lottery Church.

Christianshavn's importance in Denmark's naval history is attested to in **Orlogsmuseet** (Royal Danish Naval Museum; *see p93*), which has an extensive collection of fantastically detailed model ships. The collection was started by Christian IV and originally exhibited in Sankt Nicolaj Kirke; it was moved to the current site of Søkvæsthus, the old naval hospital, in 1989. The oldest model, of a man-of-war, dates from 1680, and there are countless replicas of later ships (including the interior of a submarine, with sound effects), as well as a comprehensive history of the Danish Royal Navy and several historic battle scenes recreated in model form. One gallery contains a splendidly ornate state barge from 1780, another is dedicated to marine archaeology. Orlogsmuseet will delight model-making enthusiasts and naval historians; it's also popular with children, who are catered for with a well-equipped playroom.

Further along historic Strandgade is **Dansk Arkitekturcenter** (Danish Architecture Centre; *see p93*). The changing exhibitions cover current Danish projects and international themes and, though fairly specialised, are usually worth a look for those with a general interest in architecture. Exhibitions are often accompanied by debates and conferences in the restaurant on the main floor.

One of Christianshavn's easily overlooked sites is **Lille Mølle** (*see p93*), a windmill dating from 1669, situated on the ramparts south-east of Christiania. It was converted into a private home in 1916 and the interior, with numerous antiques and art objects, has been perfectly preserved by Nationalmuseet, which now owns the site. Next door is **Bastionen og Løven**, an excellent café (*see p135*) and a very popular meeting place during summer.

If you head west from Christianshavn across the old defensive ramparts, you come to a part of the city that has, up until now, not really featured on the tourist itinerary: **Islands Brygge** (*photo p95*). That all changed when trendy architects Plot were commissioned to build the city's magnificent, permanent, open-air bathing complex that enables locals to swim in the ultra clean harbour water. The complex is moored on the waterfront beside Langebro and behind it, when the sun shines, you will find the lawns packed with sunbathers, basketball players and picnickers. A few trendy independent galleries have followed, as well as some decent sandwich shops – all of which points to Islands Brygge as the next big thing.

Christians Kirke

Strandgade 1 (32 54 15 76/www.christianskirke.dk). Metro Christianshavn. **Open** *Mar-Oct* 8am-6pm daily. *Nov-Feb* 8am-5pm daily. **Admission** free. **Map** p252 P16.

Dansk Arkitekturcenter

*Strandgade 27B (32 57 19 30/www.dac.dk). Metro
Christianshavn/bus 2A, 19, 350S.* **Open** 9am-5pm
daily. **Admission** free. **Map** p252 O16.

Lille Mølle

*Christianshavns Voldgade 54 (33 47 38 38/in July
phone 33 47 38 57/www.natmus.dk). Metro
Christianshavn/bus 66.* **Open** (guided tours only)
June-Sept 1pm, 2pm, 3pm Sat, Sun. *Oct-May* closed.
Admission 50kr; 40kr concessions, free under-18s.
No credit cards. **Map** p252 P18.

Orlogsmuseet

*Overgaden Oven Vandet 58 (33 11 60 37/www.
orlogsmuseet.dk). Metro Christianshavn/bus 2A, 19,
350S.* **Open** noon-4pm Tue-Sun. **Admission** 50kr;
20kr concessions; free under-18s. Free to all Wed.
Credit V. **Map** p252 P17.

Vor Frelsers Kirke

*Sankt Annægade 29 (32 57 27 98/www.vorfrelsers
kirke.dk). Metro Christianshavn/bus 2A, 66,
350S.* **Open** Church & spire are closed for
restoration until 2008. Visit website for up-to-date
information on opening hours during this period.
Map p252 P17. **Photo** *p91*.

Christiania

Christiania, or the Freetown of Christiania to
give it its full title, is a residential area unlike
any other in Denmark. This mess of historic
military buildings, makeshift housing and
ramshackle businesses, which straddles the
defensive moat and 17th-century ramparts
to the east of Christianshavn, is home to
approximately 1,000 people (exact figures

Christiania is dead, long live Christiania

The bands are still packing them in at
Loppen, the organic breakfast at
Morgenstedet is as healthy and popular
as ever, and even though the sought-after
Christiania Bikes are selling so well that
production had to be moved to Jutland,
they're still being sold at Cykelværkstedet.
Still, it must be said that Christiania has
an end of era feel to it these days.

The pressure on the 35-year-old self-
proclaimed free state is mounting on all
sides. On the community's birthday in
September 2006, the government presented
its report on the 'normalisation' of the area,
and, as expected, it included a plan for
20,000 square metres (215,000 square
feet) of new housing to be built on the
former army grounds. Also increasing
violence in Christiania reached its peak
recently when a 26-year-old resident was
killed and five were wounded in a gangland
shoot-out in April 2005.

After this, the police presence became even
larger than when now-defunct Pusher Street
was in operation, introducing a new zero-
tolerance policy to soft drugs. The
Månefiskeren bar complained that busts
could reach double figures in a single day.
Protests included keeping the score on a
chalkboard, and inviting the national press
to mark the police's 1,000th visit.

Even today, though, Christiania is not
without its supporters. The red and yellow
symbol is visible throughout the city, painted

as graffiti and printed on T-shirts sold as
merchandise to fund the community;
demonstrations to support Christiania are
well attended, as are fundraising concerts;
and the odd PR scoop continues to help the
cause. Robbie Williams, before playing a
couple of concerts at Parken in July 2006,
went walkabout in the free state with pal
Jonathan Wilkes, press in tow. He even
bought a 'Save Christiania' hoodie to show
his support. RIP Christiania? We'll see.

are difficult to come by). It attracts around three-quarters of a million visitors a year, which makes it one of Denmark's biggest tourist attractions.

Christiania is unique. Until very recently it was a community that existed within Copenhagen, but outside of its laws and conventions. With the election of the new government, and more particularly the rise to power of right-wing factions within the coalition such as the Dansk Folkeparti, Christiania has been under threat like never before. There was talk of the whole place being torn down and the first casualty was the world-famous Pusher Street, where soft drugs were being sold openly from stalls like market produce.

In January 2004 Christiania voted to tear down the booths selling ready rolled spliffs, cannabis resin and other soft drugs – before the government ordered the police to do it forcibly, as they had been threatening. This came despite the fact that the police felt it would be counterproductive to send the sale of soft drugs underground – 'You don't just make a problem like this go away with a click of the fingers,' said Copenhagen's drugs tsar at the time.

The demolition of Pusher Street did turn out to be a smart move, however, as the government's final surprise ruling was that Christiania could stay but must follow a 'legalisation' process, involving the removal of some buildings and the rental system being made more 'above board' than before.

Despite this pressure to conform, its residents remain committed to their 'alternative' lifestyle. But as recycling and other environmentally conscious practices have been adopted by the mainstream over the years, and attitudes to soft drugs have changed, just how alternative Christiania is has become open to debate.

Up until 1971, the 41-hectare (101-acre) site that Christiania now occupies was an army barracks. When the army moved out, a group of like-minded Christianshavn residents decided to knock down the fence on Prinsessegade and access the land as a playground and open space. Meanwhile, an exhibition at Charlottenborg, Noget for Noget (Give and Take), which examined the hippie movement, and an alternative lifestyle newspaper, *Hovedbladet* (Head Magazine), galvanised Copenhagen's experimentalists. The paper ran an article on the barracks with various proposals for its use, including as housing for the young. This was all the encouragement that hundreds of 'drop-outs' from across Denmark needed and soon the site began to fill up. On 13 November 1971 the new residents founded what they like to call the Freetown of Christiania, although it was promptly declared illegal by the authorities. However, the number of residents had already grown to the extent that, despite their best and often most violent efforts, the police failed to clear the barricades.

In subsequent years, as the community formed its own system of government, built schools, shops, cafés, restaurants, various co-operatives and music venues, and embarked on

The power of nature

Whether you arrived by plane at Kastrup Airport, by train from Germany or drove across the Øresund Bridge from Sweden, you will immediately have been struck by the proliferation of gigantic windmills in Denmark. Just outside the mouth of Copenhagen Harbour beyond Holmen, for instance, is a long row of these elegant wind-power generators, a fitting riposte to the massive Barsebæk nuclear power plant the Swedes built (much to the annoyance of the Danes) on the coast just a few miles from Copenhagen. This tells you two things about Denmark. One, it is very windy here, and two, the Danes are genuinely interested in a clean environment – keen enough to have put their money where their mouth is. In 2002 the world's first off-shore wind parks began generating electricity in the North Sea for

western Denmark. All this investment is beginning to pay off as the rest of the world has begun to wake up to wind power as a serious supplement to fossil fuels and has come calling on Denmark for assistance.

Today, around 65 per cent of the world's wind turbines are Danish-built. The Danish company Vestas Wind Systems is one of the world leaders in the field and has supplied wind turbines to over 35 countries. Denmark still only produces around 15 per cent of the power it needs from the wind, but it is a start, and by 2008 it hopes that will be 20 per cent.

The ultimate aim is for renewable energy to provide 35 per cent of the country's needs by 2030. So, though the Danes may well smoke like chimneys, their chimneys don't smoke quite as much as they used to.

Fancy a dip? Head for the harbour at **Islands Brygge**. See p92.

recycling programmes and nascent solar- and wind-power projects, the debate about Christiania raged. The bulldozers and batons were never far away. Charity records, concerts, PR stunts and the election to the local council of some of its residents ensured Christiania remained in the headlines and, eventually, in 1991, an uneasy truce was met with the authorities. Christiania agreed to pay rent and cover the cost of water and electricity supplies, as well as to look after the buildings that were of historical importance, while the city council agreed to allow it to continue as a 'social experiment'. In truth, were Christiania to be closed down tomorrow, the ensuing housing crisis and crime wave would prove a far greater political hot potato. The site is technically still owned by the Ministry of Defence.

Today, with the sale of drugs banished, the community earns money from its restaurants and bars, as well as the sale of its unique Christiania bicycles and handicrafts. The residents (around 70 per cent of whom receive some kind of government benefit) pay rent, which goes towards the upkeep of buildings, city taxes and services. None pays income tax.

A complex system of self-government is headed by the Common Meeting with power devolved through 15 local Area Meetings. Decisions are arrived at via consensus, as opposed to majority vote, and new arrivals must be approved by the House Meeting. A stunt by a Danish TV show revealed just how

territorial the Free State has become, however, when they turned up and tried to build a house by the lake. Christianites tore it down and assaulted the TV crew.

Christiania is divided by the moat into two distinct areas – the main commercial centre, with its music venues, shops, restaurants and bars; and Dysen, a quiet residential area on the eastern side of the moat.

Flower power staggers on in Christiania and, by way of evidence, no wall is left undaubed with murals, graffiti and, well, daubs, and large, shaggy dogs of indeterminate breed roam unhindered. There are a number of cafés and restaurants. **Spiseloppen** (*spise* means 'eat'; *loppen* means 'the flea'; *see p120*) is the best and, if you don't mind the exotic fumes from other diners, can hold its own against many more salubrious venues in the city. In the same building as Spiseloppen is the atmospheric music venue **Loppen** (*see p189*), while the 2,000-capacity **Den Grå Hal** (the Grey Hall) is Christiania's largest music venue, and has hosted gigs by the likes of Blur and Bob Dylan.

All of Christiania is open to tourists (though obviously not the private dwellings). You can pass a very pleasant afternoon wandering around the quieter parts, inspecting the extraordinary variety of housing – from pyramids, railway carriages and tree houses, to sophisticated wooden chalets and the original 17th-century barracks. It's well worth taking the time to explore this remarkable community.

Vesterbro & Frederiksberg

Boho sleaze meets park life.

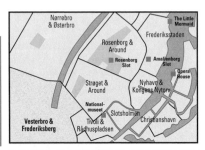

Vesterbro

Sex and drugs have long been the claim to fame of **Vesterbro** – the area stretching west from Central Station – but this notoriously sleazy, shabby district has been gentrified in recent years. The sex shops, hookers and junkies are still here, but they are now crowded out by media people, artists and students, who appreciate the area's gritty realism, ethnically diverse population and exotic food shops and restaurants. As the trendies have taken over, Bohemian cafés and indie design shops have sprung up here and there, boosting the property market in the process.

But it will take more than a few cool shops and cafés to stamp out the district's sordid character. Vesterbro has revelled in its trashy image since the 18th century, when it was the site of numerous music halls and drinking dens, and the second half of the 19th century, when it was filled by an immense block of inhuman corridor flats (to ease overcrowding in the city).

Meat markets, literal and metaphorical, have always been Vesterbro's speciality. Until recently it was the butchers' quarter of Copenhagen. Their trade was centred on Værnedamsvej, which at one time had Europe's highest concentration of dead flesh.

Halmtorvet (just south-west of Central Station) is the most visible symbol of the area's rejuvenation: it has had the sandblasters and decorators in and the cobbles relaid. The square is now a popular evening and weekend

destination, boasting several great cafés and restaurants. The fashionistas come for the trendy clothes shops, while **Vega** (*see p188*) remains one of the city's top nightspots.

Though sex tourists may find a few cheap thrills, Vesterbro has very few traditional tourist attractions, other than the city museum and planetarium. **Københavns Bymuseum & Søren Kierkegaard Samlingen** (Copenhagen City Museum & Søren Kierkegaard Collection; *see p97*) is a 15-minute walk along Vesterbrogade from Tivoli. The museum gives an excellent overview of the capital's history and includes old shopfronts and displays depicting how Copenhageners have lived over the last millennium. A special 'Copenhagen Underground' exhibition tells you more than you'd probably like to know about things subterranean – sewers, gas pipes and, metaphorically, prostitution and crime.

Tycho Brahe Planetarium (*see p97*), on Gammel Kongevej, shows a variety of IMAX movies and interplanetary displays. The largest

Sleazy **Vesterbro**.

planetarium in Western Europe, it was opened in 1989 in a cylindrical building designed by Knud Munk and is named after the great Danish astronomer (1546-1601), who, during the 16th century, painstakingly catalogued the solar system – a crucial contribution to the development of the laws of planetary motion.

Københavns Bymuseum & Søren Kierkegaard Samlingen

Vesterbrogade 59 (33 21 07 72/www.kbhby museum.dk). Bus 6A, 26. **Open** 10am-4pm Mon, Thur-Sun; 10am-9pm Wed. **Admission** 20kr; 10kr concessions; free under-18s; free to all Fri. **Credit** V. **Map** p245 Q9. **Photo** *p98.*

Tycho Brahe Planetarium

Gammel Kongevej 10 (33 12 12 24/www.tycho.dk). **Open** 9.30am-8.30pm Mon-Fri; 10.30am-8.30pm Sat, Sun. **Admission** *Exhibition* 25kr; 15kr concessions. *Exhibition & film* 95kr-105kr; 65-75kr concessions. **Credit** AmEx, DC, MC, V. **Map** p250 P10.

Frederiksberg

Though just west of Vesterbro, quiet and refined **Frederiksberg** seems worlds away from its blowsy neighbour. Its leafy, wide avenues, grand parks and elegant 18th-century royal palace make this one of the city's most desirable residential areas (slightly lower taxes for residents help), and its parks are a popular destination at weekends. The district's appealing character may be partially the result of its distinct political status: like Christiania, Frederiksberg is a separate town within the city of Copenhagen (and a stark contrast to the alternative Freetown). An independent municipality of just over 90,000 people, it has its own mayor, town hall and administration. Apartments tend to be larger and more expensive than elsewhere in the city, especially those along Frederiksberg Allé, a long, tree-lined boulevard, which could have been lifted straight from one of the more affluent arrondissements of Paris. Until the 19th century Frederiksberg lay well outside Copenhagen, with views from its hill ('berg' means 'hill') over the fields (now Vesterbro) to the city beyond. And it still has a unique sense of separateness: true, the district's conservative character doesn't make for giddy nightlife, but it does have a few sights that are worth the short bus or Metro ride from the centre of town.

The heart of the quarter is **Frederiksberg Have** (Frederiksberg Park; *see p101*), a large, rambling park that was laid out in the formal French style in the 18th century, before being given a more informal English revamp at the turn of the 19th century. With its tree-lined paths, canals and lake, Frederiksberg Have is

The observer

Every city has a writer whose work becomes synonymous with its inner workings, and in Copenhagen that writer was Dan Turèll. In his short time on earth (a 30-a-day man, he died from lung cancer in 1993 at the age of 47) he was considered the prime chronicler of Copenhagen life, ascending from a cult figure to a widely loved literary hero. When Turèll made his breakthrough in 1974 with *Karma Cowboy* – an excellent collection of poems heavily influenced by Zen Buddhism and Lucky Luke comics – he was seen as a loveable oddball, dressed in a long coat and huge hat and sporting a wicked goatee beard and painted black nails. But mass acceptance soon followed. Over the next 20 years, the workaholic Turèll wrote weekly columns in the *Politiken* newspaper as well as numerous volumes of poetry and a series of 12 noir crime novels in the style of Dashiell Hammett.

Weak on plot but heavy on atmosphere and romanticised local Vesterbro colour, these were the books that made Turèll one of Copenhagen's most treasured celebrities (he was always available for a wry comment on current events).

However, he remains unknown outside of Denmark, and his witty, modern writing style would probably be difficult to translate properly. Still, the man mirrors the contradictory essence of Copenhagen: self-publicising but shy, elitist but accessible, radical but somehow everyday.

Turèll lived primarily in Vesterbro and Frederiksberg, whose streets supplied him with many a droll observation. More than a decade after his death, the city hasn't forgotten him. In 2006 a play opened in his honour (*Onkel Danny*, Turèll's nickname). And, in Vesterbro, they named a square after him. Had he still been alive, he would probably have turned up to protest that the once-seedy square was too squeaky clean for his taste.

one of the city's most romantic spaces, particularly in spring. In its grounds are a Chinese pavilion, numerous statues and an impressive avenue of stately linden trees, dating from the 1730s.

The greenery extends across Roskildevej to **Søndermarken** common, a more informal but equally picturesque park that also features one

Sightseeing

Københavns Bymuseum. *See p97.*

of Copenhagen's most unusual museums. Entrance to **Cisternerne – Museet For Moderne Glaskunst** (the Cisterns – Museum of Modern Glass Art; *see p101*) is gained via a Louvre-style glass pyramid in the park, opposite the rear of Frederiksberg Slot. Descend the stairs into what were once sizeable underground water tanks and you will find a remarkable glass sculpture museum with modern and classical stained glass and three-dimensional works. But the extraordinary vaulted subterranean rooms leave an equally lasting impression, still dank and wet under foot with stalactites and stalagmites surviving as evidence of their former function. This is supposedly the only art museum in Europe to do without natural light, but it manages superbly thanks to the work of theatrical effects expert John Aage Sørensen.

In the south-east corner of Frederiksberg Have is **Det Kongelige Danske Haveselskabs Have** (Royal Danish Horticultural Garden; *see p101*), a formal, oriental-influenced water garden, founded in 1884. In the summer this is one of the Copenhagen Jazz Festival's most idyllic outdoor venues, while the orange stucco Spa Room is used year-round for exhibitions and concerts.

Frederiksberg has two other small parks, less frequently visited by tourists. Sheltering behind a cluster of apartment blocks on Hollændervej is the tiny **Rosenhaven** (Rose Garden), which is home to a variety of roses including the Ingrid Bergmann and Queen Elizabeth. **Landbohøjskolens Have** (Agricultural University's Garden; *see p101*) on Bülowsvej was laid out in 1858 at the time of the university's foundation. Come spring, this garden positively explodes in a riot of flora; aconite, snowdrops, crocuses and 10,000 tulips bloom each April. In summer these are succeeded by roses and 700 different summer flowers, as well as 100 or so medicinal plants and exotic trees.

On the south side of Frederiksberg Have lies **Frederiksberg Slot** (Frederiksberg Palace; *see p101*), a royal summer residence between the early 18th and mid 19th centuries. Frederik IV had been so taken by the villas he had seen while on a visit to Frascati that, between 1699 and 1703, he instructed architect Ernst Brandenburger to build a palace in the Italian style. The two side wings, which were designed by Laurids de Thurah, were added between 1733 and 1738, on the instruction of Christian VI. Today the palace is home to the Danish

Military Academy and, as such, is not open to the public other than for the occasional guided tour.

Beside Frederiksberg Slot is the **Zoologisk Have** (Zoological Garden; *see p101*), Denmark's national zoo. Founded in 1859, it is one of the oldest in the world, and has a good reputation for breeding animals in captivity. Recent new buildings for the giraffes and the elephants have helped improve the inhabitants' lot, and next up is a new savannah for African species, including a reservoir for the ever-popular hippos. The zoo is modest by international standards, but nevertheless has the usual remit of exotica, including polar bears, tigers, lions and apes, plus a new elephant house by Lord Norman Foster. An impressive indoor tropical zoo houses butterflies, crocodiles and tropical birds. The children's zoo is also a major attraction, and its main landmark is the 40-metre (131-foot) tower, built in 1905, which, on a clear day, affords spectacular views as far as the Swedish coast. The queues are invariably lengthy on sunny holidays.

Moving around Frederiksberg Have in a clockwise direction you come to the **Royal Copenhagen Porcelain Manufactory**. Further on are two small museums that offer a unique, and at times perplexing, insight into the Danish sense of humour. Danes seem to be divided as to the merits of the Frederiksberg-born artist and cartoonist Robert Storm Petersen (1882-1949), better known as Storm P.

For older Danes he typifies a traditional, aphoristic strain of Danish humour; for younger Danes he is a dusty relic of a bygone era, and about as funny as a hospital visit. At **Storm P Museet** (Storm P Museum; *see p101*) you can judge for yourself whether his social-critical cartoons display any comedic merit, or whether his symbolist-influenced paintings hold any profound philosophical meaning. There are English captions.

Behind the Storm P Museum you'll find the even more idiosyncratic **Det Danske Revymuseum** (the Museum of Light; *see p101*), containing 200 years' worth of memorabilia from traditional Danish revue theatre. The assorted photographs, programmes and costumes will be largely meaningless to foreign visitors, however, as there is no English information.

Opposite Frederiksberg Runddel stands the small, octagonal **Frederiksberg Kirke**, dating from 1734. The pretty Dutch Renaissance church regularly holds concerts and has an altarpiece depicting the Eucharist, painted by CW Eckersberg, while in its cemetery you'll find the grave of 19th-century poet Adam Oehlenschläger.

On the south side of Frederiksberg is **Bakkehusmuseet** (Bakkehus Museum; *see p101*), a converted 17th-century house containing souvenirs of Denmark's early 19th-century Golden Age. This small, eclectic collection is housed in the former home of a

Escape the crowds at **Frederiksberg Have**. *See p101.*

What lies beneath: **Cisternerne**'s underground museum for modern glass art. *See p101.*

professor of literature and publisher of the period, Knud Lyhne Rahbek. The display includes everything from death masks to Adam Oehlenschläger's dressing gown.

Bakkehus Museet lies literally in the shadow of the headquarters of what is undoubtedly Copenhagen's and probably Denmark's best-known international brand: Carlsberg. The **Carlsberg Museum** (*see p101*) is a must for beer buffs, featuring a pictorial overview of the company's operations in over 130 countries, as well as providing scientific displays about brewing and a few relics of the Jacobsen dynasty. In the entrance hall are photographs of the many VIP visitors who have sampled Carlsberg's hospitality over the years, including Danny Kaye (Hans Christian Andersen in the Sam Goldwyn film), Kenneth Branagh, Victor

On yer bike

Scandinavians are famous for using bicycles as everyday transport. And Danes cycle, on average, 600 kilometres (375 miles) per year. But Copenhagen take things a step further. Almost everyone – regardless of income or social status – cycles in this city. What's more, Copenhageners take their cycling very seriously: woe betide anyone who, during rush hour, ventures out on the city's many kilometres of cycle paths with a faint heart. Copenhagen's two-wheeled commuters take no prisoners. And there are certain cast-iron rules of which foreigners should take note. For instance, passengers at bus stops (either embarking or disembarking) have right of way: all cyclists must stop and wait until the bus doors have closed. Left-hand turns on main roads are not permitted for cyclists: you must dismount and cross the road (with the green man, of course) as a pedestrian would. As a rule you should ride on the right-hand side of the cycle path; if someone rings a bell behind you (never more

than once, that is considered rude), it is to indicate that you should move over and let them pass on the left. When you want to stop, raise your right hand (in a fey salute) to signal this to other cyclists. None of these rules seems to apply to cycle couriers, however. They do as they please.

Between April and September, the city operates a public bike rental scheme called **Bycykler** (City Bikes) where, as with shopping trolleys, you put a 20kr piece in the slot to borrow a bike from one of the 125 bike deposits around town. The sponsored, gearless bikes are only good for short journeys, however, and by midsummer many of the 2,500 have disappeared or lie in ruins. A better bet is to rent a bike from one of the city's many bike shops (*see p225* **Bike hire**). This usually costs from 70kr per day (it becomes cheaper the longer you rent) for a simple three-speeder. Bicycle theft is rampant in Copenhagen, so make sure you always lock yours up.

Italian-style **Frederiksberg Slot**, home to the Danish Military Academy.

Borge and a smattering of European royalty. The museum also has an amusing display of promotional material from the last century and a large 1:10 scale model of the brewery. Outside the museum, a little further down Ny Carlsberg Vej, are the famous Elephant Gates, flanked by two stone Indian elephants, designed by Vilhelm Dahlerup. Around the corner is the entrance to the **Carlsberg Visitors Centre & Jacobsen Brewhouse** (*see below*). The centre used to run guided tours, but these days visitors are allowed to wander through the various displays on the history of beer and the brewing processes used at Carlsberg. Naturally, visits conclude with a free sample.

Bakkehus Museet
Rahbeks Allé 23 (33 31 43 62/www.bakkehus museet.dk). Train to Valby/bus 6A, 18, 26. **Open** 11am-3pm Wed, Thur, Sat, Sun. **Admission** 20kr; 1kr concessions. **No credit cards.**

Carlsberg Museum
Valby Langgade 1, Valby (33 27 12 74/www. carlsberg.dk). Bus 18, 26. **Open** 10am-3pm Mon-Fri. **Admission** free.

Carlsberg Visitors Centre & Jacobsen Brewhouse
Gamle Carlsberg Vej 11, Valby (33 27 12 82/ www.visitcarlsberg.com). Bus 18, 26. **Open** 10am-4pm Tue-Sun. **Admission** 40kr; 25kr concessions; free under-12s.

Cisternerne – Museet for Moderne Glaskunst
Søndermarken (33 21 93 10/www.cisternerne.dk). Bus 4A, 6A, 18, 26. **Open** 2-6pm Thur, Fri; 11am-5pm Sat, Sun. **Admission** 40kr; 30kr concessions; free under-14s. **No credit cards. Photo** *p100.*

Det Danske Revymuseum
Allegade 5 (38 10 20 45/www.revymuseet.dk). Bus 18, 26. **Open** 11am-4pm Tue-Sun. **Admission** 35kr; 25kr concessions. **No credit cards.**

Frederiksberg Have
Main entrance: Frederiksberg Runddel (33 92 63 00/ www.ses.dk). Bus 18, 26. **Open** 6am-sunset daily. **Admission** free. **Photo** *p99.*

Frederiksberg Slot
Roskildevej 28 (36 16 22 44/www.ho.dk). Bus 6A. **Open** *Guided tours* Jan-May, Aug-Nov 11am, 1pm last Sat of month. **Admission** 25kr. **No credit cards.**

Det Kongelige Danske Haveselskabs Have
Pile Allé 6, Frederiksberg (36 44 98 99/www. haveselskab.dk). Bus 18, 26. **Open** 10am-sunset daily. **Admission** free.

Landbohøjskolens Have
Grønnegårdsvej 15 (35 28 21 81/www.lbh.kvl.dk). Bus 14, 15, 29. **Open** sunrise-sunset daily. **Admission** free. **Map** p245 N6.

Storm P Museet
Frederiksberg Runddel (38 86 05 23/www.stormp-museet.dk). Bus 18, 26. **Open** *May-Oct* 10am-4pm Tue-Sun; closed Mon. *Nov-Apr* 10am-4pm Wed, Sat, Sun. **Admission** 30kr; 20kr concessions; free under-18s. **No credit cards.**

Zoologisk Have
Roskildevej 32 (72 20 02 00/72 20 02 80/www. zoo.dk). Bus 4A, 6A, 26. **Open** *Mar* 9am-4pm Mon-Fri; 9am-5pm Sat, Sun. *Apr, May, Sept* 9am-5pm Mon-Fri; 9am-6pm Sat, Sun. *June, Aug* 9am-6pm daily 1st 2wks of month; 9am-10pm daily last 2wks. *Oct* 9am-5pm daily. *Nov-Feb* 9am-4pm daily. **Admission** 100kr; 60kr concessions. **Credit** AmEx, DC, MC, V.

Nørrebro & Østerbro

Head across the *bro* for a feel of real Copenhagen.

Nørrebro and Østerbro, along with Vesterbro, are often referred to as the *Brokvartererne* (literally the Bridge Quarters). These are the main residential areas outside the city's ramparts, and individual as they are, all have a flavour of 'real' Copenhagen about them that is sometimes sadly lacking in the city centre. Nørrebro can get a bit too real at times, hosting the odd riot, but overall remains a pulsating and attractive neighbourhood, while Østerbro is far more sedate and well-heeled.

Nørrebro

Along with Vesterbro, Nørrebro is one of the hippest areas of the city, thanks to its trendy clothes shops, vibrant cafés and burgeoning nightlife. Nørrebro has its epicentre on **Sankt Hans Torv**, with its two great cafés, **Sebastopol Café** and **Pussy Galore's Flying Circus** (for both, *see p138*), and the boutiques and cafés on **Blågårdsgade**, but the café-bar-restaurant **Bodega** (*see p137*) and happening **Elmegade** have spread the trendification further.

As with Vesterbro, many younger Copenhageners have found that Nørrebro's ethnic mix is a major element of its appeal as an up-and-coming residential area. But unlike Vesterbro's so-called second generation Danes, who are more established, Nørrebro's ethnic inhabitants seem less integrated into the community and are generally less prosperous. As a result, the area has suffered from that most un-Danish phenomenon, social unrest, and has even experienced some shocking violent crime, the odd riot on the occasion of a deportation or some heavy-handed policing. Nørrebro, with its dark streets and tightly packed housing, has more than its share of social problems and, as such, is probably central Copenhagen's least safe (as opposed to 'most dangerous') neighbourhood at night – though that statement should be qualified by saying that it is still a relatively secure night-time destination, particularly compared with many other European capitals.

Fælledparken. *See p103*.

Zoologisk Museum. *See p104.*

It is ironic, then, that Nørrebro's only museum is the **Politihistorisk Museum** (Police History Museum; *see below*). This well-presented museum would potentially be of interest to foreign visitors but for the lack of any significant information in English. As well as covering the history of the police force, with old uniforms, equipment and ephemera, the building also houses the Museum of Crime, which documents Copenhagen's nefarious residents (including various infamous murderers) from past centuries.

Nørrebro also has two historic cemeteries. The Jewish cemetery, **Mosaisk Kirkegård**, on Peter Fabers Gade is surrounded by a high wall and gates, and is only open for private visits arranged through the local Jewish community. **Assistens Kirkegård** (*see p104* **Dead famous**), on the other hand, is open year-round and, for a place of eternal rest, is fairly lively; it's used by many as a local park and picnic place (rehearsing musicians are a common sight). Buried among the hundreds of varieties of trees in this graceful cemetery is just about everyone of any note from Danish history over the last two centuries, including old rivals Hans Christian Andersen and Søren Kierkegaard; Niels Bohr; Carlsberg patriarch JC Jacobsen; and the artists Christen Købke, CW Eckersberg, Jens Juel, HW Bissen and Peter Skovgaard.

Of all Nørrebro's shopping attractions, the best known are its **antiques** shops, which can be found scattered throughout the quarter.

The trade centres on Ravnsborggade (just south-east of Sankt Hans Torv) and its extension Ryesgade, where just about every store has a selection of old clothes, furniture, porcelain, art, glassware, silverware, gold or bric-a-brac (*see p141*).

Assistens Kirkegård

Entrances on Jagtvej & Nørrebrogade (35 39 93 04/www.assistens.dk). Bus 5A, 18, 350S. **Open** *Mar, Apr, Sept, Oct* 8am-6pm daily. *May-Aug* 8am-8pm daily. *Nov, Dec* 8am-4pm daily. *Jan, Feb* 8am-5pm daily. **Admission** free. **Map** p248 H8.

Politihistorisk Museum

Fælledvej 20 (35 36 88 88/www.politimuseum.dk). Bus 5A, 16. **Open** 11am-4pm Tue, Thur, Sun. **Admission** 25kr; 20kr concessions; free under-18s. **No credit cards. Map** p248 J10.

Østerbro

Østerbro, which runs from the eastern side of Nørrebro across to the docks on the coast, is dominated by Denmark's national stadium, **Parken** in Fælledparken. Bordered by Nørre Allé, Blegdamsvej, Østerbrogade and Jagtvej, **Fælledparken** (**photo** *p102*) is a large, municipal park with a small lake. A more practical open space than most of Copenhagen's other more historic or ornamental gardens, this is where locals come for a game of football or hockey, to play tennis, cycle, rollerskate, jog or skateboard. During the summer, there are often free concerts here: larger-scale pop and rock concerts by big bands and artists take place in the big concrete stadium, better known as the home of **FC København** (*see p200* **The new firm**), the country's top football team.

To the west of Parken, across Nørre Allé, is the **Zoologisk Museum** (Zoological Museum; *see below*), which, though a little fusty – the mammals and birds from around the world that are displayed here are stuffed – is a good place to take children if the weather is bad.

Østerbro itself is a prosperous residential area with a mixture of century-old apartment buildings and newer high-rise blocks. There is a good mix of shops, cafés and restaurants stretching along the length of **Østerbrogade**, and the shops along Nordre Frihavnsgade and the bars on Bopa Plads are showing signs of trendification.

East of Østerbro is a large dock area that in recent years has seen a considerable amount of development. Further north in Nordhavnen, the docks become more industrial, though here you will find the cavernous modern furniture store **Paustian** (*see p157*) and a couple of stylish restaurants, as well as Copenhagen's yacht basins. In terms of new architecture, this is one of the most stimulating parts of the city – but bring a bike, the area is too big to cover on foot.

Zoologisk Museum
Universitetsparken 15 (35 32 10 01/www.zoologisk museum.dk). Bus 18, 42, 43, 150S, 173E, 184, 185. **Open** 11am-5pm Tue-Sun. In week 7 & 42 (school holidays) open 10am-5pm daily. **Admission** 50kr; 15kr-40kr concessions. **No credit cards.** **Photo** *p103.*

Dead famous

Assistens Kirkegård (Cemetery) is the final resting place of many a great Dane. Here are the CVs of a few of the better known inhabitants.

Hans Christian Andersen
Plot no: P1
Assistens' most famous lodger by far, Andersen is probably *the* most famous Dane – period. Born in Odense in 1805, he moved to Copenhagen at 14. He was a playwright, a poet and an excellent origami artist, but became world-famous first and foremost for fairytales such as *The Emperor's New Clothes* and *The Nightingale*. He died in 1875.

Søren Kierkegaard
Plot no: A17
Born in Copenhagen in 1813, Kierkegaard had a life as plagued by doubt as his existentialist philosophy. Inspired by his strongly religious father, he decided to become a pastor. But after a troubled youth and a broken engagement to the love of his life, Regine, he turned to writing philosophical masterpieces such as *Either/Or* and *The Sickness unto Death*. He died a bitter 42-year-old in 1855.

Niels Bohr
Plot no: Q4
Niels Bohr, the 1922 Nobel Prize Winner for physics, was born in Copenhagen in 1885. Living proof that footballers aren't all dim, Bohr was a fine league player at Akademisk Boldklub. He chose to pursue physics, and went on to formulate the principle of atomic fission. He won the Nobel Prize for his work on the periodic system of elements. Bohr, like thousands of Danish Jews, fled the Nazi occupation in 1943 and wound up in the US, working on the atomic bomb – though he was later to campaign against its use. He died in 1962.

Martin Andersen Nexø
Plot no: H2
A writer of socially minded works about the hardships of common folk around the turn of the 20th century, Nexø was born in 1869 in Copenhagen's early industrial slums. *Pelle the Conqueror* remains his best known work, not least because it was turned into an Oscar-winning movie by director Bille August. A communist, he fled occupied Denmark in 1941 and died in Dresden in 1954.

Dan Turèll
Plot no: B13
(*See also p97* **The observer**)

Michael Strunge
Plot no: V15
Strunge and Turèll were two of Copenhagen's most notable post-war writers. Turèll died in 1993 at the age of 47 and was a much-loved local character and bon viveur – finding beer and whisky at his graveside is by no means unusual.

Strunge was a post-punk poet who committed suicide in 1986 in central Copenhagen, diving from a fourth floor window at the age of just 28. Twenty years later, his romantically bleak Cold War poems of alienation still attract new readers.

Further Afield

Science and nature to the fore beyond the city limits.

Hellerup & Charlottenlund

The affluent coastal suburb of Hellerup, just north of the city centre via Østerbro, has some good shops and restaurants, but the star of the show is a superb museum.

Experimentarium (*see below*), Denmark's radical and inventive science museum, is filled with imaginative displays and hands-on experiments. Though aimed at children, it attracts its fair share of adults, who are mesmerised by the virtual technology (trying a human-size gyroscope, programming robots or staring at an optical illusion). The museum renders mundane or esoteric topics – alternative power, recycling and genetics – fascinating and accessible. Be warned, though: the noise can be deafening.

Continue northwards through the suburbs and you soon reach the greenery surrounding **Charlottenlund Slot** (Charlottenlund Palace), the site of a royal residence since 1690. The current baroque palace was built for Princess Charlotte Amalie in 1730, but its leafy gardens subsequently found favour among city dwellers as a popular destination for Sunday outings. Various other royals have lived in the palace, but since the 1930s it has been home to the Danish Institute for Fisheries, so only the grounds, not the house, are open to the public.

Danmarks Akvarium (*see below*), located in the palace grounds, is one of Copenhagen's perennially popular attractions. Though not the most modern of aquariums, the 90 tanks contain the usual marine attractions, including sharks, piranhas, turtles and tropical fish. It's worth a look if you are visiting **Charlottenlund Fort** (a grassy hillock with a nice campsite) and **Charlottenlund Strand** and the weather turns nasty. Charlottenlund Strand, although small, is the nearest beach to Copenhagen heading north; though most people continue up to Bellevue Beach, the former has a large, landscaped grass area. All are a pleasant forest walk from Charlottenlund station.

Culture vultures should visit **Ordrupgaard** (*see below*), an art museum containing some excellent French Impressionist and Danish art from the 19th and 20th centuries. Zaha Hadid's stunning extension, completed in 2005, has doubled the size of the museum, which contains works by Manet, Renoir, Matisse and Gauguin.

Danmarks Akvarium

Kavalergården 1, Charlottenlund (39 62 32 83/ www.danmarksakvarium.dk). Bus 14. **Open** *Feb-Apr, Sept-Oct* 10am-5pm daily. *May-Aug* 10.30am-6pm daily. *Nov-Jan* 10am-4pm daily. **Admission** 85kr; 45kr concessions. **Credit** MC, V.

Experimentarium

Tuborg Havnevej 7, Hellerup (39 27 33 33/www. experimentarium.dk). **Open** 9.30am-5pm Mon,Wed-Fri; 9.30am-9pm Tue; 11am-5pm Sat, Sun. **Admission** 125kr; 55kr-80kr concessions; free under-2s. **Credit** AmEx, DC, MC, V. **Photo** *p106.*

Ordrupgaard

Vilvordevej 110, Charlottenlund (39 64 11 83/www. ordrupgaard.dk). Train to Klampenborg or Lyngby/ bus 388. **Open** 1-5pm Tue-Sun. **Admission** 70kr; 55kr concessions; free under-18s. **Credit** MC, V.

Bispebjerg

The most striking landmark in Copenhagen's monotonous suburbs is **Grundtvigs Kirke** (Grundtvigs Church; *see below*) in Bispebjerg, 15 minutes' drive north-west of the city centre. The church is named after Nicolai Frederik Severin Grundtvig, the Danish priest, writer, composer and educational pioneer. And its construction was a family affair: it was designed by PV Jensen-Klint and completed after his death by his son, the designer Kaare Klint. The massive yellow-brick church took almost 20 years to complete (it was finished in 1940), and possesses a stark beauty.

Grundtvigs Kirke

På Bjerget 14B, Bispebjerg (35 81 54 42/www. grundtvigskirke.dk). Train to Emdrup/bus 10, 16. **Open** 9am-4pm Mon-Wed, Fri, Sat; 9am-6pm Thur; *May-Sept* noon-4pm Sun. *Oct-Apr* noon-1pm Sun. **Admission** free.

Lyngby

One of Copenhagen's greener and more attractive suburbs is **Lyngby**, eight kilometres (five miles) north of the centre, and home to Denmark's largest open-air museum, **Frilandsmuseet** (*see p106*). Not to be confused with **Frihedsmuseet** (the museum of Denmark's resistance movement), Frilandsmuseet covers an area of 35 hectares (86 acres) and is home to 110 buildings from Denmark, southern Sweden and northern

Roaring fun at **Experimentarium**. See p105.

Germany, all dating from the 17th to the 19th centuries. To see and appreciate them all takes at least a day, but to get a good cross-section of architectural styles the curators suggest you visit buildings 34, 42 and 60-72. Opened in Copenhagen in 1897, and relocated to the present site in 1901 under the auspices of Nationalmuseet, the museum features wind- and watermills, farm buildings, fishermen's cottages, peasants' houses, factories, and even a 19th-century fire station, all preserved with period decor. There aren't any information signs to set the atmosphere (though there is a useful guidebook in English). Other attractions include rare Danish cattle breeds and excellent guided tours. On the downside, an enjoyable day out at an open-air museum depends on the weather – a risky proposition – and, thanks to poor signposting (typical of Denmark), it is difficult to find by car. However, you can get off the S-train at Jægersborg and catch the local train, which winds its pretty way to the museum at Brede station.

Adjacent to Frilandsmuseet is **Brede Vaerk** (*see below*), once the Brede cloth mill industrial complex (which closed in 1956), and now preserved as a complete industrial village (with workers' cottages and the owner's country house). It's also run by Nationalmuseet. At one time this whole region was the centre for Denmark's industry and there were many factories and mills, stretching all the way from Lyngby to the coast. Brede House is a neo-classical manor, built in 1795 for the owner of the mill, Peter van Hemert, and has an exquisite Louis XVI interior. The house was intended to be a summer residence for his family, but van Hemert went bankrupt in 1805. Ironically, that bankruptcy, and the detailed inventory of the house that ensued, allowed Nationalmuseet to restore the interior accurately. There is also a superb restaurant, Brede Spisehuset (IC Modewegs Vej), nearby.

Brede Vaerk

IC Modewegs Vej, Lyngby (33 13 44 11/www. natmus.dk). Train to Jægersborg, then train to Brede/bus 184 (from Nørreport Station), 194. **Open** *Easter-Oct* 10am-5pm Tue-Sun. Closed Oct-Easter. **Admission** 50kr; 40kr concessions; free under-18s. **Credit** AmEx, DC, V.

Frilandsmuseet

Kongevejen 100, Lyngby (33 47 34 81/www. frilandsmuseet.dk). Train to Jægersborg, then train to Brede/bus 184 (from Nørreport Station), 194. **Open** *Easter-Mid Oct* 10am-5pm Tue-Sun. Closed Mid Oct-Easter. **Admission** free. **Credit** AmEx, DC, V. **Photo** *p107.*

Ishøj

The fourth of Sjælland's world-class art museums is found in the unprepossessing suburb of Ishøj, 15 minutes by train south along the coast from Copenhagen. **Arken Museum For Moderne Kunst** (Arken Museum of Modern Art; *see p107*) was built to celebrate Copenhagen's year as European City of Culture in 1996 and is almost as famous for its architecture as its exhibits. Arken is housed in an extraordinary concrete, glass and steel building, designed by the Danish architect Søren Robert Lund. His compelling and perplexing construction, with its echoes of marine architecture (both inside and out), won a competition for the design of the new gallery in 1988, and has divided critics ever since.

Some applaud its apt maritime references (the museum is near the beach), which give it the appearance of an abstract shipwreck; others say that an art museum should focus on its art, not its own architecture. Most artists hate it, claiming the exhibition spaces compete with, rather than enhance, their work. But visitors are usually won over by Lund's skewed vision.

Arken's permanent collection of paintings, sculpture, graphic art and installations includes 260 post-war works, although, disappointingly, only 50 or so of these are usually on show. This display, however, is augmented by superb temporary exhibitions, often transferred from other major European museums.

Many pieces in the permanent collection are by Danish artists, but there are also numerous foreign works. And there is something to surprise everyone, including major works by Asger Jørn, Per Kirkeby and Christian Boltanski. Probably the most famous piece in the permanent collection is the photograph *Flex Pissing/Björk er en nar* (aka Bringing It All Back Home) by Claus Carstensen and the art group Superflex (popularly known as the mildly controversial Danish Art Mob). Arken also has a small cinema, a concert hall and a café.

Arken is a few metres from **Ishøj Strand** (Ishøj Beach), an artificial but attractive seven-kilometre (four-mile) stretch of sandy beach.

Arken Museum For Moderne Kunst

Skovvej 100, Ishøj (43 54 02 22/www.arken.dk). Train to Ishøj, then bus 128. **Open** 10am-5pm Tue, Thur-Sun; 10am-9pm Wed. **Admission** free. **Credit** DC, MC, V.

Amager

Amager is the small island immediately to the east of Copenhagen. It is home to the city's international airport, but aside from that, it's mostly a flat, bleak area of industrial estates, cheap housing and farmland. Currently, the island is redeemed only by the fishing village of **Dragør**, though it also boasts the nearest (and best) beach to the centre of Copenhagen, **Amager Strandpark**.

On the east coast of Amager, among salt flats and farmland bustling with birdlife, lies Dragør, with its maze of cobbled lanes and traditional yellow cottages. Like many coastal settlements in this area it was founded upon the humble herring – shipped throughout Europe before the Reformation to provide sustenance for the Catholic faithful abstaining from meat during Lent and on Fridays – and prospered during the 14th century as a fishing port. In the 19th century it found a new lease of life as a centre for shipping and salvage, trading through the Baltic and as far away as England. That came to an end with the advent of steam ships, and since then little has changed here (part of its charm) though it's only half-an-hour's bus ride from Copenhagen.

However, Dragør's sleepy idyll can be misleading. Property prices here are high – the village is popular with affluent young professionals who commute into the city. They ensure that Dragør remains an improbably lively, almost cosmopolitan, village. There are also some smart shops on its short high street (open on Sundays during the summer), as well as several good restaurants and beer gardens, which draw the tourists. The town has a marina, a small cinema and an equally small

museum (**Dragør Museum**; *see below*), housed in the town's oldest fisherman's house (dating from 1682). If you fancy staying in Dragør, a great choice is the three-star Dragør Badehotel (Drogdensvej 43, 32 53 05 00, www.badehotellet.dk, double 765kr-1,050kr). Ask for a room with a sea view.

Five minutes' drive to the south, inland, is the charming village of Store Magleby, founded by Dutch settlers in the early 1500s. The village is home to the **Amager Museum** (*see below*), which traces the history of the Dutch immigrants in the area.

Amager Museum

Hovedgade 4 & 12, Store Magleby, Amager (32 53 93 07/www.amagermuseet.dk). Bus 30, 73, 350S. **Open** *May-Sept* noon-4pm Tue-Sun. *Oct-Apr* noon-4pm Sun. **Admission** 30kr; 15kr concessions. **No credit cards.**

Dragør Museum

Havnepladsen, Strandlinien 2 & 4, Dragør, Amager (32 53 41 06/www.dragoer-information.dk). Bus 30, 32, 73, 75E, 350S. **Open** *May-Sept* noon-4pm Tue-Sun. Closed Oct-Apr. **Admission** 20kr; free under-18s. **No credit cards.**

Frilandsmuseet. *See p106.*

Sightseeing

Eat, Drink, Shop

Designer Zoo. *See p141.*

Restaurants

There's more than just meatballs on the menu in Scandinavia's culinary capital.

When Sir Terence Conran turns his attention to a city and its cuisine, it is a sure sign that something epochal is stirring in the culinary world. As usual, Terry has been a couple of years late turning up in Copenhagen (although, admittedly, his company did have a hand in the design of Salt a few years back, *see p116*), but at the time of going to press he was about to open his latest gourmet complex in the former Malmö ferry terminal at the end of Nyhavn. The much delayed **Customs House**, as it will be called, was due to open in December 2006 with Japanese, Italian and Modern European/Scandinavian restaurants, plus a delicatessen, following the Bluebird (King's Road, London) blueprint. So it seems that the world is finally waking up to modern Scandinavian food, and discovering that Copenhagen is its true capital.

There are now more Michelin-starred restaurants in Copenhagen than in the rest of Scandinavia put together. But what is really energising the city's restaurant scene at the moment isn't the high-end market, but the good-value, expertly run local bistro with a short menu of surefire classics, an informal-verging-on-groovy atmosphere and wines by the glass. **Luns** (*see p124*) in Østerbro is probably the leader of the pack, but **Les Trois Cochons** (*see p123*), **Cofoco** (*see p123*) and **Famo** (*see p123*) are following the formula with huge success and packing the punters in night after night.

One of the pleasures of eating out in even the top restaurants in Copenhagen is their relaxed, unstuffy attitude – the snooty sommelier is a rarity here. This is probably because most waiting staff tend to be paid comparatively well, which means that, though a tip is always welcome, you shouldn't feel obliged to load on an extra 15 per cent unless you've had a really great experience. Five per cent or 10kr for meals under 100kr should suffice. The Danes are pretty mean tippers as a rule.

Be aware that many of the best restaurants close for the holidays in July and many of Copenhagen's cafés and bars serve excellent food, from light snacks to full meals. *See chapter* **Cafés & Bars**.

The best Restaurants

For cheap eats
Riz Raz. See p115.

For dining like the Danes
Restaurant Kanalen. See p121.

For herring heaven
Restaurant Ida Davidsen. See p118.

For a beer with that
Nørrebro Bryghus. See p124.

For old-school posh
Els. See p118.

For a bowl of pho bo
Lê Lê. See p123.

For haute, haute cuisine
Dining Room. See p121.

For the meal of your life
Prémisse. See p118.

Tivoli & Rådhuspladsen

Contemporary

The Paul

Tivoli, Vesterbrogade 3, Vesterbro (33 75 07 75/ www.thepaul.dk). **Open** noon-2pm, 6-8pm Mon-Sat. Closed Jan-Mar. **5-course menu** 700kr. **Credit** AmEx, DC, MC, V. **Map** p250 O11 ❶
The Paul, named after its owner, Englishman Paul Cunningham, opened in 2003 to much acclaim and received a Michelin star in 2004. The food is best described as Modern European but the real star is the venue, Glassalen, a glass-domed conservatory designed by Poul Henningsen in the 1940s and one of the most beautiful dining rooms in the whole of Copenhagen. It has a bar by the entrance; a homely, open kitchen at the end of the room; and a corridor to the loos lined with menus from some of the world's greatest restaurants. As for the light, contemporary food, as good as it is, you pay the usual Tivoli mark-up to eat here.

> ❶ Purple numbers in this chapter correspond to the location of each restaurant as marked on the street maps. *See pp244-253.*

1.th. *See p116.*

Eat, Drink, Shop

Oriental

Wagamama

Tietgensgade 20 (33 75 06 58/www.wagamama.dk).
Open noon-11pm Mon-Thur, Sun; noon-midnight
Fri, Sat. **Main courses** 95kr. **Credit** AmEx, DC,
MC, V. **Map** p250 P12 ❷

Londoners will be familiar with the Wagamama formula: cheap, simple Asian noodles, soups, rice dishes and curries eaten at communal benches in a
bustling canteen atmosphere, and it has translated
well to the Danish capital. As in London reservations aren't possible, so you can expect to queue at
weekends. There are entrances on Tietgensgade and
via Tivoli, so you don't have to pay to enter the old
playpark to dine here.

Strøget & around

Contemporary

Aura

Rådhustræde 4 (33 36 50 60). **Open** 6pm-midnight
Tue-Thur; 6pm-3am Fri, Sat. **Set menus** 325kr-
465kr. **Credit** DC, MC, V. **Map** p251 O13 ❸

Aura's modern interpretation of Mediterranean, in
tapas-style courses with plenty of seafood options,
has helped make it a great success since it opened
in what was formerly something of a restaurant
graveyard just off Nytorv. Courses tend to be larger
than the usual tapas and can be selected either à la
carte or from fixed menus (featuring eight, 11 or 14
courses – most find eight a struggle). The new cocktail menu and a DJ have helped draw the pre-club
crowd at weekends.

Den Lille Fede

*Boltens Gaard, Store Kongensgade 17 (33 33 70
02/www.denlillefede.dk).* **Open** 5.30-10pm Mon-Sat.
5-course menu 498kr. **Credit** AmEx, DC, MC, V.
Map p251 M15 ❹

This dark, concrete tunnel has always been a challenge to the city's restaurateurs. The latest owner,
Poul Erik Ferdersen, has risen to the challenge offering keenly priced modern Mediterranean cuisine
with a southern French bias – scallops with orange
braised endive and tarragon, for example. As he
only offers seven dishes, from which you can either
choose five or all seven, Poul keeps prices reasonable and quality high. The name means 'the little fat
one', by the way. Booking is advised at weekends
and there is some outside seating in summer.

MR

Kultorvet 5 (33 91 09 49/www.mr-restaurant.dk).
Open 6pm-midnight daily. **Set menus** 500kr-700kr.
Credit AmEx, DC, MC, V. **Map** p251 M13 ❺

Having previously worked at Noma and the Paul,
Mads Reflund fulfilled a dream and opened his own
restaurant in one of the city's oldest houses back in
2005. It's an ambitious place. The food is wildly
inventive, sometimes bewilderingly complicated,
but always fascinating; meanwhile the decor is
lavishly louche, with alligator skin wallpaper and

Le Sommelier. *See p119.*

chandeliers. The location, on one of the city's less glamorous shopping squares, is not ideal, but dishes like sweetbreads with crayfish, dill and wild berries or beetroot with goat's cheese and peanuts ought to distract the more curious diners.

Thorvaldsen Hus

Gammel Strand 34 (33 32 04 00/www.thorvaldsens-hus.dk). **Open** 11am-10pm Mon-Thur, Sun; 11am-midnight Fri, Sat. **Main courses** 158kr-249kr. **Set menus** 325kr-385kr. **Credit** AmEx, DC, MC, V. **Map** p251 N14 **❻**

Advantageously located on historic Gammel Strand, Thorvaldsen Hus is a stylish restaurant/bar/café complex whose tables move outside both front and back during the summer: on to the cobbles beside the canal and, at the rear, into the beautiful courtyard. It struggles to offer consistency throughout its menu, though it excels at more traditional Danish fare.

TyvenKokkenHansKoneog-HendesElsker

Magstræde 16 (33 16 12 92/www.TyvenKokken HansKoneogHendesElsker.dk). **Open** 6pm-2am Mon-Sat. **5-course menu** 550kr. **Credit** DC, MC, V. **Map** p251 O13 **❼**

It may be (mis-)named after Peter Greenaway's cannibalistic *The Cook, the Thief, His Wife and Her Lover*, but this exquisite Franco-Danish restaurant located in a tiny, elegantly simple 18th-century townhouse (formerly a brothel) near Rådhuspladsen is a firm favourite with the city's gastronomes.

Diners are offered only one fixed menu (you choose the number of courses), but from the first mouthful you'll realise that TyvenKokken's... self-confidence is totally vindicated. The menu is not quite as radically inventive as it once was, with a more refined French discipline to courses such as bisque of Norway lobster or steamed foie gras with pumpkin purée and almonds (there is an entire lobster menu too). Booking is advised.

Danish

Huset Med Det Grønne Træ

Gammel Torv 20 (33 12 87 86). **Open** 11.30am-3.30pm Mon-Fri. **Main courses** 40kr-100kr. **Credit** MC, V. **Map** p251 N13 **❽**

A kind of working man's Ida Davidsen's (*see p118*), this old-style lunch restaurant is frequented by journalists, local businessmen and lawyers from the nearby courthouse. Offering traditional Danish *smørrebrød* in a small, spartan cellar café with yellowed ceilings and wood-panelled walls, this is an authentic taste of basic Danish cuisine. Owner Peter Damgaard has run the place for over 20 years and is happy to talk you through the menu (English version available), which includes a decent range of typical open sandwich toppings.

Slotskælderen Hos Gitte

Fortunstræde 4 (33 11 15 37). **Open** 10am-5pm Tue-Sat. **Main courses** 40kr-75kr. **Credit** AmEx, DC, MC, V. **Map** p251 N14 **❾**

Everyone who comes to Copenhagen should try proper, authentic, traditional Danish food, at least once. And it doesn't come much more authentic than Slotskælderen (the castle cellar). This old-school smørrebrød restaurant is just across the canal from Christiansborg Slot (home to the Danish parliament), which means this atmospheric, low-lit venue, run by the eponymous Gitte, attracts a fair number of politicians. Simply choose your sandwiches, *frikadeller* (meatballs) and *sild* (herring) from the counter, and the attentive staff bring them to your table. Fried plaice and pickled herring are two top choices here, classically washed down with a beer and schnapps.

French

Chit Chat Brasserie
Sankt Peders Stræde 24A (33 33 93 39). **Open** 5-11pm daily. **Set menus** 275kr-325kr. **Credit** MC (5.75% surcharge for foreign credit cards). **Map** p250 N12
This simply styled, split-level café-brasserie, run by Australian Christopher Howard, serves sizeable portions of creative French and modern southern European food at competitive prices, including *filet mignon* with mushrooms, haricots verts and rösti with a port wine sauce, or duck with baked

Star quality

At the time of writing Copenhagen had more Michelin stars than any other Scandinavian city – ten in all, and few would bet against more being awarded in the next edition of the guide. Of course, counting Michelin stars is only one method of assessing a city's culinary worth, and a rarefied one at that, but it is a sure sign of an emerging foodie force: modern Scandinavian cuisine.

What was once a dead-end dining scene with a handful of stiff, stuffy classical French restaurants serving suited businessmen and Japanese tourists, is now a burgeoning culinary destination talked of in the same terms as northern Spain or southern Italy. There are some world-class restaurants here, a few of them – such as Noma, Premisse and MR – dazzlingly innovative, slick and a match for anything in New York, Paris or London. One leading chef suggested recently that if, in cooking terms, Spain was 'the new France', then the Nordic countries were the next Spain. The chef was Ferran Adrià of El Bulli.

The scene is being driven by a new generation of young Danish chefs such as Rene Redzepi (*pictured*) of Noma (*see p120*) who, over the last couple of years, have returned from journeys of discovery abroad – to France, Spain, New York and Thailand – to mount a raid on their homeland's rich but neglected natural larder, finding magnificent shellfish, flavoursome root vegetables, a lavish forest harvest – berries, mushrooms, game, wild herbs – and some of the finest dairy products and pork in the world (this is where the legendary French chef Paul Bocuse comes to pick his pigs personally).

Technical and spiritual inspiration comes from the usual suspects – Adrià, Heston Blumenthal, Thomas Keller, Alain Ducasse

and Alain Passard – but it is tempered by a rigorous respect for the seasons' bounty and an inbuilt sense of restraint. These are characteristically Danish qualities, as is the appreciation of natural light (borne of long, dark winters), and an innate sense of good design that have helped make these new restaurants such pleasurable places to dine. And even that old stalwart, herring, still puts in an appearance now and again.

It is never cheap to eat out in Copenhagen and two people can easily ring up a bill of 2,000kr for dinner with wine, but at least these days, if you have managed to choose the right spot, you won't regret it.

aubergine, mushrooms and duchesse potatoes. Handy for the cool shops and bars of the trendified district of Pisserenden.

Kong Hans Kælder
Vingårdsstræde 6 (33 11 68 68/www.kong hans.dk). **Open** 6pm-midnight Mon-Sat. *Food served* 6-10pm Mon-Sat. **Main courses** 390kr. **6-course menu** 935kr. **Credit** AmEx, DC, MC, V. **Map** p251 N15 ⓫
Kong Hans' stylish, whitewashed, vaulted cellar rooms are tucked away down a small side street. Thomas Rode Andersen is one of the most highly respected chefs in Denmark and from his open kitchen he combines the finest quality regional ingredients (Danish smoked cheese, fish from the Øresund, and the restaurant's speciality, smoked salmon) with classic French techniques. Lending gravitas to the occasion is the *kælder* (cellar) itself, dating from the 15th century and said to be the oldest building in the city still in use commercially. At one time it faced the waterfront and was the site of a vineyard (hence the name Vingårdsstraede, 'vineyard street'). Prices, of course, are set at the sort of high levels you'd expect, which means that the clientele tends to be older and more conservative than the norm. Hardly the grooviest of venues, and being in a cellar there is no view, but come purely for the food and you will not leave disappointed.

Restaurant L'Alsace
Ny Østergade 9 (33 14 57 43/www.alsace.dk). **Open** 11.30am-midnight Mon-Sat. **Main courses** 165kr-176kr. **Credit** AmEx, DC, MC.V. **Map** p251 M15 ⓬
You can hardly move for posh and pricey French restaurants in this part of town, but L'Alsace is more authentic than most, serving Alsatian delicacies like foie gras, goose and *choucroute*, along with excellent cheeses and wines. This curious venue combines a whitewashed cellar with a rough and ready conservatory, but it still manages to evoke the crucial *hyggelige* atmosphere so valued by the Danes.

Global

Peder Oxe
Gråbrødretorv 11 (33 11 00 77/www.pederoxe.dk). **Open** 11.30am-1am daily. *Food served* 11.30am-10.30pm Mon-Wed, Sun; 11.30am-11pm Thur-Sat. **Main courses** 95kr-189kr. **Credit** DC, MC, V. **Map** p251 N13 ⓭
Peder Oxe is one of Copenhagen's best-known restaurants and it is very popular with domestic and overseas tourists. A wide-ranging menu covers all the bases, from steaks and burgers (made from organic and/or free-range beef), to light, fresh Asian-influenced dishes such as tuna tartar with avocado and mango, all of which are well presented and reasonably priced. But Peder Oxe's trump card is its romantic interior, featuring original wooden floors and exquisite Portuguese tiling – ample compensation should the few tables outside be taken.

Italian

Alberto K
Radisson SAS Royal Hotel, Hammerischsgade 1 (33 42 61 61/www.alberto-k.com). **Open** 6pm-midnight Mon-Sat. *Food served* 6-10pm Mon-Sat. **Set menus** 555kr-675kr. **Credit** AmEx, DC, MC, V. **Map** p250 O11 ⓮
Named after the first general manager of the Arne Jacobsen-designed SAS Royal Hotel (*see p41*), this magnificent modern Italian/Scandinavian restaurant ranks among the best of the city's upscale/event eateries. Chef Betina Repstock's forte is robust and utterly delicious dishes such as rabbit with Alba truffles, creamed polenta and hazelnuts. The view from the 20th-floor windows helps, of course. Prices are relatively high but portions are large, and the food and service are exceptional.

Mediterranean

Riz Raz
Kompagnistræde 20 (33 15 05 75/www.rizraz.dk). **Open** 11.30am-midnight daily. **Main courses** 99kr-139kr. **Buffet** 59kr-69kr. **Credit** AmEx, DC, MC, V. **Map** p251 O13 ⓯
The bargain-priced southern Mediterranean food at this convivial cellar restaurant is a favourite with tourists and Copenhageners and consistently wins over reviewers from the Danish press. Riz Raz always seems to be packed to the gunwales with an eclectic range of diners, in for a quick bite before heading somewhere groovier. The buffet, which in many other places is just an excuse to stuff punters with cheap salads, is, in Riz Raz's case, utterly delectable, and probably the best value food on offer here. A place to return to, particularly in summer. **Other locations:** Store Kannikstraæde 19 (33 32 33 45).

Oriental

Sushi Time
Grønnegade 28 (33 11 88 99). **Open** noon-3pm, 4-8pm Mon-Wed; noon-3pm, 4-9pm Thur, Fri; noon-4pm Sat. **Sushi** from 75kr. **Credit** AmEx, DC, MC, V. **Map** p251 M15 ⓰
A no-frills, decent value sushi takeaway with a small dining area upstairs – though, if the weather is nice, it's far better to go and enjoy your nigiri in nearby Kongens Have. The best priced sushi in town.

Sushitarian
Gothersgade 3 (33 92 30 54/www.sushitarian.dk). **Open** noon-11pm Mon-Wed; noon-midnight Thur-Sat; 5.30-11pm Sun. *Food served* noon-10pm Mon-Wed; noon-11pm Thur-Sat; 5.30-10pm Sun. **Main courses** 175kr. **Credit** MC, V. **Map** p251 M15 ⓱
For a more contemporary take on sushi, try this trendy, bar-style venue at the top of Gothersgade. Sushitarian offers a wide range of nigiri, sashimi and maki rolls.

Eat, Drink, Shop

Steakhouses

Bøf & Ost

Gråbrødretorv 13 (33 11 99 11/www.boef-ost.dk).
Open 10am-1am daily. *Food served* 11.30am-
10.30pm Mon-Wed, Sun; 11.30am-11pm Thur-Sat.
Main courses 159kr-189kr. **Set menus** 295kr-
350kr. **Credit** DC, MC, V. **Map** p251 N13 🔞
The rustic wooden tables and stone floor of this
cellar restaurant are slightly at odds with the
impressive complexity and prices of its food, but the
various cuts and preparations of beef (charcoal-
grilled is the house speciality) are excellent, as are
the many luxurious seafood dishes that feature on
the menu. As you'd guess from the name ('Beefsteak
& Cheese'), the cheeseboard is one of the best in
Copenhagen. The restaurant is situated on the southern side of the square in the oldest of the so-called
Fire Houses, built after the great fire of 1728 that
razed Copenhagen. Note: if you pay by credit card,
a 4.06% surcharge will be added to your bill.

Jensen's Bøfhus

Gråbrødretorv 15 (33 32 78 00/www.jensens.com).
Open 11am-10.30pm Mon-Sat; noon-10.30pm Sun.
Main courses *Lunch* 49kr-89kr. *Dinner* 129kr-
189kr. **Set menus** 159kr-239kr. **Credit** AmEx, DC,
MC, V. **Map** p251 N13 🔞
Don't dismiss these excellent family restaurants just
because they are a chain. Expect a decent range of
grilled steak and chicken dishes (particularly good
value at lunchtime), and attentive and friendly service. There are a few variations on the standards
(such as the Tex-Mex 'Sombrero Steak'), but Jensen's
classic whisky sauce is a deserved long-standing
favourite, as is the all-you-can-eat ice-cream bar. Not
as cheap as it should be, but good if you have kids
in tow.
Other locations: Kultorvet 15 (33 15 09 84);
Axeltorv (33 12 16 66); Vesterbrogade 11A,
Vesterbro (33 25 03 66); Amagerbrogade 84,
Amager (32 84 85 03).

Nyhavn & Kongens Nytorv

Contemporary

1.th

Herluf Trollesgade 9 (33 93 57 70/www.1th.dk).
Open from 6.30pm Wed-Sat. **Set menu** 1,100kr.
No credit cards. Map p252 N16 🔞
This unique and really rather splendid restaurant
behaves more as if it were a private dinner party (or
a piece of performance art) than a commercial catering enterprise. You pay when you book (two to three
weeks in advance is best in order to be sure of a
table) and receive an invitation by return of post.
When you arrive ('promptly at seven'), you buzz a
discreetly labelled intercom on the door of an ordinary, turn-of-the-19th-century apartment block in
the quiet residential area behind the Kongelige
Teater, before being shown into a drawing room in

which other 'guests' are mingling over an aperitif.
After a while doors are opened with a theatrical
flourish to reveal a spacious dining room with an
open kitchen. The eight innovative, contemporary,
but unfussy Scandinavian dishes on the fixed menu
more than live up to this elaborate preamble. A truly
out of the ordinary experience. **Photo** *p111.*

Restaurant Ensemble

*Tordenskjoldsgade 11 (33 11 33 52/www.restaurant
ensemble.dk).* **Open** 6-10pm Tue-Sat. **6-course
menu** 600kr. **Credit** DC, MC, V. **Map** p252 N16 🔞
Under the previous chef, Mikkel Maarbjerg, this
small, discreet one-room restaurant behind the
Kongelige Teater won two Michelin stars and was
widely considered the ultimate restaurant in
Copenhagen. That was quite something for Nikolaj
Egebøl and Morten Schou to live up to when they
took over in 2005 but, having worked under
Maarbjerg here before, they knew that a devotion to
Danish ingredients and adherence to the season's
bounty was an essential part of what made this such
a great restaurant. There is only one five-course
menu on offer here, but it is among the very best
modern Danish food you will find and features local
luxuries like turbot and lobster matched with superb
root vegetables, or venison and wild mushrooms.
Unlike Noma, Ensemble does permit some foreign
ingredients so you will spot the odd cameo from
France, like foie gras or truffles.

Salt ✓

*Toldbodgade 24-28 (33 74 14 48/www.salt
restaurant.dk).* **Open** noon-4pm, 5-10pm daily.
Main courses 188kr-230kr. **Credit** AmEx, DC, V.
Map p252 M17 🔞
As a preamble to his new gastrodome, the Customs
House (due to open in December 2006), a few years
ago Sir Terence Conran was involved in the design
of this Modern Franco-Danish place, housed in a
converted corn-drying warehouse dating from 1787.
The menu changes every three weeks but is usually
loaded with lovingly prepared fish dishes as well as
local pork and game. Service is brisk but brusque;
the prices are reasonable, considering the prime location and the high quality of the food (smoked
Greenland halibut with potatoes, plum and oyster
or braised veal shank with fried foie gras, beetroot
and blackberries), and there is a cheaper, more
Danish lunch menu. Plus, for the connoisseur, every
table has three choices of salt on offer: Maldon,
Guérande and Danish Læso.

Danish

Cap Horn

Nyhavn 21 (33 12 85 04/www.caphorn.dk). **Open**
9am-1am daily. *Food served* 9am-11pm daily. **Main
courses** 89kr-189kr. **Set menu** 325kr. **Credit** DC,
MC, V. **Map** p252 M16 🔞
When Danes think of Nyhavn they usually think of
herring and *smørrebrød*, and few restaurants along
the canal do it better than Cap Horn. This is one of

Noma. *See p120.*

the most commonly recommended venues on the quayside, so it is popular with tourists, but Danes come here too, which is always a good sign. There's outdoor seating from around April to September.

French

E-go
Hovedvagtsgade 2 (33 12 79 71/www.egoisten.dk). **Open** 11.30am-midnight Mon-Thur; 11.30am-2am Fri, Sat. **Main courses** 185kr. **Credit** AmEx, DC, MC, V. **Map** p251 M15 ❷

A recent name change (from Egoisten) has been accompanied by a jazzing up and a welcome pricing down of the menu at this discreet businessman's favourite. The chef used to work at Conran's Meza, in London, and so you can get a foie gras burger for lunch or a more fusion-oriented evening meal featuring dishes such as venison with smoked beetroot, or mullet with a leek terrine, parsnip foam and lobster sauce.

Els
Store Strandstræde 3 (33 14 13 41/www.restaurant-els.dk). **Open** 11.30am-10pm daily. **Main courses** 178kr-265kr. **5-course menu** 448kr. **Credit** AmEx, DC, MC, V (4.75% surcharge for foreign credit cards). **Map** p252 M16 ❷

There is no doubting the excellence of the kitchen at this posh (and a tad stuffy) restaurant. Els has been around since Hans Christian Andersen's day (he wrote a poem in appreciation of its hospitality) and the food is steeped in classical French tradition. The restaurant's original mid 19th-century interior underscores the mood, which is more 'well-heeled tourist on a spree' than 'regular local in for a treat'.

Restaurant d'Angleterre
Hotel d'Angleterre, Kongens Nytorv 34 (33 37 06 45/www.remmen.dk). **Open** noon-3.30pm, 5.30-11pm daily. **4-course menu** 495kr. **Credit** AmEx, DC, MC, V. **Map** p251 M15 ❷

At last this grand room overlooking Kongens Nytorv in the city's grandest hotel has the decor to match the refined brilliance of its food. This used to be the Wiinblad – named after a whimsical Danish artist – but a restrained, elegant restyle involving a major rebuild of the hotel frontage, glamorous gold panelling on the walls and ankle deep carpets has once again made this a destination restaurant in the city. Expect heavyweight French classics with all the usual suspects – quail, foie gras, truffles, lobsters – rendered with a delicate, modern twist. The clientele, however, remains resolutely antediluvian.

Oriental

Wokshop Cantina
Ny Adelgade 6 (33 91 61 21/www.wokshop.dk). **Open** noon-2pm, 5.30-10pm Mon-Fri; 6-10pm Sat. **Main courses** 55kr-130kr. **Credit** DC, MC, V. **Map** p251 M15 ❷

This excellent little cellar restaurant just around the corner from Kongens Nytorv is loosely modelled on the Wagamama concept (*see p110*), with long tables and cheap, fresh and delicate dishes. The food is mostly Thai, with some other regional influences, and includes the usual noodle- and rice-based bowls.

Slotsholmen

Contemporary

Søren K
Søren Kierkegaards Plads 1 (33 47 49 49/www. soerenk.dk). **Open** noon-midnight Mon-Sat. *Kitchen closes* at 10.30pm. **Main courses** *Lunch* 55kr-110kr. *Dinner* 95kr-235kr. **Set menus** 325kr-950kr. **Credit** AmEx, DC, MC, V. **Map** p251 P15 ❷

This supercool minimalist Scandinavian restaurant on the ground floor of the Black Diamond is a very popular lunch venue with visitors. Although there are probably more atmospheric destinations for a night out in the city, it is one of the surprisingly few restaurants to take full advantage of Copenhagen's waterside location (a stiff sea breeze can blight alfresco dinners even in summer) and the food is refreshingly light, imaginatively prepared and very highly regarded by locals. Style, substance and a view – what more could you ask for?

Frederiksstaden

Contemporary

Prémisse
Dronningens Tværgade 2 (33 11 11 45/www. premisse.dk). **Open** noon-2pm, 6pm-midnight Mon-Fri; 6pm-midnight Sat. Closed 15 July-15 Aug. **6-course menu** 750kr. **Credit** AmEx, DC, MC, V (5% transaction fee). **Map** p249 L16 ❷

With wunderkind Rasmus Grønbech in the kitchen, Denmark's top sommelier Christian Aaro Jensen looking after the drinks, and a venue in the spacious, vaulted cellar of one of the city's most venerable palaces a short walk from Kongens Nytorv, Prémisse could not fail. This is perhaps the most sumptuous, sensual dining experience in the city – extravagant, rich and at times overpowering, but unforgettable. Grønbech is another of those Danish chefs preaching the use of seasonal, local ingredients, but his dedication takes things further than the norm, with often radical combinations such as wild mushroom and smoked chocolate, or veal tongue with crayfish. Expect to pay around 1,500kr per head with wine, but expect it to be worth every øre.

Danish

Restaurant Ida Davidsen
Store Kongensgade 70 (33 91 36 55). **Open** 10am-5pm Mon-Fri. **Main courses** *smørrebrød* 50kr-160kr. **Credit** AmEx, DC, MC, V. **Map** p249 L16 ❸

Ida Davidsen is generally regarded as the queen of *smørrebrød* and a visit to her poky, unostentatious cellar restaurant is the perfect introduction to the art of the open sandwich. Ida, who works behind the counter most days and is the fifth generation of her family to run this 100-year-old lunch restaurant, is the Carl Fabergé of the *smørrebrød* world, concocting ornate sandwiches that could rank as works of art in any gourmand's book. She piles high her home-made rye bread with a multiplicity of well-matched toppings, including smoked salmon, caviar, herring, tomato, dill, *akvavit*, beef tartare, raw egg yolk and just about any other ingredient that will fit. From the 250 or so sandwiches on offer, the Victor Borge, featuring fresh salmon, lumpfish roe, shrimps, crayfish and dill mayonnaise, is always popular with a clientele that includes everyone from royalty (from their gaff round the corner in Amalienborg) to local office workers.

French

Gendarmen

Sankt Annæ Plads 16 (33 93 66 55/www. gendarmen.dk). **Open** 6pm-1am Mon-Sat. **Main courses** 195kr. **3-course menu** 250kr. **Credit** AmEx, DC, MC, V. **Map** p252 M17 ③

Right next door to the Hotel Neptun is this stylish, faintly rustic Franco-Danish restaurant, taken over in 2003 by chefs Birgitte Bodorf and Knud Rüsz. Since then they have pared down the French excesses, focussing more on lightly updated Danish classics, like plaice with butter sauce and potatoes, and veal with wild mushrooms. Lunch is a traditional Danish affair, dinner more sophisticated. The three-course menu with wine is reasonable value.

Rasmus Oubæk

Store Kongensgade 52 (33 32 32 09/www.rasmus oubaek.dk). **Open** 11.30am-4pm Mon, Tue; 11.30am-4pm, 6pm-midnight Wed- Fri. **Main courses** 155kr. **Credit** AmEx, DC, MC, V. **Map** p249 L16 ③

Having bagged a Michelin star, Rasmus Oubæk – formerly of TyvenKokkenHansKoneogHendes Elsker (*see p113*) – has recently toned down the costly excesses of his food (it is exceptionally difficult to make a gourmet restaurant pay in this city) and embraced simpler brasserie fare, but he continues to impress with his perfect, posh renderings of classic French dishes, like coq au vin or scallops in brown butter. The interior is about as minimalist as it gets with white walls, white tablecloths and elegant wooden chairs.

Le Sommelier

Bredgade 63-65 (33 11 45 15/www.lesommelier.dk). **Open** noon-2pm, 6-10pm Mon-Thur; noon-2pm, 6-11pm Fri; 6-11pm Sat; 6-10pm Sun. **Main courses** 185kr-210kr. **Set menu** 365kr. **Credit** DC, MC, V. **Map** p249 K16 ③

This is one of Copenhagen's finest French restaurants, offering an unfailingly wonderful menu of solid French classics, fortified with a welcome Danish robustness in dishes such as braised lamb or quail with poached foie gras and cherries. This relaxed but stylish restaurant/brasserie has won a number of awards for its wine list and has one of the finest cellars in Copenhagen, stocked with over 800 bottles (more than 20 reds are sold by the glass) – *Wine Spectator* magazine has given the place an award of excellence. Consequently, despite being located in a fairly quiet part of town, Le Sommelier is usually busy and booking is advised at weekends and in the evenings. At lunchtime it tends to lure business types; in the evenings it draws a more mixed crowd. Either way, brace yourself for a sizeable bill if you plan to enjoy it to the full. **Photo** *p112*.

Fusion

Umami

Store Kongensgade 59 (33 38 75 00/www.restaurant umami.dk). **Open** noon-3pm, 6-10pm Mon-Thur; noon-3pm, 6-11pm Fri; 6-11pm Sat; noon-3pm Sun. **Main courses** 90kr-180kr. **Credit** AmEx, DC, MC, V. **Map** p249 L16 ②

Looking like the backdrop for a *Wallpaper** magazine shoot, this Danish take on Nobu offers an eclectic range of Asian-influenced dishes, from classic sushi in the large sushi bar on the first floor, to unexpected fusions of classic French and Japanese cuisine (seared foie gras with eel, dashi pear, black beans and seaweed salad). Fusion has become something of a dirty word these days, but ask any of the Michelin-starred chefs in the city where they like to eat when off duty, and this is the place they most often mention. Everyone in this city who has anything to do with food has the highest respect for chef Francis Cardenau – also behind Le Sommelier – and this has to be Copenhagen's most ambitious restaurant opening, well, ever. The interior, by Orbit of London (who also count Louis Vuitton among their clients), is seductive with dark stone walls, walnut floors and ebony tables, and there is a saké and cocktail bar on the ground floor. Be warned, lunch can be rather dead in what is a slightly out of the way venue, but DJs liven things up a little at weekends.

Vegetarian

Cascabel Madhus

Store Kongensgade 80-82 (33 93 77 97). **Open** 11am-4pm Mon-Thur; 11am-5.30pm Fri. **Main courses** 48kr-75kr. **Credit** MC, V. **Map** p249 K16 ③

It may not look much from the outside, or indeed on the inside for that matter, but Cascabel, despite its anti-*hyggelige* decor, is recommended for its fresh, light, vegetarian food. Above all, it's cheap. You can fill up on healthy pastas, salads and muffins for under 90kr – the sun-dried tomato pasta salad with aubergine, olives, jalapeño peppers and sunflower seeds (50kr) is a meal in itself. Understandably, Cascabel draws a loyal, local crowd of Danes and expats. Please note it's only open for lunch.

Home cooking

Posh restaurants and groovy cafés are all very well, but if you really want to get to know what makes Danes tick, it could be worth getting in touch with **Dine with the Danes**. Since 1998 this organisation has offered visitors the chance to spend an evening in the home of local people, sampling traditional Danish food and getting to know more about Denmark and Danish culture over the dinner table.

The service attempts to match you up with people of similar ages and interests. To facilitate this, it prefers potential dinner guests to make reservations via its online questionnaires at least a week in advance. You can also book via your hotel, youth hostel or campsite.

Also associated with Dine with the Danes is **Meet Gay Copenhagen** (www.meetgaycopenhagen.dk), which offers dinners and socialising organised by local gay couples.

Dine with the Danes

26 85 39 61/www.dinewiththedanes.dk. **Cost** *Dinner* 400kr. **Credit** (at tourist office) AmEx, DC, MC, V.

Rosenborg & around

French

Kokkeriet Spisehus & Catering

Kronprinsessegade 64 (33 15 27 77/www. kokkeriet.dk). **Open** 6pm-1am Tue-Sat. *Food served* 6-11pm Tue-Sat. **Main courses** 225kr. **6-course menu** 600kr. **Credit** AmEx, MC, V. **Map** p247 K15 ③⑥

Tucked away in Nyboder, this small but seductive modern French restaurant and catering company is among the most recent recipients of a Michelin star in the city. Loved by locals and hidden well off the tourist trail, Kokkeriet has thrived thanks to its superb kitchen and lively combinations, such as slow-braised pork cheek with octopus. Exceptional quality and well worth hunting out.

Global

Sult

Filmhuset, Vognmagergade 8B (33 74 34 17/ www.sult.dk). **Open** noon-4pm, 5-10pm Tue-Fri; 10am-3pm, 5-10pm Sat, Sun. **Main courses** 185kr-225kr. **Credit** AmEx, DC, MC, V. **Map** p247 L14 ③⑦

The Danish Film Institute's magnificent film centre has another draw. Chef Margrethe Kofoed Olsen successfully fuses southern European food with global influences in handsomely modern, New Yorkish surroundings (high ceilings, wooden floors, tall windows). Sult is short for *sulten*, which means 'hungry' in Danish, and is not to be confused with the equally good Salt (*see p116*), which means 'salt' in both English and Danish.

Oriental

Sticks 'n' Sushi

Nansensgade 47 & 59 (33 11 70 30/www.sushi.dk). **Open** 11am-11pm Mon-Thur, Sun; 11am-midnight Fri, Sat. *Takeaway* 11.30am-10pm Mon-Thur, Sun; 11.30am-10.30pm Fri, Sat. **Set menu** 249kr. **Credit** MC, V. **Map** p246 L11 ③⑧

If you can forgive the heinous abbreviation in the name, you will find this to be one of the city's most stylish sushi restaurants (it was also the first), with branches in two of the city's coolest residential streets. Sticks 'n' Sushi's menu varies, depending on the fish of the day, but the quality remains generally high (as do the prices). There is a well-stocked rack of magazines to peruse as you await the arrival of your sashimi.

Other locations: Øster Farimagsgade 16B (35 38 34 63); Strandvejen 195, Hellerup (39 40 15 40); Istedgade 62, Vesterbro (33 23 73 04).

Christianshavn

Danish

Noma

Strandgade 93, Christianshavn (32 96 32 97/ www.noma.dk). Bus 2A. **Open** 6pm-midnight Mon, Sat; noon-2pm, 6pm-midnight Tue-Fri. **Main courses** from 275kr. **5-course menu** 585kr. **Credit** DC, MC, V. **Map** p252 N18 ③⑨

Having worked at legendary Spanish restaurant El Bulli and the French Laundry in California, Denmark's most innovative chef, Rene Redzepi, has tried to bring their kind of out-of-the-box thinking and meticulous attention to detail to bear on Nordic ingredients, with sensational results. The proud boast is that there is not a sun-dried tomato or any olive oil to be found in the kitchen. Redzepi is a tireless forager, unearthing extraordinary 'substitute' ingredients, such as sea shanties that taste like coriander from beaches in Sweden, truffles from Gotland and herbs from the banks of Christianshavn's ramparts. One sauce uses the digestive juices from the arctic grouse (it's a favourite of Crown Prince Frederik, Redzepi tells us). Our only real criticism is that the bare wood interior of this converted 18th-century warehouse (overlooking the harbour, close to the new opera house) is rather soulless, despite the best efforts of the inhabitants of the lobster tank and the bubbling of the mineral water 'jacuzzi'. **Photo** *p117*.

Restaurant Kanalen
Wilders Plads 2, Christianshavn (32 95 13 30/
www.restaurant-kanalen.dk). Bus 2A, 350S.
Open 11.30am-midnight Mon-Sat. *Kitchen open*
11.30am-3pm, 5.30-10pm. **Main courses** *Lunch*
58kr-185kr. **Set menus** *Dinner* 238kr-490kr.
Credit AmEx, DC, MC, V. **Map** p252 O17 ④
Tucked away beside the canals in a particularly
idyllic corner of Christianshavn, Restaurant Kanalen
(which means 'the Canal') strikes a happy balance
between traditional and modern Danish cooking.
Thus you'll find excellent herring and *frikadeller*
sitting alongside more intricate dishes that blend the
freshest fish with deliciously light sauces and surprise ingredients such as air-dried Italian ham or
slow-roasted tomatoes. Usually, restaurants this
well located fail to deliver on the food front, but
Kanalen is a superb all-rounder. Alfresco dining in
summer, plus very sweet service, elevate it into the
top ten eateries in town. Reasonable prices too.

Global

Dining Room
25th floor of Radisson SAS Scandinavia Hotel,
Amagerboulevard 70, Amager (33 96 58 58/
www.thediningroom.dk). Bus 5A. **Open** 5pm-
midnight Tue-Thur; 5pm-1am Fri, Sat. *Kitchen*
open 6-10pm. **Main courses** 318kr. **Set menus**
395kr-535kr. **Credit** AmEx, DC, MC, V.
It may be stuck out of the way on charmless Amager
island but the 25th-floor restaurant of the Radisson
SAS Scandinavia is one of those places that war-
rants a special journey across town. If the stunning
views aren't enough, the food (blending predominantly modern French styles and top-quality Danish
ingredients together with the odd international
twist) is as good as anything Copenhagen has to
offer. The stylish oblong dining room, with windows
on one side overlooking the city, is one of the destination dining spots right now, and quite deservedly
so. Dress up, dust off every credit card you own,
expect to be hit hard with the drinks bill and you
won't be disappointed.

Spiseloppen
Loppen building, 2nd floor, Bådsmandsstræde 43,
Christiania (32 57 95 58/www.spiseloppen.com).
Metro Christianshavn/bus 8, 72E. **Open** 5-10.30pm
Tue-Sun. **Main courses** 165kr-215kr. **Credit** MC,
V. **Map** p252 P18 ④
What do you get when you cross an Englishman, an
Irishman, a Scotsman, a Dane, a Lebanese and an
Italian? Spiseloppen's constantly changing rota of
international kitchen staff create a different menu
every night but, for once, this isn't a case of 'too
many cooks' – the myriad influences at work here
rarely fail to conjure something really special (the
vegetarian dishes are particularly impressive). The
entrance to Spiseloppen, through an anonymous-
looking door and up some shabby stairs in one of
Christiania's warehouses, promises little, but once
you enter its low-ceilinged, candlelit dining hall its

true worth becomes clear: this is a very special
restaurant. Diners tend to be young and arty, not
minding the occasional waft of exotic cheroot.

Viva
Langebrogade Kajplads 570, Christianshavn (27 25
05 05). Bus 5A, 47. **Open** 11.30am-3pm, 5.30-10pm
Mon-Thur; 11.30am-3pm, 5.30-10.30pm Fri, Sat;
11.30am-4pm, 5.30-9pm Sun. **4-course menu** 435kr.
Credit AmEx, DC, MC, V. **Map** p251 Q14 ④
Viva is a unique and rather special floating restaurant housed aboard a ship moored next to Langebro,
across the water from the Black Diamond. Noted for
its shellfish dishes, it is owned by Thomas Veber
and Paolo Guimaraes (the half-Portuguese chef), and
is the sister restaurant to Aura (*see p112*). Like Aura,
the dishes are tapas sized, while the interior is similarly contemporary and furnished by Gubi. During
the summer the rooftop deck is a great place for a
pre-dinner cocktail with views across the harbour.

Indian

Spicey Kitchen
Torvegade 56 (32 95 28 29). Metro Christianshavn/
bus 2A. **Open** 5-11pm Mon-Wed; 6pm-midnight
Thur-Sat; 2-5pm Sun. **Main courses** 35kr-70kr.
No credit cards. **Map** p252 Q17 ④
The number of customers usually found waiting for
a table inside this frantic and cramped one-room
curry house is testament to its excellent value. The
choice of chicken, lamb or fish curries might be a little limited (the chicken and spinach curry is recommended), but that hasn't stopped Spicey Kitchen
building a reputation as one of Copenhagen's best
cheap and fast eats.

Italian

Era Ora
Overgaden Neden Vandet 33B (32 54 06 93/
www.era-ora.dk). Metro Christianshavn/bus 2A.
Open noon-3pm, 7pm-1am Mon-Sat. *Food served*
noon-3pm, 6.30-10pm. **Set menus** 680kr-880kr.
Credit AmEx, DC, MC, V. **Map** p252 P16 ④
The dedication of the chefs here is evident in the
complex yet light Umbrian dishes, using ingredients
flown in from Italy. This beautifully decorated
restaurant, with its gold leaf lighting, burnt sienna
walls and open courtyard to the rear, only serves set
menus, with a choice of fish or meat for the main
course. The wine list remains as impressive and
expensive as ever, the service efficient and formal.
The best Italian in town by a very long stretch.

Vegetarian

Morgenstedet
Fabriksområdet 134, Christiania (www.morgen
stedet.dk). Metro Christianshavn/bus 8, 72E.
Open noon-9pm Tue-Sun. **Main courses** 59kr.
No credit cards. **Map** p253 P19 ④

Les Trois Cochons. *See p123.*

This tiny place set deep in the heart of the Free City of Christiania serves a mean vegetarian curry at an even meaner price – there aren't many places in the city where you can get a meal for less than 60kr. It is a great place to fill up while on a tour of the old hippy quarter and you can be sure you won't eat quite like this anywhere else in the city.

Vesterbro & Frederiksberg

Contemporary

Cofoco
Abel Cathrinsgade 7, Vesterbro (33 13 60 60/ www.cofoco.dk). **Open** 5.30pm-midnight Mon-Sat. *Kitchen closes* at 10pm. **3-course menu** 235kr. **No credit cards. Map** p250 Q10 **45**
From the Copenhagen Food Consulting people, also behind Les Trois Cochons (*see below*) and bargain takeaway place Le Marché (Værndemsvej 2), comes this superb value local Franco-Danish kitchen. The rustic interior decor is slightly misleading as the food here is rather more than just confit and entrecôte. Dishes include salmon and rye bread with celeriac and fennel, followed by home-made blueberry ice-cream for dessert – part of the reason why this place is immensely popular with locals. All Cofoco establishments are non-smoking.

formel B
Vesterbrogade 182, Frederiksberg (33 25 10 66/www.formel-b.dk). **Bus** 6A. **Open** 6pm-1am Mon-Sat. *Kitchen closes* at 10pm. **6-course menu** 700kr. **Credit** AmEx, DC, MC, V. **Map** p245 Q6 **47**
Several of Denmark's best-known chefs have passed through the kitchen of this small, delectable, marble-lined cellar restaurant at the western end of Vesterbrogade (please note, it is a very long walk from the centre of town). But the latest owners, Christian Moeller and Rune Jochumsen (both in their early 20s), have taken the modern European food to another level with dishes such as langoustine ravioli with snow crab foam or cod with glazed turnips in blood orange sauce. formel B offers just one six-course menu for 700kr, but even at these prices that's good value – the quality of the mostly locally sourced and strictly seasonal ingredients is exceptional. The place manages to draw in a young and fashionable crowd.

French

Les Trois Cochons
Værnedamsvej 10 (33 31 70 55/www.cofoco.dk). **Open** noon-3pm, 5.30pm-midnight daily. **3-course menu** 235kr. **No credit cards. Map** p245 P8 **48**
This is the kind of restaurant – a decently priced, authentic local bistro – that this part of Copenhagen has been crying out for. Run by the same folk behind Franco-Danish Cofoco (*see above*), Les Trois Cochons dishes up similarly priced, superb value three-course French meals with locally sourced ingredients and an enjoyable lack of formality. Diners must choose main courses in pairs, but with succulent poussin in a tarragon sauce or zander with leeks and fennel (both served with potato purée and haricots verts), whatever your companion chooses it should be easy to agree. Desserts are equally fabulous: the last time we were here the chef presented a satisfying riff on rhubarb as a compote, crumble and ice-cream. **Photo** *p122.*

Italian

Famo
Saxogade 3 (33 23 22 50). **Open** 6pm-midnight Mon-Thur; 6pm-1am Fri, Sat. **Set menu** 300kr. **No credit cards. Map** p245 P8 **49**
A kind of Italian version of Les Trois Cochons (*see above*) Famo was set up by ex-Era Ora chef Fabbio Mazzon and Dane Morten Kaltoft in 2006, in what was formerly the Crystal Palace, in this quiet residential street just off Vesterbrogade. Their simple, authentic, rural Italian fare, straight from the 'slow food' school, proved an immediate hit with the well-heeled locals and booking is pretty much essential in the cramped, one-room venue. There is only one menu, beginning with a joyous plate of antipasta (air-dried hams, squash purées, artichokes, etc), followed by freshly made pasta, main course, cheese and dessert. Very much worth the effort, and very keenly priced.

Oriental

Lê Lê
Vesterbrogade 56, Vesterbro (33 22 71 35). **Bus** 6A. **Open** 11.30am-11pm Mon-Thur; 11.30am-2am Fri, Sat; 11.30am-10pm Sun. **Main courses** 98kr. **No credit cards. Map** p245 P9 **50**
This is one of the city's best oriental restaurants and also one of its better bargain eats, serving up authentic, complex Vietnamese dishes – everything from soups and noodles to curries and rice dishes. The venue is cool too, with high ceilings and massive glass windows.

Spicylicious
Istedgade 27 (33 22 85 33/www.spicylicious.dk). **Open** 5-10pm Mon-Thur; 5-11pm Fri, Sat. **Main courses** 100kr. **No credit cards. Map** p250 Q10 **51**
This recent opening at the Central Station end of Istedgade serves up excellent value contemporary Thai food, with the odd Vietnamese influence. Chef Danni Nguyen is half-Vietnamese, half-Danish and his restaurant fittingly blends authentic cooking with a Scandinavian design sensibility. Unlike the spit 'n' sawdust Ban Gaw that used to inhabit this space, Spicylicious has a cool lounge vibe and attracts a young clientele for tom yum, red curries, noodles, etc.

Eat, Drink, Shop

Nørrebro

Danish

Nørrebro Bryghus

Ryesgade 3, Nørrebro (35 30 05 30/www.noerrebro bryghus.dk). Bus 5A. **Open** 11am-midnight Mon-Wed; 11am-2am Thur-Sat; 11am-10pm Sun. *Food served* 11.30am-3pm, 5.30-10pm Mon-Wed, Sun; 11.30am-3pm, 5.30-10.30pm Thur-Sat. **Main courses** 189kr-198kr. **Credit** DC, MC, V. **Map** p246 J11 ⑫

This super-stylish, split-level modern Scandinavian take on a microbrewery serves not just great home-brewed beers and ales but also some excellent, simple Franco-Danish food. The medium-priced menu changes monthly but will typically include plenty of fresh fish, such as fried pepper mackerel with summer cabbage, plus a choice of roast meats. All washed down, of course, with some of the best beers in town.

Oriental

Kiin Kiin

Guldbergsgade 21 (33 35 75 55). **Open** 6pm-1am Mon-Sat. **7-course menu** 500kr. **Credit** AmEx, DC, MC, V. **Map** p248 H9 ⑬

Formerly of the Paul (*see p110*), chef Henrik Yde Andersen has put five years spent living in Thailand to good effect in this new three-storey Nørrebro restaurant, close to Sankt Hans Torv. Weary of being served the same five dishes in the city's unadventurous Thai restaurants, Andersen's mission has been to get Danes eating new and more interesting Thai food, and vegetables and shellfish feature strongly. There is an excellently chosen wine menu too for 400kr.

Østerbro

French

Luns

Øster Farimagsgade 12, Østerbro (35 26 33 35). **Open** 6-10pm Wed-Sat. **Main courses** 150kr. **Credit** MC, V. **Map** p247 J13 ⑭

Chef Jens Vestergaard has earned Michelin stars in the past, but with the opening of Luns he has eschewed all the table-scraping, penguin-suited brouhaha of starred dining to present his take on decent, honest, earthy French food at excellent prices. There is just one dish of the week, plus an appetiser of charcuterie, cheese and a dessert: expect to be confronted with wonderfully rich stews, delicious confits and hearty tarts. The wine list is rather more serious, as Vestergaard bought all the wine from Restaurant Ensemble (*see p116*) when it changed hands a couple of years ago. The city's restaurant critics are unanimous in their praise: this is simplicity perfected.

Le Saint-Jacques

Sankt Jakobs Plads 1 (35 42 77 07). Bus 1A, 14. **Open** 11am-midnight Mon-Wed, Sun; 11am-2am Thur-Sat. **Main courses** 135kr-198kr. **Credit** DC, MC, V. **Map** p248 C13 ⑮

This pricey but inviting French restaurant, run by accomplished French chef Daniel Letz (formerly at Kong Hans), is across the street from the national stadium, Parken, in a quiet square just off busy Østerbrogade. Impeccable service, crisp white linen tablecloths and evocative candlelight that flickers enigmatically across the glittering gold of the religious icons on the walls ensure that this is a place that the locals return to again and again for special treats or that well-earned blow-out. Home-smoked salmon is a speciality.

Further afield

Contemporary

Den Gule Cottage

Staunings Plæne, Strandvejen 506, Klampenborg (39 64 06 91/www.dengulecottage.dk). Train to Klampenborg. **Open** noon-4pm, 6pm-midnight Mon-Sat. *Food served* noon-2pm, 6-9.30pm. **3-course menu** 445kr. **Credit** AmEx, DC, MC, V.

With its fairytale location in a thatched, half-timbered cottage, set beneath oak trees on the lawns that roll down to Bellevue beach, this tiny restaurant could probably get away with serving hot dogs (in fact, it used to be an ice-cream kiosk). But this is one of the very finest restaurants in the region, serving elegant, fabulously choreographed modern Danish dishes from the freshest seasonal ingredients. Expect locally caught game, fish and meats, funky foams and extravagant desserts in this definitive *hyggelige* venue. Highly recommended.

Fusion

Restaurant Jacobsen

Strandvejen 449, Klampenborg (39 63 43 22/ www.restaurantjacobsen.dk). Train to Klampenborg. **Open** noon-midnight Tue-Sat. *Food served* noon-10pm Tue-Sat. **Set menus** 335kr-435kr. **Credit** AmEx, DC, MC, V.

When Arne Jacobsen designed the Bellavista housing complex and theatre, he didn't quite have the chutzpah to name the restaurant after himself. But with his designs now as trendy as ever, the current owners have done just that. Jacobsen 'Ant', 'Swan' and 'Egg' chairs decorate the light, white interior with views to the Øresund Sea across Bellevue beach. The food is an erratic Danish-Asian-French fusion, and the service can be sloppy, but there is ample outside seating in the summer and, architecturally, it can't be beaten. The restaurant recently started offering picnic baskets and bike rental so, if the weather is up to it, you can head to Dyrehaven for an alfresco lunch or dinner. **Photo** *p125.*

Eat, Drink, Shop

Restaurant Jacobsen. *See p124.*

Cafés & Bars

Chilled to perfection.

Copenhageners have been addicted to coffee for centuries. Despite this, café culture has only really flourished in the city in the last decade or so. In that time dozens of venues have opened up, growing in sophistication over the years from the original, grand, French-style Café Norden on Amagertorv to the quirky coffee bars on Istedgade and Halmtorvet, encompassing ambitious gourmet places and painfully hip vodka bars along the way.

Virtually all cafés serve alcohol and food of some description, and so the line between café, bar and restaurant is often blurred. To add to the confusion many change as each day progresses. Some become more bar-like, others transform into full-blown restaurants, or have DJs playing at weekends (*see chapter* **Nightlife**).

The better Copenhagen cafés can be a match for many of the city's restaurants both in terms of the quality of food they serve and the atmosphere. Brunch is still the most important meal of the day for many of Copenhagen's cafés and they vie to see who can offer the most elaborate and exotic mid-morning platter (usually for around 100kr).

Though it's not nearly as costly as in the other Scandinavian countries, alcohol is still expensive everywhere in Denmark, with spirits especially so (though, by some curious quirk of excise, wine is cheaper in Danish supermarkets than British ones). As a rule, the further the café or bar is from the centre of town, the cheaper the booze becomes. You can usually expect to pay around 45kr for a glass of wine or a small beer; this rises a little on Nyhavn and in places like Norden and Europa.

Tivoli & Rådhuspladsen

Tivoli itself has around 30 restaurants and cafés, some good, most average, and all expensive, so you are advised to seek sustenance outside.

Bjørgs
Vester Voldgade 19 (33 14 53 20/www.cafe bjorgs.dk). **Open** 10am-midnight Mon-Thur, Sun; 10am-2am Fri, Sat. **Main courses** 75kr-145kr. **Credit** AmEx, MC, V. **Map** p250 O12 **①**
This L-shaped café-bar does a passable impression of an Edward Hopper painting, with its large windows, red sofas and mirrored walls. Although it's from the same stable as Sommersko (*see p129*) and Dan Turèll (*see p130*), Bjørgs is less pretentious, and serves as both a local bar and a trendy Saturday night stop-off.

Fox Kitchen & Bar
Jarmers Plads 3 (33 38 70 30/www.hotelfox.dk). **Open** 5pm-midnight Mon-Thur, Sun; 5pm-2am Fri, Sat. **Main courses** 150kr. **Credit** AmEx, DC, MC, V. **Map** p250 N11 **②**
Every night the lobby of the funky Fox Hotel (*see p43*) draws the city's sophisticates as it transforms into the Fox Bar, serving cocktails until the wee hours. Guests lounge on low-slung sofas, slowly slipping into a kaleidoscopic haze thanks to the ever-changing psychedelic lighting and ultra-chilled ambience. The Fox Kitchen is run by chef Anders Barsøe, who has worked at the cutting-edge molecular pioneer WD-50 in New York and brings some contemporary techniques like *sous-vide* to bear on Nordic ingredients, with an emphasis on health. Quite what barman Gromit makes of that as he

① Pink numbers in this chapter correspond to the location of each café/bar as marked on the street maps. See pp244-253.

The best Cafés & bars

For a well-poured Guinness
Bloomsday Bar. See *p128*.

For live jazz
Copenhagen JazzHouse. See *p130*.

For cake cravings
La Glace. See *p131*.

For a drink with a view
Kaffesalonen. See *p138*.

For cool cocktails
Fox Kitchen & Bar. See *p126*.

For cheap beer
Studenterhuset. See *p133*.

For late, late drinks
Café Bopa. See *p138*.

For guest-list glam
Oil. See *p134*.

Café Norden. *See p128.*

mixes a unique cocktail menu to match each course is anyone's guess. Needless to say, there's a DJ on hand at weekends.

Library Bar

Sofitel Plaza Copenhagen Hotel, Bernstorffsgade 4 (33 14 92 62). **Open** noon-midnight Mon-Thur; noon-1am Fri, Sat. **Main courses** 195kr-215kr. **Credit** AmEx, DC, MC, V. **Map** p250 P11 **❸**

Though members of some of the more salubrious gentlemen's clubs in London's St James's will be underwhelmed by the scale of this quiet and faux-exclusive bar within the Sofitel Plaza Copenhagen Hotel, most visitors are taken by its characterful wood panelling, crystal chandeliers, book-lined walls and Chesterfield-style sofas. This was once voted one of the finest gentlemen's bars in the world by *Forbes* magazine. If you've any money left over, you may care to nibble on sybaritic snacks like oysters and Parma ham. Cocktails start at 80kr.

Ultimo

Tivoli, Vesterbrogade 3 (33 75 07 51/www.cafe ultimotivoli.dk). **Open** 11am-midnight daily during Tivoli opening. **Main courses** 98kr. **Credit** AmEx, DC, MC, V. **Map** p250 O11 **❹**

The latest addition to the portfolio of Copenhagen restaurant mogul Torben Olsen is this glorious conservatory restaurant in the old pleasure garden. One of the most beautiful dining rooms in the city now serves contemporary, high-end Italian food – crab ravioli with tomato sauce, chilli, orange and grilled Norwegian lobster; vitello tonnato; posh pizzas, etc. There's outside seating if the weather allows.

Strøget & around

Atlas Bar

Larsbjørnsstræde 18 (33 15 03 52). **Open** noon-midnight Mon-Sat. Kitchen closes at 10pm. **Main courses** *Lunch* 85kr-138kr. *Dinner* 110kr-200kr. **Credit** DC, MC, V. **Map** p250 N12 **⑤**

The Atlas Bar serves 'food from the warm countries', which in practice means its influences range from Asia (it does a decent Manila chicken) to Mexico (humungous burritos). To underscore the point, the tabletops are decorated with maps. This welcoming cellar bar is well located in the heart of bustling Pisserenden and so is great for a mid-shop lunch, and popular with vegetarians. Upstairs is Flyvefisken, its sister Thai restaurant.

Bloomsday Bar

Niels Hemmingsgade 32 (33 15 60 13/www. bloomsdaybar.com). **Open** noon-2am daily. **Credit** DC, MC, V. **Map** p251 M13 **⑥**

This small, low-ceilinged Irish cellar pub, owned by Englishman Phil and Irishman Jonathan, is open until 2am every night, and offers a warm welcome with a good range of Irish and British draught beers. There is live Irish music on Sunday afternoons. Big with expats but also draws keen local øl enthusiasts.

Cafeen På 4

Illum, Østergade 52, Strøget (33 18 28 63/www. illum.dk). **Open** 10am-7pm Mon-Thur; 10am-8pm Fri; 10am-5pm Sat. **Main courses** 89kr-119kr. **Credit** AmEx, DC, MC, V. **Map** p251 N14 **⑦**

To escape the maddening crowds on Strøget, take the Willy Wonka-style glass elevator to the spacious, light and airy top floor of the Illum department store (the name means 'the café on 4'). There have been various attempts to turn this into a café/restaurant over the years: right now it is Kåre Find Jensen's turn to have a go with sandwiches, salads and brunches.

Café Europa

Amagertorv 1 (33 14 28 89). **Open** 8am-midnight Mon-Fri; 9am-2am Sat; 9am-11pm Sun. **Main courses** from 99kr. **Credit** AmEx, DC, MC, V. **Map** p251 N14 **⑧**

With a location right in the heart of the shopping district on Amagertorv, Café Europa is one of the city's most popular meeting places. Its prices can be high and the service frosty, but the food isn't bad and it's a nice place to stop off for a drink during an afternoon's shopping. Sandwiches are reasonable value. There is seating outside during the summer.

Café Ketchup

Pilestræde 19 (33 32 30 30/www.cafeketchup.dk). **Open** noon-midnight Mon-Thur; noon-2am Fri; 11am-2am Sat. **Main courses** *Restaurant* 275kr-298kr. **Credit** AmEx, DC, MC, V. **Map** p251 N14 **⑨**

Ketchup is one of those places Copenhageners go to be seen, and many a tabloid star has woken to find his evening antics here plastered on the morning's papers. The ground floor is divided into a café at the front, with floor-to-ceiling windows overlooking the street, restaurant tables to the rear, and a bar along one wall. Below in the basement are more restaurant tables and an open kitchen. A DJ plays on Friday and Saturday nights when the crowds can become fairly intense. Ketchup has a sister restaurant doing much the same thing in Tivoli. Great 'world' food; very smart, very cool, very pricey.

Other locations: Tivoli, Vesterbrogade 3 (33 75 07 55).

Café Laszlo

Læderstræde 28 (33 33 88 08). **Open** 11am-2am Mon-Sat (10am-2am during the summer); noon-2am Sun. **Main courses** 48kr-90kr. **Credit** V. **Map** p251 N14 **⑩**

This well-established and extremely popular cellar café on lovely Læderstræde offers sandwiches and salads at lunchtime, and has outdoor seating in warm weather. Cosy and dark in winter, it attracts a large proportion of students.

Café Norden

Østergade 61, Strøget (33 11 77 91). **Open** 9am-midnight daily. **Main courses** from 90kr. **Credit** AmEx, DC, MC, V. **Map** p251 N14 **⑪**

This grandest and largest of all Copenhagen's cafés (it seats 350 on sunny days) overlooks Amagertorv in the heart of Strøget, but despite its vast, two-storey,

Parisian-style interior (with chandeliers and wood panelling), it's usually a challenge to find a table. Sadly, the service here is often fairly grouchy (in fact, there is no table service and you have to order at the bar), but the food is adequate (salads, sandwiches, steaks and so forth), though you will pay around 20% more for everything by virtue of Café Norden's prime location. **Photo** *p127*.

Café Sommersko

Kronprinsensgade 6 (33 14 81 89/www.sommersko. dk). **Open** 8am-midnight Mon-Wed; 8am-1am Thur; 8am-4am Fri; 9am-4am Sat; 10am-midnight Sun. **Main courses** 88kr-168kr. **Credit** DC, MC, V. **Map** p251 M14 ⓬
Sommersko was one of Copenhagen's café pioneers back in the 1980s and things have moved on since then, but its wonderfully glamorous kitsch decor (mirror mosaics, baby grand piano, red vinyl banquettes) is distinctive, which is more than you can say for many cafés. The menu is rather predictable (mussels, burgers, salads, etc) and the food can be disappointing. Service, too, often leaves plenty to be desired.

Café Stelling

Gammeltorv 6 (33 32 93 08). **Open** 9am-11pm Mon-Thur; 9am-2am Fri, Sat. Closed Sun. **Main courses** 59kr-139kr. **No credit cards**. **Map** p251 N13 ⓭
This delectable corner café was designed by the maestro Arne Jacobsen and is today another of those archetypal Copenhagen hangouts, with vast plate glass windows affording an excellent view of the comings and goings in and around the old square, and dozens of international magazines to flick through while waiting for coffee and cake.

Café Victor

Ny Østergade 8 (33 13 36 13/www.cafevictor.dk). **Open** *Café* 8am-1am Mon-Wed; 8am-2am Thur-Sat; 11am-11pm Sun. *Restaurant* noon-3pm, 6-10.30pm Mon-Thur; noon-3pm, 6-11pm Fri; noon-4pm, 6.30-11pm Sat; 6-10pm Sun. **Main courses** 120kr-270kr. **Credit** AmEx, DC, MC, V. **Map** p251 M15 ⓮
A Copenhagen institution, Café Victor is one of the city's prime see-and-be-seen venues for celebrities, football stars, politicians, journalists and the jet set. Midday it is packed with lunching ladies, wrapped in fur or Gucci. The food is ultra-classic French fare – lobster Americain, sole meuniere – of a high standard. However, you don't come here just for the food, but more to soak up the atmosphere, marvel at the mirrored, art deco interior and do battle with the supercilious staff. If you don't fancy a full meal, half a dozen oysters at the bar (85kr) washed down with a glass of champagne will give you a taste of the Victor experience. A 4.2-5.7% surcharge is added to credit card payments (except Visa).

Café Zeze

Ny Østergade 20 (33 14 23 90). **Open** 8am-midnight Mon-Thur; 8am-2am Fri; 9am-2am Sat. **Main courses** 98kr. **Credit** AmEx, DC, MC, V. **Map** p251 M15 ⓯
Some cafés spend thousands on design, finding the right chairs and the right lighting, but ultimately it is the clientele that decides if a place succeeds or

Café Victor.

Café Zeze. *See p130.*

fails, and for all its spartan appearance, there is something about Zeze that continues to draw a dream café crowd. Models, ad folk, actresses, musicians – all young and beautiful – cram this place just about every night of the week. The food is fancier than the standard café fare, but hardly remarkable. And there is limited outdoor seating in summer. A great place to start an evening, and located near to Kongens Nytorv and Strøget.

Copenhagen JazzHouse

Niels Hemmingsens Gade 10 (33 15 26 00/33 15 47 00/www.jazzhouse.dk). **Open** midnight-5am; 6pm-5am concert nights. **Credit** AmEx, DC, MC, V. **Map** p251 N14

A stalwart of the Copenhagen nightlife scene, this superb live jazz venue has two storeys with a bar on each, a large dancefloor downstairs and is a dead cert most nights for an excellent atmosphere, interesting clientele and superb music. Jazz aficionados head here particularly on Thursday, Friday and Saturday nights for the best concerts in town, but despite this the Copenhagen JazzHouse remains blessedly free of jazz snobs. *See also p189.*

Dan Turèll

Store Regnegade 3-5 (33 14 10 47/www.dan turell.dk). **Open** 9.30am-midnight Mon-Wed; 9.30am-1am Thur; 9.30am-2am Fri, Sat; 10am-10pm Sun. **Main courses** 65kr-165kr. **Credit** AmEx, DC, MC, V. **Map** p251 M15

One of Copenhagen's most famous cafés, Dan Turèll is named after a well-known late poet, writer and iconoclast and has been one of *the* places to visit on a Friday or Saturday night for as long as anyone can remember. But the food here is middling (salads and sandwiches during the day), the staff snobby and the drinks expensive.

Drop Inn

Kompagnistræde 34 (33 11 24 04). **Open** 11am-5am Mon-Fri; noon-5am Sat; 2pm-5am Sun. **Credit** MC, V. **Map** p251 O13

With live music every night (jazz, blues and folk), and an open front with pavement seating in summer, Drop Inn is one of those places that never seems to take a rest. Hardly cool or trendy, Drop Inn tends instead to attract the more dedicated drinkers, so things can get a little lively towards the end of the evening.

Det Elektriske Hjørne

Store Regnegade 12 (33 13 91 92). **Open** 11am-midnight Mon-Wed; 11am-2am Thur; 11am-5am Fri, Sat. *Food served* 11.30am-8pm Mon-Fri. **Main courses** 49kr-79kr. **Credit** AmEx, DC, MC, V. **Map** p251 M15

This grand corner café, with an ornate frontage dating from the 1890s, is well located, with dozens of the city's best bars and restaurants nearby. Wisely, the Hjørne doesn't attempt to outdo its neighbours on the food front but instead trades on its welcome spaciousness and comfy sofas. The basement has table football, darts and pool.

Danish delicacies

Traditional Danish cuisine (if that's not too grand a term for it) has endured a rather bad press over the years, and it is true to say that a blend of indigestible rye bread, vinegary herring, fried pork and processed meats holds little obvious appeal for visitors from, say, France or Spain. Together with a major smoking habit, their diet has made the Danes among the unhealthiest people on earth. But despite the health warning, Danish food, done well and in small doses, can be delicious and is definitely worth trying while you're here.

Sild

Locally caught *sild* (herring) in some form or other is the archetypal Danish ingredient. This dense, oily fish is usually salted and pickled in vinegar with a touch of sugar, some onion, white peppercorns and a bay leaf (or, for reasons best known to the Danes, a curry-style sauce), and served on dark, buttered rye bread with chopped red onion.

Smørrebrød

Herring is one of the classic toppings for the famous Danish *smørrebrød* (literally 'buttered bread'), which is traditionally eaten only for lunch. *Smørrebrød* is the name given to the classic Danish open sandwich, and toppings can vary from highly elaborate gourmet confections featuring caviar, prawns and raw egg (see **Ida Davidsen**, *p118*), to the more prosaic liver paste and cucumber. Basically anything goes as long as it's savoury, but toppings will typically include boiled egg and dill, prawns, beetroot, tinned mackerel, cucumber, roast onions, various cold meats and goose or pork dripping.

Flæske svar

With over 20 million pigs bred each year in Denmark (four for each person) pork naturally features heavily on most menus. One of the more extreme variants is *flæske svar*, a dish made from fried pig's fat. And nothing else. Danes also mince pork to make *frikadeller* (meatballs) which are usually served without sauce and, as with many meals, accompanied with a small glass of schnapps (a strong, clear spirit distilled from potatoes), and a beer or two.

Pølser

Danish street food is limited to *pølser*, a kind of hot dog served from mobile kiosks and ladled with vivid coloured sauces and fried onions. Safe to say, *pølser* cannot be considered part of a healthy, balanced diet, although it can work as an excellent prophylactic against hangovers.

Wienerbrød

Bizarrely there is no such thing as Danish pastry in Denmark. What we call Danish pastry, the Danes call *wienerbrød*; they are made from sweet, buttery, flaky pastry topped with nuts, custard, stewed apple, chocolate or cinnamon. The other classic Danish dessert is the unpronounceable *rødgrød med fløde*, a currant and raspberry coulis mixed with fresh cream.

Galathea Kroen

Rådhusstræde 9 (33 11 66 27/www.galathea-kroen.dk). **Open** 6pm-2am Mon-Thur; 6pm-5am Fri, Sat. **Main courses** 45kr-185kr. **Credit** AmEx, DC, MC, V. **Map** p251 O13 ⑳

Galathea opened in 1953 and was named after a ship that was used as a base for exploration of Pacific sea life. Inside it is decorated with mementoes from the ship's journeys. The moment you enter this charismatic, eclectic mess of a bar, past the totem poles that guard the entrance, you know that Galathea Kroen is not one of Copenhagen's more style-conscious places. Maybe it's the jazz playing on the turntable (this is a strictly vinyl-only joint) or the affable and intriguing clientele, from trendy teens to bohemian oldies; or perhaps it's the engagingly dishevelled decor. Galathea changed owners in 2005 but, happily, the place and its unique atmosphere remain unchanged.

La Glace

Skoubogade 3 (33 14 46 46/www.laglace.com). **Open** 8.30am-5.30pm Mon-Thur; 8.30am-6pm Fri; 9am-5pm Sat; 11am-5pm Sun (closed Sun Apr-Sept). **No credit cards**. **Map** p251 N13 ㉑

Copenhagen's most vaunted and venerable bakery and pâtisserie was founded in 1870 and is famous for its delectable cream cakes, which would tempt even the most fanatical of calorie-counters. The speciality is the Sports Kage (Sport Cake), an over-the-top cream, caramel and nougat mousse confection. Skoubogade is just off the west end of Strøget, which makes it perfect for weary shoppers, but also means that you have to fight your way through a scrum of devoted cocoa bean groupies most afternoons.

Grill Bar

Ny Østergade 14 (33 14 34 54). **Open** 8am-1am Mon-Thur; 8am-2am Fri, Sat. **Main courses** 85kr-149kr. **Credit** AmEx, MC, V. **Map** p251 M15 ㉒

You can wake up with breakfast at this super trendy lounge bar-café-restaurant, right next door to Zeze (see p129), and continue all the way to cocktails the next morning, confident of being surrounded by the very coolest of the coolest, here in the heart of the Danish fashion and media manor. The food is ubiquitous fusion/modern Mediterranean. There is a lounge bar and DJs play at weekends.

Kafe Kys

Læderstræde 7 (33 93 85 94). **Open** 10am-1am Mon-Thur; 10am-2am Fri, Sat. **Main courses** 52kr-75kr. **No credit cards. Map** p251 N14

This enduringly popular bar is unremarkable other than for its pleasant location and its sandwiches, which are slightly more exotic than the usual café fare. That and the fact that it seems, for some reason, to draw an unusually attractive clientele. Friday night is the hottest of the week for Kys when it is usually packed with the young and the beautiful bar-hopping their way along Copenhagen's most charming street.

K-Bar

Ved Stranden 20 (33 91 92 22/www.k-bar.dk). **Open** 3pm-1am Mon-Thur; 3pm-2am Fri; 5pm-2am Sat. **Credit** AmEx, DC, MC, V. **Map** p251 N14

This low-slung, flirty cocktail bar is just how you imagine all Scandinavian bars will be: very cool, beautifully designed and with a short but sweet cocktail list featuring tempters like 'Very Berry Caipirinha' and 'Rude Cosmopolitan'. Bartender Kirsten is a dab hand at Martinis and there are 13 to try on the menu. This jewel of a place is tucked away just around the corner from Højbro Plads, a few moments from Strøget.

Kong Christian

Sankt Peders Stræde 34 (33 32 80 80). **Open** 6pm-midnight Tue, Wed; 6pm-2am Thur-Sat. **Set menu** 200kr. **No credit cards. Map** p250 N12

This used to be a lesbian bar, but now serves 100 per cent Arabica bean coffee, sandwiches and salads to a studeny crowd. Raw brick walls and candle lights make this one of the cosier places in town, and the owner, Christian Lauritzon, has grand plans to sell vintage clothing and arrange 'happenings' with his chums from the art academy (whose paintings decorate the walls).

Krasnapolsky

Vestergade 10 (33 32 88 00/www.krasnapolsky.dk). **Open** 11am-midnight Mon-Thur; 10am-5am Fri, Sat. **Main courses** 75kr-109kr. **Credit** AmEx, DC, MC, V. **Map** p250 N12

A star during the 1980s, this bar-restaurant-club is still popular with Copenhagen's pre-clubbers at weekends, apparently unbowed by the hefty cocktail prices and unsmiling staff. The food is pretty basic fare but a welcome tart-up in 2004 has improved the atmosphere and decor, and there is now a mellow lounge with appealing orange sofas to the rear.

Kreutzberg Café & Bar

Kompagnistræde 14A (33 93 48 50). **Open** 11am-midnight Mon-Fri; 11.30am-2am Sat; 12.30-6pm Sun. **Main courses** 49kr-95kr. **Credit** DC, MC, V. **Map** p251 N13

Kreutzberg has carved a niche as a friendly, buzzing basement venue serving classic café food. It's one of several cosy, cool places on the pedestrian Strædet which runs parallel to Strøget.

Bankeråt. *See p134.*

Peder Oxe Vinbar

Gråbrødretorv 11 (33 11 00 77/www.pederoxe.dk).
Open 11.30am-1am daily. **Main courses** 95k-189kr.
Credit DC, MC, V. **Map** p251 N13 ㉓
This stylish, spacious wine bar near the centre of
Strøget opened in 1978 and is located in the vaulted
cellars beneath the venerable Peder Oxe restaurant
(*see p115*). It is one of the city's more sociable, cosy
cellar venues.

Studenterhuset

*Købmagergade 52, Copenhagen University (35 32
38 61/www.studenterhuset.ku.dk).* **Open** noon-6pm
Mon; noon-midnight Tue; noon-1am Wed, Thur;
noon-2am Fri. **Main courses** 25kr. **No credit
cards.** **Map** p251 M13 ㉙
This subsidised student drinking den and live music
venue is a few steps from the Rundetårn. The decor
is grotty-chic to match the clientele's dress sense,
and prices are set for those on a government grant
budget. The beer is cheap and there is usually something groovy happening of an evening – most
notably, a gay evening on Tuesdays; 'International
Night' on Wednesdays; jazz on Thursdays; and rock
on Fridays. It is also a participating venue in the
annual jazz festival.

Thé à la Menthe

Kompagnistræde 29 (33 33 00 38). **Open** 10am-8pm
Mon-Sat. **Main courses** 59kr-119kr. **No credit
cards.** **Map** p251 O13 ㉚
This charming little cellar café and teahouse sells
couscous, salads and curries alongside its exotic
teas. Laid-back sofas and scatter cushions complete
the chilled Moroccan vibe. An oasis in the heart of
the shopping district.

Zirup

Læderstræde 32 (33 13 50 60/www.zirup.dk).
Open 10am-midnight Mon-Thur, Sun; 10am-2am
Fri, Sat. **Main courses** 74kr-149kr. **Credit** MC, V.
Map p251 N14 ㉛
Our choice of all the many excellent cafés on this
pretty pedestrian street parallel to Strøget, with its
beautifully lit interior, good value and slightly
more adventurous fusion menu (everything from
stroganoff to curry to Mexican wraps). Tables go
outside when the weather permits. All in all, a pleasant place to pass time. The Sunday morning hangover brunch should be available on prescription.

Nyhavn & Kongens Nytorv

Café à Porta

Kongens Nytorv 17 (33 11 05 00/www.cafeaporta.dk).
Open 8am-10pm Mon-Fri; 11am-10pm Sat. **Main
courses** 95kr-225kr. **Set menu** 250kr. **Credit**
AmEx, DC, MC, V. **Map** p251 M15 ㉜
This glorious Viennese café is one of the city's oldest and grandest – it opened in 1792 – with a perfectly restored, mirrored 19th-century interior (Hans
Christian Andersen lived upstairs for a while and
was a regular). The service is brisk but not brusque
and the reliably tasty French/Danish bistro cooking
(with ample portions) ensures it is packed with a mix
of tourists and older locals.

Fisken

*Nyhavn 27 (33 11 99 06/www.skipperkroen-
nyhavn.dk).* **Open** 8.30am-1am Mon-Thur; 8.30am-
2.30am Fri, Sat; 8.30am-2am Sun. *Food served*
11.30am-11pm daily. **Main courses** 168kr-195kr.
Credit AmEx, DC, MC, V. **Map** p252 M16 ㉝
One of Nyhavn's most *hyggelige* pubs is in the cellar underneath Skipperkroen. The decor is heavy on
maritime references (although it's hard to tell how
authentic any of it really is) and there's live nightly
folky, guitar-based music.

Palæ Bar

Ny Adelgade 5 (33 12 54 71). **Open** 11am-1am
Mon-Wed; 11am-2am Thur-Sat; 4pm-1am Sun.
No credit cards. **Map** p251 M15 ㉞
This esteemed boho bar, just around the corner from
the Hotel d'Angleterre, tends to appeal to more
mature drinkers who prefer its unrushed, understated mood and rich, old-fashioned Parisian-style
boozer atmosphere. Popular with journalists and
writers, Palæ exudes a kind of old-world intellectu-
alism (or so it seems after a few glasses of wine).

Quote

Kongens Nytorv 16 (33 32 51 51/www.cafequote.dk).
Open 9am-midnight Mon-Wed; 9am-1am Thur; 9am-
2am Fri; 10am-2am Sat; 11am-midnight Sun. **Main
courses** 118kr-248kr. **Credit** AmEx, DC, MC, V
(2.5% transaction fee). **Map** p251 M15 ㉟
One of the largest café-bar-restaurant places to open
in Copenhagen for a long time is this chic, two-floor
venue next door to the national newspaper *Jyllands*

Eat, Drink, Shop

Posten. With black banquettes, white walls, mirror-tiled columns and a *Get Shorty*-style central staircase, there is an enjoyable theatricality about the place. The food, by chef Patrick de Neef (ex-Ketchup) is equally showy, with regulars such as stuffed Bresse chicken with braised cabbage or pumpkin and chilli soup with tiger shrimp. There is outdoor seating overlooking the city's grandest square in summer. A more contemporary alternative to the inns of nearby Nyhavn.

Sporvejen

Gråbrødretorv 17 (33 13 31 01). **Open** 11am-midnight Mon-Sat; noon-midnight Sun. **Main courses** 44kr-70kr. **No credit cards. Map** p251 N13 ❸❻

This unique bar is housed in an old tram of the type that used to run in the city (before they were all flogged to Egypt), but is now embedded in a wall in this historic cobbled square just off Strøget. As you'd expect, it is rather cosy inside, but there is outside seating in summer.

Zoo Bar

Kronprinsensgade 7 (33 15 68 69). **Open** 11am-midnight Mon-Wed; 11am-2am Thur-Sat. **Main courses** 75kr-110kr. **Credit** MC, V. **Map** p251 M14 ❸❼

It may be small, but by virtue of its dream location – on Copenhagen's outdoor catwalk – and its reliably hip line-up of DJs at weekends, this pared down bar is always popular with the city's fashion and media crowd.

Frederiksstaden

Café Oscar

Bredgade 58 (33 12 50 10/www.oscarcafe.dk). **Open** 9.30am-11pm daily. **Main courses** 98kr-145kr. **Credit** AmEx, DC, MC, V. **Map** p249 K16 ❸❾

A welcome refreshment stop in what is otherwise a café-free quarter, Café Oscar is located on a corner site near to Amalienborg, Kunstindustrimuseet, Kastellet and the other main sights of the area. This light, spacious and relaxed café serves the usual beverages and sandwiches, plus a short crêpe menu and a more substantial selection of beef, fish and pasta dishes. There are a few outside tables for summer munching.

Oil

Esplanaden 8 (70 22 08 70/www.oilrestaurant.dk). **Open** *Restaurant* noon-10pm Tue, Wed; noon-11pm Thur, Fri; 6-11pm Sat; 11am-3pm Sun. *Bar* 10am-midnight Tue, Wed; 10am-1am Thur; 10am-3am Fri, Sat. **Main courses** 120kr-225kr. **Credit** MC, V. **Map** p249 K16 ❸❾

With the closure of the exclusive restaurant-bar Konrad in 2005, there was something of a gap in the market for a guest-list, wannabe bar in town, but the vacancy has been amply filled by the ambitious Oil, so named as it lies beside Maersk Oil and Gas close to the harbour near Kastellet. It is part-owned by René Dif (the bald one from Aqua), but that needn't necessarily put you off as this is a great place to come for a big, dressy night out. A guest list is enforced Thursday to Saturday – but you can just ring ahead to get on it.

Rosenborg & around

Bankeråt

Ahlefeldtsgade 27-29 (33 93 69 88/www.bankeraat.dk). **Open** 9.30am-midnight Mon-Fri; 10.30am-midnight Sat, Sun. **Main courses** 75kr-89kr. **No credit cards. Map** p246 L11 ❹❶

Monster brunches, great tortillas and pasta dishes, plus the quirkiest decor of all Copenhagen's cafés set this grungy boho cave apart. Brace yourself for a sobering encounter when you descend to the basement loos, as you're confronted by a ghoulish assortment of Gothic taxidermy tableaux – animals standing upright wearing long leather coats are a favourite. And parents beware, porn awaits. A weird and wonderful place. **Photo** *p132.*

Café Oliver's

Nørre Farimagsgade 63 (33 91 45 55). **Open** 11am-10pm Mon-Thur; 11am-5am Fri, Sat; 11am-6pm Sun. **Main courses** 99kr-149kr. **Credit** MC, V. **Map** p246 L12 ❹❶

This large corner café, a short walk north from Nørreport station, used to be Skurks. Its main attractions are the late opening hours at weekends and the lively, young crowd. Steaks, salads and burgers are served until late.

Kalaset

Vendersgade 16 (33 33 00 35). **Open** 11am-1am Mon-Sat; 11am-11pm Sun. **Main courses** 89kr-129kr. **Credit** AmEx, MC, V. **Map** p246 L11 ❹❷

This strikingly coloured, purple corner café opened in 2006 and serves a good organic brunch, burgers and sandwiches. The interior is best described as 'junk shop chic'.

MJ Coffee

Gothersgade 26 (33 32 01 05). **Open** 7.30am-10pm Mon-Thur; 7.30am-11pm Fri; 11am-6pm Sat, Sun. **Bagels** 60kr. **Credit** DC, MC, V. **Map** p247 L13 ❹❸

It may have changed its name from Mojo (to avoid confusion with the similarly named blues bar across town), but the quality of the coffee, the lengthy options and the wonderful cakes thankfully remain the same. This corner café located on bustling Gothersgade is very popular and a great place to ruminate while sipping coffee and watching the world go by, thanks to its floor to ceiling windows. It is owned and run by an American émigré from Chicago, so you know that this is the real deal. Also serves soups, salads and smoothies.

Vincafeen Bibendum

Nansensgade 45 (33 33 07 74). **Open** 4pm-midnight Mon-Sat. **Tapas** plate 145kr. **Credit** MC, V. **Map** p246 L11 ❹❹

Playing a leading role in the trendification of Nansensgade, this cosy, sexy wine bar complements its more rough and ready neighbour Bankeråt (*see above*) with an extensive range of wines by the glass (unusual in beer-minded Copenhagen) and a groovy, flirty cellar ambience. The tapas plates are excellent and the staff extremely knowledgeable. Argentinian wines are a speciality.

Christianshavn

Aristo
Islands Brygge 4 (32 95 83 30/www.cafearisto.dk). **Open** 11am-midnight Mon-Thur; 11am-2am Fri; 10am-2am Sat; 10am-7pm Sun. **Set menu** 465kr. **Credit** MC, V. **Map** p251 Q14 **45**
Located in the newly hip Islands Brygge area beside Langebro, this light, modern harbourside café serves contemporary European/global food (everything from sandwiches to five-course menus) and really comes into its own in the summer when the nearby harbour baths fill up with local sun-worshippers.

Bastionen og Løven
Christianshavns Voldgade 50 (32 95 09 40/www. bastionen-loven.dk). Metro Christianshavn/bus 2A, 19, 48, 350S. **Open** 10am-midnight daily. **Main courses** 175kr-200kr. **Set menus** 315kr. **Credit** AmEx, DC, MC, V. **Map** p252 Q18 **46**
This delightful, if rather hard to find, garden café is situated in an extension of Nationalmuseet's Lille Mølle (Little Windmill) on the ramparts of Christianshavn. It's set well off the tourist trail and during the summer is usually packed with locals, but if you fancy trying one of the city's great culinary institutions – traditional Copenhagen brunch (a simple but satisfying array of cheeses, herring, bread, fruit and cold meats) – in idyllic surroundings, this is the best place to come.

Café Luna
Sankt Annæ Gade 5 (32 54 20 00/www.cafeluna.dk). Metro Christianshavn/bus 2A, 350S. **Open** 9.30am-midnight Mon-Thur; 9.30am-1am Fri, Sat; 9.30am-midnight Sun. **Main courses** 90kr-149kr. **Credit** AmEx, DC, MC, V. **Map** p252 P17 **47**
If you can't get a table at Café Wilder opposite (*see below*), Café Luna offers good, simple food, including cheap salads, pasta dishes and more traditional Danish café fare. It is a good vegetarian option, and has an extensive wine list.

Café Wilder
Wildersgade 56 (32 54 71 83/www.cafewilder.dk). Metro Christianshavn/bus 2A, 66, 350S. **Open** 9am-midnight Mon; 9am-1am Tue, Wed; 9am-2am Thur, Fri; 9.30am-2am Sat; 9.30am-midnight Sun. **Main courses** 80kr-145kr. **Brunch** 95kr. **Credit** MC, V. **Map** p252 P17 **48**
Christianshavn's loveliest café-bar is located just a short walk from the chaos of Christiania. The food is fresh, cheap and simple (pasta, salads and sandwiches), and the service charming. This small, L-shaped room is usually crowded to bursting point with trendy, arty locals at weekends, so arrive early to be sure of a seat. Supermodel Helena Christensen lives nearby and is allegedly a regular when in town.

Café Wilder.

Vesterbro & Frederiksberg

Apropos

Halmtorvet 12, Vesterbro (33 23 12 21/www.cafe apropos.dk). **Open** 10am-midnight Mon-Thur, Sun; 10am-1am Fri, Sat. **Main courses** *Café* 65kr-125kr. *Restaurant* 169kr. **Credit** MC, V. **Map** p250 Q10 ❹

Probably the best of the trendy café-restaurants to have opened on the rejuvenated Halmtorvet in the last few years, Apropos offers mid-priced, southern European café food (the 98kr tapas plate, for example), more substantial French à la carte dishes, and a limited drinks menu. What makes Apropos and its neighbours particularly popular is their great location, and the fact that Halmtorvet is now a must-see-and-be-seen-in place, especially at weekends. There is plenty of outdoor seating in summer.

Bang og Jensen

Istedgade 130, Vesterbro (33 25 53 18/www.bang ogjensen.dk). Bus 10. **Open** 8am-2am Mon-Fri; 10am-2am Sat; 10am-midnight Sun. **Main courses** 65kr-119kr. **No credit cards. Map** p245 R8 ❺

This trashy Vesterbro café has been a mainstay of the quarter's nightlife scene for years and the area's plentiful fashion victims can usually be relied upon to serve up a bit of life most nights. Though the food is the usual Copenhagen café fare, it doesn't detract from Bang og Jensen's appeal as an alluring place to while away an evening (slumped, if you're lucky, in its great squashy sofas). Breakfast, with a fine disregard for the dictates of the clock, is served until 4pm daily.

Barbar Bar

Vesterbrogade 51, Vesterbro (33 31 88 89/www. barbarbar.dk). Bus 6A, 26. **Open** 10am-midnight Mon-Thur, Sun; 10am-2am Fri, Sat. **Main courses** 59kr-98kr. **No credit cards. Map** p245 Q9 ❺

This funky Vesterbro café and bar lies in shadow during the day, but it is lively at night when it is usually full of cool locals (and they don't come much cooler than Vesterbro's). It serves sandwiches and salads at reasonable prices.

Café André Citroën

Vesterbrogade 58 (33 23 62 82). **Open** 10am-11pm Mon; 10am-midnight Tue, Wed; 10am-1am Thur; 10am-2am Fri, Sat; 10am-11pm Sun. **Main courses** 109kr-169kr. **Credit** DC, MC, V. **Map** p245 P9 ❺

With its mirrors, red banquettes and classic brasserie menu, this is like a little bit of Paris transplanted on to busy Vesterbrogade. The food, service and people-watching are all top notch. Like so many places in town, it serves up a traditional Danish lunch but more mixed bag of French, Italian and Mexican fare in the evening.

Café Viggo

Værnedamsvej 15, Vesterbro (33 31 18 21). Bus 1, 6, 14. **Open** 10.30am-1am Mon-Wed; 10.30am-2am Thur-Sat; 11am-6pm Sun. **Main courses** 79kr-140kr. **No credit cards. Map** p245 P8 ❺

This cheap, characterful French café on what was once Copenhagen's 'food street' is a gathering place for the city's French community, which is usually a good sign. Sandwiches, omelettes and salads are

Pussy Galore's Flying Circus. *See p138.*

served during the day, while the dinner menu includes heartier bistro fare like rabbit stew and roast duck.

Det Gule Hus

Istedgade 48, Vesterbro (33 25 90 71). **Open** 10am-midnight Mon-Thur; 10am-2am Fri, Sat; 10am-11pm Sun. **Main courses** 80kr-178kr. **Credit** V. **Map** p245 Q9 **54**

One of the more spacious and attractive of Istedgade's hip cafés, Det Gule Hus is light, airy and welcoming, with great people-watching potential via the gritty daily life on Copenhagen's sleaziest street. Some tables outside in summer.

Konjak

HC Ørstedsvej 46, Frederiksberg (35 35 35 52/ www.konjak.dk). **Open** 11am-1am Mon-Wed; 11am-midnight Thur; 10am-1am Fri, Sat; 10am-6pm Sun. **Main courses** 112kr-198kr. **Credit** AmEx, DC, MC, V. **Map** p245 M8 **55**

This warm, inviting corner café is located in an increasingly interesting area. Decent food, cocktails and an unpretentious air are augmented by the work of local artists on the walls.

Meyers Deli

Gammel Kongevej 107 (33 25 45 95/www.meyers deli.dk). **Open** 8am-10pm daily. **Main courses** 159kr. **Credit** MC, V. **Map** p245 O7 **56**

Klaus Meyer is one of the leading foodie figures in Denmark. Entrepreneur, TV personality and restaurateur (he is the man behind Noma, *see p120*), Meyer opened this magnificent deli-café in the heart of

bourgeois Frederiksberg back in 2005 and his healthy, innovative eat/heat/cook takeaways have proved very popular with time-poor yuppie locals.

Pegasus Bar & Café

Mysundgade 28 (33 31 80 50). **Open** 10am-11pm Mon-Wed, Sun; 10am-1am Thur; 10am-2am Fri, Sat. **Main courses** 69kr-89kr. **No credit cards. Map** p245 R8 **57**

A large, hospitable bar, which specialises in wine and fine beer (they have over 80 varieties), the Pegasus is just off Istedgade, close to Bang og Jensen and Vega, in the heart of Vesterbro.

Ricco's Coffee Bar

Istedgade 119 (33 31 04 40/www.riccos.dk). **Open** 9am-11pm Mon-Fri; 10am-11pm Sat, Sun. **No credit cards. Map** p245 R8 **58**

This tiny, narrow coffee bar and boutique, owned by Ricco Sørensen, has a devoted following among Vesterbro's dedicated coffee addicts. They take their coffee very seriously here, selling a wide range of beans, syrups and paraphernalia. There is a comfortable room out the back with long sofas and vinyl-only sounds.

Other locations: Studiestræde 24 (33 12 11 06).

Straßen

Istedgade 128 (33 22 32 41/www.strassen.dk). **Open** 10am-midnight Mon-Wed; 10am-2am Thur-Sat; 10am-11pm Sun. **Main courses** 98kr-155kr. **No credit cards. Map** p245 R8 **59**

One of the more recent arrivals on Istedgade serves run of the mill French-southern Mediterranean food and intriguing hangover cures for the morning after. Its chief draws are its vast aquarium and compelling views of the even more colourful street life.

Nørrebro

Atame

Blågårdsgade 3 (35 35 12 30/www.atame.dk). **Open** 11am-10pm Mon-Sat; noon-10pm Sun. **Main courses** 125kr. **No credit cards. Map** p248 K10 **60**

This lovely, homely Spanish place opened on the site of the old Shark House Deli in March 2006. Named after the Almodóvar film, Atame is a take-away deli and tapas bar with simple decor and a loyal local crowd.

Bodega

Kapelvej 1, off Nørrebrogade (35 39 07 07/www. bodega.dk). Bus 5A. **Open** 10am-midnight Tue; 10am-2am Wed, Thur; 10am-4am Fri, Sat; 10am-11pm Sun. **Set menu** 185kr. **Credit** MC, V. **Map** p248 J9 **61**

Formerly called Barstarten, this tucked away café-cocktail bar reopened with pretty much the same set-up (albeit with better food) as Bodega in 2006. The food is contemporary southern European fare, the coffee is excellent and the interior is effortlessly hip, with low ceilings, white walls, expensive leather chairs and a striking wooden bar and tables. DJs

Eat, Drink, Shop

play soul, funk and R&B on Thursdays and at weekends, and in summer there is limited seating outside, across the road from Assistens Kirkegård (see p104 **Dead famous**). The graveyard here is Denmark's most prestigious, providing a final resting place to Hans Christian Andersen, Søren Kierkegaard and Niels Bohr among others.

Frontpage

Sortedam Dossering 21 (35 37 38 27/www.cafe frontpage.dk). Bus 6A, 43. **Open** *Café* 11am-1am Mon-Wed; 11am-2am Thur; 10am-2am Fri, Sat; 10am-1am Sun. *Restaurant* 5.30-10pm Mon-Wed, Sun; 5.30-10.30pm Thur-Sat. **Set menu** 225kr. **Credit** (restaurant only) AmEx, DC, MC, V. **Map** p248 J11 ⑫

It remains something of a mystery why there aren't more cafés and bars located beside Copenhagen's elegant man-made lakes to the west of the city centre, since it seems such an obviously picturesque spot to dine and drink. Perhaps the reason lies hidden in the long cold of Copehagen's winter which can whip across the open water here. But we should be grateful for Frontpage, an appealing cellar bar (with outdoor tables during summer), and with a separate cellar restaurant serving excellent Franco-Danish delights next door. One of the cosiest places in the city.

Kaffesalonen

Pebling Dossering 6 (35 35 12 19). **Open** 8am-midnight Mon-Fri; 10am-midnight Sat, Sun. **Main courses** 68kr-130kr. **No credit cards**. **Map** p248 K10 ⑬

Salonen is blessed with an ideal location close to the lakes, which allows it to expand on to a large floating deck during the summer. It's the perfect place for a long, leisurely sundowner followed by a selection from the accomplished Franco-Danish menu.

Oak Room

Birkegade 10 (38 60 38 60). **Open** 7pm-midnight Tue; 7pm-2am Wed, Thur; 5pm-2am Fri, Sat. **No credit cards**. **Map** p248 J10 ⑭

This cramped venue just off trendy Elmegade is always packed and sweaty, with crowds spilling on to the pavement at weekends. After opening in 2004 it soon became the place to drink in Nørrebro, popular with pre-clubbers on their way to Rust nearby, or post-cinema goers coming from the Empire Cinema round the corner.

Pussy Galore's Flying Circus

Sankt Hans Torv 30 (35 24 53 00/www.pussy-galore.dk). Bus 3A. **Open** 8am-2am Mon-Fri; 9am-2am Sat, Sun. **Main courses** 70kr-110kr. **Credit** MC, V. **Map** p248 H10 ⑮

Located right at the centre of one of the hippest parts of Copenhagen (the area surrounding Sankt Hans Torv in Nørrebro) lies Pussy Galore's Flying Circus, the archetypal modern Copenhagen café. This busy L-shaped bar and dining area, decorated in requisite 1990s minimalist style (replete with Arne Jacobsen chairs and art by Danish rocker Lars H.U.G.), is the

trendy counterpart to the more conventional French food offered by Sebastopol next door (see below). The menu is fusion-heavy, with cheap salads and hearty burgers, but the quality can be variable. As with Sebastopol, come spring Pussy Galore's tables move out on to the square. The cocktails are reasonably priced compared with bars in the centre of town. **Photo** p136.

Sebastopol Café

Sankt Hans Torv 32 (35 36 30 02/www. sebastopol.dk). Bus 3A. **Open** 8am-1am Mon-Wed; 8am-2am Thur, Fri; 9am-2am Sat; 9am-1am Sun. **Main courses** 78kr-148kr. **Credit** AmEx, DC, MC, V. **Map** p248 J10 ⑯

Sebastopol's French staples offer tempting, good-value competition to the more erratic offerings of Pussy Galore's next door. A young and groovy clientele (musicians, journalists, advertising types) from this super cool part of town provides constant visual entertainment. Sebastopol gets very crowded on summer weekends when, like Pussy's, it bursts exuberantly outside on to the square.

Østerbro

Café Bopa

Løgstørgade 8 (35 43 05 66/www.cafebopa.dk). **Open** 10am-midnight Mon-Wed, Sun; 10am-2am Thur; 10am-5am Fri, Sat. **Main courses** 79kr-119kr. **Credit** MC, V. **Map** p248 C14 ⑰

Dark and arty by day, pulsating by night, Bopa is at the heart of this leafy square's young scene. At the weekends DJs ensure the place is packed and sweaty. Unusually late opening hours are another major plus, as are cheap cocktails.

Dag H

Dag Hammarskjölds Allé 36-40 (35 27 63 00/ www.dagh.dk). Bus 1A, 15, 40. **Open** 10am-11pm Mon-Thur, Sat; 10am-midnight Fri; 10am-10pm Sun. **Main courses** 109kr-159kr. **Credit** AmEx, DC, MC, V. **Map** p248 F14 ⑱

Formerly the coffee cathedral Amokka, this mainstay of Østerbro's café life on Lille Trianglen (Little Triangle, just along from the American Embassy) reopened with chefs Brian Damkvist and Peter Andersen at the helm in the kitchen. The coffee is still great, but not the centre of attraction as it once was. The emphasis is more on the excellent food now, which includes fancy burgers and more modern Med food.

Fru Heiberg

Rosenvængets Allé 7 (35 38 91 00/www.fruheiberg. dk). **Open** 5pm-midnight Tue, Wed; 10am-midnight Thur, Sun; 10am-2am Fri, Sat. **Main courses** 120kr. **No credit cards**. **Map** p248 E14 ⑲

This new, local Danish/French/Mediterranean restaurant has proved immensely popular since opening in 2006, thanks to excellent ingredients prepared with diligence and imagination. Cosy and old-fashioned but with a young, hip clientele.

Shops & Services

Take a hike down Europe's longest high street.

Copenhagen is a shopper's paradise, thanks to the locals' devotion to quality goods and innovative style. The city's shopping landscape reflects Denmark's egalitarian and inclusive society, offering something great for every budget. You'll find bustling branches of international high-street chains, thriving specialist shops and luscious boutiques all vying for your attention, with retailers largely clustered by type in various parts of the city.

The majority of retail therapy can be had on and around the seemingly endless **Strøget**, although shopping opportunities aren't limited to the city centre: in recent years several of Copenhagen's suburbs have become fashionable, including Vesterbro, Nørrebro, Østerbro and Frederiksberg (*see p159* **Off the beaten track**).

The only bad news is reserved for late risers or visitors on a short break. Denmark's weekend opening hours are fleeting to say the least – most stores close early on Saturdays and almost all are closed on Sundays – but late opening on Fridays provides some compensation, and there's always the option of making the half-hour train journey to Malmö in Sweden (*see p207*), where many shops are open on Sunday.

Sales tax is high at 25%, so if you live outside the EU and spend over 300kr at any of the places displaying a Global Refund Tax Free Shopping sign, it is worth asking the shop for a VAT refund cheque. When leaving Denmark, remember to make time before your flight to go to customs (Terminal 3, Arrivals hall) and get your cheques stamped; they can then be cashed at the Global Refund office for a refund of 19% of your total purchases.

One-stop shopping

Department stores

Illum

Østergade 52, Strøget (33 14 40 02/www.illum.dk). **Open** 10am-7pm Mon-Thur; 10am-8pm Fri; 10am-5pm Sat; noon-5pm 1st Sun of month. **Credit** AmEx, DC, MC, V. **Map** p251 M15.
Illum's interior design and magnificent glass dome make it the more modern of the city's two department stores. The ground floor is home to cosmetics, accessories and a fabulous range of womenswear by Scandinavian designers (Acne Jeans, J Lindeberg,

Bruuns Bazaar), while the basement houses a branch of supermarket Irma. More high-end fashion is found on the first and second floors. **Photo** *p140*.

Magasin

Kongens Nytorv 13 (33 11 44 33/www.magasin.dk). **Open** 10am-7pm Mon-Thur; 10am-8pm Fri; 10am-5pm Sat; noon-5pm 1st Sun of month. **Credit** AmEx, DC, MC, V. **Map** p251 M15.
This was Scandinavia's first department store and remains its largest, with five floors of clothes, high-class cosmetics, toys, household goods, books and fine food. Womenswear is a strong point, while families will find a Hamleys toy store, two juice bars and a comprehensive childcare area. **Photo** *p143*.

Royal Shopping

Amagertorv 10, Strøget (33 14 19 41/www.royal shopping.com). **Open** 10am-7pm Mon-Thur; 10am-8pm Fri; 10am-5pm Sat. **Credit** AmEx, DC, MC, V. **Map** 251 N14.
Royal Shopping is a one-stop wonderland for anyone looking to kit their home out in style. On hand is Illum's stylish homeware branch, Illums Bolighus (*see p157*), plus porcelain from Royal Copenhagen, Holmegaard glassware and Georg Jensen silver and jewellery design. Danish furniture, fine porcelain, crystal and silver are also represented, as are other Nordic brands including Orrefors, Kosta Boda and Iittala. There are plenty of bargains too.

The best Streets

Frederiksborggade
Map p246 K11/L12
For: crafts and fabric, outdoor sportswear, interiors and homewares.

Nansensgade
Map p246 L11 & p250 M10/M11
For: bespoke designer womenswear.

Læderstræde
Map p251 N14
For: jewellery, antiques, art and design, ethnic handicrafts.

Vestergade
Map p250 O12/N12
For: urban streetwear, second-hand clothes and records.

Eat, Drink, Shop

Illum. *See p139.*

Malls

Field's
*Arne Jacobsens Alle 12, Ørestad (70 20 85 05/
www.fields.dk). Metro/train Ørestad.* **Open** 10am-
8pm Mon-Fri, 10am-5pm Sat. *1st weekend of month*
10am-10pm Fri, 10am-5pm Sat, Sun. **Credit** varies.
This shopping and leisure centre is Scandinavia's
largest, boasting a branch of Magasin department
store, a Bilka supermarket and 70 high-street shops,
including H&M and Zara.

Fisketorvet
*Kalvebod Brygge 59, Vesterbro (33 36 64 00/
www.fisketorvet.dk). Train Kalvebod Brygge/bus 1A,
30, 65E.* **Open** 10am-8pm Mon-Fri, 10am-5pm Sat,
11am-5pm 1st Sun of month. **Credit** varies.
With 120 shops, a supermarket, 16 restaurants and
a ten-screen cinema, this enormous mall has something for all ages. All the usual chains are here
(H&M, Mango, Vero Moda), plus there's a Lego store
to placate younger punters.

Antiques, classics, decorative art

Bredgade is where all the serious antiques
stores, art dealers and auction houses are
located. Alternatively, **Ravnsborggade** has
over 20 specialist antiques stores catering to a
range of budgets (www.ravnsborggade.dk).

Antikhallen
*Sortedams Dossering 7C, Nørrebro (35 35 04 20).
Bus 5A.* **Open** 2-6pm Mon-Fri; 11am-3pm Sat.
No credit cards. Map p246 H12.
An unpretentious treasure trove of second-hand and
antique furniture. The shop is bursting with eye-
catching curiosities, from 19th-century mahogany
tables to 1970s moulded orange plastic chairs.

Antique Toys
*Store Strandstræde 20 (33 12 66 32/www.antique-
toys.dk).* **Open** 3-6pm Wed-Fri and by appointment.
No credit cards. Map p252 M16.
This has to be one of Copenhagen's cutesiest stores,
selling a huge range of antique toys in all shapes
and sizes (model cars, train sets, doll's houses), some
dating from as far back as the 17th century.

H Danielsen's Successors
Læderstræde 11 (33 13 02 74). **Open** 10am-5.30pm
Mon-Fri; 10am-2pm Sat. **Credit** AmEx, MC, V.
Map p251 N14.
Founded in 1907, this family firm owns the original
moulds of countless cutlery designs, allowing it to
reproduce long extinct silverware to order.

Green Square Copenhagen
*Strandlodsvej 11B (32 57 59 59/www.greensquare.dk).
Metro Lergravsparken, then 10min walk.* **Open** 9am-
5pm Mon, Tue; 9am-5.30pm Wed-Fri; 10am-3pm Sat.
Credit AmEx, DC, MC, V (transaction fee 6%).

Green Square occupies a massive aircraft hangar of
a building south of the city, and claims to be northern Europe's single largest antiques dealer, selling
a vast range of 18th- to 20th-century furniture.

Gregory Pepin's Danish Silver
Bredgade 12 (33 11 52 52). **Open** 10am-5pm
Mon-Fri; 10am-2pm Sat. **Credit** AmEx, MC, V.
Map p249 K16.
Pepin claims to stock the largest amount of antique
Georg Jensen creations in the city, from jewellery to
more formal sculpted pieces, as well as items from
the likes of Hans Hansen and Evald Nielsen.

Kim Anton
*Ravnsborggade 14D, Nørrebro (35 37 06 24). Bus
5A.* **Open** 9.30am-5.30pm Mon-Fri; 11am-2pm Sat.
Credit V. **Map** p248 J10.
A two-floor emporium of ornate 18th- and 19th-
century European furniture, plus a selection of fine
fabrics from Bevilacqua, whose luxurious velvets and
brocades grace grand buildings around the world.

Permanent Design
Bredgade 34 (33 15 13 50/www.gauguin.dk). **Open**
noon-5.30pm Mon, Tue, Thur, Fri. **Credit** MC, V.
Map p249 K16.
A specialist in 20th-century Danish furniture and
decorative art. Avid collectors can pick up one of
Arne Jacobsen's model 3107 chairs: designed in
1955, five million have been produced, none more
famous than the one posed on by a sultry Christine
Keeler for Lewis Morley's iconic 1960s snap.

Soelberg Kunst & Antikvitetshandel
*Kompagnistræde 21 (33 12 79 77/www.soelberg-
antik.dk).* **Open** 11am-5.30pm Mon-Fri; 11am-2pm
Sat. **Credit** AmEx, MC, V. **Map** p251 O13.
One of the city's most eclectic stores, Soelberg boasts
the likes of Russian Orthodox icons, military memorabilia and Inuit cultural artefacts – there's even a
small shrine to *Star Wars* merchandise. Bizarre.

Sølvkælderen
Kompagnistræde 1 (33 13 36 34). **Open** 9am-
5.30pm Mon-Thur; 9am-6pm Fri; 9am-2pm Sat.
Credit AmEx, MC, V. **Map** p251 O13.
A century-old purveyor of Danish silver. Certain
pieces date back as far as 1700, but there are also
more modern candlestick holders, plates and cutlery.

Art & design
The annual **Danish Arts and Crafts
Association market** (www.kunsthaand
vaerkermarkedet.dk) takes place every August
in Vor Frue Plads.

Designer Zoo
*Vesterbrogade 137, Vesterbro (33 24 94 93/
www.dzoo.dk). Bus 6A, 26.* **Open** 10am-5.30pm
Mon-Thur; 10am-7pm Fri; 10am-3pm Sat. **Credit**
MC, V. **Map** p245 Q7.

The brainchild of six young artisans who work in full view of ogling visitors (hence the name), and with furniture, glass, handmade clothes, jewellery and ceramics among the output. **Photo** *p146*.

Galerie Stamkunsten

Sankt Peders Stræde 27B (33 12 25 90/www.
stamkunsten.dk). **Open** 2-6pm Wed-Fri; noon-4pm Sat. **No credit cards. Map** p250 N11.
This charming workshop and gallery offers one-off paintings, ceramics, jewellery and clothing from a team of largely non-professional in-house artists.

Art supplies, hobbies & crafts

Grønlands Repræsentation

Strandgade 91, 3rd floor (32 83 38 00/www.ghsdk.dk).
Open 8.30am-4pm Mon-Fri. **No credit cards.**
Map p252 O17.
The best source for Greenlandic handicrafts and information, this shop sells books, jewellery, exquisitely forged, hand-ground knives, art and – animal rights supporters beware – seal fur products.

Københavns Farvehandel

Badstuestræde 9 (33 11 16 81/www.kobenhavns
farvehandel.dk). **Open** 10am-5.30pm Mon-Fri; 10am-1pm Sat. **No credit cards. Map** p251 N13.
Established in 1909, this charming shop caters to the most demanding of fine artists with a comprehensive range of creative raw materials.

Uldstedet

Fiolstræde 13 (33 91 17 71). **Open** 10am-5.30pm Mon-Fri; 10am-3pm Sat. **No credit cards.**
Map p251 M13.

A well-stocked knitting shop with quality yarns from Italy to Norway. A second branch, in suburban Lyngby, boasts an in-house knitting café.
Other locations: Gl Jernbanevej 7, Lyngby (45 88 10 88).

Auctions

Bruun Rasmussen Kunstauktioner

Bredgade 33 (33 43 69 11/www.bruun-rasmussen.dk).
Open 9am-5pm Mon-Fri. **Credit** DC, MC, V.
Map p249 K16.
Denmark's premier auction house also happens to be one of the world's top ten auctioneers, serving the prime end of the antiques and arts market. Usually themed, Rasmussen's sales of art, antiques, furniture, wine and just about everything else that could go under the gavel take place at least a couple of times each week.

Beauty

Illum and **Magasin** (*see* *p139*) both have good cosmetics departments. **Matas**, meanwhile, offers beauty products to suit all budgets and has branches throughout the city.

Pure Shop

Grønnegade 31 (33 17 00 70/www.pureshop.dk).
Open 10am-5.30pm Mon-Wed; 10am-6pm Thur; 10am-7pm Fri; 10am-3pm Sat. **No credit cards.**
Map p251 M15.
All-natural and hypoallergenic cosmetics, skincare and beauty products made from organic ingredients. Brands available include Dr Hauschka, Jurlique and Weleda.

Danish designers

What do you get if you combine well-funded art colleges with a national heritage for clothes-making and an affinity for innovation? The answer is Denmark, a country that has produced one of Europe's most dynamic fashion industries, which is finally making waves the world over. Styles and prices vary dramatically, but the following designers share an emphasis on quality and originality.

JENS LAUGESEN

London-based and Paris-trained, this critically acclaimed Danish designer is known for his cerebral yet highly wearable takes on fashion classics. A master of streamlined formalwear in black, white and neutrals, his clothes are sold at Selfridges and Antipodium in London and in countless boutiques across Japan.
www.jenslaugesen.com

CAMILLA STÆRK

London-based Camilla Stærk's dark, edgy yet eminently feminine womenswear has been featured in *Paris Vogue*, *Grazia* and *UK Elle*. Her trademark contrast of black and neutrals with delicious splashes of colour has made her work much coveted in the world's fashion capitals. www.camillastaerk.co.uk

HENRIK VIBSKOV

Beck's Futures prize winner and Central St Martin's-trained Henrik Vibskov is one of Denmark's hottest young designers. His streetwise clothes, recognisable for their distinctive prints, are sold all over the world in fiercely cool shops such as Colette in Paris, Oak in New York and Pineal Eye in London.
www.henrikvibskov.com

Magasin – Scandinavia's grandest department store. *See p139.*

Books

The Latin Quarter boasts a large number of bookshops, although those people seeking second-hand and vintage volumes should head to Fiolstræde.

Antiquarian/second-hand

Peter Grosell
Læderstræde 15 (33 93 45 05/www.grosell.dk).
Open 10am-5pm Mon-Fri; by appointment Sat.
Credit AmEx, DC, MC, V. **Map** p251 N14.
This large dealer in rare, second-hand and antiquarian books is particularly strong on art and design books, as well as Scandinavian first editions.

General

Arnold Busck
Købmagergade 49 (33 73 35 00/www.arnoldbusck.dk).
Open 10am-6pm Mon; 9.30am-6pm Tue-Thur;
9.30am-7pm Fri; 10am-4pm Sat; noon-4pm 1st Sun
of month. **Credit** DC, MC, V. **Map** p251 M14.
Busck is one of Denmark's leading book retailers, and this three-storey branch – its biggest – has a large department dedicated to English-language paperbacks and guides. **Photo** *p151.*
Other locations: Købmagergade 50 (33 15 44 66); Fiolstræde 24 (33 73 35 45); Statens Museum For Kunst, Sølvgade 48-50 (33 74 86 68).

Politikens Boghallen
Rådhuspladsen 37 (33 47 25 60/www.politikens boghal.dk). **Open** 10am-7pm Mon-Fri; 10am-4pm Sat. **Credit** AmEx, DC, MC, V. **Map** p250 O12.
Along with Arnold Busck (*see above*), Politikens Boghallen is one of the city's biggest bookshops, with a huge range of English-language titles available in store.

Newsagents

The two best sources of international magazines and newspapers are **Magasin's** vast basement newsstand (*see p139*) and the newsagent at **Central Station.**

Specialist

Cinematekets Bog- og Videohandel
*Filmhuset, Vognmagergade 8B (33 74 34 21/
www.dfi.dk).* **Open** noon-6pm Tue-Sun. **Credit**
AmEx, DC, MC, V. **Map** p251 M14.
There's no safer haven for cinefiles than Filmhuset – headquarters of the Danish Film Institute – and its affiliated bookshop is the best place to pick up that elusive tome on Scandinavian cinema.

Diamantboghandlen
*Det Kongelige Bibliotek, Søren Kierkegaards Plads 1
(33 47 49 47/www.diamantboghandlen.dk).* **Open**
9.30am-6pm Mon-Fri; 10am-5pm Sat. **Credit** DC,
MC, V. **Map** p251 P15.

The glittering waterfront Black Diamond building is home to the Royal Library bookshop, one of Copenhagen's most reliable sources of English-language books about Danish culture.

Nordisk Korthandel
Studiestræde 26-30 (33 38 26 38/www.scanmaps.dk).
Open 10.30am-5.30pm Mon-Fri; 9.30am-3pm Sat.
Credit DC, MC, V. **Map** p250 N12.
Copenhagen's best source of maps, travel books and globes, staffed by knowledgeable travel enthusiasts.

Ceramics

Butik for Borddækning
Møntergade 6 (33 32 61 01). **Open** noon-6pm Wed-Fri; 11am-2pm Sat. **Credit** AmEx, MC, V. **Map** p251 M14.
A reputable purveyor of handmade ceramics from the prosaic to the positively outlandish, with everything from sleek sushi sets and enigmatic espresso cups to artfully wonky water pitchers.

Helbak/Scherning
Badstuestræde 4 (20 61 04 77/www.helbak-scherning.dk). **Open** 11am-5.30pm Wed, Thur; 11am-6pm Fri; 10am-3pm Sat. **Credit** AmEx, MC, V. **Map** p251 N13.
High-quality earthenware vessels and delicate porcelain jewellery by Malene Helbak and Mette Scherning, all hand-decorated in playful colours.

Fashion

Budget

H&M
Amagertorv 21, Strøget (70 10 23 31/www.hm.com). **Open** 10am-6pm Mon-Thur; 10am-7pm Fri; 10am-5pm Sat. **Credit** AmEx, DC, MC, V. **Map** p251 N14.
This Swedish retail giant needs no introduction. With two branches on Strøget alone, H&M is a Danish favourite for affordable fashion.
Other locations: throughout the city.

Children

Exit
Østergade 21-23, Strøget (33 14 70 15/www.exit-kids.com). **Open** 10am-6pm Mon-Thur; 10am-7pm Fri; 10am-5pm Sat. **Credit** AmEx, DC, MC, V. **Map** p251 M15.
A Danish-owned chain store stocking a popular range of childrenswear with the emphasis on fashion rather than frugality.
Other locations: Field's, Arne Jacobsens Alle 12, Ørestad (32 62 12 42); Fisketorvet, Kalvebod Brygge 59, Vesterbro (33 12 20 70).

Hugin & Mugin
Kompagnistræde 12 (33 91 81 24/www.hugin-mugin.com). **Open** 11am-6pm Mon-Fri; 10am-4pm Sat. **Credit** AmEx, DC, MC, V. **Map** p251 O13.

A range of clothing for children aged 11 and under, most of it undeniably Scandinavian in design, with cheerful stripes and bright prints galore.

Pluto Børne Sko
Rosengården 12 (33 93 20 12). **Open** 10am-5.30pm Mon-Fri; 10am-2pm Sat. **No credit cards**. **Map** p251 M13.
For nascent foot fetishists everywhere, this children's shoe shop sells trendy footwear for kids whose parents are prepared to pay designer prices.

Designer

Acne Jeans
Gammel Mønt 10 (33 93 93 28/www.acnejeans.com). **Open** 11am-6pm Mon-Thur; 11am-7pm Fri; 10am-4pm Sat. **Credit** AmEx, DC, MC, V. **Map** p251 M14.
A flagship store for this increasingly popular Swedish brand of men's and women's clothing. Streetwise denim is the order of the day, although suits, shoes and plenty of T-shirts are also on offer.

Birger Christensen
Østergade 38, Strøget (33 11 55 55/www.birger-christensen.com). **Open** 10am-6pm Mon-Thur; 10am-7pm Fri; 10am-4pm Sat. **Credit** AmEx, DC, MC, V. **Map** p251 M15.
Mens- and womenswear, shoes and accessories from a range of top international designers including YSL, Prada, Chanel and Paul Smith, as well as a selection of ostentatious seal and sable furs.

Bruuns Bazaar
Kronprinsensgade 8-9 (33 32 19 99/www.bruuns bazaar.com). **Open** 10am-6pm Mon-Thur; 10am-7pm Fri; 10am-4pm Sat. **Credit** AmEx, DC, MC, V. **Map** p251 M14.
Set up by the two brothers Bruun in the mid 1990s, Bruuns Bazaar has since found its way on to catwalks around the world. Its mainstays are creative but wearable designs in attractive colours and top-of-the-range fabrics. The women's shop also sells a good range of tiny, delicate, deliciously colourful footwear.

By Malene Birger
Antonigade 6 (35 43 22 33/www.bymalenebirger.dk). **Open** 10am-6pm Mon-Thur; 10am-7pm Fri; 10am-4pm Sat. **Credit** AmEx, DC, MC, V. **Map** p251 M14.
Luxurious ready-to-wear clothing is the remit of Malene Birger's elegant flagship store, with glamorous but highly wearable designs in beautiful fabrics that have taken the fashion world by storm.

Companys
Frederiksberggade 24, Strøget (33 11 35 55). **Open** 10am-7pm Mon-Thur; 10am-8pm Fri; 10am-5pm Sat. **Credit** AmEx, DC, MC, V. **Map** p251 O12.
Highlights include By Malene Birger clothing, Marc Jacobs shoes, Miu Miu bags for women and Tiger of Sweden for men. Lower-priced Danish brands InWear, Part II and Matinique can also be found at this one-stop shop for label lovers of both sexes.

Eat, Drink, Shop

Designer Zoo. *See p141.*

Eat, Drink, Shop

DAY Birger et Mikkelsen
Pilestræde 16 (33 45 88 80/www.day.dk). **Open**
10am-6pm Mon-Thur; 10am-7pm Fri; 10am-4pm Sat.
Credit AmEx, MC, V. **Map** p251 M14.
DAY's flagship store is the only place offering every
one of the brand's bohemian glamour lines under
one roof, from sophisticated mens- and womenswear
to a charming range of cool clothing for kids.

Filippa K
Ny Østergade 13 (33 93 80 00/www.filippa-k.com).
Open 11am-6pm Mon-Fri; 11am-4pm Sat. **Credit**
AmEx, DC, MC, V. **Map** p251 M15.
Filippa Kihlborg creates understated clothes with a
distinct but internationally relevant Scandinavian
style, which many other Copenhagen designers have
since struggled (and largely failed) to imitate.

Henrik Vibskov
Krystalgade 6 (33 14 61 00/www.henrikvibskov.com).
Open 11am-6pm Mon-Fri; 10am-5pm Sat. **Credit**
AmEx, DC, MC, V. **Map** p251 M13.
Henrik Vibskov's cutting-edge designs are top of
every Danish fashion insider's wish list. This flagship
store offers the complete Vibskov experience, with
the full collection of his coveted, edgy designs on sale.

J Lindeberg
*Christian IX Gade 1 (33 13 11 77/www.jlindeberg.
com).* **Open** 11am-6pm Mon-Thur; 11am-7pm
Fri; 10am-4pm Sat. **Credit** AmEx, DC, MC, V.
Map p251 M14.
A Swedish lifestyle brand with a deep-seated rock
'n' roll aesthetic, J Lindeberg's quality men's and
women's tailoring is perennially popular with those
seeking unfussy fashion with an underground edge.

Mads Nørgaard
*Amagertorv 15, Strøget (33 32 01 28/www.mads
norgaard.dk).* **Open** 10am-6pm Mon-Thur; 10am-
7pm Fri; 10am-5pm Sat. **Credit** AmEx, DC, MC, V.
Map p251 N14.
A wide range of international labels – Prada, Miu
Miu, Dries Van Noten, John Smedley and Carhartt –
alongside Mads Nørgaard's own-brand clothing.
Other locations: Frederiksberggade 24, Strøget
(33 12 18 28).

Moshi Moshi
*Dag Hammarskjolds Allé 34, Østerbro (35 38 70
78/www.moshimoshi.dk).* Bus 1A, 14. **Open** 11am-
6pm Mon-Fri; 11am-3pm Sat. **Credit** AmEx, MC, V.
Map p247 G14.
Effortlessly stylish womenswear from the likes of
Sonia Rykiel, Vanessa Bruno and Acne Jeans. A second, more spiritual branch, Moshi Moshi Mind (Dag
Hammarskjolds Allé 40, 35 38 70 79), sells everything from yoga costumes by Filippa K to skincare
products from the Organic Pharmacy.

Munthe plus Simonsen
*Grønnegade 10 (33 32 03 12/www.muntheplus
simonsen.dk).* **Open** 10am-6pm Mon-Thur; 10am-
7pm Fri; 10am-4pm Sat. **Credit** AmEx, DC, MC, V.
Map p251 M15.

Luxurious muted colours abound at Munthe plus
Simonsen. The shop is reportedly a favourite of
both supermodel Helena Christensen and Crown
Princess Mary.

Sabine Poupinel & Co
Kronprinsensgade 12 (33 14 44 34). **Open** 10am-
6pm Mon-Thur; 10am-7pm Fri; 10am-4pm Sat.
Credit AmEx, MC, V. **Map** p251 M14.
The old adage that 'if you have to ask how much it
costs, you probably can't afford it' gets a shot in the
arm at this store, which dispenses with price tags
altogether. Hand-crafted, individually tailored, reas-
suringly expensive clothing.

Sand
*Østergade 40, Strøget (33 14 21 21/www.sand-
europe.com).* **Open** 10am-6pm Mon-Thur; 10am-
7pm Fri; 10am-5pm Sat. **Credit** AmEx, DC, MC, V.
Map p251 M15.
Divine men's and women's clothes from this archetypal Copenhagen designer store. Sand's simple, elegant style is the epitome of high-end Scandinavian
clothing design, but it doesn't come cheap.

Stig P
Kronprinsensgade 14 (33 14 42 16). **Open** 10am-
6pm Mon-Thur; 10am-7pm Fri; 10am-5pm Sat.
Credit AmEx, DC, MC, V. **Map** p251 M14.
Home to local names like Dico, MAVI and Ganni
next to Cacharel, Paul & Joe and Marc Jacobs, not to
mention Stig P's highly desirable own-label products. The Nørrebro branch has men's clothing too.
Other locations: Ravnsborggade 18, Nørrebro
(35 35 75 00).

Storm
Store Regnegade 1 (33 93 00 14). **Open** 11am-
5.30pm Mon-Thur; 11am-7pm Fri; 10am-6pm Sat.
Credit AmEx, DC, MC, V. **Map** p251 M15.
Line Storm's high-end boutique offers labels like
Dries Van Noten, Dior Homme and Raf Simons for
the men, plus women's clothes from the likes of
Veronique Branquinho, Balenciaga, Chloé and
APC. The clean, sparse atmosphere gives the fea-
tured clothing the space it needs to breathe, and
you may need to take a bit of a deep breath when
you see some of the prices.

Wettergren & Wettergren
Læderstræde 5 (33 13 14 05). **Open** 10am-6pm Mon-
Fri; 10am-4pm Sat. **Credit** MC, V. **Map** p251 N14.
Beautifully made womenswear from Danish brands
Graumann and Tara Jarmon alongside a small col-
lection of vintage cocktail dresses, every one of them
altered to bring them bang up to date.

Zone 1
Nikolaj Plads 7 (33 12 13 43). **Open** 11am-6pm
Tue-Fri; 11am-4pm Sat. **Credit** AmEx, DC, MC, V.
Map p251 N15.
Proprieter Jan Machenhauer's own sharply tailored
men's and women's clothes are complemented by
T-shirts from John Smedley, shoes by Emma Hope
and the lavish scarves of French designer Epice.

Eat, Drink, Shop

Erotic

Lust

Mikkel Bryggers Gade 3A (33 33 01 10/www.lust.dk).
Open 11am-7pm Mon-Thur; 11am-9pm Fri; 11am-6pm Sat. **Credit** AmEx, DC, MC, V. **Map** p250 O12.
Lust took Copenhagen's sex shop scene out of the dark ages when it opened in 1999, with a mainstream attitude, central location and an eminently female-friendly atmosphere.

Underwear for Gentlemen

Gothersgade 27 (33 14 04 84/www.underwearfor gentlemen.dk). **Open** 11am-6pm Mon-Thur; 11am-7pm Fri; 11am-4pm Sat. **Credit** MC, V. **Map** p251 M15.
These bold, provocative underwear designs for men are the kind of second skin to wear at foam parties on Ibiza nights. Caution: the designs can be seriously body-conscious. A huge amount of self-confidence and a reality check could be handy. If it all ends in tears don't say we didn't warn you. **Photo** *p149.*

Lingerie

There are comprehensive lingerie departments at both **Illum** and **Magasin** (*see p139*).

Agent Provocateur

Pilestræde 6 (33 91 99 31/www.agentprovocateur. com). **Open** 10am-6pm Mon-Fri; 10am-2pm Sat. **Credit** AmEx, DC, MC, V. **Map** p251 M14.
Agent Provocateur's Copenhagen debut allows Danish women to spice up their underwear drawers with some of the sexiest smalls on the planet.

Fogal

Østergade 2, Strøget (33 14 86 84/www.fogal. com). **Open** 10am-6pm Mon-Thur; 10am-7pm Fri; 10am-5pm Sat. **Credit** AmEx, DC, MC, V. **Map** p251 M15.
It may look tiny from the outside, but this Swiss purveyor of fine hosiery – a favourite of Queen Margrethe – is the place to find tights and stockings in exactly the right shade, sheerness or size.

Mid-range

Invasion

Vestergade 10 (33 11 00 26/www.invasion.dk). **Open** 10am-6pm Mon-Thur; 10am-7pm Fri; 10am-5pm Sat. **Credit** DC, MC, V. **Map** p250 O12.
Invasion has a huge stock of painfully trendy clothes that, in one of life's tragic ironies, only skinny teenagers can get away with wearing but only the over-20s are able to afford.
Other locations: Frederiksborggade 12 (33 93 79 77); Falkoner Allé 45, Frederiksberg (38 33 35 34).

InWear/Matinique

Østergade 27, Strøget (33 14 20 41/www.inwear. com). **Open** 10am-7pm Mon-Thur; 10am-8pm Fri; 10am-5pm Sat. **Credit** AmEx, DC, MC, V. **Map** p251 M15.

A quality mens- and womenswear chain with stores in 28 countries worldwide, offering affordable alternatives to current designer trends and a great line in stylish suits and glamorous eveningwear.

Sweater Market

Nytorv 19, Strøget (33 15 27 73/www.sweater market.dk). **Open** 10am-6pm Mon-Thur; 10am-7pm Fri; 10am-5pm Sat. **Credit** AmEx, DC, MC, V. **Map** p250 O12.
If the wind is whistling down Strøget, dive inside this wonderful woollens store where you'll find traditional Scandinavian jumpers, socks, gloves and scarves to keep you toasty, all featuring elaborate and quintessentially Nordic knit patterns.

Vero Moda

Østergade 7-9, Strøget (33 15 88 15/www.vero moda.dk). **Open** 10am-6pm Mon-Thur; 10am-7pm Fri; 10am-4pm Sat. **Credit** AmEx, DC, MC, V. **Map** p251 M15.
With three branches along Strøget alone, this Danish chain is clearly making a name for itself among women who want wearable, work-friendly versions of catwalk trends at high-street prices.
Other locations: throughout the city.

Zara

Vimmelskaftet 28, Strøget (33 32 39 77). **Open** 10am-7pm Mon-Thur; 10am-8pm Fri; 10am-5pm Sat. **Credit** AmEx, DC, MC, V. **Map** p251 N13.
The Spanish fashion chain has brought its successful formula to Copenhagen. Catwalk-driven mens-, womens- and childrenswear over three floors.
Other locations: Field's shopping centre, Arne Jacobsens Alle 12, Ørestad (32 48 45 00).

Plus sizes

There are plus size departments for both men and women at **Magasin** (*see p139*).

JE Lingerie

Ryesgade 4, Nørrebro (35 37 61 62/www.je-lingerie.dk). Bus 5A. **Open** 10am-5.30pm Tue-Fri; 10am-2pm Sat. **Credit** MC, V. **Map** p246 J11.
A popular plus size lingerie specialist stocking beautiful pieces by Anita, Goddess, Ulla and Prima Donna, with nightwear and stockings also on hand.

Søstrene Nielsen

Christian IX Gade 1 (33 16 30 08/www.sostrene nielsen.dk). **Open** 11am-6pm Mon-Fri; 10am-2pm Sat. **Credit** AmEx, DC, MC, V. **Map** p251 M14.
An impressive selection of plus size womenswear, from inexpensive jeans and T-shirts to higher-end formalwear and designer pieces (Denmark's Benedikte Utzon is a favourite).

Second-hand

Head to Vestergade (*see p139* **The best streets**) for the widest selection of second-hand and vintage clothes shops.

Eat, Drink, Shop

Underwear for Gentlemen. *See p148*

Atelier Decor

Rømersgade 9 (33 14 80 98). **Open** noon-6pm
Mon-Fri; 10am-4pm Sat. **Credit** V. **Map** p246 L12.
Located next to the Israels Plads Saturday flea market, this wonderful store offers Copenhagen ladies
the chance to unearth quality vintage clothing at
bargain prices, while Edith Piaf sets a suitably nostalgic tone on the shop stereo.

Boutique Chic

Naboløs 4 (33 11 42 60). **Open** 10am-5.30pm
Mon-Thur; 10am-7pm Fri; 10am-4pm Sat. **No credit
cards. Map** p251 N14.
This dress agency sells quality used clothing and
accessories for women by designer labels, including
suits by Chanel, Escada and Max Mara.

Kitsch Bitch

Læderstræde 30 (33 13 63 13). **Open** noon-6pm
Mon-Thur; noon-7pm Fri; 11am-4pm Sat. **Credit**
MC, V. **Map** p251 N14.
A fabulous little treasure trove of a shop, loaded
with 1950s, '60s and '70s fashion gems. There's also
the kind of kitschy Swedish kitchenware that would
have caused death by social embarrassment any
time earlier than the 21st century.

Street

Adidas Originals

*Pilestræde 6-8, Strøget (33 93 63 60/www.
adidas.com).* **Open** 10am-6pm Mon-Thur; 10am-
7pm Fri; 10am-4pm Sat. **Credit** AmEx, MC, V.
Map p251 M14.
This place is a sanctuary for Adidas classics, with
hard-to-find trainers, clothing (Carlo Gruber skiwear,
for example) and accessories with an emphasis on
Adidas's golden years from the 1960s to the '80s.

Diesel

Købmagergade 19 (33 32 90 70/www.diesel.com).
Open 10am-6pm Mon-Thur; 10am-7pm Fri;
10am-4pm Sat. **Credit** AmEx, DC, MC, V.
Map p251 M14.
An impressive showcase for Diesel's slightly
skewed, self-proclaimed 'haute couture of casual'
streetwear for men and women. However, if you
want to look street and you're on a tight budget,
head to the factory outlet which sells bundles of
second line clothing for cheap.
Other locations: Diesel Factory Outlet, Langelinie
Alle 14 (35 43 45 43).

timeout.com

The hippest online guide to over 50 of the world's greatest cities

IL
Gråbrødretorv 4 (33 91 10 00/www.il-cph.dk). **Open**
11am-6pm Mon-Thur; 11am-7pm Fri; 11am-5pm Sat.
Credit MC, V. **Map** p251 N13.
Only high-end menswear makes it into this happening
little store in one of the hippest corners of Copenhagen.

Miss Sixty
Købmagergade 36 (33 93 82 52/www.misssixty.com).
Open 10am-6pm Mon-Thur; 10am-7pm Fri; 10am-
5pm Sat. **Credit** MC, V. **Map** p251 M14.
Fun, flimsy items in vibrant colours and upbeat
urban styles typify Miss Sixty's reasonably priced
clubbing and partying threads for younger women.

Urban Outfitters
*Østergade 42, Strøget (33 17 05 00/www.urban
outfitters.co.uk).* **Open** 10am-6pm Mon-Thur;
10am-7pm Fri; 10am-5pm Sat. **Credit** MC, V.
Map p251 M15.
Denmark's is the 100th branch of this popular US
fashion and homewares chain.

Suit hire

Amorin
*Vesterbrogade 45, 1st floor, Vesterbro (33 21 20 21/
www.amorin.dk). Bus 6A, 26.* **Open** 9am-5.30pm Mon-
Fri; 9am-1pm Sat. **No credit cards. Map** p250 P10.
Formalwear and fancy dress costume rentals, from
fine tuxes and tails to saucy French maid's outfits.

Fashion accessories

Bags
Gucci, Hermès, Mulberry and Louis Vuitton all
have shops on Strøget; Loewe and Burberry are
sold at **Magasin** and **Illum** respectively.

Friis & Company
Købmagergade 41 (33 91 01 70/www.friis-co.dk).
Open 10am-6pm Mon-Thur; 10am-7pm Fri; 10am-
5pm Sat. **Credit** AmEx, MC, V. **Map** p251 M14.
Affordable bags, shoes and accessories adorned
with the distinctive fleur-de-lys motif and diamanté
crown of this popular Danish brand. Staff are
particularly helpful so don't be afraid to ask them
for a recommendation.
Other locations: Østerbrogade 44, Østerbro
(35 38 00 57).

Neye
*Vimmelskaftet 28, Strøget (33 69 28 33/www.
neye.dk).* **Open** 10am-6pm Mon-Thur; 10am-7pm
Fri; 10am-4pm Sat. **Credit** AmEx, DC, MC, V.
Map p251 N13.
The city's largest bag shop, with handbags, luggage
and – that staple of Copenhagen accessories –
rucksacks to suit most mainstream tastes. Well-
known brands include Samsonite, Carlton and
Florentine manufacturer Bridge, which offer a nice
line in leather suitcases and satchels.

Arnold Busck – three whole storeys of stories. *See p143.*

Eat, Drink, Shop

Hats

Chapeaux Petitgas
Købmagergade 5 (33 13 62 70). **Open** 10am-5.30pm
Mon-Fri; 10am-2pm Sat. **Credit** AmEx, DC, MC, V.
Map p251 N14.
Nothing much has changed over the century-and-
a-half that Chapeaux Petitgas has been furnishing the
heads of Copenhagen's gentlemen – but that, of
course, is all part of its charm.

Samarkand
Dag Hammarskjölds Allé 32 (35 38 14 45/
www.samarkand.dk). Bus 1A, 14, 40. **Open** by
appointment. **No credit cards. Map** p247 G14.
Eberlein makes only 100 luxurious Mongolian-style
embroidered silk and fur hats a year, and Queen
Silvia of Sweden and Hillary Clinton are among the
well-to-do heads she has covered in the past.

Susanne Juul
Store Kongensgade 14 (33 32 25 22). **Open** 11am-
5.30pm Tue-Thur; 11am-6pm Fri; 10am-2pm Sat.
Credit MC, V. **Map** p249 L16.
Designs range from Tibetan-inspired wool beanies to
wide-brimmed chic chapeaux from the milliner of
Denmark's Crown Princess Mary.

Shoes

A Pair
Ny Østergade 3 (33 91 99 20/www.apair.dk). **Open**
10am-6pm Mon-Thur; 10am-7pm Fri; 10am-4pm Sat.
Credit AmEx, DC, MC, V. **Map** p251 M15.
One of Copenhagen's most popular mid- to high-end
shoe shops, selling shoes, boots and bags, with own-
brand designs on offer alongside international labels.
Other locations: Nansensgade 39 (33 33 99 24);
Copenhagen airport (32 51 99 24).

Bruno & Joel
Kronprinsensgade 2 (33 13 87 78). **Open** 10.30am-
6pm Mon-Thur; 10.30am-7pm Fri; 10am-4pm Sat.
Credit AmEx, DC, MC, V. **Map** p251 M14.
Unbelievably chic Danish-designed, Italian-made
women's foot candy for quality shoe junkies, with a
men's branch on nearby Pilestræde (No.41).

Lola Pagola
Classensgade 4, Østerbro (35 42 66 00). Bus 1A.
Open 11am-6pm Tue-Fri; 10am-2pm Sat. **Credit**
AmEx, MC, V. **Map** p248 F14.
Østerbro's refuge for the city's more demanding feet,
stocking only the most exclusive shoes and boots
from Alexander McQueen and Bottega Veneta.

Bruno & Joel.

Textiles

Albot

Kompagnistræde 24 (33 32 50 60). **Open** 11am-6pm Mon-Sat. **Credit** AmEx, MC, V (transaction fee 6%). **Map** p251 O13.

A tranquil, unassuming shop selling textiles and crafts from across Asia. Exotic dyed silks from Cambodia, Burma and Malaysia jostle for space alongside antique statues from the Philippines, sumptuous modern kimonos from Japan and Korea and colourful woven baskets.

Flowers

Bremerholm Blomster

Bremerholm 3, Magasin Torv (33 14 58 85). **Open** 10am-6pm Mon-Thur; 10am-7pm Fri; 10am-5pm Sat. **Credit** AmEx, MC, V.

Bremerholm Blomster explodes on to the pavement in a floral spectrum of reds, violets, yellows and greens. The philosophy here is simplicity itself: lots of flowers for very little money. As a result, it's as popular with locals popping in for a bunch to brighten their homes as it is with those seeking posh posies to give away as gifts.

Tage Andersen

Ny Adelgade 12 (33 93 09 13). **Open** 10am-6pm Mon-Thur; 10am-7pm Fri; 10am-5pm Sat. **Credit** AmEx, MC, V. **Map** p251 M15.

Calling Tage Andersen a florist is rather like calling the *QE2* a boat; the term just isn't quite grand enough for what is one of Copenhagen's most astonishing and, it has to be said, pretentious shops (you've got to laugh at the audacity of charging a 40kr entry fee). Opulent and over the top, Andersen's is part florist, part garden gallery, but it's worth a visit just to wander among the caged tropical birds and ornate flower sculptures. Keep your beta blockers to hand when asking the prices, though.

Food & drink

Bakeries & pâtisseries

Conditoriet La Glace

Skoubougade 3-5, Strøget (33 14 46 46). **Open** 8.30am-5.30pm Mon-Thur; 8.30am-6pm Fri; 9am-5pm Sat. **Credit** V. **Map** p251 N13.

The city's oldest pâtisserie and tea salon is an institution among Danes with a taste for the sweeter things in life. Generous slices of the dozen or so fairy

Eat, Drink, Shop

tale-sized cakes in the window are available to take out, as are the delightfully dainty cream cakes and traditional Danish pastries.

emmerys
Vesterbrogade 34, Vesterbro (33 22 77 63/ www.emmerys.dk). Bus 6A, 26. **Open** 7am-6pm Mon-Thur; 7am-7pm Fri; 7am-3pm Sat; 7.30am-3.30pm Sun. **Credit** MC, V. **Map** p250 P10.
One bite of chewy emmerys bread and you'll be sold. The ingredients (only organic flour, salt and water) sound about as exciting as a piece of dry cracker, but emmerys claims to use a 5,000-year-old method in its production. The same bread is used for the (pricey) lunchtime sandwiches with fillings like serrano ham, marinated artichokes and parsley pesto. **Other locations**: throughout the city.

Lagkagehuset Bageri og Konditori
Torvegade 45, Christianshavn (32 57 36 07). **Open** 6am-7pm daily. **No credit cards**. **Map** p252 P16.
Fresh bread, cakes and divine pastries are sold at this busy Christianshavn bakery, considered by many to be the best in town. The perfect place to sample an authentic Danish pastry. **Photo** *p155*.

Butchers

Slagteren ved Kultorvet
Frederiksborggade 4 (33 12 29 02/www.kultorvet.dk). **Open** 8am-5.30pm Mon-Fri; 8am-2pm Sat. **No credit cards**. **Map** p247 L13.
Butcher Jens Slagter – whom you'll often find quoted in the Danish media for his 'you are what you eat' views – has built up a huge customer base for his quality products. This is a great place to try one of the several types of Danish salami or bacon — the smell of the place alone (the smoking oven is in the back) will make your stomach rumble.

Chocolate & confectioners

Peter Beier
Skoubougade 1 (33 93 07 17/www.peterbeier chokolade.dk). **Open** 10am-6pm Mon-Thur; 10am-7pm Fri; 10am-4pm Sat. **Credit** AmEx, MC, V. **Map** p251 N13.
The essence of chocolate chic, this modern shop, run by the charming Bagger family, offers premium quality chocolates in customisable gift boxes, plus dessert and port wines to accompany more refined tasting sessions. Prices start at 52kr for 100g.

Sømods Bolcher
Nørregade 24 & 36 (33 12 60 46/www.soemods-bolcher.dk). **Open** 9.15am-5.30pm Mon-Thur; 9.15am-6pm Fri; 10am-2.30pm Sat. **Credit** AmEx, DC, MC, V. **Map** p250 M12.
There has been a traditional boiled candy factory and shop here on Nørregade since 1891, and you can still watch the multicoloured sweets being made by the fourth generation of the Sømod family (sweet boilings take place nine times a day).

Coffee & tea

AC Perchs Thehandel
Kronprinsensgade 5 (33 15 35 62/www.perchs-the.dk). **Open** 9am-5.30pm Mon-Thur; 9am-7pm Fri; 9.30am-2.30pm Sat. **Credit** MC, V. **Map** p251 M14.
Copenhagen's most venerated and venerable tea emporium dates from 1834 and is currently in the hands of the sixth generation of the Perch family. The glorious, wood-panelled interior is lined with old-fashioned jars of tea leaves (own blends as well as some more exotic brands), and the staff are only too happy to help you choose. Also the Darjeeling First Flush comes highly recommended.

Østerlandsk Thehus
Nørre Voldgade 9 (33 13 10 00/www.osterlandsk thehus.dk). **Open** 10am-6pm Mon-Fri; 10am-2pm Sat. **Credit** MC, V. **Map** p246 L12.
What Perchs is to tea, Østerlandsk Thehus is to Copenhagen's coffee scene. The interior of the shop is currently being restored to its former glory, originally decorated by the designer behind Tivoli's Chinoiserie decor. The stock incorporates the finest coffee beans from around the world, own blends and a dazzling assortment of gleaming coffee makers.

Delicatessens

Værnedamsvej in Frederiksberg is deli street, with dozens of gourmet food shops.

Kiwi & Mango
Værnedamsvej 5, Frederiksberg (33 23 23 64). Bus 6A, 15. **Open** 8am-7pm Mon-Fri; 8am-4pm Sat; 9am-4pm Sun. **No credit cards**. **Map** p245 P8.
This is no ordinary fruit stand. Supreme quality in-season fruits and veggies – beautifully presented – plus Greek and Spanish olives, chillies, and an array of gourmet oils, syrups and other goodies.

Løgismose
Nordre Toldbod 16 (33 32 93 32/www.loegismose.dk). **Open** 10am-7pm Mon-Fri; 10am-3pm Sat. **Credit** AmEx, DC, MC, V. **Map** p249 J18.
What started out as a wine importer attached to the renowned restaurant Kong Hans Kaelder has grown into the best gourmet supermarket in town, with an eclectic mix of items, from Harvey Nichols tins and jars to delicious Valhrona chocolates. The shop also produces its own serve-yourself meals and there is an in-house butcher's and baker's to boot.

Fish

Gammel Strand stall
Gammel Strand (no phone). **Open** 10am-2pm Mon-Fri. **No credit cards**. **Map** p251 N14.
The last remnant of Gammel Strand's fishing heritage is this sole fish seller. Strange to think that this single stall is all that remains of a city that was founded on herring landed from the Øresund.

Lagkagehuset. *See p154.*

OUR CLIMATE NEEDS
A HELPING HAND TODAY

Be a smart traveller. Help to offset your carbon emissions
from your trip by pledging Carbon Trees with Trees for Cities.

All the Carbon Trees that you donate through Trees for Cities
are genuinely planted as additional trees in our projects.

Trees for Cities is an independent charity working with local
communities on tree planting projects.

www.treesforcities.org   Tel 020 7587 1320

Trees for Cities
Charity registration number 1032154

Health & organic food

Egefeld
Gammel Kongevej 113, Frederiksberg (33 28 20 20/ www.egefeld.dk). Bus 14, 15. **Open** 10am-8pm Mon-Fri; 10am-5pm Sat, Sun. **Credit** MC, V. **Map** p250 O7.
An award-winning, comprehensively stocked one-stop shop for the city's eco-friendly. As wide a selection of organic products as you'll find anywhere.

International

Abigail's
Peder Hvidtfeldts Stræde 17 (33 16 41 79). **Open** 10.30am-5.30pm Mon-Thur; 10am-6pm Fri; 10am-4pm Sat. **No credit cards. Map** p251 M13.
Who'd have thought there'd be a market for selling British sweets, tinned food and crisps to the Danes? A few doors down from the Americana Company *(see below)*, this is the place to come when only British teabags, sausages and baked beans will do.

Americana Company
Peder Hvidtfeldts Stræde 13 (33 93 78 70/www. americana.dk). **Open** 11am-5.30pm Tue-Thur; 11am-6pm Fri; 11am-3pm Sat. **No credit cards. Map** p251 M13.
A small mini-mart doing a roaring trade in root beer, peanut butter and candy from across the Atlantic. Popular with both expats and Danes who've sampled the joys of American cuisine abroad.

Wines, beers & spirits

Kjær og Sommerfeldt
Gammel Mønt 4 (33 93 34 44/www.kogs.dk). **Open** 10am-5.30pm Mon-Thur; 10am-6pm Fri; 10am-2pm Sat. **Credit** AmEx, DC, MC, V. **Map** p251 M14.
Sommerfeldt's wood-panelled interior is more akin to a gentleman's club than an off-licence. The shop speciality is Bordeaux wines, but it also has an entire room dedicated to Scottish and Irish single malts.

Ølbutikken
Oehlenschlægersgade 2, Vesterbro (33 22 03 04/ www.olbutikken.dk). **Open** 3-7pm Wed-Fri; 11am-3pm Sat. **No credit cards. Map** p245 Q8.
The microbrewery movement has only recently come to Copenhagen, but this beer shop has risen to the challenge magnificently, selling a selection of Danish micro beers and international alternatives.

Furniture

Casa Shop
Store Regnegade 2 (33 32 70 41/www.casagroup. com). **Open** 10am-5.30pm Mon-Thur; 10am-6pm Fri; 10am-3pm Sat. **Credit** DC, MC, V. **Map** p251 M15.
Casa is one of the country's premier retailers of contemporary furniture, but there are plenty of smaller, quirkier pieces to catch, such as Nemo lamps and Ron Arad's flexible Bookworm bookshelf.

Hay CPH
Pilestræde 29-31 (99 42 44 00/www.hay.dk). **Open** 10am-6pm Mon-Fri; 10am-3pm Sat. **Credit** AmEx, DC, MC, V. **Map** p251 M14.
Walking into Hay's you might be forgiven for thinking you've stumbled on a chic version of the *Teletubbies* house. Simple, rounded forms and modular, felt-covered units in primary colours abound. Tinky Winky is no fool, however, for these Danish designs are supremely comfortable. There's a second showroom upstairs and the website gives a good idea of what's in store. **Photo** *p160.*

Illums Bolighus
Royal Shopping, Amagertorv 10, Strøget (33 14 19 41/www.royalshopping.com). **Open** 10am-7pm Mon-Thur; 10am-8pm Fri; 10am-5pm Sat. **Credit** AmEx, DC, MC, V. **Map** p251 N14.
The homeware arm of department store Illum boasts a selection of premium brands including Orrefors, Arabia and Alessi, while connecting doors lead into the Royal Copenhagen, Holmegaard and Georg Jensen shops.

Paustian
Kalkbrænderiløbskaj 2, Østerbro (39 16 65 65/ www.paustian.dk). Bus 26. **Open** 9.30am-5.30pm Mon-Thur; 9.30am-6pm Fri; 10am-3pm Sat. **Credit** AmEx, DC, MC, V.
It's a bit of a trek to get over here, but Paustian's stunning warehouse – designed by Jørn Utzon of Sydney Opera House fame – makes the trip worthwhile. Inside, you'll find the likes of Aalto, Eames, Starck and Jacobsen.

Gifts & souvenirs

Danish Souvenir
Frederiksberggade 2, Strøget (33 14 74 00). **Open** 10am-7pm Mon-Fri; 10am-5.30pm Sat; 11am-4pm Sun. **Credit** AmEx, DC, MC, V. **Map** p250 O12.
Cheesy Danish souvenirs, including (but not limited to) dolls in national costume, plastic Viking helmets and replicas of the Little Mermaid.

Hi-fi/home entertainment

Bang & Olufsen
Kongens Nytorv 26 (33 11 14 15/www.bang-olufsen.com). **Open** 10am-6pm Mon-Thur; 10am-7pm Fri; 10am-5pm Sat. **Credit** AmEx, DC, MC, V. **Map** p251 M15.
Danes are justifiably proud of this top-notch brand of televisions, stereos and telephones, the minimalist modern masterpieces of which constantly dominate the world's fashion and design bibles. Second-hand Bang & Olufsen pieces can be found at AA Audio (Gothersgade 58; 33 14 14 53). *See also p35* **Sound engineers.**
Other locations: Nørre Voldgade 8 (33 12 33 08); Fisketorvet shopping centre, Kalvebod Brygge 59, Vesterbro (33 11 34 50).

Eat, Drink, Shop

Fona

Østergade 47, Strøget (33 15 90 55/www.fona.dk).
Open 10am-6pm Mon-Thur; 10am-7pm Fri; 10am-5pm Sat. **Credit** AmEx, DC, MC, V. **Map** p251 M15.
Denmark's largest home entertainment chain stocks plenty of well-known home entertainment and computer brands, including the likes of Apple and Bang & Olufsen.

Homewares

Bodum Hus

Østergade 10, Strøget (33 36 40 80/www.bodum.dk).
Open 10am-6pm Mon-Thur; 10am-7pm Fri; 10am-5pm Sat. **Credit** AmEx, DC, MC, V. **Map** p251 M15.
This flagship store for the world famous Danish kitchenware chain is a veritable temple to teatime, laden with stylish coffee- and tea-making kit.

Le Klint

Store Kirkestræde 1 (33 11 66 63/www.leklint.com).
Open 10am-5.30pm Mon-Thur; 10am-6pm Fri; 10am-2pm Sat. **Credit** AmEx, DC, MC, V. **Map** p251 N14.
This is the main stockist for Kaare Klint's trademark concertina-style lampshades, including his perennially popular 'Model 1', folded by hand since 1943.

Normann Copenhagen

Østerbrogade 70, Østerbro (35 55 44 59/www.normann-copenhagen.com). Bus 14, 15, 650S. **Open** 10am-6pm Mon-Thur; 10am-7pm Fri; 10am-4pm Sat. **Credit** AmEx, DC, MC, V. **Map** p248 E14.
Normann Copenhagen's home accessories take centre stage in this former theatre, with a huge range of effortlessly sleek and streamlined domestic designware, from arty vases to achingly modern salad sets.

Rosenthal Studio Haus

Frederiksberggade 21, Strøget (33 14 21 01/ www.rosenthal.dk). **Open** 10am-6pm Mon-Thur; 10am-7pm Fri; 10am-5pm Sat. **Credit** AmEx, DC, MC, V. **Map** p250 O12.
The main outlet for Bjørn Wiinblad's popular porcelain creations, Rosenthal also sells Lin Utzon vases and tableware by the likes of Versace and Bulgari.

Søstrene Grene

Amagertorv 29, Strøget (no phone/www.grenes.dk).
Open 10am-6pm Mon-Thur; 10am-7pm Fri; 10am-5pm Sat. **No credit cards. Map** p251 N14.
People either love Søstrene Grene's lucky dip potential or loathe its often brazenly poor quality stock, but there's no denying that there are gems aplenty lurking among its collection of oddball crockery, toys, bedding, glassware and miscellaneous gifts.

Vi Ses

Valkendorfsgade 3 (33 12 33 15/www.blindes-arbejde.dk). **Open** 8am-3.30pm Mon-Thur; 8am-1pm Fri. **No credit cards. Map** p251 N13.
Whether it's for bottles, hair or nails, Vi Ses has the brush for you, plus there's a nice line in wooden toys to amuse kids while parents browse the bristles. Great for obsessive compulsives with a cleaning complex.

Jewellery

Galerie Metal

Nybrogade 26 (33 14 55 40/www.galeriemetal.dk).
Open noon-5.30pm Wed-Fri; 10am-2pm Sat.
No credit cards. Map p251 N12.
Fine modern jewellery-making and craftsmanship make this high-end exhibition space a treat to visit, with a selection of work from over 20 jewellers on display at any given time.

Georg Jensen

Amagertorv 4, Strøget (33 11 40 80/www.georg jensen.com). **Open** 10am-6pm Mon-Thur; 10am-7pm Fri; 10am-5pm Sat. **Credit** AmEx, DC, MC, V. **Map** p251 N14.
The undisputed daddy of Danish silver design, Jensen's showroom boasts elaborate flower arrangements artfully complementing the ornate jewellery on display. There's also a museum at the back showcasing the history of the company.

Halberstadt

Østergade 4 (33 15 97 90/www.halberstadt.com).
Open 9.30am-5.30pm Mon-Fri; 10am-2pm Sat.
Credit AmEx, DC, MC, V. **Map** p251 M15.
Since 1846 Halberstadt has been selling elaborate, often bespoke jewellery with an emphasis on Danish amber. Even if you don't feel like stepping inside, it's worth checking out the Golden Train, a solid gold, diamond-encrusted toy pulling a cargo of real rubies, sapphires and emeralds inside the window.

Monies

Nordre Toldbod 17 (33 91 33 33/www.monies.dk).
Bus 1A. **Open** 11am-6pm Tue-Fri; 11am-3pm Sat.
Credit AmEx, DC, MC, V. **Map** p249 J18.
Spectacular formal jewellery by designer couple Gerda and Nikolai Monies, who use jade, bone, wood and amber, among other materials, to create truly original sculptural statements.

Museums Kopi Smykker

Grønnegade 6 (33 32 76 72/www.museum-jewelry.dk).
Open 10am-6pm Mon-Thur; 10am-7pm Fri; 10am-2pm Sat. **Credit** AmEx, DC, MC, V. **Map** p251 M15.
Artistry from the ancestors of today's Danish jewellery designers – from the Bronze Age to the Viking Age – is here reproduced in silver, bronze and gold. Pick up your Thor's Hammer necklace or any number of bizarre but beautiful Viking designs.

Musical instruments

Aage Jensen

Landemærket 29 (33 18 19 00/www.aage.dk). **Open** 10am-6pm Mon-Thur; 10am-7pm Fri; 10am-3pm Sat.
Credit AmEx, DC, MC, V. **Map** p247 L14.
With the Musikhistorisk Museet and Sony's Danish HQ nearby, this area rivals Pisserenden as the city's most musical quarter. Guitars, keyboards and drums dominate in this, Denmark's largest musical instrument store.

Off the beaten track

The four areas of Vesterbro, Nørrebro, Østerbro and Frederiksberg, which lie outside the city's old gates, are all bursting with independent shops on thriving high streets.

VESTERBRO

Vesterbrogade, the main street, is teeming with shopping opportunities, although Istedgade has an interesting collection of smaller, more streetwise fashion shops. Highlights include **Donn Ya Doll** (No.55; 33 22 66 35), which offers a mix of quirky gift items, casual clothes and accessories; **Asfalt** (No.83; 33 22 51 74), which boasts second-hand and customised clothing; and **Girlie Hurly** (No.101; 33 24 22 41), which sells 1950s-style novelty gifts.

NØRREBRO

Ravnsborggade, best known for its antique and second-hand furniture shops, has become a thriving fashion centre with **Stig P** (No.18; 35 35 75 00) and **Dico** (No.21; 35 34 24 90) among its biggest designer emporiums, while **LLLP** (No.18; 35 36 60 04), on nearby Fælledvej, has hip brands like Camilla Stærk and Jens Laugesen alongside its functional custom furniture. Elmegade, meanwhile, has an abundance of trendy clothing shops including **Carhartt** (No.13; 35 36 53 70) and **Bark** (No.26; 33 12 12 55).

ØSTERBRO

Østerbro is the height of chic. Classensgade has plenty of quality fashion and jewellery boutiques, as well as fabulous shoes from **Lola Pagola** (No.4; 35 42 66 00) and eminently stylish homeware accessories from **Weber Furniture** (No.25; 33 23 77 17). Beside the lake, Østerbrogade is home to the flagship store of **Normann Copenhagen** (No.70; 35 55 44 59), a veritable temple to modern Danish design housed in a former theatre, while neighbouring Nordre Frihavnsgade offers a variety of shops – from traditional grocers and antiques dealers to trendy gift shops.

FREDERIKSBERG

Værnedamsvej is fit to burst with specialist food stores, including gourmet butchers, bakers and bagel makers, while Gammel Kongevej offers a mix of clothing and accessory shops to rival the best in the city centre, including **Vadumsrum** (No.92; 33 25 11 19) and **B.APS** (No.88; 33 21 58 00), the latter selling a gorgeous selection of quality women's brands including Chloé, Cacharel and D&G. Foodies, meanwhile, should head for **Meyer's Deli** (No.107; 33 25 45 95), the gourmet food shop and café of celebrity chef Claus Meyer.

Super Sound

Skindergade 27 (33 32 50 88/www.eskildsen.dk). **Open** 10am-6pm Mon-Thur; 10am-7pm Fri; 10am-3pm Sat. **Credit** MC, V. **Map** p251 N13.
A well-stocked shop complementing a good range of more traditional instruments with plenty of high-tech software for budding dance producers.

Music

Accord

Vestergade 37 (70 15 16 17/www.accord.dk). **Open** 10am-6pm Mon-Thur; 10am-7pm Fri; 10am-4pm Sat; noon-5pm Sun. **Credit** AmEx, DC, MC, V. Note there is a 10% surcharge for foreign credit cards. **Map** p250 O12.
Stacks of old and new vinyl, including a whole floor of 78s, along with hundreds of CDs and DVDs make this a good hunting ground for those who want to pick up a bit of music. Techno, house, rock, pop and world music are the main genres. There's also a good selection of new release titles and the prices are competitive as well.
Other locations: Østerbrogade 92 (35 42 00 39).

Bånd & Plade Centret

Vognmagergade 9 (33 11 22 51). **Open** 10am-5.30pm Mon-Thur; 10am-6pm Fri; 10am-2pm Sat. **Credit** DC, MC, V. **Map** p251 M14.
Unpretentious, mildly chaotic but as comprehensive as you'll get, this is Scandinavia's largest classical music store. Stock is mainly new CDs, but there's some second-hand vinyl available too.

Jazz Kælderen

Skindergade 19 (33 91 22 45/www.jazzmusic.dk). **Open** 11am-5.30pm Mon-Thur; 11am-6.30pm Fri; 11am-3pm Sat. **Credit** MC, V. **Map** p251 N13.
A large jazz specialist boasting a wide range of CDs and vinyl, as well as a decent café. There are also live performances on the first Thursday of every month.

Moskito Music World

Nørregade 38 (33 93 28 00). **Open** 11am-5.30pm Mon-Thur; 11am-6pm Fri; 11am-2pm Sat. **No credit cards**. **Map** p250 M12.
Since it opened in the mid 1990s, Moskito has been the country's leading world music store, covering just about every style and trend of music from across the planet, both contemporary and classic.

Hay CPH. See p157.

Sex Beat Records
Studiestræde 18 (33 12 82 92/www.sexbeat records.dk). **Open** 11am-6pm Mon-Thur; 11am-7pm Fri; 11am-3pm Sat. **Credit** MC, V. **Map** p250 N12.
New and used British and American indie rock and metal is the speciality at Sex Beat Records, where the staff are extremely knowledgeable about everyone from 16 Horsepower to White Zombie. It's also one of the best places in town to pick up tickets for local gigs.

Opticians & eyewear

Poul Stig Briller
Østergade 24, Strøget (33 15 52 52). **Open** 9.30am-6pm Mon-Thur; 9.30am-7pm Fri; 9.30am-4pm Sat. **Credit** AmEx, DC, MC, V. **Map** p251 M15.
Smart, minimal and consistently cool eyewear in the only boutique in Denmark offering products from the venerable Poul Stig.

Outlet shopping

Langelinie Pier
Langelinie Alle. **Open** 11am-6pm daily. **Credit** varies. **Map** p249 H18.
There are over a dozen outlet stores under the arches of Langelinie Pier. Casual clothing by Danish labels such as Noa Noa and Friis Company mingle with international brands like Diesel and Miss Sixty, with the end result that only the most obstinate spendthrift will be able to leave empty-handed.

Royal Copenhagen Factory Outlet
Søndre Fasanvej 9, Frederiksberg (38 34 10 04/ www.royalcopenhagen.com), Bus 4A, 14. **Open** 10am-5.30pm Mon-Fri; 10am-2pm Sat. **Credit** AmEx, DC, MC, V.
Reduced prices on items from the prestigious Royal Copenhagen group (including silver from Georg Jensen and glass by Holmegaard), mostly end-of-line products or seconds with no discernible flaws.

Pharmacies

Steno Apotek
Vesterbrogade 6C (33 14 82 66). **Open** 24hrs daily. **No credit cards**. **Map** p250 P10.
A 24-hour chemist facing Central Station. Please note that there is a small surcharge (15kr) on purchases made outside normal business hours.

Photography & film processing

Kontant Foto
Købmagergade 44 (33 12 00 29/www.kontant foto.dk). **Open** 10am-6pm Mon-Thur; 10am-7pm Fri; 10am-4pm Sat. **Credit** AmEx, DC, MC, V. **Map** p251 M14.
Conveniently located film processors.

Photografica
Skindergade 41 (33 14 12 15/www.photografica.com). **Open** 9.30am-5.30pm Mon-Thur; 9.30am-6pm Fri; 9.30am-3pm Sat. **Credit** AmEx, DC, MC, V. **Map** p251 N13.
An Aladdin's cave of top brands (Hasselblad, Leica), equipment and accessories.

Second-hand

Hot Kotyr
Nørrebrogade 76, Nørrebro (35 39 02 74/www.hot kotyr.dk). Bus 5A. **Open** 11am-6pm Mon-Fri; 10am-2pm Sat. **No credit cards**. **Map** p246 J10.
Lamps of all shapes and sizes (with at least a few Danish 'PH' models), in addition to cluttered shelves of Rolling Stones puzzles, Beatles pillows, cartoon lunchboxes and antique Danish signs.

Sonny Boy
Nordre Frihavnsgade 86, Østerbro (35 42 73 63). Train to Nordhavn/bus 3A. **Open** noon-6pm Mon-Fri. **No credit cards**. **Map** p248 D15.
Ever wonder how you've gone so long without a mechanical Mao Tse-tung wristwatch? Or an original propeller blade from an old SAS aircraft? Look no further than Sonny Boy, a shop with simply everything you want but nothing you need.

Services/repairs

Dry cleaning & alterations

Schleisner Rens
Vester Voldgade 12 (33 11 00 37). **Open** 8am-5.30pm Mon-Fri; 10am-2pm Sat. **No credit cards**. **Map** p250 O12.
Same-day cleaning on items brought in before 10am.

Hair salons

X-Salonen
Sankt Peders Stræde 45 (33 32 32 76). **Open** noon-8pm Mon-Sat. **No credit cards**. **Map** p250 N12.
A den of industrial glam in the Latin Quarter.

Key cutting & shoe repairs

Hælebaren
Østergade 16, Strøget (33 91 02 20). **Open** 8am-6pm Mon-Thur; 8am-7pm Fri; 9am-3pm Sat. **Credit** DC, MC, V. **Map** p251 M15.
Centrally located key cutter and shoe repairer.

Watch repairs

Vintageure & Urmager
Kompagnistræde 10 (33 12 10 94/www.woollhead.dk). **Open** 11am-5pm Tue-Thur; Fri by appointment. **No credit cards**. **Map** p251 N13.
Repairs, plus a range of vintage timepieces.

Eat, Drink, Shop

Sport

Christiania Cykler
Refshalevej 2, Christiania (32 95 45 20/www. pedersenbicycle.dk). **Open** *Sept-May* 10am-5.30pm Mon-Fri. *June-Aug* 10am-5.30pm Mon-Thur; 10am-6pm Fri. **No credit cards. Map** p253 O19.
Christiania Cykler's most interesting item is the idiosyncratic Pedersen bike. Based on a design from the early 20th century, the bike was the work of Mikael Pedersen, who was tired of getting a sore backside from riding. He devised a swinging hammock-like leather seat, then built a unique pyramid-style frame to support it. Today, the shop builds 40 to 50 specially ordered Pedersen bikes a year, about half of which are shipped abroad.

Eventyr Sport
Nørre Voldgade 9 (33 93 66 21/www.eventyrsport.dk). **Open** 10am-6pm Mon-Fri; 10am-3pm Sat. **Credit** AmEx, DC, MC, V. **Map** p250 L12.
Eventyr Sport sells camping equipment, climbing gear, clothing for heavy duty outdoor use and all the usual accoutrements required for survival in the wilderness (or Copenhagen in winter).

Sögreni of Copenhagen
Sankt Peders Stræde 30A (33 12 78 79/www. sogreni.dk). **Open** noon-6pm Mon; 10am-6pm Tue-Thur; 10am-7pm Fri; 11am-3pm Sat. **Credit** AmEx, MC, V. **Map** p250 N12.
This high-end bicycle maker produces a limited quantity of traditional-looking yet ultra-modern bikes, several of which have been featured in *Wallpaper** magazine and sell at the Conran Shop in London. Prices start at 6,000kr and go up to 12,000kr.

Stationery

Ordning & Reda
Grønnegade 1B (33 32 30 18/www.ordning-reda.com). **Open** 10am-6pm Mon-Thur; 10am-6pm Fri; 10am-4pm Sat. **Credit** MC, V. **Map** p251 M15.
Delectable designer paper, folders, photo albums and other stationery from this stylish Swedish chain. **Other locations**: Kongens Nytorv 13 (33 18 21 46).

Supermarkets

Irma
Rådhusarkaden, Vesterbrogade 1 (33 11 37 91/ www.irma.dk). **Open** 9am-8pm Mon-Fri; 9am-5pm Sat. **Credit** MC, V. **Map** p250 O12.
A high-end central supermarket boasting a good selection of fine food and wine.
Other locations: Irma City, Vesterbrogade 46 (33 79 02 39).

REMA 1000
Hammerichsgade 1 (33 93 68 63). **Open** 8am-8pm Mon-Fri; 9am-5pm Sat-Sun. **Credit** MC, V. **Map** p250 O11.
Well stocked and centrally located.

Ticket agents

BilletNet (www.billetnet.dk) is Denmark's online ticket agent; **Sex Beat Records** (*see p161*) also sells tickets to local concerts.

Toys

Build-a-Bear Workshop
Vesterbrogade 3 (33 13 80 30/www.buildabear.dk). **Open** 11am-7pm Mon-Thur; 11am-8pm Fri; 10am-5pm Sat, Sun. **Credit** MC, V. **Map** p251 O11.
A wildly successful stuffed toy shop where visitors put together their own furry friends from scratch.

Dansk Håndværk
Kompagnistræde 20 (33 11 45 52). **Open** 11am-5.30pm Tue-Thur; 11am-6.30pm Fri; 11am-3pm Sat. **No credit cards. Map** p251 O13.
Local craftsman Lars Jensen has been producing traditional wooden toys for almost 30 years, and this small cellar shop is full of hand-crafted, brightly coloured playthings for under-fives.

Fætter BR
Frederiksberggade 11 (33 13 74 70/www.br-leg.dk). **Open** 10am-6pm Mon-Thur; 10am-7pm Fri; 10am-5pm Sat. **Credit** AmEx, DC, MC, V. **Map** p250 O12.
Denmark's biggest toyshop chain, with lots of Lego as well as international brands.
Other locations: Bremerholmen 4 (33 14 08 73); Købmagergade 9 (33 14 14 64).

Faraos Cigarer
Skindergade 27 (33 32 22 11/www.faraos.dk). **Open** 11am-5.30pm Mon-Thur; 11am-6pm Fri; 10am-3pm Sat. **Credit** AmEx, DC, MC, V. **Map** p251 N13.
Copenhagen's answer to London's Forbidden Planet is a meeting place for people who collect comics, role-playing games and *Star Wars* merchandise.

Krea
Vestergade 4-6 (33 32 98 58/www.krea.dk). **Open** 9.30am-5.30pm Mon-Thur; 9.30am-7pm Fri; 9.30am-3pm Sat. **Credit** AmEx, DC, MC, V. **Map** p250 O12.
Krea caters mainly to under-tens, and does so with a broad range of educational and fun toys for boys and girls. Staff are friendly and patient.

Solspejlet
Frederiksborggade 41 (33 33 72 12/www. solspejlet.dk). **Open** 11am-5pm Mon-Fri; 11am-2pm Sat. **Credit** AmEx, DC, MC, V. **Map** p246 L12.
Hand-made toys including painted wooden fruit and veg for budding shopkeepers and miniature wicker shopping baskets for aspiring shopaholics.

Travel

STA Travel
Fiolstræde 18 (33 14 15 01/www.statravel.dk). **Open** 9.30am-5.30pm Mon-Thur; 10am-5.30pm Fri. **Credit** MC, V. **Map** p251 M13.
The Student Travel Association's Copenhagen HQ.

Arts & Entertainment

Features

Black Diamond. *See p190.*

Festivals & Events

From summer jazz to Christmas pixies, Copenhagen knows how to celebrate.

Scandinavians aren't exactly renowned for their love of festivals or public expressions of joy, but Copenhagen nevertheless has a wealth of annual cultural, artistic and festive events that hold a great appeal for visitors. The events listed in this chapter are just the highlights: individual chapters have a wider selection and more information. For further details and precise dates of the year's events in the city, the lavishly named **Wonderful Copenhagen Tourist Information Bureau** (70 22 24 42/ www.visitcopenhagen.dk) has a superb English website with up-to-the minute listings and publishes *Copenhagen This Week*, which, despite its name, is a monthly magazine with detailed listings and reviews of sporting and cultural events. Pick up a free copy from tourist information centres, hotels and libraries.

For those who want to avoid the queues, Danish school holidays begin around the end of June and finish in the first week of August. For a list of public holidays, *see* chapter **Directory**.

Spring

NatFilm Festivalen

33 12 00 05/www.natfilm.dk. **Date** Mar-early Apr.
Approaching its 20th year, this is Denmark's premier film festival in terms of audience, attracting over 30,000 people and showing films from around the world. Often the directors themselves turn up to talk about their work after the screenings, which take place day and night throughout the city's many cinemas. The Danish answer to the Oscars, the Bodils, are awarded during the festival, with 2006's top award going to Per Fly's *Drabet*.

The Queen's Birthday

Date 16 Apr.
The Danes are united by their fondness for their multi-talented Queen Margrethe II and her birthday is cause for celebration across the country. The Queen herself makes an appearance on a balcony at Amalienborg Slot at noon, while the Royal Life Guards mark the occasion by parading in their finest ceremonial dress.

May Day

Fælledparken, Østerbro. Bus 15. **Map** p248 E12.
Date 1 May.
Head to Østerbro for this trades unions-led festival of the working man, complete with live music and ethnic food.

Ølfestival (Beer Festival)

Valbyhallen, Jul Andersens Vej 3, Valby (36 17 44 00/www.haandbryg.dk/www.ale.dk). *Train to Valby*. **Tickets** 75kr. **No credit cards**. **Date** 3 days mid May.
The growth of microbreweries has finally challenged the stronghold of Carlsberg and interest in beer is growing fast in Denmark. This is the country's leading festival, drawing crowds of over 10,000. Tastings, talks and, of course, monster hangovers are all part of this annual three-day event.

Copenhagen Marathon

35 26 69 00/www.sparta.dk. **Admission** 400kr-450kr. **No credit cards**. **Date** 3rd weekend in May.
Professional and amateur runners from around the world pound the cobbles from Vesterbro to Nørrebro to Østerbro and Vester Voldgade.

Copenhagen Whitsun Carnival

Østerbrohuset, Århusgade 103, Østerbro (35 38 85 04/www.karneval.dk). **Admission** free.
Map p248 E12. **Date** Whitsun weekend.
This is Copenhagen's stab at a Rio Carnival-type event, with lashings of South American spirit, costumes, parades and floats. The three-day festivities are centred on Østerbro's Fælledparken.

Summer

Sommerscene

33 15 15 64/www.kit.dk. **Tickets** phone for details. **Credit** varies. **Date** June-Aug.
An annual three-month festival of international dance, theatre and circus, Sommerscene occurs in venues across the city. The line-ups are impressive and have included Philip Glass and the RSC.

Danish Derby

Klampenborg Galopbane, Klampenborgvej, Klampenborg (39 96 02 15/www.galopsport.dk). *Train to Klampenborg/bus 388*. **Admission** 100kr; 50kr concessions; free under-18s. **No credit cards**. **Date** late June.
Denmark's premier equine event takes place at Klampenborg racecourse, to the north of the city.

Round Sjælland Yacht Race

Helsingør. Train to Helsingør. **Date** late June.
Sailors compete in one of Europe's largest yacht races over three days.

Sankt Hans Aften

Date 23 June.
Sankt Hans Aften (St Hans Night) is one of the biggest celebrations of the festival calendar for

Danes, who have marked the longest day of the year since pagan times with bonfires and songs. The biggest gatherings are usually held on the beaches or in the parks.

Roskilde Festival

Roskilde (www.roskilde-festival.dk). Train to Roskilde. **Tickets** phone for details; within Denmark: 70 15 65 65 10am-9pm daily/www.billetnet.dk; from UK: The Way Ahead 0115 912 9000. **Credit** varies. **Date** late June/early July.

Held over four days, Roskilde is renowned as Scandinavia's largest outdoor music event. In 2006 crowds of 80,000 enjoyed headline acts including Bob Dylan, Kanye West, Arctic Monkeys and Kaiser Chiefs. The festival is famous for its relatively crime-free party atmosphere, and for many teenage Danes their first Roskilde Festival is an important coming-of-age milestone. A shuttle bus runs from Roskilde Station to the festival grounds on the outskirts of this ancient town in the centre of Sjælland.

Copenhagen Jazz Festival

33 93 20 13/33 93 25 45/www.jazzfestival.dk. **Tickets** varies; phone for details. **Credit** varies. **Date** 1st Fri-2nd Sun in July.

As soon as Roskilde is over, the Copenhagen Jazz Festival gets under way. The Danes love their jazz, and, thankfully, that passion isn't limited to the Dixieland tourist-fodder you'll hear on Nyhavn of a summer's afternoon. The festival is a delightfully ad hoc affair, with impromptu gigs, jam sessions, improvisations, free outdoor concerts and street parades happening all over the city. Naturally, you need to book early for any big names. **Photo** *p167*.

Kulturhavn (Culture Harbour)

Islands Brygge, central Copenhagen (33 66 38 50/ www.kulturhavn.dk). **Date** 1st weekend in Aug.

Over 80 events from diving to dance, water polo to dragon boat races, and theatre to fireworks, on and around the water beside Islands Brygge.

Shakespeare at Kronborg

Kronborg Slot, Helsingør (49 20 08 11/www.hamlet sommer.dk). Train to Helsingør. **Tickets** phone for details. **Credit** varies. **Date** Aug.

Productions of *Hamlet* have been staged at Kronborg since 1816, many by British companies. Laurence Olivier and his wife Vivien Leigh played here in 1937, but John Gielgud's 1939 Hamlet is generally regarded as the definitive performance. Since then, Richard Burton, Michael Redgrave, Derek Jacobi, Kenneth Branagh and, recently, Simon Russell Beale have all given notable Hamlets.

Copenhagen Pride

Throughout Copenhagen (www.copenhagenpride.dk). **Date** mid Aug.

Previously known as Mermaid Pride, this is the festival of the year for the city's gay and lesbian community, drawing crowds of up to 50,000.

DCCD Images Festival

Nytorv 17 (33 17 97 00/www.dccd.dk). **Tickets** vary; phone for details. **Credit** varies. **Date** Aug-Sept.

An annual celebration of the non-Western world, including theatre, dance, visual arts, handicrafts, photography, music, architecture and literary events, held in various venues around Denmark.

Roskilde Festival.

Arts & Entertainment

Copenhagen Film Festival

Gothersgade 157, 1123 Copenhagen (33 45 47 49/ www.copenhagenfilmfestival.dk). **Date** Aug-Sept.

The consensus when this event began in 2003 was that the last thing Europe needed was another film festival, and Copenhagen already had its popular Natfilm Festival. But this ten-day festival of European-only films is starting to gather momentum, with more events than the Natfilm Festival and more money behind it. It takes place at cinemas throughout the city. Around 100 films are shown and last year Lars von Trier premiered his film *The Boss of it All* at the festival.

Art Copenhagen

Forum, Julius Thomsens Plads, Frederiksberg (32 47 20 00/www.artcph.com). **Date** late Sept.

This new annual contemporary art fair features around 60 galleries from Scandinavia, as well as discussions and artist interviews.

Copenhagen Blues Festival

Venues throughout the city (www.copenhagen bluesfestival.dk; tickets: BILLETnet 70 15 65 65). **Date** late Sept.

The city's leading blues event featuring local and international blues musicians in over 60 concerts. Main venues include Mojo (*see p189*).

Autumn

Kulturnatten

33 25 74 00/www.kulturnatten.dk. **Tickets** vary. **Date** 1st night of autumn half-term in mid Oct. *See below* **For one night only.**

Tivoli Halloween Opening

Vesterbrogade 3 (ticket centre 33 15 10 12/ www.tivoli.dk). **Tickets** phone for details. **Credit** AmEx, DC, MC, V. **Date** mid-late Oct. **Map** p250 P12.

Tivoli opened for Halloween for the first time in 2006 with special spooky activities for children and a Halloween market.

Copenhagen Gay & Lesbian Film Festival

33 93 07 66/www.cglff.dk. **Tickets** phone for details. **Credit** varies. **Date** late Oct.

Ten days of mainstream and underground gay and lesbian films arranged by the Danske Film Institut. One of the biggests film fests on the Danish calendar.

Junge Hunde

35 43 20 21/35 43 23 24/www.jungehunde.dk; tickets: BILLETnet 70 15 65 65. **Tickets** prices vary. **No credit cards**. **Date** Oct-Nov.

Previously confined to Copenhagen, the Junge Hunde (Young Dogs) international dance festival now takes place simultaneously in Århus and Malmö. It features many of the stars of tomorrow and has a reputation for being avant-garde.

Winter

Copenhagen Irish Festival

Store Kannikestræde 19 (38 79 21 09/www.irish festival.dk; tickets: BILLETnet 70 15 65 65/ www.billetnet.dk). **Tickets** phone for details. **Credit** varies. **Date** early Nov.

Events with an Irish theme over four days, most at the above address.

CPH:Dox

Axeltorv 12 (33 93 07 34/www.natfilm.dk). **Date** mid Nov.

Copenhagen's International Documentary Festival takes place in cinemas throughout the city for a week during mid November. Now in its fifth year, the festival has already grown into the third largest of its kind in Europe.

For one night only

Although autumn can be beautiful in Copenhagen as the trees on Kongens Nytorv change colour, there is no mistaking the hint of foreboding in the air as the long, dark, wet Danish winter approaches. To help stave off the gloom each year, around the middle of October (12 Oct 2007) Copenhagen lets rip with one last cultural hurrah during **Kulturnat** (Culture Night; www.kulturnatten.dk). For one night only the festival sees many of the city's museums and palaces stay open until midnight. Around 300 venues take part in the night, inaugurated in 1992, including churches, galleries and other exhibition spaces – even Parliament and the Supreme Court open their doors. There is usually a

craft fair in Rådhuspladsen, performances galore on Strøget, countless concerts and performances, and rare displays of historic weaponry at the Tøjhusmuseet. Kulturnat brings a unique atmosphere to the venues and the city. It is the epitome of the Danish *hygge*, or 'cosiness', phenomenon – in which visitors, usually including a good proportion of very excited children, get to see a new side of familiar institutions, visit artists' studios, hear music in unlikely venues and meet artists and writers to discuss their work. Leading up to the event you can buy a Kultur pass – currently 70kr – which includes access to the majority of the events, plus bus and local train travel.

Copenhagen Jazz Festival. *See p165.*

Tivoli Christmas Season

Tivoli (33 15 10 01/www.tivoli.dk). **Admission** 75kr, 35kr concessions. **Credit** AmEx, DC, MC, V. **Map** p250 P12. **Date** mid Nov-Christmas.
From mid November Tivoli turns into a vast Christmas grotto with a special Christmas market, ice skating, Yuletide grub and an infestation of *nisser* (Danish Christmas pixies). It attracts up to a million visitors, so expect crowds.

Christmas Fairs & Parade

www.visitcopenhagen.dk. **Date** from end Nov.
Like most European cities, Copenhagen is decked out in decorations and illuminations at this time of year. But, unlike most, the atmosphere is less commercial and more authentically 'Christmassy' (maybe the sub-zero temperatures have something to do with it). At the end of November Father Christmas parades through the city in the Great Christmas Parade. In past years a popular artificial ice rink has been constructed in the centre of Kongens Nytorv. Look out too for the Hotel d'Angleterre's spectacular Christmas decorations.

Christmas

www.visitcopenhagen.dk. **Date** 24 Dec.
The Danes give a great Christmas, both in the privacy of their own homes, with elaborate rituals, feasting and decorations, and on a more grand public scale. Like all Danes, Copenhageners celebrate on Christmas Eve, and judge other nations to be perfectly bizarre for doing otherwise. Having already gone out into the woods to chop down their own tree, Danes will decorate it the night before Christmas

and hang it with real candles. Once these are lit, the family dances around the tree holding hands and singing carols, before settling down to a traditional Christmas dinner of roast duck, potatoes and red cabbage followed by rice pudding with a hidden almond (whoever gets the almond wins a present).

New Year

Date 31 Dec/1 Jan.
Rådhuspladsen is the place Danes gather on New Year's Eve for the traditional celebration. In recent years the firework displays throughout the city (both private and public) have been ever more breathtaking. But be warned, the Danes are not too hot on firework safety.

Winter Jazz Festival

33 93 20 13/www.vinterjazz.dk. **Tickets** phone for details. **Credit** varies. **Date** end Jan-early Feb.
This is a smaller, more low-key ten-day version of the famous summer jazz festival.

Fastelavn

www.karneval.dk. **Date** late Feb/early Mar.
Fastelavn could be considered the Danes' Halloween, in which children dress up in costumes and gather together wielding sticks with which they beat the hell out of a wooden barrel. This is mild compared with what used to happen when the barrel, containing a live cat, would be suspended from a tree by a rope so that the youths of a town could gallop past it on a horse and wallop it until the bottom fell out. These days, the traumatised feline has been replaced by hundreds of sweets.

Arts & Entertainment

Children

It's Tivoli time.

One almost wonders if Copenhagen was created just for children. The city is full of imaginatively designed play parks and fairytale palaces; there are several museums just for kids and many of the others have special departments for children; every restaurant has high chairs; every bus can take prams (they favour the Victorian Mary Poppins-style ones here); the Metro has lifts (are you listening, Paris and London?); and every bicycle seems to have a kid's seat on the back. During the holidays there are dozens of performances laid on for children in the theatres and parks. There are nappy changing facilities in most public buildings and much of the city centre is pedestrianised. And then, of course, there is Tivoli, the world's cosiest amusement park.

Great days out

A good way to see Copenhagen with a child is to adopt a geographical approach and base a day's activities around one area of the city.

Tivoli & Rådhuspladsen

A must for every child visiting Copenhagen is **Tivoli** (*see p54*; **photo** *p169*), open throughout the summer. Located right next to Central Station, the old amusement park can still make every child's heart beat faster. The world's tallest carousel (80 metres/262 feet), shooting galleries, Valhalla Castle and the Pantomime Theatre are among the attractions that provide action and fun for kids (and many adults), while the flowers and gardens, open-air cafés and restaurants offer parents tranquillity and time to breathe. Food is expensive in Tivoli (take advantage of the plentiful picnic areas) and rides cost extra, but the fireworks on Wednesday and Saturday nights are free, as are many performances on the open-air stage. For children of nappy age, there's a family amenity centre with baby-changing tables, free nappies and microwave ovens for heating baby food.

Across Rådhuspladsen from here is the fun **Ripley's Believe It or Not Museum** (*see p62*) and the not so impressive **Hans Christian Andersen Museum** (*see p62*). **Nationalmuseet** (National Museum; *see p60*) can be an interesting place to take children (after all, who can resist the Vikings?).

Every new exhibition is accompanied by a children's area, with specially designed activities, plus there's a toy museum on the top floor and an excellent hands-on children's museum in the basement.

West of Tivoli is the **Tycho Brahe Planetarium** (*see p97*), with its small exhibition on astronomy and space travel, but the real attraction here is the **IMAX cinema**, which is just as likely to show films about skateboarding or skydiving as the stars. (Ask for headphones with English narration at the ticket office – children must be over three.)

South of Tivoli, older kids will definitely get something from a visit to the newly renovated **Ny Carlsberg Glyptotek** (*see p59*), especially if they are promised a trip to the popular swimming centre **Vandkulturhuset** (within the DGI-Byen sports complex; *see p201*) nearby, which contains a baby pool with fountains, a swimming pool, waterslides, diving boards, climbing walls and a spa where parents can recharge their batteries.

The magnificent open-air pool in the city harbour by **Langebro** is open throughout the summer and has a children's area. Alternatively, a short bus ride away is the **Amager Strand** lagoon (*see p107*), a spectacular new sandy beach development with gently sloping shallows and plenty of children's entertainment laid on during the summer.

Strøget & around

The long pedestrian street **Strøget** can be fun for kids, partly because of its shops (there's a toy store, Fætter BR, near the Rådhuspladsen end), but mostly because of the street performers. Towards the Kongens Nytorv end are the **Guinness World Records Museum** and **Mystic Exploratorie** (*see p64*), which children seem to enjoy.

Get away from the noise of the street by climbing the 17th-century **Rundetårn** (Round Tower; *see p65*) on Købmagergade. Instead of steps there is a 209-metre (686-foot) long ramp, which spirals up inside the tower: a real challenge for buggy pushers.

For something completely different, rent out a kayak from **Kajak-Ole** on Gammel Strand (*see p53*). A guide leads the group through the canals, telling local anecdotes on the way;

Whatever you do, make sure you take the little tykes to **Tivoli**. *See p168.*

a drink at a café in Christianshavn is included in the price. No experience is necessary, as the kayaks are very stable, but children must be 11 or older for a two-person kayak and 15 for a single-person kayak.

South of Gammel Strand on Slotsholmen, the double-handed swords, suits of armour and other military paraphernalia at **Tøjhusmuseet** (Royal Arsenal Museum; *see p79*) nearby are usually a hit, especially with boys. The charismatic **Thorvaldsens Museum** (*see p78*) is surprisingly interesting for kids too. Also on Slotsholmen, older children might like the spooky atmosphere of the **Ruinerne Under Christiansborg** (Ruins Under Christiansborg; *see p76*). The excavated ruins of the original castle of Bishop Absalon (the founder of Copenhagen), jumbled together with those of later castles on the site, are situated directly below the current Christiansborg Slot.

Rosenborg & around

Five minutes' walk north of the east end of Strøget lies **Kongens Have**. This is a wonderful place for a picnic. The park has a unique wooden playground for one- to four-year-olds, and alongside is one of the most charming traditional attractions in Copenhagen: the **Marionet Teater** (Marionette Theatre; *see p193*; **photo** *p170*). Performances for children up to five years take place every day in the summer (except Monday) at 2pm and 3pm.

Across the park, **Rosenborg Slot** (Rosenborg Palace; *see p89*) is packed with historical treasures, and is also the place to watch the Queen's Life Guards (who live in barracks next door) in training. The rooms of special interest to children are the Treasury, the Long Hall and Room 10. The atmospheric Treasury houses the Danish crown jewels, while the impressive Long Hall is decorated in golden stucco and has three silver lions guarding the thrones of the king and queen. Room 10 features a curious picture that shows the children of Frederik IV – when you look at it from the left, you see a girl; from the right, you see a boy.

Two minutes' walk south of Rosenborg is the **Musikhistorisk Museum** (Musical History Museum; *see p89*), worth visiting with a musically minded child. Audio sets play the sounds of old instruments, including Highland pipes from Scotland, launeddas from Greece and hurdy-gurdys from the Czech Republic. You cannot play the historical instruments, but the museum does have a kids' room where children can use up some of their energy on drums, stringed instruments and xylophones.

A couple of minutes' walk north of Rosenborg is the excellent **Statens Museum for Kunst** (National Gallery; *see p87*). It features a children's gallery and a workshop, and offers guided tours for children on Saturdays, Sundays and throughout the Danish school holidays. Tours start at 1pm and are

Arts & Entertainment

followed by a workshop from 2pm to 4pm, where children can sculpt, draw and paint (budding Rodins may even take their work home with them). The guided tours are, not surprisingly, mainly in Danish, but English-speaking children are well catered for in the workshops.

If you need a little down-time from the kids, behind the gallery stretches **Østre Anlæg park** which contains some of the best playgrounds in Copenhagen.

Christianshavn

Vor Frelsers Kirke (Church of Our Saviour; *see p91*), close to Christianshavns Kanal, has a unique tower with a spiral staircase that twists around the outside of the spire. It's a fun (if a little scary) climb up 400 steps, with a great view compensating for the effort it takes to actually get to the top. Although be warned: when windy, the tower can start to sway a little. Back on terra firma, the kids will love a trip to the **Orlogsmuseet** (Royal Danish Naval Museum, *see p92*). While you may be drawn to the wonderful collection of model ships and maritime art, the kids might prefer to climb aboard the submarine Spækhuggeren, the interior of which has been partially recreated so that visitors can enter the command centre, the radio/radar room and the officers' mess, and even have a peep through the periscope.

From nearby Holmen you have a great view from the Opera House across the water to **Amalienborg Slot**, the royal palace (*see p82*), which can be reached by hopping aboard one of the harbour buses. The changing of the guards takes place at Amalienborg every day at noon and all the pomp and pageantry is a major event for kids.

Frederiksberg

To the west of central Copenhagen lies **Frederiksberg Have** (*see p97*), a beautiful garden that is perfect for a picnic, with its dozens of secluded, leafy corners. To find out more about the royal gardens, take one of the guided boat trips on the lake. The neighbouring **Zoologisk Have** (Zoological Garden; *see p99*) is one of the most attractive in Europe, with plenty of space for its animal residents plus a new elephant house by Lord Norman Foster. It has a special petting zoo where the smallest children can touch and play with the usual range of not-so-dangerous beasties. Other kiddie attractions include pony rides, climbing the zoo tower or just looking at the numerous baby animals. Be warned, though: queues can be long on sunny summer days.

Opposite the rear of Frederiksberg Slot, beneath the lawns of Søndermarken park, is a subterranean glass museum, **Cisternerne – Museet for Moderne Glaskunst** (The Cisterns – Museum of Modern Glass Art; *see p98*), housed in former underground water cisterns. Though not aimed at kids, it is dank, spooky and rather fun.

Østerbro & further north

Just outside the city centre, north along the harbour front, are the ancient battlements and moat surrounding **Kastellet** (*see p83*), a base for the Danish army for several centuries and still a fun and atmospheric place to take kids. Nearby is the much maligned **Den Lille Havfrue** (The Little Mermaid, *see p83*), probably more familiar to most children these days from the Disney cartoon than the creepy HC Andersen fairytale.

Marionet Teater. *See p169.*

Lego's dark secret

The original Legoland lies three-and-a-half hours away from Copenhagen by train, on the other side of the country in Billund, Jutland, making it just about possible for a heroic day trip from the capital by truly Lego-obsessed kids. But perhaps if those children knew the 'dark truth' behind the Lego legend they might think again.

Visit the Lego website and you can read about the history of the company. It was founded in 1934 by Ole Kirk Christiansen, a carpenter who moved into making toys when his company struggled following a workshop fire. In 1949, Christiansen began producing plastic building bricks with eight studs on the top and he never looked back.

Sounds straightforward enough, but the truth is that the Lego brick concept as we know it today was in fact invented by a long-forgotten Englishman, Hilary Harry Fisher Page, and originally built by his company Kiddicraft as 'self-locking building bricks'. Page was one of the first people to approach toy design from an educational and psychological point of view and his product was reasonably successful. Lego – which comes from the Danish 'Leg godt' ('play well') got their hands on some Kiddicraft bricks, saw the potential and began manufacturing their own version. Page committed suicide in 1957 and Lego introduced its bricks to the English market a year later, finally buying the rights to the Kiddicraft system in 1981.

Lego developed the idea beyond Page's wildest imaginings, of course, creating an absorbing and educational toy system that would be sold around the world. In the late 1950s they added the tubular supports that gave the bricks their strength and usability; they created the double-size Duplo sets for younger children in the late '60s; opened Legoland in Billund in 1968, Denmark's second most popular tourist attraction after Tivoli; and introduced the iconic Lego man in 1973 (they have since made almost four billion of these curiously asexual, racially ambivalent, emotionless figures). In 2000 the British Association of Toy Retailers named the Lego brick the Toy of the Century, and few people would disagree with them.

The Christiansen family, today headed by Ole's grandson Kjeld, remains one of the wealthiest in Denmark and the company still has its base in Billund – the town is essentially Legoville, and its airport, Denmark's second largest, owes its continued existence to the theme park. But most of the manufacturing has long since been outsourced to cheaper foreign labour markets.

Curiously, there is no dedicated Lego store in Copenhagen, but you can buy most of the range of Lego products in the Fætter BR toy chain, which has two outlets on Strøget (see p161).

Legoland Billund

Nordmarksvej 9, Billund (75 33 13 33/ www.legoland.dk). **Open** Apr-Oct (opening times vary, check website for details). **Admission** 225kr; 195kr concessions; free under-3s. **Credit** AmEx, DC, MC, V.

In Østerbro lies the extensive **Fælledparken** (*see p103*), which has several playgrounds, a skateboard park and an indoor swimming pool. In the summer several festivals, carnivals and playdays for children are held here. Another summer attraction in the park is Pavillionen, an outdoor café and restaurant that does very good barbecues.

Older children might find the stuffed animals a little static, but for younger kids the **Zoologisk Museum** (Zoological Museum; *see p104*), just west of Fælledparken, is a real hoot (especially the full-size replica mammoth). The **Experimentarium** (*see p105*), further north in Hellerup, is one of Copenhagen's great children's attractions. This science centre explores nature and technology, the environment and health issues through more than 300 interactive exhibits. In the kids' pavilion – aimed at children between three and six – there are crazy mirrors, water wheels and other delights to explore.

In **Danmarks Akvarium** (Danish Aquarium; *see p105*) in Charlottenlund, you can learn about the sea life that inhabits polar seas and tropical waters. On Saturdays and Sundays, when the touch pool is open, children can get up close and personal with marine life of all kinds. Don't miss feeding time at 2pm on Wednesdays, Saturdays and Sundays. During the school holidays there are daily activities but the aquarium does get crowded at weekends.

The oldest amusement park in the world, **Bakken** (*see p215; photo p172*), is located in the forest of Dyrehaven, further north of the city at Klampenborg. Open from late spring to

Arts & Entertainment

early autumn, Bakken has all the usual amusement park attractions, including rollercoasters, shooting galleries and daily shows for children, but you should note that, although entrance to the park is free, the attractions are not. A pleasant way to see the rest of Dyrehaven is by pony. If you do feel like it, little ponies, which can be led by parents, are available at **Fortunens Ponyudlejning**. Alternatively, take a horse and cart ride or simply stroll around in the forest. Right next to Dyrehaven is one of the best beaches in the Copenhagen area – **Bellevue** (*see p215*).

Further north, just a short train journey from the center of town, the beautifully situated **Louisiana Museum For Moderne Kunst** (Louisiana Museum of Modern Art; *see p216*) has a children's wing offering daily artistic activities such as drawing and model making. Louisiana also has a wonderfully designed park, perfect for a picnic, and there's a small swimming beach in front of the museum.

Fortunens Ponyudlejning

Ved Fortunen 33, Lyngby (45 87 60 58). Train to Klampenborg, then bus 388 towards Lyngby or train to Lyngby, then bus 388 towards Helsingør. **Open** *noon-6pm Mon-Fri; 9am-6pm Sat, Sun. School holidays 9am-6pm daily.* **Rates** 160kr/hr; 130kr/hr under-11s. **No credit cards.**

Horse around in the forests of **Dyrehaven**.

Other attractions

Axelborg Bowling

Axeltorv 3A (33 32 00 92/www.axelborg-bowling.dk). **Open** 11am-10pm Mon-Thur; 11am-midnight Fri, Sat; 11am-11pm Sun. **Prices** *Lane hire* 100kr-300kr; *shoe hire* 10kr. **Credit** DC, MC, V. **Map** p250 O11.
While the children practise their moves, there is a bar available for grown-ups and karaoke too if you're feeling in the mood. For other bowling alleys, *see p202.*

Park Bio Cinema

Østerbrogade 79, Østerbro (35 38 33 62/www.park bio-kbh.dk). Bus 1A, 14. **Open** *baby screening* 9am-1pm Fri. **Tickets** 50kr-65kr. **No credit cards.** **Map** p248 C13.
This cinema offers so-called baby screenings for parents with small children at 10.30am every Friday (except during July). There's also a nappy-changing intermission, and spare nappies are provided free of charge.

Cafés & restaurants

Virtually all cafés and restaurants welcome children, many with baby seats, children's menus and even a play area.

Café Hovedtelegrafen

Købmagergade 37 (33 41 09 86/www.postogtele museet.dk). **Open** 11am-5pm Tue, Thur-Sat; 11am-8pm Wed; noon-4pm Sun. **Credit** MC, V. **Map** p251 M14.
A rooftop café with an outdoor terrace might not sound the most child-friendly recommendation, but it is, of course, perfectly safe and there is plenty of space for the children to 'express themselves'.

La Rocca

Vendersgade 23-25 (33 14 66 55). **Open** 1-10.30pm daily. **Credit** AmEx, DC, MC, V. **Map** p246 L11.
This decent, authentic Italian restaurant is great for families with kids as it offers both a children's menu and a well-equipped play room.

Wagamama

Tietgensgade 20, Tivoli (33 75 06 58/www. wagamama.dk). **Open** noon-11pm Mon-Thur, Sun; noon-midnight Fri, Sat. **Credit** MC, V. **Map** p250 P12.
Opened in spring 2006, this first Danish branch of the worldwide noodle chain has a well-priced kids' menu plus ice lollies for dessert.

Online information

www.karneval.dk

Provides information on the range of activities for children available during Copenhagen's yearly carnival. Also offers details of the children's biennial festival in Kongens Have and several other musical and entertainment events.

Film

Doing it Dogme style.

Grand Teatret. See p176.

The Danes have a prodigious movie-making history. From the silent era of black-and-white film with piano accompaniment to the more recent spate of releases, Danish filmmakers have had an impact on cinema disproportionate to the country's size and population. This can be credited to the Danes' true love of and devotion to film, as well as government subsidies to create quality products for the international market. There is also the famous Danish Film School (Den Danske Filmskole) with its steady flow of talented graduates, who have brought Danish cinema several notable triumphs during the last three decades.

MOVIE PIONEERS

Denmark's filmmakers were among the key pioneers in European cinema and in the decades leading up to World War II had a notable influence on its development. The establishment of the Nordisk Film Kompagni in 1906 galvanised the industry, and in 2006 it celebrated its centenary. Nordisk Film was the first studio in Europe to focus solely on feature films and it thrived (until the emergence of the American film industry, from around 1913), thanks to its technical superiority and the talent of its directors. As extraordinary as this may

sound, in the early days of cinema Denmark was the world's biggest producer of films.

After facing near bankruptcy with the advent of sound, Nordisk Film re-established itself in 1929 as a producer of talkies. It is still the oldest working film studio in the world and its polar bear logo is said to have inspired the use of a lion as MGM's symbol.

FILM FUNDING

Among the most important innovators of early cinema were filmmakers **Benjamin Christensen** and **Carl Theodor Dreyer**. In front of the camera, the world fell in love with **Asta Nielsen**, one of the first great movie stars.

The popularity of cinema – particularly documentaries – exploded in Denmark during the 1930s and, as a result, a Film Act was passed in 1938, establishing the Film Council, the Film Fund and the National Film Board.

Between World War II and the early 1980s, Danish cinema experienced something of a lull in international terms, with the country's filmmakers focusing their energies on television production. When feature films were made, they were often worthy social dramas or soft pornography (the industry having been derestricted in 1969). Yet in this period, director

Henning Carlsen created the masterful *Knud Hamsun's Hunger* (1964), which is one of the ten official film entries in the recently established 'canon' of Danish culture (www.kulturkanon.kum.dk).

Government subsidies for film production started in the 1960s, and by the mid '70s most Danish films were made with some element of government aid. By 1989 an even more radical system was introduced, whereby a filmmaker could demand 50 per cent of the film's budget (with no creative strings attached) from the government if the director could match it with private funding.

INTERNATIONAL SUCCESS

In 1988 **Gabriel Axel**'s film adaptation of Karen Blixen's short story *Babette's Feast* won the Oscar for Best Foreign Language Film, which led the way to many more international successes for Danish cinema, including the unprecedented double triumph when **Bille August**'s *Pelle the Conqueror* won in the same category the following year. The great Swedish actor, Max von Sydow, received a nomination in the Best Actor category. The film, adapted from Martin Andersen Nexø's novel telling the bleak tale of Swedish immigrants coping with life on 19th-century Bornholm (the Danish island in the Baltic), also won the Palme d'Or at Cannes.

ENFANT TERRIBLE

Danish cinema continued to hog the limelight in the 1990s with the international success of director **Lars von Trier**, and the advent of

Palads. *See p176.*

Dogme 95, the cinema-ascetic movement of which he was a co-founder. Von Trier's (the 'von' is an aristocratic affectation) string of successes over the last decade has earned him a virtually unrivalled reputation for stylistic experimentation, provocative scripts and less than reverential treatment of actors. He established his name on the international art house circuit with such films as *The Element of Crime* (1984), *Epidemic* (1987) and *Europa* (1991).

Von Trier's spooky and disturbing 1994 TV series, *The Kingdom*, set in Copenhagen's main hospital, was a huge international success. However, it was his 1996 feature, *Breaking the Waves*, that finally launched him on the world stage. A torrid and occasionally crudely manipulative film (the first of his so-called 'Trilogy of Goodness'), the film cast the die for his future relationship with the world's film critics, who continue to be violently polarised in their opinions of his work. The film did, however, win him a top prize at Cannes and Emily Watson earned an Oscar nomination for Best Actress with her moving performance.

More controversy followed with his 1998 Dogme release, *The Idiots*, featuring explicit sex and a less than politically correct look at mental illness. Von Trier's 2000 feature, the bleak musical *Dancer in the Dark*, starred Björk, who famously ate her costume in frustration at working with the obsessive director. Again the film divided critics, but it went on to win the Palme d'Or at Cannes.

Dogville (2004), starring Nicole Kidman, was a barely concealed attack on American culture and again very well received. It was intended to spawn two further films starring Kidman, who instead pulled out of Lars's flop, *Manderlay* (2006). Created in *Dogville*'s bare studio style, the film tackles themes of slavery in an imaginary Louisiana town in the 1930s.

Von Trier owns his own film company, Zentropa, so the failure of *Manderlay* was hardly enough to scupper him in the long term. His latest film, *The Boss of it All*, is a shot at comedy and a return to the lo-fi aesthetic of the Dogme films.

DOGME STYLE

Founded in Copenhagen, the Dogme collective was the brainchild of four Danish directors – von Trier, **Thomas Vinterberg**, **Søren Kragh-Jacobsen** and **Kristian Levring**. Dogme's mission was to discard the 'trickery' of modern filmmaking to refocus on the characters' emotional journey.

The Dogme directors declared that Hollywood movies deceived their audience by mythologising the process of filmmaking. But to set themselves aside from all the other bleating, under-funded independent directors, they made it clear that their creed (called the Vow of Chastity) need not preclude Hollywood-sized budgets. As Vinterberg commented: 'The Dogme 95 Manifesto does not concern itself with the economic aspects of film-making. A Dogme film could be low-budget or it could have a $100m budget.' The 'Vow' included such draconian commandments as 'Shooting must be on location only', 'The director can receive no credit' and 'Films cannot be of a specific genre'. No dubbing, tripods, artificial lighting or optical effects were allowed either.

The movement spawned several notable successes, prime among them Vinterberg's successful second feature film, *Festen (The Celebration)* (1998), a disturbing tale of family secrets, set against the backdrop of a 60th birthday party.

EMERGING TALENT
Resonant dramas such as *Facing the Truth* (2002), *Inheritance* (2003) and *Brothers* (2004) are key examples of the intelligent and high-quality movies made by established directors such as **Nils Malmros**, **Per Fly** and **Susanne Bier**, who continue to make waves internationally. Meanwhile a new generation of young filmmakers is redefining genre-oriented films with forceful stories told in highly aesthetic packages, such as **Nikolaj Arcel**'s political thriller *King's Game* (2004), **Nicolas Winding Refn**'s raw and violent drug trilogy *Pusher* (1996), and **Christoffer Boe**'s modern romances such as *Reconstruction* (2003) and *Allegro* (2005). Comedies such as *Adam's Apples* and *The Green Butchers*, both by **Anders Thomas Jensen**, and **Jonas Elmer**'s fable of a modern Bridget Jones-style single woman named *Nynne* (2005) have also been major box-office successes.

Danish children's films have a very long tradition of winning international awards, and have rolled with the times to deliver first-class CGI animation movies such as *Terkel in Trouble* (2004) and *The Ugly Duckling and Me* (2006).

NEW DANISH SCREEN
In 2006 the creation of a fund called New Danish Screen, based on a subsidy scheme of risk capital, provided a solid financial platform for innovative ideas in filmmaking. Under this umbrella, major film festivals around the world have already had the opportunity to experience a new wave of Danish experimental cinema, including **Pernille Fischer Christensen**'s *A Soap* and Christoffer Boe's *Offscreen* at the 2006 Berlin Film Festival.

My Copenhagen
Thomas Vinterberg

Film director Thomas Vinterberg shot to international fame in 1998 with the very first Dogme film, 'Festen (The Celebration)', which was subsequently transformed into a critically acclaimed West End show. Since then, he has attempted to break through into the English language market with 2003's futuristic romance, 'It's All About Love', starring Joaquin Phoenix and Claire Danes; and 'Dear Wendy' (2005), a critique of American gun culture starring Jamie Bell.

'There are two places I like to visit in Copenhagen because of the memories they bring back from my childhood and it's great that they still exist today.

'First I would visit **Dyrehaven** (*see p215*), the 'Deer Garden', which is a huge, wild, wooded park a few miles north of Copenhagen where you can see deer roaming freely. The old Bakken amusement park is here too, but I would skip the funfair and go to the park instead. The king had it built in the 15th century as his own private hunting grounds – now anyone is allowed to walk around it.

'I grew up in a commune and we always used to come to Dyrehaven for birthdays. We'd fly kites, and I'd be this naked hippy kid running around, surrounded by all the other happy, naked hippy kids. What would often start as a child's party usually grew into an excuse for an all-night drink fest. I've been coming back to this place since I was born, although you can't get naked any more. I don't know, maybe it disturbs the deer or something?

'Later I'd go to **Christiania** (*see p91*), which is still standing even though the authorities have been trying to close it down for the last 35 years. A whole culture of squatters and hippies developed after it opened in 1971. There were so many cultural events there in the 1970s, when it grew into a colourful hippy town full of ideologies, theatre groups and happy people. My first cultural experiences were here: the first play I ever saw was at the Grey Hall and was full of wild stuff, not your average trip to the theatre. Christiania is definitely the place for experimentation.'

Arts & Entertainment

CINEMA-GOING

There are plenty of top-quality screens in Copenhagen's city centre, with a choice of multiplexes and art houses as well as the dynamic **Cinemateket** (*see below*). This all points to the locals' insatiable cinemania, which means even the largest cinema in Scandinavia, the **Imperial** *(see below)*, is usually packed to capacity during blockbuster openings.

Almost four million people go to the cinema annually in Copenhagen, yet cinephiles have learned to be patient in this town: occasionally, American movies can take up to a year to arrive on their screens, yet at times Copenhageners can get to see major releases a little before Londoners. Fortunately, the vast majority of foreign films are shown in their original language with Danish subtitles with tickets usually costing around 80kr.

Filmhuset/Den Danske Filminstitut Cinemateket

Gothersgade 55 (33 74 34 00/www.dfi.dk). **Open** *Café* noon-midnight Mon-Fri; 11am-midnight Sat; 11am-10pm Sun. Closed July. *Bookshop* noon-6pm Tue-Sun. *Documentary archive* 2pm-midnight Tue-Fri; 4-8pm Sat, Sun. *Library* noon-7pm Tue, Thur; noon-4pm Wed, Fri. **Admission** free; prices vary for cinema. **Map** p251 M15.

This world-class film complex is devoted to Danish and international cinema. Among its facilities are a shop selling difficult-to-find film books, posters and videos, a restaurant, a documentary archive (open to non-members) and three cinemas.

Multiplexes

CinemaxX

Fisketorvet Shopping Center, Kalvebod Brygge 57 (70 10 12 02/www.cinemaxx.dk/koebenhavn). **No credit cards**. **Map** p251 Q13.

This multiplex in a shopping mall has Copenhagen's biggest screen. Comfortable but costly.

Dagmar Teatret

Jernbanegade 2 (33 14 32 22/www.dagmar.dk). **No credit cards**. **Map** p250 O11.

A multiplex devoted to projecting quality films. The main cinema is decent, the smaller screens less so.

Empire Bio

Guldbergsgade 29F (35 36 00 36/www.empirebio.dk). **No credit cards**. **Map** p248 H9.

Nørrebro's local multiplex manages to show both art-house movies and blockbusters.

Imperial

Ved Vesterport 4 (70 13 12 11/www.biobooking.dk). **No credit cards**. **Map** p250 O10.

This is Copenhagen cinema par excellence. A large, old-fashioned theatre that used to be the biggest screen in Scandinavia before the CinemaxX giant came to town.

Metropol

Vesterbrogade 1 (70 13 12 11/www.biobooking.dk). **No credit cards**. **Map** p250 O12.

These three decent-sized screens are devoted to a more grown-up audience than Nordisk Film's other multiplex, Palads.

Palads

Axeltorv 9 (70 13 12 11/www.biobooking.dk). **No credit cards**. **Map** p250 O11.

Copenhagen's family multiplex is nicknamed 'the birthday cake' for its pink exterior. **Photo** *p174*.

Park Bio

Østerbrogade 79 (35 38 33 62/www.parkbio-kbh.dk). **No credit cards**. **Map** p248 C13.

A charming neighbourhood cinema showing three different movies a day.

Art house cinemas

Gloria

Rådhuspladsen 59 (33 12 42 92/www.gloria.dk). **No credit cards**. **Map** p250 O12.

Small underground art house cinema located in the heart of town.

Grand Teatret

Mikkel Bryggers Gade 8 (33 15 16 11/www.grand teatret.dk). **No credit cards**. **Map** p250 O12.

This beautiful old building is home to a distinguished cinema screening an impeccable selection of international and art house titles. **Photo** *p173*.

Husets Biograf

Huset, Magstræde 14, 2nd Floor (33 32 40 77/ www.husetsbio.dk). **No credit cards**. **Map** p251 O13.

Art house, student-oriented cinema with a predilection for the unusual.

Posthus Teatret

Rådhusstræde 1 (33 11 66 11/www.posthus teatret.dk). **No credit cards**. **Map** p251 O13.

Travel back in time in this tiny cinema, which could almost be mistaken for a puppet theatre from the outside. Screens international art house films.

Vester Vov Vov

Absalonsgade 5 (33 24 42 00/www.vestervovvov.dk). **No credit cards**. **Map** p245 Q9.

Vesterbro's charming local cinema has a really cosy feel to it, with comfy reclining airline seats in its screening rooms.

IMAX

Tycho Brahe Planetarium Omnimax

Gammel Kongevej 10 (33 12 12 24/www.tycho.dk). **Credit** AmEx, DC, MC, V. **Map** p250 P10.

This ultra-modern landmark contains an exhibition space and also features Copenhagen's spectacular IMAX cinema, projecting family-friendly science and nature films.

Galleries

For cutting-edge contemporary, skip the centre and head out to the industrial suburbs instead.

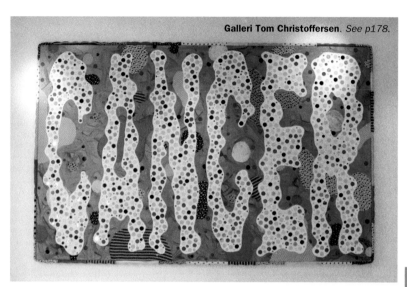

Galleri Tom Christoffersen. *See p178.*

The interest, and thus the market, for contemporary art in Denmark has had a remarkable growth in recent years. Copenhagen has always had a strong portfolio of galleries dealing in art from all ages, but in recent years the opening of several new galleries in the formerly unloved areas of Islands Brygge and industrial Valby has reinvigorated the scene.

For general updates on cultural events in Copenhagen, check out **www.kultunaut.com** for established, museum-oriented art and culture news, and **www.kopenhagen.dk** for details of openings and interviews with artists. Comprehensive listings can also be found at **www.aok.dk**, **www.kunstonline.dk**, or the website of the English-language newspaper, *Copenhagen Post*, at **www.cphpost.dk**. Meanwhile, for information about online art, software art, and other computer based art forms, visit **www.artificial.dk**.

The most significant events are the September art fairs hosted by Art Copenhagen (**www.artcopenhagen.dk**), the leading art shows in the Nordic countries with around 60 galleries and more than 450 artists represented.

Centre

Charlottenborg Udstillingsbygning
Nyhavn 2 (33 13 40 22/www.charlottenborg-art.dk). **Open** 10am-5pm Mon, Tue, Thur-Sun; 10am-7pm Wed. **Admission** 30kr; 20kr concessions. **No credit cards. Map** p252 M16.
This huge gallery alternates between Danish and international exhibitions of contemporary art, architecture and decorative arts. The hall was built in 1883 at the request of an influential group of Danish artists and is now run by the Ministry of Culture.

Clausens Kunsthandel
Toldbodgade 9 (33 15 41 54/www.clausenskunst handel.dk). **Open** 11am-5pm Tue-Sat. **No credit cards. Map** p249 K17.
Clausens has been working in the art trade since 1953 and the two-floor gallery houses an impressive selection of graphic work by some of Denmark's most established artists.

Fotografisk Center
Gammel Strand 48 (33 93 09 96/www.photography.dk/ www.digitalroom.org). **Open** 11am-5pm Tue-Sun. **Admission** 25kr; 15kr concessions. **Credit** MC, V. **Map** p251 N14.

Holding six annual exhibitions of mostly contemporary photography, the Fotografisk Center is also the only art book shop in Denmark that specialises solely in the photographic arts.

Galleri Christian Dam
Bredgade 23 (33 15 78 78/www.gcd.dk). **Open** noon-5pm Mon-Fri; noon-3pm Sat; closed 3wks July. **No credit cards. Map** p249 K16.
Galleri Christian Dam concentrates on the COBRA artists and their later artistic heirs. The gallery owns a great many works by the likes of Robert Jacobsen, Asger Jørn and Lise Malinovsky, and hosts four to six exhibitions annually so that you can own them too.

Galleri Nørby
Vestergade 8 (33 15 19 20/www.galleri-noerby.dk). **Open** noon-6pm Wed-Fri; 11am-4pm Sat. **Credit** AmEx, DC, MC, V. **Map** p250 O12.
For the last decade Galleri Nørby has represented the most celebrated ceramic artists in Denmark. With a showroom and studios on the premises, this is the primary resource for ceramic-oriented art in the country.

Galleri Specta
Peder Skrams Gade 13 (33 13 01 23/www.specta.dk). **Open** noon-5.30pm Tue-Fri; 11am-2pm Sat. **No credit cards. Map** p252 N16.
Gallery owner Else Johannesen was one of the most well respected figures in the art scene in Århus, Denmark's second largest city. She moved down to Copenhagen in 1992, establishing Galleri Specta. She represents the likes of Sylvie Fleury, Clay Ketter, Anders Moseholm, Sven Daalskov and Eva Steen Christensen. Specta sells well, thanks to its collection of smaller works and collectibles by some of the more cutting-edge Danish artists.

Galleri Susanne Ottesen
Gothersgade 49 (33 15 52 44/www.susanne ottesen.dk). **Open** 10am-1pm, 2-6pm Tue-Fri; 11am-3pm Sat. **No credit cards. Map** p247 L14.
Like Galerie Asbæk (*see below*), Susanne Ottesen represents the established generation of contemporary artists. The gallery opened back in 1989 and has had an impressive string of exhibitions, including Per Kirkeby, Kirsten Ortwed, Cindy Sherman and Kehnet Nielsen.

Galleri Tom Christoffersen
Skindergade 5 (33 91 76 10/www.christoffersen art.dk). **Open** noon-6pm Wed, Thur; noon-8pm Fri; noon-3pm Sat. **No credit cards. Map** p251 N13.
Tom Christoffersen's gallery positions itself right at the very heart of the Scandinavian contemporary art scene. It aims to work with the youngest, most forward-thinking artists on the international scene, and does so by putting on roughly ten exhibitions every year. **Photo** *p177.*

Galleri Veggerby
Ny Østergade 34 (70 20 31 11/www.galleri veggerby.dk) **Open** 11.30am-5.30pm Tue-Fri; 11am-3pm Sat. **Credit** MC, V. **Map** p251 M15.
Jens Veggerby used to be a professional cyclist in both the Tour de France and Giro d'Italia until his dream to own a professional gallery took centre stage. This gallery was established in conjunction with art historian Helle Kamvig, and has been instrumental in promoting artists both established and upcoming.

Galerie Asbæk/Martin Asbæk Projects
Bredgade 20 (40 75 86 16/www.asbaek.dk/ www.maprojects.dk). **Open** 11am-6pm Mon-Fri; 11am-4pm Sat. **Credit** AmEx, DC, MC, V. **Map** p249 K16.
Since its inception in 1975, Asbæk has been one of Denmark's leading galleries. Patricia and Jacob Asbæk have collected an impressive stable of modern artists and their prices are commensurately high, with works easily running up to 100,000kr. In the gallery's shop, graphic works, books and posters, as well as international art magazines, line the walls. Martin Asbæk Projects is an independent extension of the gallery, working exclusively with the younger artists represented.

Galerie Birthe Laursen
Bredgade 30 (33 36 27 07/www.birthelaursen.com). **Open** noon-6pm Wed-Fri; 10am-4pm Sat. **Credit** AmEx, MC, V. **Map** p249 L16.
In 1997 Birthe Laursen opened her first gallery in Paris, and in 2003 expanded her activities in Copenhagen. She presents Danish contemporary art from both established and upcoming artists across the disciplines of photography, sculpture, painting

Galerie Asbæk.

and graphics. Moreover, the gallery also exhibits international contemporary art alongside its sister gallery in Paris.

Galerie Mikael Andersen
Bredgade 63 (33 33 05 12/www.gma.dk). **Open** noon-6pm Tue-Fri; 11am-3pm Sat. **No credit cards.** Map p249 K17.
Mikael Andersen opened in 1989 and is now a major force in the Copenhagen art scene, representing a number of artists who debuted in the mid 1980s and who have gone on to become internationally significant across the art world. Works on show come from the likes of Kaspar Bonnén, Mogens Andersen, Günther Förg, Poul Gernes and Øivind Nygård.

Kunstforeningen
Gammel Strand 48 (33 36 02 60/www.kunst foreningen.dk). **Open** 11am-5pm Tue, Thur-Sun; 11am-8pm Wed. **Admission** 45kr; 15kr-30kr concessions; free under-16s. **Credit** DC, MC, V. Map p251 N14.
Kunstforeningen was built in 1825 and has been an institution in Danish art ever since. With five exhibitions a year, it focuses its attention on presenting shows reflecting on our age, often through retrospectives or by importing group shows from abroad.

Nikolaj – Copenhagen Contemporary Art Center
Nikolaj Plads 10 (33 18 17 80/www.nikolaj-ccac.dk). **Open** noon-5pm daily. **Admission** 20kr; 10kr concessions; free under-15s and all Wed. **No credit cards.** Map p251 N14.
The former Sankt Nikolaj Kirke has long been associated with contemporary art. Carlsberg Brewery founder Carl Jacobsen turned the church into a cultural centre in 1917 and it was the location of a number of avant-garde happenings during the 1960s, including some of Fluxus's first international performances. With a small permanent collection and four exhibition spaces, Nikolaj certainly has room for the constant flow of (mostly group) shows that pass through its doors. Fluxus artist Eric Andersen created a fascinating permanent installation here, the Crying Room, which is adorned with all kinds of things that can make you cry (onions, needles, etc).

Peter Lav Photo Gallery
Sankt Peders Stræde 51 (28 80 23 93/www.pl gallery.dk). **Open** 5-7pm Thur; noon-6pm Fri; noon-3pm Sat. **Credit** MC, V. Map p250 N12.
This is the first gallery in Copenhagen to focus exclusively on contemporary photography. Peter Lav's exhibition space profiles both up-and-coming and more established photographers.

Christianshavn

Frederiks Bastion
Refshalevej 80 (32 57 08 51/www.nordenifokus.dk). Bus 48, then 5min walk. **Open** noon-5pm Tue, Thur-Sun; noon-7pm Wed. **Admission** 20kr; 10kr concessions. **No credit cards.** Map p253 M21.

My Copenhagen
Marco Evaristti

Chilean-born artist Marco Evaristti became a household name in Denmark after putting live goldfish in working food blenders as part of the group show 'Eyegoblack' in 2000. He didn't press the 'on' button, but a visitor to the show did and the gallery director was charged with animal cruelty. He was later acquitted. Since then, Evaristti has painted an iceberg red, covered Strøget in a red carpet and made meatballs from his own surgically removed fat – 'polpette al grasso di Marco'.

'If I had to be a tourist in my own city, I would go for brunch in **Nyhavn**, to watch people moving around and to be near the water. Afterwards I'd visit **Charlottenborg Udstillingsbygning** (Academy of Art; *see* p177) on Kongens Nytorv; I studied art there and it was my home for seven years, so I'd go and see an exhibition in the gallery. I'd have lunch in the Academy's canteen, which is where I used to go when I was a student – the chef is a Spanish woman who prepares great organic food.

'Then I'd take a walk to **Nørreport**, except I wouldn't go along Strøget; instead I'd walk along the little side streets, which are full of second-hand clothes and record shops. From there I would go on to **Nørrebrogade**, because the subculture is more interesting there now than in Vesterbro. Vesterbro has become too fancy for me – it just takes concepts from other places and imports it, while Nørrebro still has a soul.

'For a romantic evening, I would start off with a movie at the **Imperial** (*see* p176) with its large screen, and then go to eat in one of the city's many Thai restaurants. I don't have a particular favourite, but I love Thai food and the beautiful way it's presented. I'd have a nostalgic drink at one of the cafés I used to go to when I was younger, and finish with dancing at **Luux** (Nørregade 41, 33 13 67 88, www.luux.dk); it's a good place to go after midnight.

'Though most people seem to prefer Copenhagen in the summer, I like wintertime. In winter, people move very quickly and the city is empty – you can see every little detail of the architecture.'

Arts & Entertainment

Frederiks Bastion is one of a series of bastions, built in 1744 to defend the city against (usually British) naval attack. Now that Admiral Nelson has disembarked this life, it's been turned into a gallery with a large permanent collection and various temporary exhibitions, concentrating on Nordic art in a wide variety of styles.

Overgaden

Overgaden Neden Vandet 17 (32 57 72 73/www. overgaden.org). Metro Christianshavn/bus 2A. **Open** 1-5pm Tue, Wed, Fri-Sun; 1-8pm Thur. **No credit cards. Map** p252 P16.
Overgaden is a two-floor open exhibition space for younger experimental artists. A three-person committee has the thankless task of panning through hundreds of applications for artistic gold, but the shows it selects often strike the motherlode.

Islands Brygge

Andersen S Contemporary

Islands Brygge 43 (46 97 84 37/www.andersen-s.dk). Metro Islands Brygge/bus 33, 34, 40. **Open** noon-5pm Tue-Fri; 11am-3pm Sat. **No credit cards.**
Situated right on the habour of Islands Brygge, this gallery features the most succesful Danish artist in recent years, Olafur Eliasson, alongside works by many of his national contemporaries and the occasional international exhibition.

Galleri Christina Wilson

Sturlasgade 12H (32 54 52 06/www. christinawilson.net). Metro Islands Brygge/ bus 40. **Open** noon-5pm Tue-Fri; noon-3pm Sat. **No credit cards.**
This gallery deals in installations, photography and paintings by emerging Danish and foreign artists. Wilson's mission is to present a range of ambitious international shows.

Galleri Nicolai Wallner

Njalsgade 21, Building 15 (32 57 09 70/www. nicolaiwallner.com). Metro Islands Brygge/bus 33, 40. **Open** noon-5pm Tue-Fri; noon-3pm Sat. **No credit cards.**
This is one of the most significant contemporary art galleries in Copenhagen. Wallner changed the art scene here in the early 1990s, and a large stable of artists make sure it remains both important and relevant. Definitely worth getting aboard the Metro and paying a visit to the suburbs.

Vesterbro & Valby

Bendixen Contemporary Art

4th floor, Carl Jacobsensvej 20 (36 16 03 25/ www.bendixen-art.dk). Train to Valby. **Open** noon-5pm Tue-Fri; 11am-2pm Sat. **No credit cards.**
As part of the thriving new art district that has grown up in Valby, Bendixen focuses on young Danish and international artists working across a variety of media.

Graffitigalleriet.dk

Vesterbrogade 171 (26 18 12 27/www.graffiti galleriet.dk). **Open** 4-7pm Thur-Fri; 1-5pm Sat. **No credit cards. Map** p245 R6.
As the name implies, it's all about graffiti and the mission to spread the word regarding this most misunderstood of urban art forms.

Helene Nyborg Contemporary

Entrance 6, 2nd floor, Carl Jacobsens Vej 16 (36 45 23 07/www.helenenyborg.com). Train to Valby. **Open** noon-5pm Tue-Fri; noon-3pm Sat, or by appointment. **No credit cards.**
Helene Nyborg's gallery was established in 2006 within this giant industrial estate, which rightly claims to represent the cutting edge of Copenhagen's art scene. The gallery pushes a mix of funky and futuristic creations from an army of young artists including Kalim Yoon, Peter Rune Christiansen and Peter Callesen.

Mogadishni

Entrance 6, 3rd floor, Carl Jacobsens Vej 16 (32 54 35 35/www.mogadishni.com). Train to Valby. **Open** 11am-4pm Tue-Fri; noon-3pm Sat, or by appointment. **No credit cards.**
Mogadishni is an ultra-modern space hosting long-term exhibitions of contemporary art. The gallery was established by students from the Jutland Art Academy in a shrewd move to give their own art a showcase in Copenhagen. In 2001 Christian Chapelle took over the space, which is now used to profile the best in cutting-edge Danish artists such as Julie Nord and Fie Norsker.

Øksnehallen

Halmtorvet 11 (33 86 04 00/www.oeksnehallen.dk). **Open** times vary, depending on exhibition. **Credit** MC, V. **Map** p250 Q10.
This was once the largest slaughterhouse in town but, after many dormant years, it was turned into a cultural centre in 1996. At a massive 5,000sq m (53,700sq ft), Øksnehallen is ideal for larger events, such as trade shows and conventions. Exhibitions tend to concentrate on photography and design.

Nørrebro & Østerbro

Galleri Grønlund

Birketoften 16A, Værløse (44 44 27 98/www.glass art.dk). Bus 165. **Open** by appointment; phone for details. **No credit cards.**
The only gallery in Copenhagen specialising solely in glass art, and housing both a permanent collection and a showroom with moderately priced work for sale. A new branch of Galleri Grønlund is due to open in the heart of Copenhagen in 2007.

Galerie Pi

Dag Hammerskjölds Allé 33 (35 43 82 84/www. galeriepi.dk). Bus 1A, 15. **Open** 10am-5.30pm Mon-Fri; 10am-2pm Sat. **No credit cards. Map** p247 G14.
A small contemporary gallery focusing on sculpture, graphics and ceramics.

Gay & Lesbian

Proof, if proof were needed, that size isn't everything.

Denmark is so tolerant of same-sex relationships that there hasn't been much need for specialised venues. The result is a gay and lesbian scene that more than makes up for its diminutive size with an overwhelming air of warmth and openness that few cities can match.

Nor is this a nation dragging its heels when it comes to promoting gay culture. In 2009 Denmark will be hosting the gay and lesbian sporting Outgames; there's also **Copenhagen Pride** in August (www.copenhagenpride.dk) and the annual **Gay and Lesbian Film Festival** in October (www.cglff.dk).

For an excellent English overview of gay life in Copenhagen, visit **www.copenhagen-gay-life.dk**, **www.out-and-about.dk** and **www.gayguide.dk**.

Organisations

Landsforeningen for Bøsser og Lesbiske (LBL) – Danish National Association of Gays & Lesbians

Teglgårdsstræde 13, Baghuset, 1452 Copenhagen K (33 13 19 48/www.lbl.dk). **Open** *Phone enquiries* 11am-3pm Mon-Fri. **Map** p250 M12.
Denmark's national gay and lesbian association was founded in 1948, and prides itself on being at the vanguard of gay politics. The LBL publishes *PAN*,

a free monthly magazine that is available at most gay venues and provides information on gay events, as well as running an English-language website.

Stop Aids

Amagertorv 33, 1160 Copenhagen K (33 11 29 11/ www.stopaids.dk). **Open** *Phone enquiries* 10am-4pm Mon-Fri. **Map** p251 N14.
Stop Aids has been promoting safe sex in Denmark since 1986. Its refreshing approach has included putting up condom-and-lube compartments in cruising parks, offering numerous free workshops and courses, distributing safe sex kits in gay bars and larger one-off parties, and offering free massages in exchange for a chat about safe sex.

Bars & clubs

Admission is free unless otherwise stated.

Amigo Bar

Schønbergsgade 4, Frederiksberg (33 21 49 15). Bus 6A, 14. **Open** 10pm-6am daily. **No credit cards. Map** p245 P8.
Amigo attracts an unpretentious mix of gay men, lesbians and straights. A bit of a trek to get to, but then it is one of the very few karaoke venues in town, with plenty of late-night singalongs catering to off-key amateurs. Be prepared for a late one as things only start to hot up around midnight.

Oscar Bar & Café.

BLUS at Studenterhuset
Købmagergade 52 (35 32 38 60/www.blus.dk).
Open *Sept-June* 8pm-1am Tue. **No credit cards.**
Map p251 M13.
Gay students meet weekly for Tuesday GayDay, although you don't have to be studying to join in with the laidback poetry readings, political discussions, lectures and music performances. Biannual gay parties pack the place to the rafters.

BOIZ
Magstræde 12-14 (33 14 52 70/www.boiz.dk). **Open** *May-Aug* 11am-2am Mon-Thur, Sun; 11am-5am Fri, Sat. *Sept-Apr* 4pm-2am Mon-Thur; 4pm-5am Fri; noon-5am Sat; noon-2am Sun. **Credit** AmEx, DC, MC, V. **Map** p251 O13.
Copenhagen's largest gay bar/café/restaurant combines a relaxed vibe with weekly drag shows. Cheap shots, a fun crowd and good-looking bar staff virtually guarantee a decent night out.

Café Intime
Allégade 25, Frederiksberg (38 34 19 58/www.cafe intime.dk). Metro Frederiksberg. **Open** 6pm-2am daily. **No credit cards.**
This pint-sized but eminently popular piano bar has been around since 1920, and these days draws everyone from older Marlene Dietrich obsessives to younger jazz connoisseurs.

Centralhjørnet
Kattesundet 18 (33 11 85 49/www.central hjornet.dk). **Open** noon-2am daily. **No credit cards.** **Map** p250 N12.
Copenhagen's most famous gay bar has been around for more than a century, offering a friendly pub atmosphere that's popular with everyone from the local 'countessa' to gay carpenters downing a pint or three after work. Holidays see the owner's notorious taste for wild decoation come to the fore.

Chaca
Studiestræde 39 (33 73 10 20/www.chaca.dk).
Open 4pm-midnight Thur; 4pm-5am Fri, Sat.
No credit cards. **Map** p250 N12.
This is Copenhagen's latest lesbian bar, café and restaurant. The owner has created a warm, well-lit meeting place combining music, drinking and dancing over two intimate floors.

Cosy Bar
Studiestræde 24 (33 12 74 27/www.cosybar.dk).
Open 10pm-6am Mon-Thur, Sun; 10pm-8am Fri, Sat.
No credit cards. **Map** p250 N12.
If you're still out and about after a long evening on the town, chances are you'll end up in this dark, boisterous and cruise-oriented bar, where the tiny dancefloor gets ridiculously packed at weekends.

Jailhouse Copenhagen
Studiestræde 12 (33 15 22 55/www.jailhouse cph.dk). **Open** *Bar* 2pm-2am Mon-Thur, Sun; 2pm-5am Fri, Sat. *Restaurant* 6pm-midnight Thur-Sat (kitchen closes 11pm). **Credit** AmEx, DC, MC, V.
Map p250 N12.
This two-level gay bar and restaurant is decorated with prison bars and jail-related paraphernalia. Not nearly as hardcore as it sounds, the downstairs bar is noted for being surprisingly relaxed. As a bonus, staff are friendly and easygoing, despite being dressed in full prison guard regalia.

Men's Bar
Teglgårdsstræde 3 (33 12 73 03/www.mens bar.dk). **Open** 3pm-2am daily. **No credit cards.**
Map p250 N12.
The only real men's bar on the scene: jeans, semi-leather, dimly lit. You know the sort of thing.

Never Mind
Nørre Voldgade 2 (33 11 88 86/www.nevermind bar.dk). **Open** 10pm-6am daily. **Credit** AmEx, DC, MC, V. **Map** p250 N11.
A lively bar churning out pop and disco hits to a mainly male crowd with late-night revellers tending to bounce between this place and Cosy. Being situated just across from Copenhagen's cruisiest park boosts its appeal dramatically.

Oscar Bar & Café
Rådhuspladsen 77 (33 12 09 99/www.oscarbar cafe.dk). **Open** noon-2am daily. **Credit** MC, V.
Map p250 O12.
Take some sexy bartenders, mix with reliable café food and garnish with talented DJs spinning some of the funkiest house and dirtiest disco around, and you're some way to understanding the popularity of Oscar. The atmosphere here is trendy but laidback, and people-watching is always at the top of the menu, making this a must for both first-timers and seasoned pros in Copenhagen.

PAN Disco
Knabrostræde 3 (33 11 19 50/www.pan-cph.dk).
Open 11pm-5am Fri; 11pm-6am Sat. **Credit** AmEx, DC, MC, V. **Map** p251 N13.

Copenhagen's number one gay club also happens to be the hottest three-floor, five-level affair in town. The main floor plays house beats, the second blasts out cheesy euro-pop and the top floor is home to a popular karaoke bar. Things tend to really warm up after midnight.

Events

For details of the **Copenhagen Gay & Lesbian Film Festival** and **Copenhagen Pride**, *see chapter* **Festivals & Events**.

Fitness & sauna

Amigo Sauna

Studiestræde 31 (33 15 20 28/www.amigo-sauna.dk). **Open** noon-7am Mon-Thur, Sun; noon-8am Fri, Sat. **Credit** MC, V. **Map** p250 N12.
Copenhagen's largest gay sauna is very dark, very lively and definitely a place for some serious action, especially on weekends.

Copenhagen Gay Center

Istedgade 34-36 (www.copenhagengaycenter.dk). **Open** 10am-1am Sun-Thur; 10am-3am Fri, Sat. **No credit cards.** **Map** p250 P10.
A small sauna and gay shop in Copenhagen's red light district complete with an intimate cinema for gay film screenings.

Frederiksberg Svømmehal

Helgesvej 29, Frederiksberg (38 14 04 00/ www.frederiksbergsvoemmehal.dk). Metro *Frederiksberg.* **Open** 7am-9pm Mon-Fri; 7am-4pm Sat; 9am-4pm Sun. **Admission** 30kr; 125kr incl aromabath, massage chair, Turkish bath & jacuzzi. *Sauna* 42kr. **Credit** AmEx, DC, MC, V.
Indoor public swimming venues are popular among gays as rumours about cruisy shower rooms abound. While the reality doesn't reflect the rumours, the cruising did become sufficiently notable that signs were posted up in the shower rooms encouraging 'proper behaviour'.

Where to stay

Carsten's Guest House

5th floor, Christians Brygge 28, Slotsholmen, 1559 Copenhagen V (33 14 91 07/www.carstensguest house.dk). **Rates** 165kr dormitory; 395kr-450kr single; 495kr-550kr double; 750kr-1,250kr studio or apartment. **Credit** MC, V. **Map** p251 Q14.
Queens will definitely fall in love with this gay and lesbian guest house: from the outside, it looks just like a cake castle; inside, it's a luxurious (but surprisingly affordable) B&B. Past guests have only good things to say about the amiable proprietors and their warm, personal service.
Non-smoking rooms. Parking. TV.

Copenhagen Rainbow

4th Floor, Frederiksberggade 25C, Strøget, 1459 Copenhagen K (33 14 10 20/fax 33 14 10 25/ www.copenhagen-rainbow.dk). **Rates** 675kr-850kr single; 750kr-940kr double. **Credit** AmEx, DC, MC, V. **Map** p250 O12.
This friendly gay penthouse B&B opened in summer 2000 and has proved very popular thanks to its prime location, right on Strøget and in the heart of the gay district.
Non-smoking rooms. TV.

PAN Disco. See p182.

Arts & Entertainment

Nightlife

From superclubs to seedy cellar jazz joints.

For such a small city, Copenhagen's nightlife is surprisingly vibrant. Sure, there isn't the same diverse range of sub-cultural 'scenes' that flourish in other European capitals – crate-digging audiophiles are largely notable by their absence – but various forms of electronic music are well represented, with top-name international DJs being regularly booked at clubs such as Culture Box, Rust and Vega.

First-time visitors, however, may initially find Copenhagen's party scene a little elusive. There are a few superb clubs and a multitude of über-stylish venues packed with armies of attractive punters, but the best nights are mainly promoter- rather than venue-led, which means that it's possible to turn up randomly on an off-night even at some of the more dedicated clubs – including **Rust** (*see p188*), **Vega** (*see p188*) and **Stengade 30** (*see p188*) – and find the place a little lacking in atmosphere.

That said, there are a few safe bets when it comes to long-running nights, like Stengade's Rub-a-Dub Sundays and Rust's MidWeek Brakes on a Wednesday (*see p187*), both of which guarantee a good night out.

As with everywhere else this side of the millennium, Copenhagen is experiencing a blurring of the boundaries in terms of pre-clubbing restaurant, café, bar and lounge venues that don't fit into the typical club mould, but which can be equally worthy of a night out in themselves. **Boutique Lize** (*see p186*), **Barbarellah** (*see below*) and **Gefährlich** (*see p186*) are just a few such hybrids, where it's as easy to throw down a few cocktails before heading elsewhere as it is to spend the whole evening partying if you don't have the inclination to move on.

PRACTICALITIES

Due to the price of alcohol, locals usually don't get going until late, preferring to pre-party at home, so don't expect to hang with the hipperati before midnight. Luckily, there is a plethora of places to begin the night and once they get started, many clubs and large bars stay open until 5am on Friday and Saturday nights.

The places listed here are the city's main nightlife venues, but it's also worth checking the local press for updates on regular nights and one-offs. The best online resource in English for venues, cafés and bars is **www.aok.dk**. For up-to-date information on forthcoming events, check out the *Copenhagen Post* – a Danish newspaper in English, available from kiosks and cafés – as well as *Citadel*, which is a free Danish-language listings paper.

For more regular visitors, **Human Productions** (www.humanwebsite.com), a group of organisers, artists and party people, sends out a weekly email that keeps a finger on the pulse of underground art, culture and nightlife events, while the Danish website **www.hifly.dk** puts flyers for electronic and house music up on its calendar. As always, record stores are another good place to pick up flyers, as are funky clothing stores: check out Amoeba Records on Hyskenstræde and Wasteland clothing store on Studiestræde.

Finally, a word about stimulant use: it may not be as rampant as in other European capital cities, but toilets without lids and one-in-a-cubicle policies demonstrate that it's definitely present. Remember that security do search for drugs and will expel you immediately if they find any.

Pre-clubbing & lounges

Barbarellah

Nørre Farimagsgade 41 (33 32 00 61/www. barbarellah.dk). **Open** 4pm-2am Mon; noon-2am Tue-Thur; noon-4am Fri, Sat. **Admission** free. **Credit** AmEx, DC, MC, V. **Map** p250 M11.
Right in the heart of the boho Nansensgade quarter, Barbarellah is a large, friendly café lounge-cum-cocktail bar, with good vibes and DJs dropping beats until the small hours. Owner Barbara also sells her own designer clothes and fully customised Danish furniture in the shop next door.

Bar Rouge

Hotel Skt Petri, Krystalgade 22 (33 45 98 22/ www.sktpetri.com/barrouge). **Open** 4pm-1am Mon-Thur, Sun; 4pm-2am Fri, Sat. **Admission** free. **Credit** AmEx, DC, MC, V. **Map** p251 M13.
Hosting everything from the main MTV Music Awards after-party to regular gatherings of top-end model agencies, it's all been happening at Hotel Skt Petri, and that's probably all thanks to the svelte trappings of Bar Rouge. It's good to note that members and hotel guests have priority when it comes to entry, although a timely email can usually secure a much coveted place on the guestlist even on a weekend. Music-wise, evenings ususally start with a bit of Buddha Bar chill and work their way up to Ibiza-style house.

Rust. *See p188.*

Boutique Lize

Enghave Plads 6 (33 31 15 60). **Open** 8pm-midnight
Wed; 8pm-2am Thur; 8pm-4am Fri, Sat. **Admission**
free. **No credit cards**. **Map** p245 S7.
Boutique Lize is one of the best cocktail bars in the
city, with queues of people trying to get in from
11pm onwards. It attracts a lot of the area's more
mature trendsetters with its hip Vesterbro ambience
and reasonably priced cocktails.

Café Bopa

*Løgstørgade 8, Østerbro (35 43 05 66/www.cafe
bopa.dk). Bus 1A, 14.* **Open** 10am-midnight
Mon-Wed, Sun; 10am-2am Thur; 10am-5am Fri,
Sat. **Admission** free. **Credit** DC, MC, V. **Map**
p248 B14.
A friendly café, bar and restaurant popular with
trendy locals. Disco and mainstream dance comprise
the tunes of choice, and in summer the café spills out
on to leafy Bopa Plads, where there are deckchairs,
rugs and games of pétanque.

Gefährlich

*Fælledvej 7, Nørrebro (35 24 13 24/www.gefahrlich.
dk). Bus 5A.* **Open** 5pm-1am Tue, Sun; 5pm-2am
Wed; 5pm-3am Thur-Sat. **Admission** free. **Credit**
MC, V. **Map** p248 J10.
Gefährlich (German for 'dangerous') claims to be a
restaurant, bar, art gallery, coffee shop, record
store, cultural centre and nightclub all rolled into
one. It may sound a bit over-conceptualised and
ambitious, but in reality it's a rather small, low-key
affair with an eclectic programme of regular and
one-off events, including a rare soul night on the
first Saturday of every month.

Ideal Bar

*Enghavevej 40, Vesterbro (33 25 70 11/www.
vega.dk). Bus 3A, 6A, 10.* **Open** 7pm-4am Wed;
7pm-5am Thur-Sat. **Admission** free. **No credit
cards**. **Map** p245 S7.
Part of the Vega complex (*see p188*), this classic
lounge bar is ideal for pre-club drinks or even
after-partying (the Peaches and Chicks on Speed
after-event parties have been recent highlights).
Thursdays are especially popular, with regular
night HipHopKontoret (Hip Hop Office) guaranteed
to pull in the beat junkies, while Fridays cater to the
rock and indie kids and other nights see everything
from Latin grooves to funk or reggae.

Oak Room

*Birkegade 10, Nørrebro (38 60 38 60/www.
oakroom.dk). Bus 5A.* **Open** 7pm-midnight
Tue; 7pm-2am Wed, Thur; 5pm-2am Fri, Sat.
Admission free. **No credit cards**. **Map**
p248 J10.
A tiny, stylish lounge bar tucked around the corner
from trendy Sankt Hans Torv, the Oak Room is literally that: a single, narrow room dominated by a
huge wooden bar. When it's packed (which seems to
be every weekend), it's very hard to sit in the little
wooden booths opposite the bar without getting
your drinks knocked over by passers-by; for some,
however, this seems to be a legitimate means for
meeting members of the opposite sex.

Stereo Bar

Linnésgade 16A (33 13 61 13/www.stereobar.dk).
Open 4pm-3am Wed-Sat. **Admission** free. **Credit**
DC, MC, V. **Map** p246 L12.

Lakeside love action at **Søpavillionen**'s Saturday meat market. *See p188*.

Dance nation

In addition to the venues listed, there are some established promoter-led nights that have stood the test of time and are as worth hunting down as any individual club or bar, assuming you're in the right place at the right time (venues vary, so check the websites for details of forthcoming events).

Backstreet Northern Soul
www.copenhagen-soul.dk.
A monthly soul night offering rare grooves for more discerning music lovers – a little self-consciously 'bijou', perhaps, but mercifully low on drunken pervs.

Copenhagen Distortion
www.cphdistortion.dk.
Started out by hosting mobile raves in unusual locations (buses and boats, for example), but has since grown into a week-long festival of music and conceptual art every June, with occasional one-off parties throughout the year.

Kill Your Telly
www.killyourtelly.dk.
Currently hosts Copenhagen's hottest electro parties, with a genuine blend of rave and street cultures, at Culture Box, Rust, Vega and Distortion.

Lækker Lytter
www.ghettoblaster.dk.
Lækker Lytter's 'mobile love sound system' is powered by car batteries and mounted on a bike – they've even built a dodgy raft, allowing them to host gigs on Copenhagen's canals – and their mainly outdoor events are promoted by text message and email less than 24 hours before taking place.

Midweek Brakes
www.midweekbrakes.dk.
A hugely successful night dedicated to electro, hip hop, breakbeat and drum 'n' bass for a youthful crowd of B-boys and fly girls. Takes place every Wednesday at Rust.

After a change of owners, this long-time cornerstone of Copenhagen revelry is attempting a mini revival with a new programme of nights to bring in the punters. With its retro decor and 1960s lighting fixtures, the venue is modish without being pretentious and underground without being oppressive.

Zoo Bar
Kronprinsensgade 7 (33 15 68 69). **Open** 11am-midnight Mon-Wed; 11am-2am Thur-Sat. **Admission** free. **Credit** MC, V. **Map** P251 M14.
It might no longer be the most fashionable bar in town, but Zoo is still a popular central spot to meet and warm up with a few drinks before heading out clubbing, and it occasionally throws a decent party in its own right. It's intimate (read: small) and the superb window seats are perfect for a spot of people-watching on trendy Kronprinsensgade.

Clubs

Celcius
Rådhuspladsen 16, 1st Floor (70 33 35 55/ www.celcius.dk). **Open** 11pm-5am Fri, Sat. **Admission** 60kr-150kr. **Credit** AmEx, DC, MC, V. **Map** p250 O12.
With amazing views down over the main square of Rådhuspladsen, Copenhagen's answer to Piccadilly Circus, Celcius is the latest club to hit the city centre and was already garnering a painfully trendy crowd of regulars at the time of going to press. That said, Celcius's craving for glamour could ultimately be its downfall.

Culture Box
Kronprinsessegade 54A (33 32 50 50/www.culture-box.com). **Open** from 8pm Thur (closing time depends on event); 8pm-5am Fri, Sat. **Admission** 30kr-80kr. **No credit cards**. **Map** p247 K15.
Copenhagen's premier techno palace regularly plays host to DJ legends like Derrick May and Jeff Mills. The sound system has by far the most penetrating bass in town, the VJ shows are superb and the more sedate downstairs dancefloor is perfect for hipsters who don't want to sweat for hours on the main floor of 'the Box'.

Emma
Lille Kongensgade 16 (33 11 20 20/www.emma.dk). **Open** 11pm-5am Thur-Sat. **Admission** 60kr Thur; 70kr Fri; 80kr Sat. **Credit** AmEx, DC, MC, V. **Map** p251 M15.
Located close to Kongens Nytorv in the city centre, this spacious non-smoking bar, restaurant and club caters to more mainstream partygoers who just want to dance the night away to pop classics.

NASA
Boltens Gård, Kongens Nytorv (33 93 74 15/ www.nasa.dk). **Open** midnight-6am Fri, Sat. **Admission** 100kr, subject to doorman's discretion. **Credit** AmEx, DC, MC, V. **Map** p251 M15.
A long time ago (in a galaxy far, far away), NASA supposedly represented the cream of the cream of Copenhagen clubbing. These days that accolade seems to refer only to the bio-morphic, all-white interior, inspired by the glamour of space travel and

Arts & Entertainment

Stanley Kubrick's sanitised visions of the future. While it used to be a members-only nightspot with a reputation for being even harder to get into than a pair of hotpants, the trendy patina has worn off and it's now a far less discriminatory venue, swearing instead by a policy of 'massclusivity': namely, if you can afford to pay for a table there, then you're in. Nevertheless, NASA remains one of the most amazing-looking clubs in the world, with some nights – including those hosted by party legend Jean Eric von Baden – that are still good enough to eclipse the air of studied self-consciousness.

Park Café
Østerbrogade 79, Østerbro (35 42 62 48/www.
parkcafe.dk). Bus 6A, 14, 15, 650S. **Open** 11pm-
4am Thur; 11pm-5am Fri, Sat. **Admission** 70kr.
Credit DC, MC, V. **Map** P248 B13.
With three dancefloors, a restaurant and a capacity of 2,000, it's not surprising that Park attracts a more mature, dressed-up crowd. From Thursday to Saturday (after the restaurant closes), the whole venue turns into a nightclub, featuring mainstream house, pop and R&B.

Rust
Guldbergsgade 8, Nørrebro (35 24 52 00/www.
rust.dk). Bus 5A. **Open** 9pm-5am Wed-Sat.
Admission 50kr Wed; 30kr Thur (free with student card); 50kr Fri, Sat; prices vary according to events. **Credit** DC, MC, V. **Map** p246 H10.
Rust is one of the city's best venues for both concerts and clubbing, and an integral part of Copenhagen's nightlife. Its evolution over the years (from political café through to dubious rock club and finally the more polished venue seen today) is all the more impressive for its retention of an experimental edge and an ability to roll with the times.
The small cocktail bar, Living Room, is a minimalist interpretation of a 1970s lounge, complete with groovy low seating, mellow lighting and a chilled ambience. There's also the sweaty downstairs area, Bassment, living up to its name with plenty of growling beats. **Photo** *p185*.

Søpavillionen
Gyldenløvesgade 24 (33 15 12 24/www.
soepavillionen.dk). **Open** 10pm-5am Fri; 9pm-
5am Sat. **Admission** 90kr-125kr. **Credit** MC, V.
Map p246 M10.
This beautiful white pavilion on the lake holds one of the meatiest Saturday night meat markets in town: a seventh heaven for divorced thirtysomethings looking to groove to innocuous pop hits. The building, designed by architect Vilhelm Dahlerup in the 1890s, is spectacular, especially when it's lit up at night. **Photo** *p186*.

Stengade 30
Stengade 30 (35 36 09 38/www.stengade30.dk).
Bus 5A, 69, 250S. **Open** 9pm-2am Tue, Wed;
9pm-5am Thur; 10pm-5am Fri, Sat. **Admission** varies. **No credit cards**. **Map** p248 K9.
Part live music venue and part club, Stengade's no-frills decor and eclectic booking policy give it an unpretentious outlaw feel with a charmingly scruffy atmosphere (although some might argue that it's becoming a little too worn around the edges for its own good). Nights here cover everything from raw, trashy rock and electro-clash through to hip hop, jazz and some serious reggae and dancehall, so don't expect just to roll up randomly and find your scene.

Vega
Enghavevej 40, Vesterbro (33 25 70 11/www.
vega.dk). Bus 3A, 10, 16. **Open** 11pm-5am Fri, Sat.
Admission 60kr (free before 1am). **Credit** MC, V.
Map p245 S7.
Vega, opened in 1996, is the queen of Copenhagen's nightlife, a listed landmark building featuring a large and small concert hall (1,200 and 550 capacity respectively), the latter of which doubles up as a

Vega.

nightclub, plus a lounge and cocktail bar, the Yankee Bar and the street-level Ideal Bar, a party institution in itself. The list of famous names to have played at Vega in recent years is a testament to its popularity, from secret gigs by Prince and David Bowie to concerts from the likes of Björk. The interior is superb, the service hugely professional and the array of resident DJs among the best in town.

Music venues

See also *p187* **Clubs**.

Jazz, blues & folk

Copenhagen JazzHouse
Niels Hemmingsens Gade 10 (33 15 26 00/www. jazzhouse.dk). **Open** *Concerts* 6pm-5am Thur-Sat; open when concerts on Mon-Wed, Sun. *Club* JazzHouse midnight-5am Thur-Sat. **Admission** *Club* JazzHouse free Thur; 60kr after midnight Fri, Sat. *Concerts* prices vary. **Credit** AmEx, DC, MC, V. **Map** p251 M13.
The JazzHouse builds on the legacy of the legendary but long gone Copenhagen Montmartre jazz club of the 1960s. Now the country's premier jazz venue, JazzHouse is subsidised by the government and showcases both international and local musicians. It offers consistently good gigs on Thursdays, Fridays and Saturdays (and sometimes on other nights of the week) throughout the year. When concerts finish, the large downstairs dancefloor is filled by a younger disco-loving crowd, while famous VIPs can occasionally be spotted in the upstairs bar area.

La Fontaine
Kompagnistræde 11 (33 11 60 98/www.lafontaine. dk). **Open** 8pm-5am daily. **Admission** free Mon-Thur, Sun; 50kr Fri, Sat. **No credit cards**. **Map** p251 O13.

Though it has a capacity of only 60 people, this cosy, dingy and low-key jazz venue is well known for its legendary jam sessions and late, late nights. It attracts music students and other jazz lovers to its weekend swing and mainstream concerts, and also boasts one of the very few bars in town that are open until 5am every day of the week.

Mojo
Løngangstræde 21C (33 11 64 53/www.mojo.dk). **Open** 8pm-5am daily. **Admission** varies according to event. **No credit cards**. **Map** p251 O13.
Grubby but friendly little blues venue, featuring live entertainment every night.

Rock & pop

Amager Bio
Øresundsvej 6 (tickets 70 15 65 65/information 32 86 02 00/www.amagerbio.dk). Metro *Lergravsparken, then 5min walk*. **Open** varies according to event. **Admission** varies according to event. **No credit cards**.
One of the largest concert spaces in Copenhagen, with a capacity of 1,000. The programme is strong on old-school rock, blues and country.

Loppen
Christiania (32 57 84 22/www.loppen.dk). Metro *Christianshavn, then 5min walk*. **Open** 9pm-2am Mon-Thur, Sun; 10pm-3am Fri, Sat. **Admission** 50kr-150kr. **No credit cards**. **Map** p252 P18.
Since opening in 1973, Loppen has built an excellent reputation for live music despite its dilapidated surroundings, and its predilection for rock predates Copenhagen's rock revival. The booking policy is adventurous, covering the whole spectrum from jazz to rock, but with a strong emphasis on alternative sounds. Loppen is unconcerned with refinement, wallowing languorously in the unique environment of Copenhagen's former hippie enclave.

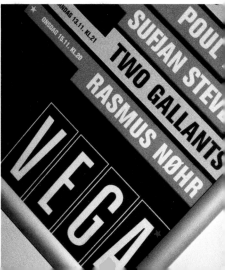

Performing Arts

The city is buzzing with cultural spaces – from an old beer factory to the imposing new opera house.

Classical Music & Opera

Copenhagen is known the world over for its jazz scene (*see chapter* **Nightlife**), but the city also has much to offer the classical music lover. Not only can you enjoy professional outfits like the **Danish National Symphony Orchestra**, but the seemingly limitless number of atmospheric churches offer a range of regular concerts.

ENSEMBLES

Foremost among the professional choirs is **Musica Ficta** (www.ficta.dk), a chamber choir led by composer and conductor Bo Holten and performing mostly Renaissance and contemporary music. **Camerata Chamber Choir** (www.camerata.dk), meanwhile, is one of Denmark's oldest; founded in 1965, it has attracted some of the best choral singers in the country, many of them students at the musical department of the University of Copenhagen. For something completely different, try **Concerto Copenhagen** (www.coco.dk), Scandinavia's leading baroque orchestra and one of the more interesting early music groups in Europe.

COMPETITIONS

Relative to its size, Denmark hosts an impressive range of competitions. The most important competition for conductors is named after Nikolai Malko, a conductor who brought the Danish National Symphony Orchestra to prominence after World War II. The **International Nikolai Malko Competition for Young Conductors** (www.malko.dk) happens every three years, with the next one due to take place in 2009.

In 2006 cellist Yo-Yo Ma won the coveted **Léonie Sonning Music Prize** – a $100,000 (£53,800) award given out annually to an internationally acknowledged composer, musician, conductor or singer. This prestigious prize has previously been given to artists such as Keith Jarrett, Leonard Bernstein, Gidon Kremer, Janet Baker and flautist **Michala Petri**. Petri, a grown-up child prodigy,

still occasionally plays in Copenhagen, so keep your eyes peeled as tickets are often hard to come by.

Other Danish singers and musicians to look out for include baritone **Bo Skovhus** (currently living in Vienna), soprano **Tina Kiberg** and tenor **Stig Fogh Andersen** (both world-renowned interpreters of Wagner), as well as the brilliant young violinist **Nikolaj Znaider**.

FESTIVALS

Copenhagen hosts a number of festivals. In the summer you can usually find organ festivals, a baroque festival and Tivoli Koncertsal's season of mini festivals (from April to September). Every other year national broadcaster Danmarks Radio puts on a competition for young ensembles and chamber musicians at the Danish Radio Concert Hall/Radiohusets Koncertsal, while the **Copenhagen Summer Festival** (www.copenhagensummerfestival.dk) is an annual showcase for both young talents and established names in the classical music world. The festival takes place in the Charlottenborg Festival Hall in Kongens Nytorv and boasts 15 concerts in 18 days, many with free admission.

Contact the **Wonderful Copenhagen Tourist Information Bureau** (70 22 24 42/www.visitcopenhagen.com) for further details of all the above, as well as information on its free Wednesday concert series, held at various venues at 5pm throughout the year.

Free publication *Copenhagen This Week* (www.ctw.dk) is a good source for regular listings of classical music events in English.

Major venues

The long-delayed **Danish Radio Concert Hall** in Ørestad, designed by architect Jean Nouvel, is due to be inaugurated in summer 2008, and looks set to become Scandinavia's top concert hall.

Black Diamond

Søren Kirkegaards Plads 1 (33 47 47 47/www.kb. dk). **Box office** 1hr before performances (or from BILLETnet 70 15 65 65). **No credit cards**. **Map** p250 P15.

The concert hall in the Black Diamond is panelled with Canadian maple and ornamented with black tapestries woven with quotations from Hans Christian Andersen's fairytales. The ensemble in residence plays six times a year, with a repertoire covering everything from modern classics and newly composed works to experiments in the borderlands between musical styles.

Radiohusets Koncertsal

Julius Thomsens Gade 1, Frederiksberg (35 20 62 62). Metro Forum/bus 2A, 68. **Box office** (DR-butikken, Julius Thomsens Gade 12) noon-5pm Mon-Wed, Fri; noon-6pm Thur; 11am-2pm Sat. **Credit** MC, V. **Map** p248 M9.

Every Thursday the beautiful Radio Concert Hall hosts a concert by one of Denmark's finest orchestras – the Danish National Symphony Orchestra (www.dr.dk/dnso) – which is also broadcast on radio (channel P2). There are also concerts on Fridays and Saturdays in the main hall, and smaller concerts in Studio 2 (Rosenørns Allé 22, 35 20 30 40/box office: Vesterbrogade 3, 35 20 62 62), which specialises in modern music.

Tivolis Koncertsal

Tivoli, Vesterbrogade 3 (Tivoli information line 33 15 10 01/ticket centre 33 15 10 12/www. tivoli.dk). **Box office** *Mid Apr-mid Sept, mid Nov-23 Dec* 11am-8pm daily. *Mid Sept-mid Nov, 24 Dec-mid Apr* 9am-5pm Mon-Fri. **Credit** MC, V. **Map** p250 P12.

Throughout summer (mid April to late September) there is jazz and other popular music in the various little pavilions dotted around the park, while the concerts in the Koncertsal vary from musicals to chamber music.

Other venues

Christianskirke

Strandgade 2 (32 54 15 76/www.christianskirke.dk). Metro Christianshavn/bus 2A, 19, 48, 350S. **No credit cards. Map** p252 P16.

Concerts in this 16th-century church cover the full spectrum of musical genres, from gospel to chamber music, and are held throughout the year.

Garnisons Kirken

Skt Annæ Plads 4 (33 91 27 06/www.garnisons kirken.dk). **No credit cards. Map** p252 M16.

The venue itself is unremarkable, but this church hosts a number of enjoyable concerts throughout the year. The gaudy gold and red organ may not be easy on the eye, but it rarely fails to please the ear.

Holmens Kirke

Holmens Kanal (33 13 61 78/www.holmenskirke.dk). **No credit cards. Map** p252 O15.

Every Easter and Christmas Holmens Kirke hosts performances of Bach's sublime Passions – both the *St John* and the *St Matthew* – and Handel's *Messiah*. There's also music throughout the evening on the annual Culture Night in October (*see p166* **For one night only**).

Kastelskirken

Kastellet (33 91 27 06/www.kastelskirken.dk). Bus 15, 19. **No credit cards. Map** p249 H17.

This beautifully restored yellow-painted church has unique acoustics and is often used for recordings as well as concerts. Sometimes a military brass band performs on the square outside the church, mixing up the usual military marches with the occasional Abba number.

Arts & Entertainment

The new **Opera House**. See p192.

Ny Carlsberg Glyptotek

Dantes Plads 7 (33 41 81 41/www.glyptoteket.dk).
Credit MC, V. **Map** p251 P13.

Both the atmosphere and the acoustics in this dark red hall are exceptional. Some afternoons the Winter Garden, with its palm trees, fountains and sculptures, also hosts concerts, many of which are free. For admission prices and opening times of the adjoining museum, *see p61*.

Opera

Musikteatret Undergrunden

Åkandevej 20, Værløse (44 47 49 44/www. undergrunden.com).

Underground Music Theatre is a touring opera company for children founded in 1977 by Niels and Kaja Pihl. The theatre works in a wide range of styles, from avant-garde experiments to repertory works, with puppet operas a regular fixture since 1989.

Operaen

Ekvipagemestervej 10 (33 69 69 69/www. operaen.dk). **Box office** 10am-7pm Mon-Sat.
Credit DC, MC, V. **Map** p249 L18.

It's an exciting time for opera in Copenhagen after the inauguration of the stunning new harbourside Opera House in January 2005. Designed by Henning Larsen, the building is nine floors high, covers 41,000 square metres (376,000 square feet) and is home to two separate stages: the grandiose main stage and the neighbouring 'Takkelloftet', the latter used for more experimental productions and opera for younger audiences. Meanwhile artistic director Kasper Bech Holten continues to strengthen contemporary Danish opera while remaining loyal to the classics, with everything from Tchaikovsky to hip hop fusion on the programme. **Photo** *p191*.

Operationen

Hedebygade 26, 1754 København V (27 52 22 29/ www.annebarslev.dk). **Map** p245 R7.

This young company is making a name for itself by dragging opera into the 21st century, updating a large number of baroque productions by staging them in the most unlikely locations, and attracting a wealth of open-minded young talent as a result.

Theatre

The language barrier means that much of what happens on Copenhagen's stages remains inaccessible to visitors, but many of the city's most interesting directors come from abroad. As a result, it is possible for non-Danes to enjoy a night at the theatre – although it might mean trudging through an abandoned industrial estate to get there.

Recent cuts in public funding have resulted in many of the city's more experimental venues being closed (the much missed Kanonhallen, for example). Undaunted, less stage-based groups have opted to use unconventional venues that reflect the change in Copenhagen's architectural landscape: these range from Trekroner fort, on a tiny island in the harbour, to the industrial wasteland around Nordhavn docks.

Established theatres, meanwhile, have become more rooted in the Danish language: good for the country, perhaps, but not so handy for foreign tourists. There is a small but talented coterie of English language dramatists, actors and playwrights. Many of them, like Vivienne McKee's **London Toast Theatre** (*see below*), have become much loved fixtures.

What follows is an overview of the organisations, venues, groups and festivals that make up the Copenhagen theatre scene. More general information can be found at **www.kulturnaut.dk**, **www.aok.dk** and **www.cphpost.dk**.

Companies

Cantabile 2

55 34 01 19/www.cantabile2.dk.

Many of Cantabile 2's pieces are site-specific, while those performed in theatres can often see the space totally transformed. The company is responsible for the biennial Waves festival, which gathers performers from around the world in the town of Vordingborg every other August.

Copenhagen Theatre Circle

www.ctcircle.org.

The only amateur English-language theatre group in Denmark, composed of non-professionals working in their spare time and aiming to stage at least one production per year. Recently performed playwrights include Dario Fo and Harold Pinter.

Holland House

35 55 26 40/www.hollandhouse.dk.

Holland House was founded in 1988 by Danish artist Ane Mette Ruge and Dutch opera director Jacob Schokking. Since then the company has pushed at the boundaries of both modern theatre and opera, generating a buzz the world over.

Hotel Pro Forma

32 54 02 17/www.hotelproforma.dk.

Kirsten Dehlholm, the founder of HPF, has a background in textile design as well as the hippie movement of the 1960s – both factors that have influenced the group's shows, which are often radical in subject matter and performed in the most unconventional of theatrical spaces.

London Toast Theatre

33 22 86 86/www.londontoast.dk.

The enormously successful LTT was established in 1982 by British actress, writer and director Vivienne McKee and her Danish husband Søren Hall. Its

Child's play

In addition to an annual festival of youth theatre (www.teatercentrum.dk/festival) and a National Children's Theatre Ensemble, Corona-la-Balance (38 79 28 22/www.corona-la-balance.dk), there are plenty of children's theatre groups in Denmark. Standard ticket prices are usually around 110kr for adults and 45kr for children.

Anemoneteatret
Suhmsgade 4 (box office 33 32 22 49/ www.anemoneteatret.dk). **Box office** 9.30am-3.30pm Tue-Fri. **Map** p251 M13.
Anemoneteatret was founded in 1988 and has been producing quality theatre for three- to 12-year-olds ever since, both from its large theatre (seats 150) and on tour.

Comedievognens Broscene
Griffenfeldsgade 7, back building, Nørrebro (35 36 61 22/www.comedievognen.dk). **Box office** 10am-2pm Mon-Fri, 10am-noon Sat, Sun. **Map** p248 J9.
This company, among the oldest of Denmark's children's theatres, began experimenting with gibberish as an art form and continues to use the universal language of humour to enthral young audiences.

Dansk Rakkerpak
21 78 47 48/www.danskrakkerpak.dk
Copenhagen's international street theatre company was founded in 1994 and produces comic pieces that often tackle controversial topics, despite the clownish behaviour.

Det Lille Teater
Lavendelstræde 5-7 (33 12 12 29/box office 33 12 27 13/www.detlilleteater.dk). **Box office** 9am-noon Tue-Fri, noon-3pm Sat, Sun. **Map** p250 O12.
Det Lille Teater (The Little Theatre) celebrated its 40th birthday in 2006. In-house productions tend to combine a good story with plenty of simple songs and are always superbly staged.

HMF Brændende Kærlighed
20 23 14 09/www.braendende kaerlighed.com
Founded in 1986, HMF Brændende Kærlighed (Burning Desire) produces silent outdoor theatre of the highest quality, using large abandoned objects as central props in their original works.

Marionet Teater i Kongens Have
Kronprinsessegade 21 (35 42 64 72). **Open** June-Sept. **Map** p247 L15.
For 40 years now the Marionette Theatre has put on two performances daily during the summer months in the lovely King's Garden.

Zangenbergs Teater
Pilestræde 59 (33 14 50 05/www. zangenbergs-teater.dk). **Box office** 10am-2pm daily. **Map** p251 M14.
An established family theatre in central Copenhagen with space for 115. The company's production of *Nikio and the Great Samurai* was given a Reumert award in 2004.

ecclectic English-language repertoire spans everything from the moderns and Shakespeare to stand-up comedy and murder mysteries. Its lighthearted Christmas cabarets have become a stalwart of the Tivoli Christmas season.

Meridiano Teater
45 20 20 90/www.meridiano.dk.
Italian director Giacomo Ravicchio has earned a glowing reputation for strong visual design and ingenious stagecraft at Meridiano, which he founded in 1995 with actors Elise Müller and Lars Begtrup. Many of the performances are aimed at audiences from six years upwards.

Odin Teatret
97 42 47 77/www.odinteatret.dk.
Denmark's oldest surviving contemporary theatre company. In 2006 Odin was chosen to perform the annual reinterpretation of *Hamlet* at Kronborg Castle in Helsingør.

Signa
www.signa.dk.
Venues for Signa's performance installations are as likely to be abandoned buildings or campsites as established theatres. With topics like fictitious cults and eastern European prostitution cropping up in recent pieces, Signa's work has created something of a stir in the city.

That Theatre Company
33 13 50 42/www.that-theatre.com.
Known for his satirical tragi-comic monologues, Ian Burns co-founded That Theatre Company in 1997. Since 2001, one or two productions a year have been staged at Østerbro's small Kruddtønden venue and the repertoire ranges from thought-provoking dramas to lighter mood pieces. However, all are highly professional despite being made on a shoestring and are worth seeking out by those who like the theatre with bite to it.

Arts & Entertainment

Ticket prices vary dramatically, although most venues offer good discounts to under-25s.

Aveny-T

Frederiksberg Allé 102, Frederiksberg (33 23 31 00/ box office 70 20 10 31/www.aveny-t.dk). **Box office** 2-6pm Mon-Fri; 2-4pm Sat. **No credit cards.** **Map** p245 P6.

This charming theatre dates right back to 1918, but didn't make much of an impression until it was taken over in 1992 by creative ensemble Dr Dante. From July 2007 Aveny-T is to merge with another Frederiksberg theatre, the Rialto, to become Teater X under the artistic leadership of Kaleidoskop's Mette Hvid Davidsen.

Folketeatret

Nørregade 39 (33 12 18 45/administration 33 12 54 45/www.folketeatret.dk). **Box office** 1-6pm Mon-Fri; 12-4pm Sat. **No credit cards.** **Map** p250 M12.

Despite starting out as a down-to-earth competitor to the Royal Theatre, the 'People's Theatre' – which celebrates its 150th birthday in 2007 – now offers an eclectic mix of more modern performances across three stages, and has been given a new lease of life by Danish Dance Theatre, which has been in residence there since summer 2005.

Grønnegårds Teatret

Bredgade 66 (33 16 22 12/box office 33 32 70 23/ www.groennegaard.dk). **Box office** *Mid June-Sept* 2-7.30pm daily. **No credit cards.** **Map** p249 K17.

Grønnegårds Teatret enjoys a unique outdoor location, nestling under the linden trees in the garden of the Danish Museum of Art and Design. The season runs throughout the summer and features a visit by the Royal Danish Ballet each July, with pre-performance picnic baskets from the museum's restaurant.

Kaleidoskop

(35 39 01 00/box office 35 36 53 02/www. kaleidoskop.dk). **Box office** 10am-4pm Mon-Fri. **No credit cards.** **Map** p246 J10.

Founded in 1994, Kaleidoskop has received nationwide recognition for its innovative productions, many of which serve as astute social commentaries. Performances in English are rare, but highly visual movement-based pieces are regularly staged at one of two venues: K1, the original, 140-seat black box playhouse in Nørrebro (Nørrebrogade 37); and K2, a new premises in Østerbro (Østerfælled Torv 37).

Det Kongelige Teater

Stærekassen, Tordenskjoldsgade 5 (main box office 33 69 69 69/www.kgl-teater.dk). **Box office** 10am-7pm Mon-Sat. **Credit** DC, MC, V. **Map** p252 N16.

With the opening of the new Opera House *(see p192)*, the function of the the Royal Theatre has shifted for the first time in its history, though it remains a theatre of many arts. What's more, as it's Denmark's national theatre tickets are subsidised by the government, so you can see world-renowned productions for as little as 50kr.

A stunning new three-stage playhouse is being built by the Copenhagen harbourfront, and will open in 2008. Its arrival will mark the broadening and modernising of the Royal Theatre's role in Danish performing arts. The appointment of director Mikkel Harder Munck-Hansen in 2004 has done much to reinvigorate the repertoire, with more experimental drama and guest international companies spicing up an already diverse programme.

Østre Gasværk Teater. *See p195.*

Madeleines Madteater

*Drechselsgade 10, Islands Brygge (33 14 05 55/
www.madeleines.dk)* **Open** 6pm-midnight Tue-Sat.
No credit cards.
At 1,200kr a ticket, a night at Madeleines Madteater
(food theatre) is the height of decadence in every
sense, a combination of expensive dining with experimental performance theatre. The venue, located in
the old Tuborg beer factory in the hip Islands
Brygge neighbourhood, is the brainchild of theatre
designer Nikolaj Danielsen and culinary doyen
Mette Sia Martinussen. Tickets must be booked in
advance through www.billetnet.dk (70 15 65 65).

Mungo Park

*Fritz Hansensvej 23, Allerød (48 13 13 00/box
office 48 13 13 09/www.mungopark.dk).* **Box
office** 10am-8pm Mon-Fri; 4-8pm Sat, Sun.
No credit cards.
A small theatre in a leafy suburb 30 minutes north-
west of Copenhagen by train may seem of little rel-
evance, but Mungo Park's fearlessness in tackling
difficult topics has attracted a lot of attention. Anna
Bro's *Sandholm*, for example, was a study of living
conditions at a nearby refugee camp.

Det Ny Teater

*Gammel Kongevej 29, Vesterbro (box office 33 25
50 75/www.detnyteater.dk).* **Box office** noon-6pm
Mon; noon-7.30pm Tue-Fri; noon-8pm Sat; noon-4pm
Sun. **Credit** MC, V. **Map** p245 P8.
The misleading New Theatre (it opened in 1908) is
best known for staging Danish versions of money-
making international musicals (*Beauty and the
Beast*, *The Producers*, etc), but it also has a restaurant, Teater Kælderen, where actors wait on tables
and perform routines between servings.

Østre Gasværk Teater

Nyborggade 17 (39 27 71 77/www.oestre-gasvaerk.dk).
Box office 2-6pm Mon-Fri; 2-3pm Sat. **Credit** DC,
MC, V. **Map** p248 A14.
This old building – a former gas storage facility –
regularly plays host to visually dazzling, big-
budget productions which often feature plenty of
international performers, but English-language
pieces are few and far between. **Photo** *p194.*

Plan-B Teater

*Huset, Magstræde 14 (33 91 11 77/box office 33
12 58 14/www.plan-b-teater.dk).* **Box office** 4-6pm
Tue-Fri. **No credit cards.** **Map** p248 A14.
Plan-B was founded in 2002, but theatre has been
performed in Huset since its days as a hub of the
grass roots radicalism that engulfed Copenhagen in
the 1960s and '70s. Premieres from the likes of
Teater Grob and Mammutteatret are staged alongside works by smaller, more experimental groups.

Plex

*Kronprinsensgade 7 (33 32 38 30/booking 33 32
55 56/www.plex-musikteater.dk).* **Box office** 4-6pm
Tue-Fri; 11am-3pm Sat; 1hr before performances.
No credit cards. **Map** p251 M14.

My Copenhagen
Vivienne McKee

*Actress Vivienne McKee made her name
in Britain in theatre, television (including
roles in 'Coronation Street' and
'Crossroads') and films, before marrying
a Dane and moving to Copenhagen in
1980. Together with her husband Søren
Hall she formed the London Toast Theatre,
which has gone on to become Denmark's
foremost English-language theatre
company. Her annual Crazy Christmas
Cabaret at Tivoli attracts crowds of
50,000 and is one of the city's best-
loved yuletide institutions.*

'On a Sunday morning when the sun is
shining I like to go out for a late breakfast
at one of my favourite brunch cafés.
There is a great one near my place on
Gammel Kongevej in Frederiksberg called
Meyer's Deli (*see p137*) – it's very stylish
and the prices are a bit high, but it has a
great atmosphere.

'Then I'll take a bike ride. My favourite
route at the moment is to cycle over to
Fisketorvet shopping centre at Kalvebod
Brygge (the on-site CinemaxX is a good
place to see a movie if it starts to rain;
see p176). Behind the centre there's a
brand new and very stylish pedestrian/
cycle bridge over the waterway to Islands
Brygge, from where you can continue along
the waterfront all the way to the island of
Christianshavn and further on to Holmen
and the site of the magnificent new
Opera House. Along the way, there are
amazing views across the harbour to the
Royal Palace. On the return ride, I'll take
a detour to 'the Free City' of Christiania for
a delicious vegetarian snack at the tiny
Morgenstedet (*see p123*).

'In the evening, one of my favourite places
to dine out is **Les Trois Cochons** (*see
p123*) on Værnedamsvej in Frederiksberg.
It is very cosy (or as the Danes say,
hyggeligt) and reasonably priced too. Then,
if the energy lasts for an evening out,
my preference is always the **Copenhagen
Jazzhouse** (*see p130*) in the centre of
the city. It has a bar upstairs that's quiet
enough to actually talk in without having to
scream your head off and a there's also a
terrific dancefloor down in the basement.'

In 2006 experimental venue Den Anden Opera changed its name to Plex in order to reflect a more international profile, but the theatre still fills every floor of its beautiful old Pentecostal church with installation and sound art, video, dance and experimental music performances.

Organisations

BILLETnet
70 15 65 65/www.billetnet.dk.
The biggest ticket-selling organisation in Denmark.

Danish International Theatre Institute & Theatre Union (DITITU)
Nørre Voldgade 12 (33 86 12 10/www.dititu.dk).
Open *Office* 10.30am-3pm Mon-Fri. **Map** p245 Q7.
Established in 1948 to support Danish theatre groups and venues.

Copenhagen International Theatre (K.I.T.)
33 15 15 64/www.kit.dk.
Since its foundation in 1979 by a Brit, Trevor Davies, K.I.T. has organised more than 40 international festivals in Denmark. It's most visible in the summer months, with the annual Sommerscene circus festival showcasing some of the best acrobatic talents in Europe, while Hamletsommer brings a production of Shakespeare's *Hamlet* to the prince's 'true' home, Kronborg Castle in Helsingør (Elsinore).

Dance

Gone are the days when the Royal Theatre and occasional one-off festivals provided the only venues for dance in Copenhagen. This cultural monopoly was broken in 1979 with the foundation of the Patterson independent dance group. In 1981 Patterson changed its name to Nyt Dansk Danse Teater (New Danish Dance Theatre). In 1982 American dancer and choreographer Warren Spears joined the company and began a tradition of inviting choreographers and dancers from abroad, which has since become the lifeblood of contemporary Danish dance. Brit Tim Rushton took over as artistic director at NDDT in 2002, shortening the company name to **Danish Dance Theatre** and helping to popularise contemporary dance with lavish multimedia productions like *Requiem*, which took over the entire Opera House with its enormous video backdrop back in 2005.

Dansescenen (*see p197*) remains the sole venue entirely dedicated to modern dance performance in Copenhagen, while the **Royal Danish Ballet** (based at the Royal Theatre) is recognised as one of the world's top five ballet companies.

Companies

Åben Dans Productions
35 82 06 10/www.aabendans.dk.
Åben Dans (Open Dance) is one of the most well-toured modern dance companies in Denmark. The majority of performances are accompanied by a series of lectures, workshops and audience debates.

Danish Dance Theatre
35 39 87 87/www.danskdanseteater.dk.
Over the course of its 25-year history, Danish Dance Theatre has redefined modern dance and experimental ballet in Denmark with its high-quality productions, and the new artistic director, Tim Rushton, continues to take this incredibly prolific company from strength to strength.

Granhøj Dans
86 19 26 22/www.granhoj.dk.
Choreographer Palle Granhøj founded Granhøj Dans in 1989 with set designer Per Victor in Århus, Jutland, where the company still has its own theatre.

Living Creatures
35 81 77 76/www.livingcreatures.dk.
A small but strong company led by Camilla Stage, whose modern performances – imbued with a unique expression and loaded with sensuality – have garnered her a formidable reputation.

Peter Schaufuss Ballet
97 40 51 22/www.schaufuss.com.
One of Denmark's biggest ballet stars, Peter Schaufuss has had an enormous influence on the development of modern ballet in the country. His company, based in Jutland, presents several full-length productions every year on the most eclectic topics: 2006's *Satisfaction*, for example, was based on the life and work of the Rolling Stones.

(Stilleben)
33 12 12 62 /www.anderschristiansen.dk.
Anders Christiansen, the artistic director and choreographer of (Stilleben) (Still Life) has achieved cult status in the Copenhagen dance world with his deeply poetic, trance-like performances.

Uppercut Danseteater
35 82 11 71/www.uppercutdance.dk.
One of Denmark's first professional dance theatre groups. In 1999 the company began a new project, Dance in the North-West, which aims to promote modern dance among young people in Copenhagen's multi-ethnic north-western neighbourhood.

X-Act
32 54 07 03/www.kittjohnson.dk.
With a background in martial arts, butoh and German expressive theatre, X-Act co-founder Kitt Johnson has made a name for herself as a dancer, teacher and choreographer, taking part in more than 20 site-specific performance projects all over Europe.

Dansescenen.

Venues

Bellevue Teatret

Strandvejen 451, Klampenborg (39 63 64 00/ administration 39 63 49 00/www.bellevueteatret.dk). **Box office** 3-6pm Mon-Fri. **No credit cards**. Since 2003 the seafront Bellevue Theatre has broadened its appeal by collaborating with Copenhagen International Ballet to produce the famous Summer Ballet under the careful direction of choreographer Alexander Kølpin.

Dansescenen

Østerfælled Torv 34 (35 43 83 00/box office 35 43 20 21/www.dansescenen.dk). **Box Office** 2-6pm Mon-Fri. **No credit cards**. **Map** p248 B12.

The heart of the city's dance milieu, Dansescenen puts on more than 130 performances a year, including an annual competition for young choreographers, Dansolution, where the audience get to vote for their favourite. Dansescenen also organises development programmes for young artists, and its Junior Company regularly performs at youth festivals.

Tivoli

Vesterbrogade 3 (information 33 15 10 01/www. tivoli.dk). **Credit** MC, V. **Map** p250 P12. Tivoli's concert hall regularly hosts some of the biggest international dance companies, including the New York City Ballet. Elsewhere, the Plænen open-air stage hosts many international events, while the Pantomime Theatre is a favourite for children's shows.

Sport & Fitness

Sport for all, from midnight dips to rooftop rallies.

Denmark is filled with sports nuts. The traditional cuisine may be somewhat on the solid side and the population may be beset by the same bad habits as the rest of the western world, but the statistics don't lie: half of all adults and three out of four children participate in sports. Every town has its own football, handball or gymnastics club, and it's all arranged with characteristic Danish efficiency.

The capital has plenty to offer too, from the groundbreaking **DGI-Byen** swimming complex (*see p201*) to shooting ranges, perfect conditions for yachting, a beautiful racecourse, a harbour for swimming in, and an indoor skateboarding dreamland – plus the nation's top two football sides and a great national stadium with 42,000 seats and a roof, right in the centre of town. And all of it is expertly overseen by the **Danish Sports Council** (43 26 26 26, www.dif.dk), which can help out if your sport is not listed here.

Participation sports

Athletics

In mid May, international runners mingle with visitors and locals in a carnival atmosphere as the Copenhagen Marathon signals the start of summer. Although not on the same scale as its counterparts in London or New York, this has become an attractive date in the international athletics calendar (*see p164*).

Badminton

Denmark has a proud badminton tradition and can boast several of the world's elite. Contact the **Danish Badminton Association** (43 26 21 44, www.badminton.dk) for more details.

Copenhagen Badminton Club

Krausesvej 12, Østerbro (35 38 72 92/www.kbk net.dk). Train to Nordhavn, then 5min walk or bus 3 to Randersgade. **Open** 7am-11pm Mon-Fri; 8am-2pm Sat; 8am-8pm Sun. **Prices** non-members 150kr/hr. **No credit cards. Map** p248 C14.

Fitness centres

Fitness centres are popular, with prices generally ranging from 55kr to 150kr for a single session. The **SATS** chain (www.sats.com) runs a series

of well-equipped clubs throughout the city and suburbs (day membership is 150kr). Its central Copenhagen branches include Gothersgade 8F (33 93 33 95), Vesterbrogade 2E, 5th floor (33 32 10 02), Vesterbrogade 97 (33 25 13 10), Bragesgade 8, Nørrebro (35 81 27 81) and Øster Allé 42E, Østerbro (35 55 00 78). For further venues *see p201* **Sports centres**.

Sporting Health Club

Gothersgade 14, 2nd floor (33 13 16 12/www. sportinghealthclub.dk). **Open** 6.30am-9pm Mon-Thur; 6.30am-8.30pm Fri; 9am-6pm Sat; 10am-6pm Sun. **Prices** 75kr. **Credit** DC, V. **Map** p247 L13.

Vesterbro Motionscenter

Angelgade 4 (33 22 05 00/www.fritidkbh.dk). Train to Enghave/bus 1A, 3A, 10. **Open** 10am-9pm Mon; 7am-7pm Tue-Thur; 7am-6pm Fri; 9am-2pm Sat, Sun. **Prices** 56kr. **No credit cards. Map** p245 T6.

Football

Fælledparken, in the shadow of the national stadium (Parken), holds amateur tournaments each Sunday (Apr-Nov). If you want to join a team, just show up around 10am. Alternatively, there are indoor and outdoor pitches throughout the city. For further information or help with booking a pitch, call the **Council Sports Office** on 35 42 68 60.

Go-karting

City Go Kart

Saltværksvej 6-12, Kastrup (70 20 53 11/www.city gokart.dk). Bus 2A, 12, 36, 250S. **Open** 10am-10pm Mon-Sat; 10am-6pm Sun. **Prices** from 300kr/hr. **Credit** MC, V.

Fart & Tempo Go Kart Bane

Tempovej 35, Ballerup (44 66 60 04/www.fart ogtempo.dk). Train to Malmparken, then 10min walk. **Open** 10am-10pm daily. **Prices** 170kr/15mins. **Credit** AmEx, DC, MC, V.

Golf

Among Sjælland's main golfing draws is Europe's biggest indoor venue, the massive Copenhagen Indoor Golf Center, with space for 60 tees as well as two golf simulators and an indoor putting green. For al fresco golfers courses tend to be busy all year (though the

DGI-Byen. *See p201.*

The new firm

You couldn't really call Copenhagen a football hotbed, so whenever local rivals FC København or Brøndby IF win another title – which they do, year after year – don't expect the streets to be bursting with Danes jumping in canals and honking their car horns until the small hours. This is, after all, a country where the top players were all amateurs less than 30 years ago. That said, the atmosphere at a league match at Brøndby or Parken certainly gets a lot more intense than anything the Roligans, Denmark's fans, can come up with.

That's not to say that you should dread going; Danish league matches are among the most relaxed in Europe, and the biggest risk to your health is a dodgy hot dog.

Talking of hot dogs, they are an essential part of blending in, along with lots of Carlsberg or Faxe, which you're free to bring into the stands. Games are on Saturday or Sunday afternoons, with live TV games following in the evening.

FC København

Parken, Øster Allé 50, Østerbro (35 43 31 31/www.fck.dk). Train to Østerport/bus 1A, 14, 15. **Tickets** *Club matches* 140kr-210kr; 70kr-115kr concessions. *Internationals* 230kr-410kr; 185kr-215kr concessions. **No credit cards. Map** p248 D12.
Formed by the merger of KB and B1903 in 1992, København had a rough ride after skipping to the title in their first season in existence. The 1990s saw the club with financial problems, and even after they started making cash by the sackload, success still eluded them. That all changed after Roy Hodgson led them to their second title in 2001. FCK have now won four of the last six titles, enjoy the biggest crowds and boast a number of internationals in the squad, but

their claim to succeeding Brøndby as the leading club was finally justified when they qualified for the Champions League in 2006.

Brøndby IF

Brøndby Stadion 30, Brøndby (43 63 08 10/ www.brondby.com). Train to Brøndbyøster, then bus 135 or train to Glostrup, then bus 166. **Tickets** 110kr-220kr; 60kr-130kr concessions. **Credit** MC, V.
Brøndby IF revolutionised the Danish game. Formed in 1964 in the western suburbs of Copenhagen, they were the first club to turn fully pro in a league that only allowed amateur football until 1978. They were also the first to make a real impression on Europe, and they've won medals in all but one season since their first Danish title in 1985. Recent times, however, have seen rivals København overtake them, and Brøndby do not seem comfortable as the nation's second team. Michael Laudrup may have been a great player, but he was no good as a coach, and since his departure Brøndby have found themselves in another period of rebuilding.

FC Nordsjælland

Farum Park 2, Farum (44 34 25 00/ www.fcnfodbold.dk). Train to Farum, then 10min walk. **Tickets** 110kr-150kr; 50kr-75kr concessions. **No credit cards.**
Another new name in an area where the traditional clubs like B1903 and KB have merged, or just fallen by the wayside in the case of AB and B93, Nordsjælland are an attractive and underrated side, and potentially a genuine alternative to the two big clubs – if only people would come and watch them. Located in sleepy Farum, Copenhagen's northernmost suburb, they inhabit a lovely new stadium but only manage to fill about half a stand.

high season runs from March to October), and a round plus equipment hire doesn't come cheap (around 350kr on weekdays, 500kr at weekends – be sure to book in advance).

Golfing enthusiasts might also like to consider a trip to southern Sweden, which boasts some excellent courses, the best of which is Barsebäck, regular host of the Scandinavian Open. The **Danish Golf Union** can be reached on 43 26 27 00 (www.dgu.org). **Malmö Tourist Information** (00 46 40 30 01 50, www.malmo.se) can provide details of Swedish courses.

Copenhagen Indoor Golf Center

Refshalevej 177B (32 66 11 00/www.cigc.dk). Bus 47. **Open** *Mid Sept-June* 11am-10pm Mon-Thur; 11am-9pm Fri; 9am-7pm Sat, Sun. *June-mid Sept* closed. **Prices** non-members 70kr-80kr/30mins; 120kr-145kr/hr. **Credit** AmEx, DC, MC, V. **Map** p253 O17.

Hørsholm Golf Klub

Grønnegade 1, Hørsholm (45 76 51 50/www. hoersholm-golf.dk). Train to Rungsted Kyst/ bus 381. **Open** phone for details. **Prices** Mon-Fri 450kr/round; Sat, Sun 550kr/round. **Credit** DC, MC, V.

Københavns Golf Klub

*Dyrehaven 2, Klampenborg (39 63 04 83/www.
kgkgolf.dk). Train to Klampenborg.* **Open** 8am-
2.45pm Mon, Thur; 11am-dusk Fri; 1pm-dusk
Sat, Sun. **Prices** Mon-Fri 350kr/round; 200kr
concessions. Sat, Sun 450kr/round; 200kr
concessions. **Credit** DC, MC, V.

Rungsted Golf Klub

*Vestre Stationsvej 16, Rungsted (45 86 34 44/
booking 45 86 34 14/www.rungstedgolfklub.dk).
Train to Rungsted Kyst.* **Open** 8.30am-dusk Mon-Fri;
noon-dusk Sat, Sun. **Prices** Mon-Sun 550kr/round;
250kr-350kr concessions. **Credit** AmEx, DC, MC, V.

Horse riding

Mattssons Rideklub

*Bellevuevej 10-12, Klampenborg (39 64 08 22/www.
mattsson.dk). Train to Klampenborg, then 5min
walk.* **Open** 6.45am-9pm Mon-Fri; 6.45am-5pm Sat,
Sun. **Prices** phone for details. **No credit cards**.

Ice skating

Each winter outdoor public ice skating rinks
spring up at locations across the city, with
hot chestnut stalls and romantic lights adding
to the chocolate-box atmosphere. The most
central winter skating rink is usually situated
on Kongens Nytorv, where skate hire is
available and a small fee is charged. The
popular **Østerbro Indoor Skating Rink**
charges around 25kr plus skate hire, but is
closed in the summer.

Østerbro Indoor Skating Rink

PH Lings Allé 6 (35 42 18 65). Bus 1A, 14, 15.
Open *Oct-Mar* noon-2.45pm Mon-Fri; 4-6.30pm
Sun. **Prices** 25kr; 12kr under-16s; skate rental 30kr.
No credit cards. **Map** p248 D12.

Jogging

Copenhagen is relatively flat, making jogging
an attractive proposition. The city's numerous
parks are both safe and spacious, and joggers
can outnumber walkers in some areas. In the
city centre, try Ørstedsparken near Nørreport
Station, or the lakes above at Nørre Søgade.
Further out, Søndermarken by the zoo in
Frederiksberg and, for more serious runners,
Dyrehaven in Klampenborg are also popular.

Pool & snooker

Many bars have a billiard table, but Danish
billiards (a game that features small skittles)
is often the only game on offer. However, for
those wanting to make like Paul Newman,
American-style pool can also be played at some
central bars and cafés including **Pub & Sport**

(Vester Voldgade 9, 33 15 08 10). Snooker is
growing in popularity but, while the standard
is surprisingly high, tables are still in short
supply. **Albertslund Billiards Club**
(Hedemarksvej 14, 43 62 21 79, train to
Albertslund) is one venue, while the **Pool
Pub** (Rentemestervej 67, 38 88 00 29, train to
Nørrebro, bus 5A, 350S) also caters for snooker
enthusiasts. Call the **Danish Billiards
Association** on 43 26 20 82 (www.ddbu.dk)
for further details.

Rollerblading/skateboarding

Experienced skaters can do as the locals do
and risk life and limb on the city's cycle paths.
Those looking to live past 30 can move indoors
at the fine **Copenhagen Skatepark**
(Enghavevej 78, 33 29 00 29, train to Enghave,
bus 3A), with a selection of ramps and rails
more suited to tricks than transportation.

Rowing

Rowing clubs exist to the north and south of
the city centre. Beginners and experienced
rowers can contact **Københavns Roklub**
(Copenhagen Rowing Club, Tømmergravsgade
13, 33 12 30 75, www.koebenhavnsroklub.dk).
The **Danish Rowing Association** can be
reached on 44 44 06 33 (www.roning.dk).

Rugby union

It often comes as a surprise to learn that rugby
union has a devoted following in Copenhagen.
The season runs from the end of March to the
end of June, and from August to October. The
local top team is **Frederiksberg** who play on
grounds at Jens Jessensvej (take the train to
Peter Bangsvej Station). For more info call the
Danish Rugby Association on 43 26 28 00
(www.rugby.dk).

Sports centres

For most of the many racket sports played
in Copenhagen, plus basketball, table tennis
and occasionally martial arts or swimming,
Copenhagen's many sports centres remain your
best bet. For sporting cool there's **DGI-Byen**,
while **Grøndal Centret**, though a little way
out of the centre, is northern Europe's largest
sports complex and features everything from
aerobics to bowling.

DGI-Byen

Tietgensgade 65 (33 29 80 00/www.dgibyen.dk).
Open *Jan-May, Sept-Dec* 6.30am-midnight, Mon-
Thur; 6.30am-7pm Fri; 9am-5pm Sat, Sun. *June-
Aug* 6.30am-6pm Mon, Fri; 10am-6pm Tue, Thur;

Arts & Entertainment

6.30am-8pm Wed; 9am-4pm Sat, Sun. **Admission** phone for details. **Credit** AmEx, DC, MC, V. **Map** p250 Q11. **Photo** *p199*.

Grøndal Centret

Hvidkildevej 64, Vanløse (38 34 11 09/www.groendal centret.dk). Train to Fuglebakken/bus 21. **Open** 7.30am-10.30pm Mon-Fri; 9.30am-5.30pm Sat, Sun. **Prices** 50kr-100kr/hr. **No credit cards.**

Nørrebrohallen

Bragesgade 5, Nørrebro (35 31 05 50/www. noerrebrohallen.dk). Train to Nørrebro/bus 5A, 16. **Open** 6.30am-11.30pm Mon-Thur; 6.30am-9.30pm Fri; 7.30am-9.30pm Sat, Sun. **Opening hours** may vary in June-Aug, phone to check. **Prices** 55kr-85kr/hr. **No credit cards.**

Svanemøllehallen

Østerbrogade 240, Østerbro (39 20 77 01/www. fritidkbh.dk). Bus 1A, 4A, 14. **Open** 7am-11pm Mon-Thur; 7am-10pm Fri; 8am-8pm Sat; 9am-10pm Sun. **Opening hours** may vary in June-Aug, phone to check. **Prices** 60kr-70kr/hr. **No credit cards.** **Map** p248 C13.

Squash

Squash courts can be hired at many sports halls in the city, including **Grøndal Centret** and **Nørrebrohallen** (for both, *see above*). For more information, the **Danish Squash Association** can be reached on 66 19 08 22/ www.dsqf.dk.

Swimming

The most central place for a swim is **DGI-Byen** sports centre (*see p201*). This state-of-the-art building is fine for a dip, but tends to be monopolised by families, and is pricier than council-run venues. The pools stay open until midnight on weekdays, however, for a quieter swim. If you don't mind colder water, you should also check out the fantastic, open-air harbour bathing complex **Islands Brygge**. It's free, but only open during the summer.

Fælledbadet

Borgmester Jensens Allé 50, Østerbro (35 39 08 04/www.fritidkbh.dk). Bus 150S, 184, 185. **Open** *June-Sept* 7am-5pm Mon, Wed; 7am-8pm Tue; 10am-5pm Thur; 10am-4pm Fri-Sun. *Oct-May* 7am-6pm Mon, Wed; 7am-8pm Tue; 7am-3pm Fri; 9am-3pm Sat, Sun. **Prices** 28kr; 13kr concessions; free under-5s. **No credit cards.** **Map** p248 C11.

Hillerødgade Swimming Pool

Sandbjerggade 35, Nørrebro (35 85 19 55/www. fritidkbh.dk). Bus 69. **Open** *Sept-May* 10am-4pm Mon; 7am-9pm Tue; 7am-4.30pm Wed; 7am-7pm Thur; 7am-4pm Fri; 8am-2pm Sat, Sun. *June-Aug* 10am-4pm Mon; 7am-7pm Tue-Thur; 7am-4pm Fri; 8am-2pm Sat, Sun. **Prices** 28kr; 13kr concessions. **No credit cards.**

Øbro-Hallen

Gunnar Nu Hansens Plads 3, Østerbro (35 25 70 60/www.fritidkbh.dk). Bus 1A, 14. **Open** 7am-8pm Mon, Tue, Thur, Fri; 10am-8pm Wed; 9am-3pm Sat, Sun. **Prices** 28kr; 13kr concessions. **No credit cards.**

Vesterbro Swimming Pool

Angelgade 4, Vesterbro (33 22 05 00/www. fritidkbh.dk). Train to Enghave/bus 1A, 3A, 10. **Open** *May-Aug* 10am-9pm Mon; 7am-5.30pm Tue,Thur; 7am-7pm Wed; 7am-4.30pm Fri; 9am-2pm Sat, Sun. **Prices** 28kr; 13kr concessions. **No credit cards.** **Map** p245 T6.

Tennis

Tennis courts are in pretty short supply in Copenhagen and many belong to private clubs, so you will need to know a member in order to gain access. An additional factor is the cost of hiring a court: most central venues charge between 100kr and 150kr per hour (sometimes with an additional fee for non-members), so a proper five-set marathon can prove expensive.

Most central is the **Hotel Mercur**, which rents out its own private, rather rundown rooftop courts to non-residents. **KB Tennis Club** has indoor and outdoor courts; reservations required. **B93 Sports Club** is another tennis-friendly venue. More information is available from the **Danish Tennis Association** on 43 26 26 60 (www.dtftennis.dk).

B93 Sports Club

Ved Sporsløjfen 10 (39 27 18 90/www.b93.dk). Train to Svanemøllen/bus 1A, 14. **Open** 7am-10pm daily. **Prices** 75kr. **No credit cards.**

Hotel Mercur

Vester Farimagsgade 17 (33 12 57 11/www.accor hotel.dk). **Open** 10am-7pm daily. **Prices** 130kr/hr (incl racket); 90kr/hr (without racket). **No credit cards.** **Map** p250 N11. **Photo** *p203*.

KB Tennis Club

Peter Bangsvej 147, Frederiksberg (38 71 41 50/ www.kb-boldklub.dk). Train to Peter Bangs Vej/bus 15. **Open** *Sept-Apr* 7am-11pm Mon-Fri; 8am-5pm Sat, Sun. *May-Sept* 8am-dusk daily. **Prices** 100kr/hr per person. **No credit cards.** **Other locations**: Pile Allé 14 (36 30 23 00).

Ten-pin bowling

Ten-pin bowling, which is usually accompanied by drinks and/or a meal, is a very popular night out in Copenhagen. Remember to call and reserve a lane in advance, especially if you want to play at the weekend. Contact the **Danish Bowling Association** (43 26 29 11, www.spilbowling.dk) for details.

Hotel Mercur. *See p202.*

Big Bowl

Gl. Jernbanevej 31, Valby (70 10 07 00/www.big bowl.dk). Train to Valby, then bus 4A, 18, 26. **Open** 11am-midnight Mon-Thur; 10am-2am Fri, Sat; 10am-10pm Sun. **Prices** 125kr-300kr. **Credit** DC, MC, V.

Bowlehuset

DGI-Byen, Tietgensgade 65 (33 29 80 20/www.dgi-byen.dk). **Open** 4-11pm Mon; 2-11pm Tue-Thur; 11am-1am Fri, Sat; 10am-8pm Sun. **Prices** 115kr-275kr per lane; 10kr shoe hire. **Credit** AmEx, DC, MC, V. **Map** p250 Q11.

Walking

All right, Denmark is flat. Maybe not as level as Holland, but still pretty horizontal. Nevertheless there are plenty of picturesque walking routes just a short bus or train ride from the city centre. **Amager Nature Reserve** is a real wilderness just five kilometres (three miles) from Central Station (Metro Islands Brygge, DR Byen or Sundby). Another alternative is the former royal hunting ground, **Dyrehaven**, a few minutes' walk from Klampenborg Station, 25 minutes north of the city.

Windsurfing

While there may be 'water, water everywhere' and quite probably more wind than most Copenhageners know what to do with, the city's windsurfers are truly blessed by these geographic coincidences. There are several places to rent boards. **Nautic Surf & Ski**, near to Arken art gallery, is the closest.

Spectator sports

Athletics

The biggest event is the annual marathon (*see p164*). Athletics meetings take place at the city's **Østerbro Stadion** (Gunnar Nu Hansens Plads 11, Østerbro, 35 25 33 26, bus

1A, 14), but Malmö in Sweden is the place to catch the more famous names. Call Malmö Tourist Information on 00 46 40 34 12 00 for details of events.

Boxing

Banned in Sweden and Norway, professional boxing is popular in Denmark. Bouts are regularly held in arenas such as **KB Hallen** (Peter Bangsvej 147). Try www.billetlugen.dk for tickets.

Cricket

Surprisingly popular. Devotees can catch a game at a number of venues throughout the suburbs such as Kløvermarken (bus 47). Contact the **Danish Cricket Association** (43 26 21 60, www.cricket.dk) for details of match schedules or **Københavns Boldklub** (38 71 41 50, www.kb-boldklub.dk) for information on games in the capital.

My Copenhagen
Kim Milton Nielsen

Kim Milton Nielsen, IT manager in Copenhagen, is better known as the no-nonsense former top FIFA referee who sent off David Beckham during England's infamous match against Argentina in the 1998 World Cup in France.

'I'd stick to the city centre for a day out. My offices are right next to **Christiansborg** and the canals around **Slotsholmen**, and I love that old part of town. To start off, I'd go for a boat trip around the harbour. Seeing the city from the water gives you a real grasp of the city's history. For lunch, I'd stop at **Croissanten** (Østergade 61, 33 32 99 58) on Strøget, opposite the Illum department store. It's a simple takeaway place that does sandwiches in home-baked bread. I wouldn't eat in – I'd walk down to **Kongens Nytorv** and eat lunch sitting on the docks.

'In the evening I'd go to **Tivoli** (*see p54*). I still think it's a really special place. I'd eat at **Hercegovina** (Bernstorffsgade 3, 33 15 63 63) and then take in a concert on the Plænen open-air stage. Afterwards – well, I rarely hit the town these days, but I might go for a cocktail at the **K Bar** (Ved Stranden 20, 33 91 92 22) before heading home.'

Golf

There are a staggering 25 full-sized 18-hole courses in the Greater Copenhagen area alone. Hardly surprising, then, that the country has produced two of Europe's top golfers, Thomas Bjørn and Anders Hansen. Major events are regularly held on Zealand. For more information contact the **Danish Golf Union** (43 26 27 00/www.dgu.org).

Handball

The nation's favourite indoor sport, handball is unique in that the women's game is far more popular than the men's version. The rules are simple and games are easy to follow, fast-moving and exciting. **FC København** have top male and female sides to supplement the football team in winter (Frederiksberghallen, Jens Jessens Vej 20, 35 43 31 31). Contact the **Danish Handball Association** (43 26 24 00, www.dhf.dk) or Copenhagen's **Håndbold Forbund** (43 26 20 84) for details of up-and-coming local games.

Horse racing

For chariot-style trotting racing, take a ride out to the **Travbane** course at Charlottenlund (Traverbanevej 10, 39 96 02 02, www.travbanen.dk). Nearby is Denmark's only flat racing course, **Klampenborg Galopbane** (39 96 02 13/www.galopbane.dk), home to the Scandinavian Open and the Danske Derby (held on the last Sunday in June).

Ice hockey

When football breaks for winter, ice hockey takes over. Denmark hosted the world 'B' Championships in 1999 and the national team has produced some impressive recent results. Top teams near Copenhagen are the **Nordsjælland Cobras**, north of the city (Stadion Allé 11, Rungsted Kyst, 45 76 30 31, www.cobrashockey.dk) and the **Rødovre Mighty Bulls** (Rødovre Parkvej 425, Rødovre, 36 72 17 79, www.rodovremightybulls.dk) in the south. For details of forthcoming matches, contact the **Danish Ice Hockey Association** (43 26 26 26, www.ishockey.dk).

Tennis

Denmark's flagship event is the **Copenhagen Open** (33 12 72 44), held every year in February or March. For details of the event, call the **Danish Tennis Association** on 43 26 26 60 or visit www.dtftennis.dk.

Trips Out of Town

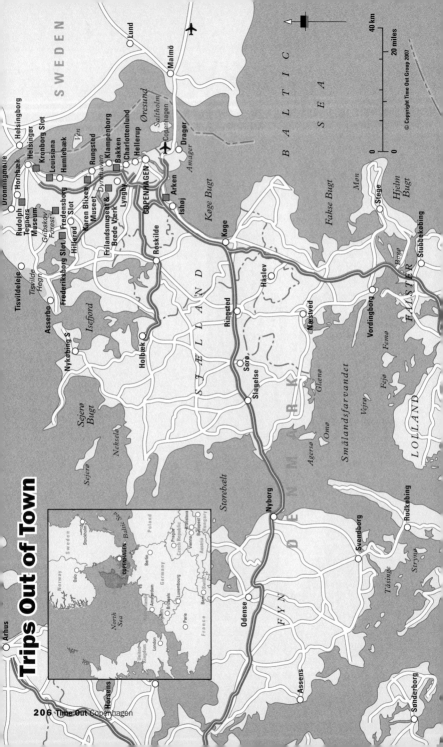

Trips Out of Town

Malmö

It's just a short hop across the sea to one of Sweden's most vibrant cities.

Treasure trove: **Slottet Malmöhus**. *See p208.*

Copenhagen ought to have more than enough to occupy you for at least a long weekend, but another city – smaller but equally scintillating – lies just 30 minutes away by train. It happens to be in another country and across a sea, but Malmö – Sweden's third largest city – is worth the short trip via the spectacular **Øresund Bridge**. Its unusually cosmopolitan population includes 15,000 university students, who give Malmö a youthful, vibrant energy, and it is also an eminently liveable place. There are some excellent art museums, an atmospheric castle, a sizeable sandy beach and some unique shops. At night most people head for the cobbled square of **Lilla Torg** with its lively bars and restaurants, but as a whole the city is awash with great nightlife venues.

> ❶ Green numbers in this chapter correspond to the location of each hotel on the street map. ❶ Purple numbers in this chapter correspond to the location of each restaurant and bar on the street map. *See p209.*

Particularly during summer, Malmö's long sandy beach, **Ribban** (a short walk west from the city centre), its beautiful parks and its peaceful, almost southern European atmosphere are hard to resist. The city has some excellent cultural facilities and a varied ethnic mix (around 40 per cent of its total population of 270,000 are originally from Eastern Europe, Latin America, the Middle East and Africa). The **Malmö Festival**, the oldest city festival in Sweden, takes place at venues throughout the city in August each year and attracts 1.5 million visitors with live music, theatre and a massive crayfish binge (www.malmo.se).

The most recent addition to the city has been in the Western Harbour area. This was once one of the most important dockyards in Europe but the decline of industry in the 1980s threatened the city's entire economy. In recent years, however, a radical housing project, **Bo01** ('bo' is the Swedish for 'to dwell' and '01' for the year it was founded as an international European housing expo), has sprung up beside the sea. This environmentally sustainable, expertly built and highly desirable housing has won

Trips Out of Town

architectural plaudits from around the globe for its 'organic' approach to planning, diverse use of materials and environmentally friendly trappings (natural gas is extracted from waste and energy comes from wind turbines). The restaurants, harbour, bathing deck, cafés, promenades, leisure facilities and shops here are now a major attraction, as is the Exhibition and Convention Centre which is housed in a former Saab factory nearby.

Some critics say Bo01 is a yuppie ghetto which is unrepresentative of the city's diverse population, but there are lower cost housing developments being built nearby. At the centre of it all is the astonishing **Turning Tower** by Santiago Calatrava (*see p210* **Twisted logic**).

Sightseeing

The historic heart of Malmö is a beguiling mix of timbered buildings, wide canals, beautiful parks and a sizeable pedestrian shopping area, Södergatan, which connects the **Stortorget** and **Gustav Adolfs Torg** squares before continuing down Södra Förstadsgatan to Triangeln, the triangular area in front of the Scandic Hotel. All are within easy reach of one another, with the railway station and beach also nearby.

While Södergatan is no Strøget, it does boast good international chain stores and independent shops, as well as plenty of restaurants and bars – the Davidhallstorg shopping area has recently undergone a major trendification. A little further south you come to **Möllevångstorget**, which has several Asian, African and Eastern European shops and restaurants. Delve a little deeper and you'll find a couple of decent bars as well as a large produce market (8am-2pm Mon-Sat), while to the north-west sits the beach, **Ribban** (*see p208*).

The centre of Malmö is encircled by a canal, and a pleasant way to get your bearings is to take a canal tour. **Rundan Canal Tours'** boats (*see p212*) leave every hour from a berth opposite Central Station (available from May to September) and the tour takes 45 minutes. You can also hire pedalos from City Boats, which is based on Södertull and open between April and September. The latter option will allow you to do the tour under your own steam (although give yourself plenty of time if you intend to pedal the full circuit).

Malmö might not offer the rich cultural and historical tapestry of Copenhagen, but it does have one or two museums and galleries that are worth spending some time in. Conveniently for the day tripper, most of them are located on a single site within the walls of **Slottet Malmöhus** (Malmö Castle).

The Danish king Erik of Pomerania was the first to build a castle on the site (which at that time was right on the seafront) in 1434, and for a while afterwards it was the home of the Danish mint. In the 16th century the castle underwent a major rebuild under Christian III of Denmark, with the addition of ramparts, four red cannon towers (two of which still stand) and a moat. The castle's usefulness continued long after the Swedes liberated this part of the country from the Danes in 1658, so much so that, Christian V tried unsuccessfully to take it back again. Up until 1937 the castle served as a prison, and only then was it converted to house the museums.

Today a rather stern, functionalist extension within the walls of the old castle contains the city's most important museums. **Naturmuseet** (Natural History Museum) boasts an enjoyably chaotic collection of stuffed animals (including one gargantuan moose), a small aquarium, various live insects and reptiles and a fascinating nocturnal room.

Upstairs on the left, you'll find the **Malmö Konstmuseum** (Malmö Art Museum; *see p211* Malmö Museums), which gives visitors a bite-size tour of Scandinavian art and design. The museum has an important collection of modern art, featuring a range of ceramics, paintings, sculpture, furniture, silverware and glassware.

The **Stadsmuseet** (City Museum; *see p211* Malmö Museums), which is to the right and up the stairs, covers the history of Malmö from the flint miners and reindeer hunters of 1000 BC onwards. This leads into the castle itself and its collection of tapestries, weaponry, art, furniture and other pieces from the 16th and 17th centuries (English information is available).

On the opposite side of the road, a short walk along Malmöhusvägen in the direction of Ribban (Malmö's beach) is **Teknikens och Sjöfartens Hus** (Technology and Maritime Museum) which opened in 1978. The highlight of the exhibits is a 1943 U3 submarine – a claustrophobe's idea of hell.

Just before you reach the museum, if you turn right into Banérskajen you will come to **Fiskehoddorna**. This row of pretty, coloured wooden fishermen's huts looks like a relic from the town's herring fishing past, but the local fishermen still sell their fresh catches from stalls in front of the houses every morning (except Sunday and Monday).

Ribersborgs Stranden (Ribersborgs Beach, otherwise known as **Ribban**), Malmö's fine, two-kilometre (one-mile) long sandy beach, further west, is the town's unique selling point, but this wasn't always the case. The beach is actually a fake, constructed on a festering swamp in the 1920s. These days, however, it

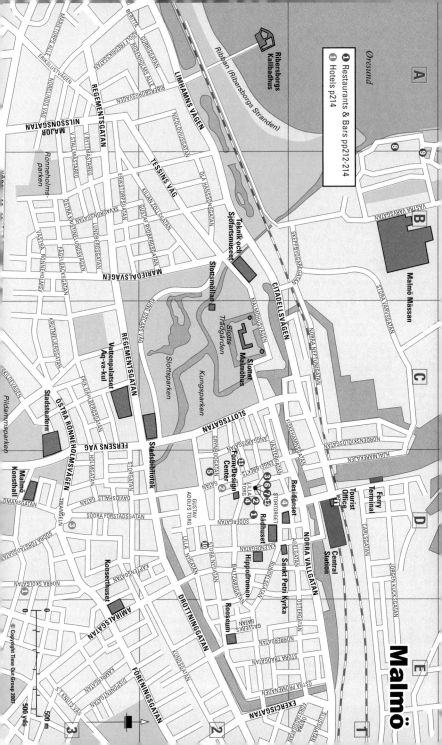

Malmö

Restaurants & Bars pp212-214

Hotels p214

Øresund

© Copyright Time Out Group 2007

Twisted logic

Drive over the Øresund Bridge from Denmark to Sweden and one building dominates the horizon on the Swedish coast. The **Turning Tower** is Scandinavia's most impressive construction project since the Øresund Bridge itself, and a real challenge to the supposed architectural dominance of neighbouring Denmark. Like a lightning conductor, it marks the location of the city's radical new housing development in the Western Harbour, built over the last five years on a former industrial site just outside the city centre.

The tower was designed by the Spanish architect Santiago Calatrava after the MD of developers HSB saw a two-metre white marble sculpture of a human torso by the architect. 'That would look great in aluminium and glass, 190 metres high,' thought the developer, and he commissioned Calatrava. The result was completed in November 2005. It's the tallest building in Sweden, and boasts an extraordinary external 'spine' of steel framework that twists through 90 degrees as it lifts nine stacks of white aluminium cubes – in all 54 storeys of, mostly, apartments. With its bombastic scale and show-stopping theatricality it could hardly be less Swedish. And some have criticised the high cost of the apartments while residents complain of living in a 'goldfish bowl'. However, most have embraced their new city symbol and are immensely proud of it.

The apartments themselves – which are rental only – dispense with the conventions of rectangular, regular rooms, in favour of all manner of curves and angles. The views, needless to say, are breathtaking. And Calatrava's next project? Like most of the great architects of our time he is involved in the rebuilding of New York's Ground Zero, but his next great apartment block, planned for Chicago, will supposedly be the tallest building in America.

Meanwhile, the neighbouring HSB Turning Torso Gallery is due to open in March 2007, with design-oriented shops, restaurants and an exhibition about the tower.

has given the city a very attractive seafront, the water is crystal clear and the sand slopes gently out into the sea – perfect for children. The first stretch of beach as you walk from the town centre is an unmarked nudist (and sometime gay cruising) area, but from then on there is a more family-oriented mix of sand, picnic areas, cafés and ice-cream vendors.

For an authentically Swedish experience, a visit to the **Ribersborgs Kallbadhus** (Ribersborgs Cold Bath House; *see p211*) is worth a gamble depending on the weather. This charming green wooden bathhouse, dating from 1898, is at the end of a short pier located on the eastern end of the beach. Walk through the café at the front, pay the entrance fee and you enter the segregated open-air deck areas (men to the left, women to the right), with their bracing sea water plunge baths and saunas. It goes without saying that nudity is the norm here. A masseur is on hand to pummel weary bodies and there is also a solarium.

In the south-east corner of Kungsparken, in one of Malmö's grander quarters, is the town's answer to Copenhagen's Black Diamond, the **Stadsbibliotek** (Town Library). As with the Black Diamond, Malmö's 19th-century red brick library received an uncompromising, modern glass extension in 1999, designed by Danish architect Henning Larsen and nicknamed the 'Cathedral of Light'.

Lovers of contemporary Scandinavian and European interior design should head for the **Form/Design Center** (*see p212*), housed in a converted warehouse. The first floor contains a changing programme of design-related exhibitions. On the second floor is an excellent design shop selling everything from garden furniture to jewellery, kitchenware and clothes.

The Center – one of numerous excellent design shops to be found throughout the city centre – is located in a courtyard adjacent to Malmö's prettiest square, **Lilla Torg** (**photo** *p212*). By night Lilla Torg is the hub of Malmö's mainstream nightlife scene. As well as its many pubs, the city also claims to have more restaurants per square kilometre than any other city in Sweden, and this is where you'll find some of the best. Lilla Torg dates from 1591 when it developed as an overflow for Stortorget. In 1903 the square was given its own roof, but that was demolished in 1967 and the area was recobbled. These days it is packed with busy bars and restaurants and has a convivial, party atmosphere in the spring and summer.

Just west of Lilla Torg is **Gamla Väster**, the pretty historic heart of the city with its rows of small, pastel-coloured 18th- and 19th-century houses interspersed with the odd designer shop and restaurant.

During the 16th century nearby Stortorget was one of the largest market squares in Scandinavia. At its centre is a statue of the comically rotund King Carl X Gustav (who was responsible for the chain of events that climaxed with the Treaty of Roskilde), astride his horse, Hannibal. Surrounding the statue stand some grand old buildings which include: on the east side, Malmö's **Rådhuset** (Town Hall; **photo** *p214*) dating from 1546 but rebuilt in 1812 in the neo-classical style; on the western side, the 16th-century home of the former Danish mayor and controller of the Mint, Jörgen Kock; on the north side the splendid **Scandic Hotel Kramer** (*see p213*), said to be modelled on Copenhagen's Hotel d'Angleterre; and also

on the north side **Residenset** (Governor's Residence), dating from the early 18th century but rebuilt most recently in 1851. It was on the balcony here that the kings of Norway, Sweden and Denmark met in 1914 to confirm their joint statement of neutrality. Shortly after the summit the balcony was found to be on the brink of collapse (it was, in fact, held on by a couple of rusty screws), which could have had serious repercussions, not only for Scandinavia but the whole of Europe. Around the corner is the wonderful art nouveau Hotel Savoy where Lenin dined en route to Russia in 1917.

An unsuccessful attempt at a coup by Danish sympathisers in the 1650s resulted in a number of grisly retaliatory executions in Stortorget. In 1678 the Danish nobleman Jörgen Krabbe, who lived in the castle at Krageholm in Sweden, was beheaded here after being (probably wrongly) accused of plotting against Sweden. Much later, in 1811, executions and floggings took place here following an uprising by farmers and peasants opposed to conscription to fight Napoleon in Europe. During the August festival, Stortorget hosts another, slightly more palatable massacre: the world's largest crayfish party.

Behind Stortorget and to the east is **Sankt Petri Kyrka** (St Peter's Church), Malmö's main place of worship, built at the beginning of the 14th century. It has many similarities with other Hanseatic churches of the period, particularly Marienkirche in Lübeck. Like most other Catholic churches at that time, Sankt Petri Kyrka suffered during the Reformation and in 1555, in an act of artistic vandalism, its medieval frescoes were whitewashed over (some have been restored and can be seen in the nearby Krämer Chapel).

As well as the Konstmuseum, Malmö has one other highly regarded art space. **Malmö Konsthall** (*see p212*), built in neo-brutalist style in 1975, holds around ten temporary exhibitions of contemporary art a year in its capacious rooms (at 2,000 square metres/ 21,500 square feet this is one of the largest contemporary art sites in northern Europe). It also has a fine bookshop as well as a courtyard café that hosts the occasional jazz concert. Sadly, at the time of going to press, the future of the city's most controversial contemporary art space, **Rooseum**, was in doubt due to financing issues.

Malmö's striking **Stadsteatern** (Town Theatre) was built on the corner of Fersens Väg and Östra Rönne in 1944 and, with three separate stages, is one of the largest theatres in Europe. Ingmar Bergman was dramatic director there in the 1950s and these days it is often visited by foreign ballet, opera and theatre

Lilla Torg. *See p211.*

Malmö Museums & Art Museum

Malmöhusvägen, Slottet Malmöhus (040 34 10 00/ www.malmo.se/museer). **Open** *Sept-May* noon-4pm daily. *June-Aug* 10am-4pm daily. **Admission** 40Skr; 10Skr-12Skr concessions; free under-6s. **Credit** MC, V. **Map** p209 C2.
The listings above cover Malmö Konstmuseum, Stadsmuseet, Naturmuseet and Teknik och Sjöfartsmuseet.

Ribersborgs Kallbadhus

Ribersborgs Stranden (040 26 03 66/www.ribban. com). **Open** *Baths* noon-7pm Mon-Fri; 9am-4pm Sat, Sun. *Sauna* noon-7pm Mon-Fri; 9am-4pm Sat, Sun. *Café* noon-7pm Mon-Fri; 10am-4pm Sat, Sun. **Admission** 50Skr; 35Skr concessions; free under-7s; 20Skr towel hire (30Skr deposit). **No credit cards.** **Map** p209 A2. **Photo** *p213.*

Rooseum

Gasverksgatan 22 (040 12 17 16/www.rooseum.se). **Open** 2-8pm Wed; noon-6pm Thur-Sun. **Admission** 40Skr; 20Skr concessions; free under-16s; free to all Fri. **Credit** MC, V. **Map** p209 E2.

Rundan Canal Tours

Central Station (040 611 74 88/www.rundan.se). **Open** *May-June* 11am-4pm daily. *July, Aug* 11am-7pm daily. *Sept* 11am-3pm daily. *Oct-Apr* closed. **Tickets** 75Skr; 40Skr concessions. **Credit** MC, V. **Map** p209 D1.

Stadsbibliotek

Kung Oscars väg 11 (040 660 85 00/www.malmo. stadsbibliotek.org). **Open** 10am-8pm Mon-Thur; 10am-6pm Fri; 11am-4pm Sat, Sun. **Admission** free. **Map** p209 C2.

Where to eat & drink

Caramello

Stortorget 25 (040 30 43 70/www.caramello.se). **Open** 5pm-1am Mon-Thur; 5pm-2am Fri, Sat. **Main courses** 155Skr. **Credit** AmEx, DC, MC, V. **Map** 209 D2 ❶
The newest and coolest arrival on Stortorget, Caramello is a combination of restaurant, bar and nightclub designed by local architect Abelardo Gonzalez. The food is best described as modern Mediterranean with touches of fusion.

Centiliter & Gram

Stortorget 17 (040 12 18 12). **Open** 5.30pm-1am Wed, Thur; 5pm-3am Fri; 7pm-3am Sat. **Main courses** 65Skr-179Skr. **Credit** AmEx, DC, MC, V. **Map** p209 D2 ❷
Just around the corner from Lilla Torg on the city's main square is this large, open-plan bar whose dressy, mature clientele usually spill outside if the weather allows.

Klubb Plysch

Lilla Torg 1 (040 12 73 60). **Open** 10pm-3am Fri, Sat. **Admission** 50Skr after 11pm. **Credit** AmEx, DC, MC, V. **Map** p209 D2 ❸

groups. In 1985 Malmö gained **Konserthuset** (Concert House), situated on the corner of Föreningsgatan and Amiralsgatan, now home to the respected Malmö Symfoni Orkester (Malmö Symphony Orchestra).
A little south of the city centre is the newest arrival on Malmö's thriving cultural and nightlife scene, **Kulturhuset Mazetti** (Mazetti Culture Centre; *see below*). Housed in a former Fazer chocolate factory, this is now home to several organisations with a cultural bent, as well as a hotel, nightclub and, nearby, a rather more exclusive *chocolatier*.

Form/Design Center

Lilla Torg (040 664 51 50/www.formdesigncenter. com). **Open** 11am-5pm Tue, Wed, Fri; 11am-6pm Thur; 11am-4pm Sat, Sun. **Admission** free. **Map** p209 D2.

Kulturhuset Mazetti

Bergsgatan 29 (040 34 48 65/www.malmo.se/ mazetti). **Open** *phone enquiries* 8.30am-8pm Mon-Wed; 10am-8pm Thur; 8.30am-6pm Fri. **Credit** varies.
This new centre houses a wide variety of cultural organisations as well as a nightclub and hotel.

Malmö Konsthall

St Johannesgatan 7 (040 34 12 93/www.konsthall. malmo.se). **Open** 11am-5pm Mon, Tue, Thur-Sun; 11am-9pm Wed. **Admission** free; charges applicable for some larger exhibitions. **Credit** MC, V. **Map** p209 D3.

Trips Out of Town

Located above Victors (*see p213*), this painfully cool club/bar/lounge is arranged in a grand, five-room, L-shaped apartment. A DJ plays at weekends and there is a small dancefloor. A haven for Malmö's beautiful people (models, media folk, musicians, millionaires), and trust us, they are beautiful. Entrance is supposedly for members only (and members must be resident in Sweden) but you can get in as a guest of a member, or, if you fancy a challenge, through sheer guile and chutzpah.

Koi
Lilla Torg 5 (040 757 00/www.koi.se). **Open** 11.30am-11pm Mon-Thur; 11.30am-5am Fri, Sat; noon-11pm Sun. **Main courses** 98Skr-295Skr. **Credit** AmEx, DC, MC, V. **Map** p209 D2 ❹
This Lilla Torg stalwart is still going strong, noted for its inventive, quality 'New Japanese' cuisine and excellent cocktails.

Lemon Grass
Grynbodgatan 9 (040 30 69 79/www.lemongrass.se). **Open** 6pm-midnight Mon-Thur; 6pm-1am Fri, Sat. **Main courses** 126Skr-198Skr. **Credit** AmEx, DC, MC, V. **Map** p209 D2 ❺
More Asian-influenced fusion magic is on offer in this stylish, minimalist eaterie.

Mellow Yello
Lilla Torg 1 (040 30 45 25/www.melloyello.se). **Open** 4pm-1am Mon-Fri; 11am-2am Sat; 11am-11pm Sun. **Main courses** 121Skr-199Skr. **Credit** AmEx, DC, MC, V. **Map** p209 D2 ❻
One of the prime bars in Lilla Torg with a great atmosphere and a young-ish clientele. All of the venues on Lilla Torg come equipped with outdoor rain covers and parasol heaters.

Moosehead Bar & Restaurant
Lilla Torg 1 (040 12 04 23/www.moosehead.se). **Open** 4pm-1am Mon-Fri; noon-2am Sat; noon-11pm Sun. **Main courses** 69Skr-162Skr. **Credit** AmEx, MC, V. **Map** p209 D2 ❼
Another recommended Lilla Torg eaterie, this time serving hearty steaks and burgers but with a local twist (moose meat burgers, for one). Great atmosphere, especially outside on a summer evening.

Salt & Brygga
Sundspromenaden 7, Västra Hamnen (040 611 5940/www.saltobrygga.se). **Open** 11.30am-2pm, 6-10pm Mon-Fri; 5-10pm Sat. **Main courses** 255Skr. **Credit** AmEx, DC, MC, V. **Map** p209 A1 ❽
If you are visiting the fabulous new Western Harbour residential area, this is a great summer restaurant serving modern Scandinavian-Italian cuisine in a light, trendy venue beside the water.

Restaurang Smak
Scaniaplatsen 2A (040 12 50 35/www.restaurang smak.se). **Open** 11.30am-10pm Mon-Thur; 11.30am-11pm Fri, Sat. **Main courses** 155Skr. **Credit** AmEx, MC, V. **Map** p209 A1 ❾
This contemporary seafood restaurant is one of the newest restaurants to open in the hot, new Western Harbour area.

Spot
Stora Nygatan 33 (040 12 02 03). **Open** 9am-4pm Mon-Sat. **Main courses** 65Skr-85Skr. **Credit** AmEx, MC, V. **Map** p209 D2 ❿
Desirable and refreshingly modern Italian cooking in a stylish setting close to the centre of town. As with most of Sweden's restaurants, despite the chic design children are very welcome here. An in-house

Ribersborgs Kallbadhus. *See p210.*

delicatessen is an extra bonus. Spot also has a branch in the trendy Bo01 dockside area of the city (Sundspromenaden 1; 040 30 60 51) with an outdoor terrace and lounge bar.

Trappaner
Tegelgårdsgatan 5 (040 57 97 50). **Open** 6-10pm Mon-Thur; 6-11pm Fri, Sat. **Main courses** 210Skr-245Skr. **Credit** AmEx, DC, MC, V. **Map** p209 C2 ⑪
Recently moved to more contemporary surroundings, this modern Italian/French/Swedish restaurant has been a great success with locals.

Victors
Lilla Torg 1 (040 12 76 70/www.victors-bar.com). **Open** 11.30am-10.30pm Mon-Sat. **Main courses** 149Skr-195Skr. **Credit** AmEx, DC, MC, V. **Map** p209 D2 ⑫
Experience modern Scandinavian cooking in this quintessential Swedish bar/restaurant which, come night-time, transforms into a club space. The food offers good value and Victors boasts its own bartending academy, so, as you would expect, the selection of cocktails is excellent.

Where to stay

If you want to stay overnight and can't get into the places listed below, contact **Malmö Tourist Hotel Booking** (040 10 92 10, www.malmo.se/turist).

Hooked on classics: **Rådhuset**. *See p211.*

Accome Hotel Apartment Mazetti
Norra Skolgatan 24 (040 641 30 00/www.accome. com). **Rates** 1-room apartment with kitchenette for 1-2 persons for 1-2 nights 1,095Skr. **Credit** AmEx, DC, MC, V. **Map** p209 D3 ❶
This apartment hotel near Möllevången is based in a converted chocolate factory.

Clarion Hotel Malmö
Engelbrektsgatan 16 (040 710 20/www.choice hotels.se). **Rates** 1,595Skr single; 1,895Skr double; 2,900Skr family room. **Credit** AmEx, DC, MC, V. **Map** p209 D2 ❷
One of Malmö's oldest hotels (dating from the turn of the 19th century) retains many of its period features and, although it is not the finest hotel in town (that accolade goes to the pricier Hotel Kramer), it is centrally located and is good value.

Hilton Malmö City
Triangeln 2 (040 693 47 00/www.hilton.com). **Rates** 1,090Skr-1,795Skr single; 1,090Skr-1,995Skr double. **Credit** AmEx, DC, MC, V. **Map** p209 D3 ❸
Modern high-rise international hotel chain with a decent restaurant, the Lean Grill & Bar. The hotel is located at the southern end of Malmö's pedestrian shopping area.

Scandic Hotel Kramer
Stortorget 7 (040 693 54 00/www.scandic-hotels. com). **Rates** 1,190Skr-1,595Skr single; 1,190Skr-1,895Skr double. **Credit** AmEx, DC, MC, V. **Map** p209 D2 ❹
Malmö's poshest hotel is a smaller replica of Copenhagen's swanky French chateau-style Hotel d'Angleterre, but without the overbearing snobbery of its Danish counterpart. It was built at the end of the 19th century and thus, unlike later hotels, enjoys a prime location right in the centre of town.

Resources

For speedy exploration, you can rent a bicycle at **Fridhems Cyklar** (Tessinsväg 13, 040 26 03 35) or **Cykelkliniken** (Carlsgatan, right behind the railway station, 040 611 66 66).

Tourist information
Malmö Tourist Office, Central Station (040 34 12 00/www.malmo.se). **Open** *June-Aug* 9am-7pm Mon-Fri; 10am-5pm Sat, Sun. *May, Sept* 10am-6pm Mon-Fri; 10am-2pm Sat, Sun. *Oct-Apr* 9am-5pm Mon-Fri, 10am-2pm Sat, Sun. **Credit** AmEx, DC, MC, V. **Map** p209 D1.
The Malmö Card (1 day 130Skr, 2 days 160Skr, 3 days 190Skr) is valid for one adult and one child under 15 and is worth considering. It provides free transport on local buses, free parking and discounts on travel to Copenhagen. In addition, use it to gain free or discounted entrance to a number of Malmö's sights, including Malmöhus Castle and the Malmö Museums. Should you decide to linger a while in town, the card also procures discounts on car, bike and pedalo hire.

The Danish Riviera

Keeping up with the Jensens.

Join the models on the beach at **Klampenborg**.

Known variously as the 'Danish Riviera', the 'whisky belt' or the 'Beverly Hills' of Copenhagen (this is where most of the showbiz and sports stars reside), the road that leads north along the coast from the capital is flanked by some of the most expensive housing in the country. As well as the architectural horrors and delights that wealthy Danes have constructed here, there are several interesting attractions for visitors.

Chief among them – and the main reason visitors leave Copenhagen and travel half an hour north in this direction – is the stunning modern art museum, Louisiana Museum For Moderne Kunst. As well as this, there is the beautiful home of Karen *Out of Africa* Blixen and, at the end of your journey north, Hamlet's home town, Helsingør, with its indomitable castle.

The coast road, Strandvejen, often comes within metres of the sea, and is frequently congested during the height of summer. Happily, the train service to Helsingør also runs parallel to the water, stopping at most of the towns and villages along the way. As is

usual in Denmark, it is quick, efficient and reasonably priced, and there are stations roughly every ten minutes.

The Riviera begins at **Charlottenlund**, with its pleasant beach and camping area. Next is **Klampenborg** with another popular beach, **Bellevue**, **Bakken** amusement park (*see p217*) and a large wild deer park.

Tivoli may be Denmark's most famous amusement park, but Dyrehavesbakken (known as Bakken for short) is equally popular with Danes. Bakken was founded in 1583 and claims to be the oldest amusement park in the world. It is, nevertheless, usually seen as Tivoli's downmarket cousin and does have more of a funfair/beer hall atmosphere but that doesn't mean less enjoyment. There are 100 or so rides (which tend to be cheaper than Tivoli's), as well as 35 cafés and restaurants. Admission to the park is free.

Bakken is on the edge of a 1,000-hectare (2,470-acre) former royal hunting ground, now a rather more serene deer park, **Dyrehaven**. Dyrehaven, as it's better known, dates from 1231 and is to Copenhagers what Richmond

Bakken. See p217.

Park is to Londoners. The park is closed to traffic; all the better for its large herds of free-roaming deer and the many walkers who come here from the city. Expensive horse-drawn carriage rides are also available. In its grounds is the enigmatic former hunting lodge, Eremitagen, which has wonderful views to the sea (but is not open to the public). Nearby is Klampenborg's **Galopbane** (*see p204*), a racing and trotting course.

Close to Bellevue Beach and Klampenborg Station are two notable restaurants: **Den Gule Cottage** and **Restaurant Jacobsen** (for both, *see p217*). The latter is housed in a building designed by the legendary Danish architect and designer Arne Jacobsen and features many of his most famous furniture designs. It is part of the famous Bellevue housing and theatre complex, which was one of his earliest and most influential works.

Dyrehaven, Bakken and Bellevue Beach are within easy walking distance of Klampenborg Station, 18 minutes by train from Copenhagen.

The next major point of interest along the coast is **Rungstedlund**, the former home of the Danish novelist Karen Blixen, now the site of

Karen Blixen Museet (*see p217*). The internationally acclaimed author spent much of her life (apart from 17 years in Kenya) in Rungstedlund. Blixen is buried in the gardens of Rungstedlund, at the foot of Ewald's hill, beneath a large beech tree. This simple, early 19th-century house set in 16 hectares (40 acres) of gardens also acts as a bird sanctuary. Its north wing has been preserved as if Blixen had just left, with her furniture, paintings and even her distinctive flower arrangements as they were when she lived here. There's a gallery of Blixen's drawings and paintings, and a biographical exhibition, library and small cinema upstairs.

The house was also once the residence of another eminent Danish writer, Johannes Ewald (1743-81). He lived here in 1773 and wrote several of his lyric poems and heroic tragedies in verse in the same room in which Blixen also chose to write. Rungstedlund is about ten minutes' walk from the nearest railway station, Rungsted Kyst. Alternatively, you can catch a train to Klampenborg and take bus number 388.

Between Rungstedlund and Helsingør are several more small harbours, but the main attraction is the **Louisiana Museum For Moderne Kunst** (Louisiana Modern Art Museum; *see p217*). There may be larger modern art collections in the world, but none is located in more blissful surroundings than Louisiana. A more peaceful setting for this diverse collection of modern art amid leafy gardens that cascade down to the shore would be hard to imagine.

Louisiana began life as a purely Scandinavian art collection. It was founded in 1954 by the industrialist and art collector Knud Jensen, but international works were added thanks to donations from the Ny Carlsberg Foundation. Architects Jørgen Bo and Vilhelm Wohlert added new galleries to the existing 19th-century villa (which already had the name Louisiana after the previous owner's three wives who, bizarrely, were all named Louise), and the resulting, much enlarged, complex is characterised by a vaguely Japanese style.

The irregular-shaped, open-plan, whitewashed rooms with their large windows blur the divide between the galleries and the outside sculpture park, giving Louisiana its uniquely tranquil atmosphere. Somehow, the reassuring proximity of beech trees, lawn and sea (with the Swedish coast in the distance) creates a harmony between the buildings and their environment that counterbalances the frequently confrontational, disturbing and/or impenetrable nature of the works on display. And the light here is unique.

The first pieces bought by the museum were by Danish artists like Richard Mortensen, Asger Jørn (one of the founders of the abstract COBRA Group; the name was formed from COpenhagen, BRussels and Amsterdam, home cities of the artists involved) and the constructivist sculptor and graphic artist Robert Jacobsen. The collection soon grew to encompass works by many notable post-war French sculptors like Herbin, Albers, Gabo and Alexander Calder and, from the 1950s, Louisiana acquired paintings by Dubuffet, Bacon, Rothko and Reinhardt. Paintings from several of Picasso's periods are among the museum's highlights, while the Pop Art movement of the '60s is also well represented (in fact, the whole museum has something of a flower-power feel) with pieces by, among others, Warhol, Lichtenstein, Oldenburg and Rauschenberg. Louisiana's collection of '70s German art is strong. Bringing things right up to date are a few contemporary pieces, including a video installation by British artist Sam Taylor Wood.

The museum's south wing was added in 1982 and a corridor built connecting it to the old buildings. Along the corridor now hang the colourful geometric paintings of Richard Mortensen. In 1991 a subterranean wing exhibiting graphic art opened.

In the garden you'll find sculptures by Calder, Henry Moore, Joan Miró, Max Ernst and Giacometti, among others (Giacometti also features inside the gallery in a dedicated room that is one of the highlights of the museum). The gardens are very popular with children, who also benefit from their own indoor area, Bornehuset (Children's House).

Louisiana holds regular lectures, film screenings and concerts and is famed for its superstar retrospectives (there are usually around six temporary exhibitions each year). It has a large shop selling everything from trendy garden tools to books and posters, plus a superb café with a terrace overlooking the Øresund towards Sweden, graced by one of Calder's amusing sculptures.

Bakken

Dyrehavsbakken, Dyrehavevej 62, Klampenborg (39 63 35 44/www.bakken.dk). **Open** *Last Thur Mar-1st Mon Sept* noon-midnight daily. *1st Tue Sept-last Wed Mar* closed. **Admission** free, rides extra (reduced prices Wed). **Credit** (most restaurants and cafés, but not rides) DC, MC, V. **Photo** *p216.*

Karen Blixen Museet

Rungstedlund, Rungsted Strandvej 111, Rungsted (45 57 10 57/www.karen-blixen.dk). **Open** *May-Sept* 10am-5pm Tue-Sun. *Oct-Apr* 1-4pm Wed-Fri; 11am-4pm Sat, Sun. **Admission** 40kr; 35kr concessions; free under-18s. **Credit** AmEx, DC, MC, V.

Louisiana Museum For Moderne Kunst

Gammel Strandvej 13, Humlebæk (49 19 07 19/www.louisiana.dk). **Open** 10am-5pm Mon, Tue, Thur-Sun; 10am-10pm Wed. **Admission** 80kr; 60kr-73kr concessions; free under-18s. **Credit** AmEx, DC, MC, V.

Where to eat

Den Gule Cottage

Staunings Plæne, Strandvejen 506, Klampenborg (39 64 06 91/www.dengulecottage.dk). **Open** *Restaurant* noon-4pm, 6pm-midnight Mon-Sat. *Kitchen* noon-2pm, 6-9.30pm Mon-Sat. **Main courses** 3 courses 445kr. **Credit** AmEx, DC, MC, V. For full review, *see p124.*

Restaurant Jacobsen

Strandvejen 449, Klampenborg (39 63 43 22/www.restaurantjacobsen.dk). **Open** noon-midnight Tue-Sat. *Meals served* noon-10pm Tue-Sat. **Main courses** *Lunch* 80-285kr; *Dinner* 165-225kr. **Credit** AmEx, DC, MC, V. For full review, *see p124.*

Getting there

By train

There are trains at least every 20mins heading north along the coast from Central Station via Nørreport. It takes 18mins to get to Klampenborg, 30mins to reach Rungsted Kyst and 41mins to Humlebæk.

Louisiana Museum.

North Sjælland

Take a dip with the Danes.

Frederiksborg Slot.

If you find yourself in Copenhagen for more than a few days and fancy a breath of old-fashioned, fresh seaside air, then a trip to the timewarp fishing villages and glorious beaches of the northern coast of Sjælland could be just the ticket. Many Copenhageners have summer houses in the region, and much of the city decamps to the beach from late June to the end of July so it can get crowded then, although there are plenty of campsites and holiday homes to rent.

On your way north to the coast – about an hour's drive from Copenhagen, a little longer if you take the train – you would do well to stop off at one of Denmark's most important castles. **Frederiksborg Slot** (not to be confused with Frederiksberg Slot in Copenhagen), is half an hour north of Copenhagen by train. This majestic early 17th-century Dutch Renaissance red-brick castle, with its ornate copper spires and sandstone façade, stands on three small

islands in Slotsø (Castle Lake), in the middle of the town of Hillerød. The castle is complemented by elegant baroque gardens and an English garden with a chateau.

The castle was gutted by fire in 1859 and for a while it looked as though it would remain a ruin. Fortunately, JC Jacobsen volunteered to use some of his considerable Carlsberg wealth to restore Frederiksborg and subsequently helped found **Det Nationalhistoriske Museum** (Museum of National History) within 70 or so of its rooms. The museum opened in 1882 and charts Denmark's history through paintings arranged in chronological order.

One of the decorative highlights of Frederiksborg is its chapel, which, between 1671 and 1840, was used for the coronations of Denmark's absolute monarchs. Since 1693 it has also been the chapel for Danish knights, whose shields hang on the walls; remarkably, it's also the local church. Its altar and pulpit are the work of the Hamburg goldsmith Jakob Mores, while the priceless Compenius organ, dating from 1610 and boasting 1,000 pipes, is played every Thursday between 1.30pm and 2pm. It is worth timing a visit to hear it.

From Frederiksborg Slot it is a short journey north to the fishing towns of Hornbæk, Gilleleje and Tisvildeleje, ranged along the northern coast of Sjælland. In between are expansive, natural stretches of sand, with shallow, clean water and all the facilities required for a day at the beach (though they are usually kept well out of sight of the beach itself). The beaches are typically fronted by grassy dunes, rugged heathland and ancient forests.

Hornbæk became popular during the 19th century with artists such as PS Krøyer and Kristian Zahrtmann, who took a shine to the picturesque life of the local fishermen. Its beach is excellent for children as it shelves gently. There is wheelchair access. As with all the beaches mentioned, it is possible to walk from the nearest railway station.

Hornbæk has a wide range of accommodation and several restaurants, mainly located in the town centre, but for cheap, fresh snacks you are best off heading for the seafood kiosks in the harbour. For more information, contact the local tourist office (49 70 47 47, www.hornbaek.dk).

Dronningmølle (Queen's Mill), the next stop five kilometres (three miles) along the road west towards Gilleleje, also has a great beach. Alternatively, you could take the road south towards Villingerød and turn left at the church to reach **Rudolph Tegners Museum** (*see below* **The world's worst sculptor?**).

Gilleleje (tourist office: 48 30 01 74/www.gilleleje.dk) is the most northerly town in Sjælland, the island's largest fishing harbour and was one of the main escape routes for Danish Jews in 1943 (there is an exhibition on this in Gilleleje Museum). Many of the Jews hid in the roof of Gilleleje Kirke in Hovedgade, which dates from the 16th century. Gilleleje has a bustling fishing harbour and a 14-kilometre (nine-mile) long beach.

Tisvildeleje (tourist office: 48 70 74 51/www.helsinge.com) is another attractive coastal village west of Gilleleje. Its long, broad, sandy beach is a short walk downhill from the railway station, past 18th-century fishermen's cottages, most of which are now summer

The world's worst sculptor?

A couple of kilometres inland from Dronningmølle on the north coast of Zealand lies one of Denmark's most idiosyncratic museums. The **Rudolph Tegners Museum** is dedicated to the work of a Danish artist who was either a crazy genius or the world's worst sculptor, depending on whom you believe.

Born in 1873, Rudolph Tegner considered himself a great artist. The difference between Tegner and your average arty megalomaniac was that, thanks to his wife Elna's inherited fortune, he had the financial wherewithal to realise his vision. In 1916 Tegner bought a piece of heath beside the coast and, over the next decades, set about preserving his life's work for future generations.

Tegner had had limited success in persuading the rest of Denmark to appreciate his symbolist/art nouveau/Nietzschean-influenced sculptures, and critics were rarely positive. *Berlingske Aften*, the leading evening paper, wrote of one of his pieces: 'The most disheartening thing about Tegner's plaster monstrosity is not... its purely sculptural mediocrity, but the mentality it expresses. If you have studied the statue long enough and close your eyes, you can hear boots tramping in time and bombastic band music,

and before your inner eye rise the contours of Haus der Deutschen Kunst in Munich.'

Today Tegner's monumental, histrionic works can be seen both dotted among the heather in the 46-acre sculpture park and inside the museum building. This sinister, virtually windowless, raw concrete bunker, built in 1937, squats among the grazing sheep like the villain's lair from a low-budget Bond movie. It's certainly in stark contrast to the exceptionally beautiful landscape of Rusland that surrounds it.

It is hard to pick out 'highlights', but *Sankt Peder med Nøglen* (St Peter with the Key) is notably dreadful – a monstrously ugly figure with oversized thighs. To be fair, Tegner did occasionally create something with genuine grace and beauty; it's just that his bad stuff is so much more entertaining.

Rudolph Tegners Museum

Museumsvej 19, Dronningmølle (49 71 91 77/www.rudolphtegner.dk). Train to Kildekrog or Dronningmølle. **Open** *Mid Apr-May, Sept, Oct* noon-5pm Tue-Sun. *June-Aug* 9.30am-5pm Tue-Sun. *Nov-mid Apr* closed. **Admission** 40kr; 20kr concessions; free under-12s. **No credit cards.**

houses. Nearby is one of Denmark's largest forests, **Tisvilde Hegn**, planted 200 years ago to stop coastal erosion, which offers bracing walks (the tourist office has maps).

Frederiksborg Slot

Hillerød (48 26 04 39/www.frederiksborgmuseet.dk). Train to Hillerød. **Open** *Apr-Oct* 10am-5pm daily. *Nov-Mar* 11am-3pm daily. **Admission** 60kr; 15kr-50kr concessions; free under-6s. **Credit** MC, V.

Gilleleje Museum

Pyramiden, Vesterbrogade 56, Gilleleje (48 30 16 31/ www.holbo.dk). **Open** *June-Aug* 1-4pm Mon, Wed-Sun. *Sept-May* noon-4pm Wed-Fri; 10am-2pm Sat. **Admission** 25kr; free under-18s. **No credit cards**.

Where to eat

Jan Hurtigkarl

Nordre Strandvej 154, Ålsgårde (49 70 90 93/ www.hurtigkarl.dk). **Open** noon-4pm, 6-10pm Tue-Sun. **Set menu** 625kr. **Credit** MC, V.
The eponymous Jan travels around the world to bring back inspiration for his themed seasonal menus at this wonderful seaside restaurant that has won rave reviews from the Danish press.

Restaurant Søstrene Olsen

Øresundvej 10, Hornbæk (49 70 05 50/www. soestreneolsen.dk). **Open** noon-4pm, 6-9pm Thur-Mon. **Main courses** 250kr. **Credit** AmEx, DC, MC, V.
The location for this restaurant– a pretty thatched cottage overlooking the beach – couldn't be better, and the food is just as good. Seafood a speciality.

Where to stay

Gilleleje Badehotel

Hulsøvej 15, Gilleleje (48 30 13 47/www.gilleleje badehotel.dk). **Rates** 1,190kr-1,390kr double. **Credit** AmEx, DC, MC, V.
This freshly renovated 'bathing hotel' makes an excellent base for a visit to the north coast.

Hotel Villa Strand

Kystvej 2, Hornbæk (49 70 00 88/www.villa strand.dk). **Rates** 500kr-850kr single; 750kr double. **Credit** AmEx, DC, MC, V.
Peaceful and serene accommodation option close to the centre of town and the beach.

Resources

Tourist information

Gilleleje *Gilleleje Hovedgade 6F (48 30 01 74/ www.gilleleje-turistbureau.dk).* **Open** 10am-4pm Mon-Fri; 10am-noon Sat.
Hornbæk *Hornbæk Bibliotek, Vestre Stejlebakke 2A (49 70 47 47/www.hornbaek.dk).* **Open** 1-7pm Mon; 10am-5pm Wed, Fri; 1-5pm Thur; 10am-2pm Sat.

Getting there

By train

To get to Hornbæk and Dronningmølle, take trains from Central Station and change at Helsingør (about 1hr 30mins in total, 1 train an hour). To reach Gilleleje or Tisvildeleje, take the S-tog from Central Station and change at Hillerød (1hr 20mins in total, around 2 trains an hour).

Sjælland's glorious coastline.

Trips Out of Town

Directory

Features

Illums Bolighus. *See p157.*

Directory

Getting Around

By air

Copenhagen Airport (also known as Kastrup) is often voted best in the world by air passengers. It receives direct flights from 128 cities worldwide and 18 million passengers pass through.

Flight time from London is about one-and-a-half hours; direct flights from New York (Newark) take seven-and-a-half hours; while the fastest direct flight from the west coast is nine-and-a-half hours (from Seattle; coming from LA or San Francisco you'll have to change and journey time is approximately 14 hours). International flights arrive and depart from **Terminals 2** and **3**. (Terminal 1 is for domestic flights only.) The airport is ten kilometres (six miles) south-east of Copenhagen on the island of Amager.

A **train** service links the airport (the station is located under Terminal 3, just walk straight ahead out of the arrivals hall and you can't miss it) to Central Station and the journey time is only **12 minutes**. The single fare is **27kr**. Trains leave **every 10 minutes from platform 2** from 4.40am every day. The last train leaves at 12.44am. There are also seven trains an hour from Central Station out to the airport (at 03, 15, 23, 27, 35, 43 and 55 minutes past the hour), starting at 4.03am. The last train runs at 3.03am. For additional information

contact **DSB** (Danish State Railways) on 70 13 14 15/ www.dsb.dk.

There are plentiful **taxis** at Terminals 1 and 3; the fare into the centre of the city should be around 200kr. Tips are not expected in Danish taxis.

Local **buses** (12 or 96N, the nightbus, to Rådhuspladsen; and 30 or 250S to Central Station) run from Terminal 3 every 10 to 20 minutes (the night bus is twice an hour), but most visitors take the train as the bus fare is only slightly cheaper and the journey longer.

For further information on bus services, contact **HUR** (Hovedstadsområdets Udviklingsråd) on 36 13 14 15/www.hur.dk.

A free transit bus runs every ten to 15 minutes between international and domestic terminals.

AIRPORT FACILITIES

The airport's facilities include shops and restaurants, banks (most open 6am-10pm daily) in the Transfer Hall and Terminals 2 and 3, as well as cash machines (ATMs) in Terminals 1, 2 and 3. There are lockers in Terminals 1 and 2 and left luggage facilities in Arkaden between Terminals 2 and 3 (*see p227*). Though Copenhagen is a pedestrian-friendly city, there are car hire desks in Terminals 1 and 3 (*see p225*).

Copenhagen Airport
Central switchboard 32 31 32 31/ flight info 32 47 47 47/www.cph.dk. The website gives details of live information on arrival and departure times. For more specific flight information, call the relevant handling agent: Novia (32 47 47 47); British Airways (70 12 80 22); Mærsk Air (70 33 33 70); Premier, Luxair

(33 91 60 91); Iberia (70 10 01 52); Pulkovo (33 91 76 74); Air Baltic (70 10 20 00); Turkish Airlines (33 14 40 55); SAS (70 10 20 00); Servisair (32 31 40 76); KLM (70 10 07 47); Air France (82 33 27 01); Alitalia (70 27 02 90); Swiss (70 10 50 64).

By rail

DSB (De Danske Statsbaner – Danish State Railways) connects Copenhagen with all of continental Europe's capitals. It also connects to the UK, though you have to change trains in the Netherlands. All international trains arrive and depart from **Central Station (Hovedbanegård)**.

Central Station (Københavns Hovedbanegård)
(33 14 04 00/www.hovedbane gaarden.dk). **Open** 4.30am-2am Mon-Sat; 5.30am-2am Sun. **Map** p250 P11.
The website is in Danish only.

By road

The Danish capital is 300 kilometres (186 miles) from the German border, and only a half-hour drive to Malmö.

Eurolines runs express coaches to Copenhagen.

Danish Road Directorate
Niels Juels Gade 13 (33 41 33 33/80 20 20 60/Traffic Information Centre 70 10 10 40). **Open** *Traffic Information Centre* 24hrs daily. Route, roadworks and traffic information for Denmark and the rest of Europe.

Eurolines
Halmtorvet 5 (70 10 00 30/ www.eurolines.com). **Open** 8am-5pm daily. **Credit** DC, MC, V. **Map** p250 P11.
The Eurolines station is located near Central Station.

By sea

There are direct ferries
between Copenhagen
and Oslo (16 hours) and
Swinoujscie in Poland
(10 hours). In addition, there's
a ferry route from Helsingør
(47 km/28 miles north of
Copenhagen) to Sweden, from
Esbjerg (200 km/124 miles
west) to the UK, from Rødby
(150km/93 miles south)
to Germany, and from
Frederikshavn or Hirtshals
(450 km/280 miles north-west)
to Sweden and Norway.

DFDS Seaways

Copenhagen–Oslo; Esbjerg–Harwich.
*Dampfærgevej 30, Østerbro (33 42
30 00/www.dfdsseaways.dk).* **Open**
Phone enquiries 9am-5pm daily.
Credit MC, V.

Polferries

Copenhagen–Swinoujscie.
*Dampfærgevej 30, Østerbro (33 11
46 45/www.polferries.dk).* **Open**
10am-4pm, and at times of departure
Mon-Fri. **No credit cards**.

Scandlines

Helsingør–Helsingborg.
*Copenhagen Office: Dampfærgevej
10, Østerbro (33 15 15 15/www.
scandlines.dk). Train to Helsingør.*
Credit AmEx, DC, MC, V. **Open**
phone enquiries 24hrs daily.

Public transport

Trains, Metro & buses

Copenhagen is blessed with an
efficient network of local buses
(**HUR**; Hovedstadsområdets
Udviklingsråd), trains (**S-tog**),
run by Danish State Railways
(**DSB**; *see p225*), and since
2003 the smart new **Metro**
system. The Metro has two
lines, M1 and M2, both of
which run through Nørreport,
Kongens Nytorv and
Christianshavn. It does not
yet go as far as the airport,
terminating at Ørestad
and Legravesparken, and
Frederiksberg and Vanløse in
the west and north-west of the
city respectively. Trains run
from 5am to midnight daily
and through the night at

weekends. For further
information call 33 11 17 00
or visit www.m.dk.

The S-tog local train system
is made up of 11 different lines,
ten of which pass through
Central Station.

Buses, S-tog trains and
the Metro all use the same
ticket system and zoned fare
structure. There is a map of
the S-tog system and Metro
lines on p256 of this guide.

Trains and buses run from
5am Monday to Saturday
(from 6am on Sundays) until
around half past midnight,
although some of these buses
do run through the night.

HUR

*Rådhuspladsen (36 13 14 15/www.
hur.dk).* **Open** *Phone enquiries* 7am-
9.30pm daily. **No credit cards**.
Map p250 O12.
The HUR office can supply you
with timetables, journey plans,
discount cards and lost property
information.

Tickets & discount cards

The Copenhagen metropolitan
area is split into seven zone
rings, radiating out from the
centre of the city. The **basic
ticket** allows passengers to
travel within two zones on a
variety of transport: buses,
trains and the Metro. It costs
18kr (9kr for children). As
the two central zones include
almost every attraction, hotel,
restaurant and bar covered in
this guide, it's unlikely that
visitors will need to buy
anything more than this
basic ticket. Such a ticket
also allows transfers between
buses and trains, providing
that the transfer is made
within an hour. All tickets
are stamped with the date,
time and departure zone.
Two- and three-zone tickets
are valid for a period of one
hour from the stamped time;
four- to six-zone tickets can
be used for one-and-a-half
hours; all-zone tickets are
valid for two hours.

Tickets are on sale at all
railway station ticket offices.
They can also be purchased
from machines at stations and
from bus drivers. Coloured
zone maps can be found
at bus stops and also in
railway stations.

CHILDREN

Two children aged under
12 can travel for free when
accompanied by an adult.
Children aged 12 to 15
pay the child fare or can
use a child's discount card.
Two 12- to 15-year-olds can
travel on one adult ticket or
on one clip of an adult's
discount card.

DISCOUNT CARDS

Discount clip cards
(*klippekort*) are available
for ten journeys within two,
three, four, five, six or all
zones (two-zone cards cost
115kr; 55kr children under
16). When you start your
journey, you must punch
your card in the yellow
machine on the bus or in
the station.

One clip covers you for
travel within the zones printed
on the card. If you want to
travel beyond those zones,
then several simultaneous clips
are needed (for example, if you
have a two-zone card, two clips
allow you to travel within
three or four zones, three clips
allow five or six zones, and so
on). Cards can be bought from
stations, most ticket machines
and HUR ticket offices.

24-HOUR TICKET

This ticket allows unlimited
travel for 24 hours on
Copenhagen's buses and
trains. It costs **105kr** (53kr
children) and should be clipped
in the yellow machines in
buses and stations at the start
of the journey. Two children
under ten can travel free with
an adult holding a 24-hour
ticket. The ticket can be
bought from manned rail
stations and HUR offices.

Directory

Airline flights are one of the biggest producers of the global warming gas CO_2. But with **The CarbonNeutral Company** you can make your travel a little greener.

Go to **www.carbonneutral.com** to calculate your flight emissions then 'neutralise' them through international projects which save exactly the same amount of carbon dioxide.

Contact us at **shop@carbonneutral.com** or call into the office on **0870 199 99 88** for more details.

CarbonNeutral®flights

COPENHAGEN CARD

As well as free admission to more than 60 museums, galleries, attractions and sights, the **Copenhagen Card** offers unlimited travel by bus and train within Greater Copenhagen. Cards are available in two formats: 24 or 72 hours. For prices, *see p52*. The card can be bought from HUR ticket offices in Rådhuspladsen and Toftegårds Plads. It can also be purchased at main stations, most tourist offices and from many hotels.

National rail system

For mapping out journeys and itineraries, **DSB** (Danish State Railways) boasts an excellent integrated journey planner (for the English version; see www.dsb.dk/english) on its website for rail (and bus) journeys within Denmark.

DSB

Central Station (domestic & international journeys 70 13 14 15/S-tog 33 53 00 33/www.dsb.dk). **Open** 7am-10pm daily. *S-tog* 6.30am-11pm daily. **Credit** AmEx, DC, MC, V. **Map** p250 P11.

Waterbuses

During the summer DFDS runs three hop-on, hop-off waterbus routes around the harbour area. One-day tickets (valid on all routes) are **50kr** (25kr children). For more details, visit www.canaltours.dk.

Driving

When it comes to driving, we have one simple word of advice: don't. The Danes, or rather their government, detest private cars and do everything to discourage their use. If you can't do without wheels, here are some tips.

The Danes drive on the right. When turning right, drivers give way to cyclists coming up on the inside and to pedestrians crossing on a green light. You must drive with dipped headlights during the day.

In most places drivers have to pay for parking within the city centre from 8am to 8pm Monday to Friday, and from 8am to 2pm on Saturdays.

Car rental

The prices below are for basic rental of the cheapest car class.

Avis

Kampmannsgade 1 (70 24 77 07/www.avis.com). **Open** 7am-7pm Mon-Fri; 7am-5pm Sat, Sun. **Map** p250 N10.
Terminal 3, Copenhagen Airport (32 51 20 99). **Open** 24hrs daily. **Rates** 962kr/day; 2,757kr/week. **Credit** AmEx, DC, MC, V.

Budget Rent a Car

Vester Farimagsgade 7 (33 55 05 00/www.budget.com). **Open** 8am-6pm Mon-Fri; 8am-1pm Sat, Sun. **Map** p250 P10.
Terminal 3, Copenhagen Airport (32 52 39 00). **Open** 7am-10pm daily. **Rates** 632kr/day; 3,335kr/week. **Credit** AmEx, DC, MC, V.

EuropCar/Pitztner Auto

Gammel Kongevej (33 55 99 00/www.europcar.dk). Bus 14, 15. **Open** 7.30am-7pm Mon-Fri; 8am-4pm Sat; 8am-7pm Sun. **Map** p245 P8.
Terminal 3, Copenhagen Airport (32 50 30 90). **Open** 7am-11pm daily. **Rates** 485kr-815kr/day; 2,555kr-4,270kr/week. **Credit** AmEx, DC, MC, V.

Hertz

Ved Vesterport 3 (33 17 90 20/www.hertzdk.dk). **Open** 7am-6pm Mon-Thur; 7am-7pm Fri; 7am-5pm Sat; 8am-5pm Sun. **Rates** 691kr/day; 2,835kr/week. **Credit** AmEx, DC, MC, V. **Map** p250 O10.

National Car Rental

Kastruplundgade 11, Copenhagen Airport (32 52 04 31/www.nationalcar.dk). **Rates** 731kr/day; 3,315kr/week. **Open** 9am-5pm Mon-Fri. **Credit** AmEx, DC, MC, V.

Breakdown services

Falck Redningskorps

Emergency 70 10 20 30. **Open** 24hrs. **Rates** Non-members approx 600kr/hr Mon-Fri; 1,200kr/hr Sat, Sun. **No credit cards**.

Taxis

Taxis can be flagged down just about anywhere in Copenhagen. If the yellow 'Taxa' light on the roof of the car is on, the taxi is available for hire. The basic fare is 24kr plus 14kr per kilometre (rising to 16kr at night-time and weekends). Fares include a service charge, so there's no need to tip. Most cabs accept credit cards (though, take note: you are supposed to tell the driver at the start if you intend to pay with a card).

Cycling

Cycling is hugely popular. During the summer you can borrow a City Bike from one of the many ranks throughout the city centre for a deposit of 20kr (*see p100* **On yer bike**).

Bike hire

Københavns Cyklebørs

Gothersgade 157 (33 14 07 17/www.cykelboersen.dk). **Open** 9am-5.30pm Mon-Fri; 10am-1.30pm Sat. **Rates** 60kr-150kr/day; 200kr-500kr deposit. **Credit** MC, V. **Map** p247 L14.

Københavns Cykler

Reventlowsgade 11, Central Station (33 33 86 13/www.copenhagen-bikes.dk). **Open** 8am-5.30pm Mon-Fri; 9am-1pm Sat. **Rates** 75kr-200kr/day; 500kr-1,000kr deposit. **Credit** MC, V. **Map** p250 P11.

Organisations

Dansk Cyklist Forbund

Rømersgade 5 (33 32 31 21/fax 33 32 76 83/www.dcf.dk). **Open** 10am-noon, 1-3pm Mon-Fri. **Map** p246 L12. The Dansk Cyklist Forbund has good cycling maps, an excellent website and runs cycling tours.

Walking

Compact, flat Copenhagen is the ideal walking city. Even the main shopping street, Strøget, is pedestrianised. For details of organised walking tours, *see p53*.

Directory

Resources A-Z

Age restrictions

In Denmark, you have to be 16 to drink in a bar. You also have to be 16 to buy cigarettes. You can drive at 18 and have sex at 15.

Business services

Couriers

De Grønne Bude
Vermundsgade 40A, Østerbro (70 10 31 03/39 12 92 00). **Open** 24hrs. **Prices** from 65kr in the city centre. **No credit cards**. Deliveries to Copenhagen and beyond.

Equipment hire

COMTECH
Broenge 8, Ishøj (70 13 10 50/ www.comtech.dk). **Open** 8.30am-4.30pm Mon-Fri. **No credit cards**. COMTECH rents out audio-visual equipment for conferences.

Photocopying/ printing

Vester Kopi
Vesterbrogade 69, Vesterbro (33 27 88 33/www.vesterkopi.dk). **Open** 9am-5pm Mon-Fri. **Map** p245 P9.
Nørregade 7 (33 14 58 33). **Open** 9am-5pm Mon-Fri. **Map** p250 M12.

Gothersgade 12 (33 32 58 33). **Open** 9am-5pm Mon-Fri. **Map** p251 M15. **Credit** MC, V.
Copying and printing services.

Secretarial

Manpower
Rådhuspladsen 75 (70 20 10 00/ www.manpower.dk). **Open** 7.30am-5pm Mon-Thur; 7.30am-4pm Fri. **No credit cards**. **Map** p250 M12.
Manpower matches clients with secretaries who speak two or more languages. Rates vary.

Translation

Check also the *Yellow Pages* under *'Oversættelse'*.

Berlitz
Vimmelskaftet 42A, Jorck's Passage (70 21 50 10/www.berlitz.com). **Open** 8am-9pm Mon-Fri. **Credit** MC, V. **Map** p251 N13.
A global company that offers translators and interpreters in most languages. Prices vary according to requirements. For online translations, check out the website.

Customs

The following can be imported into Denmark without incurring customs duty by non-Danish residents arriving from an EU country with duty-paid goods purchased in an EU country:

● 10 litres of spirits
● 20 litres of sparkling/ fortified wine (under 22 per cent)
● 90 litres of table wine
● 800 cigarettes
● 400 cigarillos
● 200 cigars
● 1,000 grammes of tobacco
● 110 litres of beer.
Residents of non-EU countries entering from outside the EU with goods purchased in non-EU countries can bring in to Denmark:
● 1 litre of spirits or 2 litres of sparkling/fortified wine (maximum 22 per cent)
● 2 litres of table wine
● 200 cigarettes or 100 cigarillos or 50 cigars or 250 grammes of tobacco
● 500 grammes of coffee or 200 grammes of coffee extracts
● 100 grammes of tea or 40 grammes of tea extracts
● 50 grammes of perfume
● 250 millilitres of eau de toilette
● 10 litres of fuel
● other articles, including beer: 1,350kr.
Only those aged 17 or over can use the alcohol and tobacco allowances; coffee and coffee extracts allowances are valid only for those aged 15 or over. It is forbidden to import fresh foods into Denmark unless they are vacuum packed.
Although duty-free goods within the EU were abolished in 1999 and there is now no legal limit on the quantities of alcohol and tobacco travellers may import into most EU countries (provided they are for personal use), Denmark, Finland and Sweden will continue to impose limits for the foreseeable future.
For enquiries about customs regulations, phone 72 37 18 18 or check out the website www.skat.dk.

Travel advice

For current information on travel to a specific country – including the latest news on health issues, safety and security, local laws and customs – you should contact your home country's government department of foreign affairs. Most of them have websites with useful advice for would-be travellers.

Australia
www.smartraveller.gov.au

Canada
www.voyage.gc.ca

New Zealand
www.safetravel.govt.nz

Republic of Ireland
http://foreignaffairs.gov.ie

UK
www.fco.gov.uk/travel

USA
http://travel.state.gov

Directory

Disabled visitors

Facilities for disabled people in Copenhagen are generally excellent relative to other European capitals. *Access in Denmark – A Travel Guide for the Disabled* is available from the Danish Tourist Board in London at 55 Sloane Street, SW1X 9SY (020 7259 5959).

In addition, much Danish tourist literature, including the Wonderful Copenhagen website (www.woco.dk), lists places that are wheelchair-accessible plus useful information on specific facilities for the disabled.

Two Danish organisations may be able to offer help:

Dansk Handicap Forbund

Hans Knudsens Plads 1A, 2100 Copenhagen Ø (39 29 35 55). **Open** *Phone enquiries* 8.15am-4pm Mon-Thur; 8.15am-2pm Fri. Staff members speak English and may be able to help tourists. However, members of the organisation have priority.

Videnscenter for Bevægelseshandicap

PP Ørumsgade 11, 8000 Århus (89 49 12 70/fax 89 49 12 76/www.vfb.dk). **Open** 10am-3pm Mon-Thur; 10am-2pm Fri. The Danish Information Centre for Physical Disability collects, develops, adapts and disseminates information about a variety of subjects relating to physical disability in Denmark.

Electricity

Denmark, in common with most of Europe, has 220-volt AC, 50Hz current and uses two-pin continental plugs. Visitors from the UK will need to buy an adaptor for their appliances, while North Americans won't be able to use their 110/125V appliances without a transformer.

Elevators/lifts

To reach the ground floor you will usually have to press a button marked 'S', for 'stuen'.

Embassies & consulates

American Embassy

Dag Hammarskjöld Allé 24, 2100 Copenhagen Ø (35 41 71 00/www.usembassy.dk). **Open** *Phone enquiries* 2-4pm daily. **Map** p247 G15.

British Embassy

Kastelsvej 36-40, off Classensgade, 2100 Copenhagen Ø (35 44 52 00/www.britishembassy.dk). Train to Østerport Station, then 10min walk. **Open** 9am-5pm Mon-Fri. *Visa dept* 9am-11am Mon-Fri. **Map** p248 F15.

Canadian Embassy

Kristen Bernikowsgade 1, 1105 Copenhagen K (33 48 32 00/www.canada.dk). **Open** 8.30am-4.30pm Mon-Fri. **Map** p251 M14.

Irish Embassy

Østbanegade 21, 2100 Copenhagen Ø (35 42 32 33). Train to Østerport Station, then 6min walk. **Open** 10am-12.30pm, 2.30-4.30pm Mon-Fri. **Map** p249 G16.

Emergencies

To contact the police, the ambulance service or the fire service in an emergency, phone **112** (free of charge). For central police stations, *see p230.*

Health

All temporary foreign visitors to Denmark are entitled to free medical and hospital treatment if they are taken ill or have an accident.

Accident & emergency

The following (relatively centrally located) hospitals have 24-hour emergency departments. Note that the largest and most central hospital in the city, the Rigshospital, does not have an accident and emergency department.

Amager Hospital

Italiensvej 1, Amager (32 34 32 34/www.amagerhospital.dk). Bus 4A, 12. Emergency department: Kastrupvej 63 (32 34 35 00). Bus 4A, 12.

Bispebjerg Hospital

Bispebjerg Bakke 23, Bispebjerg (35 31 35 31/www.bispebjerghospital.dk). Bus 21, 69.

Frederiksberg Hospital

Nordre Fasanvej 57, Frederiksberg (38 16 38 16/www.frederiksberg hospital.dk). Bus 29, 831.

Contraception

Condoms are widely available and are sold in most supermarkets and pharmacies as well as from vending machines in bars and on the street. Birth control pills can be obtained from pharmacies but require a doctor's prescription.

Dentists

Tourist offices (*see p233*) can refer foreign visitors to local dentists.

Dental Emergency Service

Oslo Plads 14 (35 38 02 51). **Open** 8am-9.30pm Mon-Fri; 10am-noon Sat, Sun. **No credit cards.** **Map** p247 H15. Personal enquiries only. Treatment must be paid for in cash.

Doctors

Lægevagten

70 13 00 41. **Price** from 400kr per visit. EU citizens are not charged.

Insurance

Citizens of other EU countries are entitled to have free medical treatment and essential medication.

The UK has a reciprocal health agreement with Denmark, which means that, in addition to free emergency treatment, UK citizens can usually obtain free medical care from a doctor, and hospital treatment if referred by a doctor.

The European Health Insurance Card (EHIC) has replaced the defunct E111. The free card entitles you to the same state-provided treatment as a resident in European

Directory

Economic Area countries and is valid for three to five years. For more information visit www.doh.gov.uk/travellers.

Citizens of non-EU countries should make sure they have adequate health insurance before travelling.

Pharmacies

There is no shortage of pharmacies in Copenhagen; look for the '*apotek*' sign.

City Helse
Vendersgade 6 (33 14 08 92). **Open** 9.30am-5.30pm Mon-Thur; 9.30am-6pm Fri; 9.30am-2pm Sat. **No credit cards**. **Map** p246 L12. City Helse stocks a good selection of health food and natural medicine.

Steno Apotek
Vesterbrogade 6, by Central Station (33 14 82 66). **Open** 24hrs daily. **No credit cards**. **Map** p250 P11.

Internet

Most hotels in Copenhagen provide internet access. *See pp38-50* **Where to Stay** for more details.

Internet cafés

Boomtown
Axeltorv 1 (33 32 10 32/www. boomtown.net). **Open** 24 hours daily. **Map** p250 O11.

Faraos Cigarer
Skindergade 27 (33 32 22 11/ www.faraos.dk). **Open** 9.30am-5.30pm Mon-Thur; 9.30am-7pm Fri; 9.30am-3pm Sat. **Map** p250 O12.

Nethouse 2000
Amagerbrogade 44 (32 95 21 20/ www.nethouse.dk). Metro Amagerbro. **Open** 24 hours daily.

Language

See p235 **Vocabulary**. For information on language classes, *see p231*.

Left luggage

Airport

Copenhagen Airport's left luggage facility is located in

Terminal 2 and is open from 6am until 10.30pm daily (32 31 23 60). You can store your belongings there for a period of up to four weeks. Charges start from **30kr** per day. Self-service baggage lockers are located next to the left luggage facility and next to the Service Centre in **Terminal 1**. The charge for a locker is **20kr-50kr** per 24 hours. The maximum rental period for use of the lockers is 72 hours.

Rail station

There are left luggage lockers by the Reventlowsgade entrance of Central Station. Prices are 30kr or 40kr for 24 hours, depending on the size of the locker. Prices for personally supervised storage (available 5.30am-1am Mon-Sat; 6am-1am Sun) depend on the quantity and size of the items and vary from 30kr to 40kr per day.

Lost property

The main Copenhagen lost property office is:

Copenhagen Police
Slotsherrensvej 113, Vanløse (38 74 88 22). Train to Islev. **Open** 9am-2pm Mon, Wed, Fri; 9am-5.30pm Tue, Thur.

Airport

If you lose luggage or other possessions on a plane, contact the relevant airline or:

Copenhagen Air Services/Novia services
Copenhagen Airport (32 47 47 25). **Open** 8am-8pm daily.

Buses/trains

If you lose something on a bus, call HUR general information (36 13 14 15; 7am-9.30pm daily); if you lose it on a train or Metro train, phone the relevant terminus or the central S-tog information office (33 53 00 33; 7am-10pm daily).

Taxis

Call the taxi company. After a couple of days items will be transferred to the central lost property office (*see p229* **Police headquarters**).

Media

Newspapers & magazines

Most of the national newspapers in Denmark started out as pamphlets for political parties. Today they target a wider readership. But with their comparatively small readerships and minuscule pool of journalists (most from the same training course), Danish newspapers struggle to achieve a consistently high standard. Denmark also has its tabloid papers, which can be just as distasteful, sexist and enjoyable as those in the UK.

Berlingske Tidende
A conservative, right of centre broadsheet with decent coverage of Copenhagen. *Berlingske Tidende* is well designed and tries hard but can be slow with international news.

Børsen
Børsen keeps tabs on the latest stock market developments, economic predictions and the major players in the Danish financial world.

BT
A tabloid paper that lags a little way behind *Ekstrabladet* in the sleaze and celebrity stakes and so in recompense places an emphasis on football and other sports.

Ekstrabladet
The most controversial of the Danish tabloids, *Ekstrabladet* relies heavily on celebrity sleaze, opinionated editorials and endless reactionary campaigning. As well known in Denmark as *The Sun* in the UK.

Information
Information was founded as 'the newspaper of the Danish Resistance' on the night of Denmark's liberation at the end of World War II. Today

the paper has no significant political leaning, its objective being to give its readers important background information on current affairs. Weighty, dry but respected.

Jyllandsposten

The most royalist and conservative of the national papers.

Kristeligt Dagblad

A Christian publication that focuses on questions concerning ethics, belief and religion.

Politiken

Once the paper of the Social-Liberal Party, *Politiken* now focuses on cultural issues. Strong on Copenhagen matters.

English-language press

Most of the major British and American newspapers are available from one or two outlets on Strøget, or the newsagents in Central Station, Illum and Magasin du Nord department stores.

Copenhagen Post

www.cphpost.dk
This weekly paper features some Danish news and Copenhagen listings in English.

Copenhagen This Week

Misleadingly titled monthly tourist board listings mag.

Radio

Copenhagen's biggest radio stations are all run by the state-owned Danmarks Radio (the Danish Broadcasting Corporation), which has a fine tradition of high quality programming. It's also possible to pick up a number of foreign radio stations from Sweden and Germany. Radio news in English is broadcast on weekdays at 10.30am, 5.10pm and 10pm on Radio Denmark International (1062 Mhz), which also offers a telephone news service (70 26 80 80) and a good website at www.dr.dk/news.

P1

90.8 Mhz
Typical broadcasts include a good range of radio plays, current affairs magazines, documentaries and news. Broadcasts from 6am to midnight.

P2 & P4/ Københavns Radio

96.5 Mhz
Broadcasting through the night (6.50pm-6.10am), P2 is mainly a classical music station, but also plays jazz from time to time. The same frequency is occupied by P4/ Københavns Radio during the day (6.10am-6.30pm), which features pop music (including the Danish pop

charts), listeners' requests, phone-ins, local news and traffic reports.

P3

93.9 Mhz
Targeted mainly at Danish youth, this station features young comedians and DJs who play pop and chart music during the day, with programmes offering more alternative content during the night. Broadcasts 24 hours a day.

POPFM

104.4 Mhz
Plays pop 24 hours a day.

The Voice

104.9 Mhz
A 24-hour chart/dance music station, the Voice is the only commercial station with more than a million listeners a week. Some of the station's DJs also play at Copenhagen's nightclubs.

Television

Founded as a public service organisation and funded by individual licence fees, Danmarks Radio still dominates the television scene (it actually enjoyed a monopoly on radio and TV broadcasting until 1986). However, over recent years, the old stations (DR1 and DR2) have been steadily losing ground to younger, more challenging, commercial

Weather report

	Average daily max temperature (°C/°F)	Average nightly temperature (°C/°F)	Daily hours of sunshine	Monthly rainfall (mm/inches)
Jan	2/36	-2/28	1	49/1.9
Feb	2/36	-3/27	2	39/1.5
Mar	5/41	-1/30	4	32/1.3
Apr	11/52	3/37	6	38/1.5
May	16/61	8/46	8	42/1.7
June	20/68	11/52	9	47/1.9
July	22/72	14/57	8	71/2.8
Aug	21/70	14/57	7	66/2.6
Sept	18/64	11/52	6	62/2.4
Oct	12/54	7/45	3	59/2.3
Nov	7/45	3/37	1	48/1.9
Dec	4/39	1/34	1	49/1.9

Directory

broadcasting companies that are not subject to any public service obligations.

DR1
The first television channel in Denmark, DR1's strengths include news and current affairs, documentaries, and children's and youth programming.

DR2
The little sister to DR1 and a slightly more alternative watch.

TV2
Despite introducing morning television and *Wheel of Fortune* to the Danes, TV2 pretty much resembles DR1, principally because TV2 is also a licence-financed station, with similar public service obligations.

TV3/TV3+
Targeting young people and families with kids, TV3 is a commercial station that aims to provide quality light entertainment, with Danish soap operas and docu-soaps among the most popular programmes. Its sister channel TV3+ is the leading station for sport.

Kanal 5
Most of the programmes on Kanal 5 (previously known as TVDanmark1) are American sitcoms and soap operas, though it occasionally broadcasts Danish docu-soaps.

Money

The Danish *krone* (crown) is divided into 100 *øre*. There are coins in denominations of 25 *øre*, 50 *øre* (both copper), one *krone*, two *kroner*, five *kroner* (all three silver in colour, the latter two with a hole), ten *kroner* and 20 *kroner* (brass). Notes come in 50, 100, 200, 500 and 1,000 *kroner* denominations. In this guide the abbreviation 'kr' is used, though you may also see 'DKK' or 'KR' before the figure in question.

At the time of writing, £1 = 11.05kr; €1 = 7.45kr; US$1 = 5.94kr, but this of course is likely to have changed.

There is no limit to the amount of foreign or Danish currency you can bring into the country, though you

may be required to explain the source of amounts over 100,000kr.

ATMs/cash machines

The majority of Danish banks have ATMs, which offer a convenient way of withdrawing Danish kroner on a credit or debit card. Most major cards are accepted.

Banks & bureaux de change

Banks in Denmark as elsewhere do not keep long hours, tending to open from 10am to 4pm on weekdays, with late opening until 5.30pm on Thursdays. Some in the centre of town (on Amager Torv, for instance) have longer hours and open on Saturdays. Most will change foreign currency and travellers' cheques, as will the plentiful bureaux de change. There are also a number of machines scattered throughout the city that will exchange foreign currency for kroner.

Lost or stolen credit cards

Emergency numbers:
American Express 33 11 25 00 (8am-5pm); 80 01 00 21 (5pm-8am).
Diners 36 73 73 73 (24hrs).
MasterCard/Eurocard 80 01 60 98 (24hrs).
Visa 80 01 85 88 (24hrs).
For other credit cards, call the 24-hour **Danish PBS Hotline** (44 89 25 00).

Money transfers

Usually, Den Danske Bank can make money transfers within 12 hours. Ask for a so-called 'swift address' and a registration number, which you pass on to the local bank in your home country. Then contact your local bank concerning the amount of money you wish to transfer.

Transactions normally cost around 150kr. Den Danske Bank has a number of branches in Copenhagen, including:

Den Danske Bank
Frederiksberggade 1, Strøget (45 12 09 00). **Open** 10am-4pm Mon-Wed, Fri; 10am-5.30pm Thur. **Map** p250 O12.

Opening hours

The majority of shops in Copenhagen open from 10am to 6pm or 7pm on weekdays and from 10am to 2pm or 5pm on Saturday, with only bakers, florists and souvenir shops open on Sunday. Office hours are usually 9am to 4pm from Monday to Friday.

Police & security

Crime is not really an issue as far as tourists are concerned, though from time to time there are stories of confidence tricksters pretending to be policemen and, of course, the very entertaining card sharps in Strøget. Otherwise Copenhagen is generally safe compared with other cities in Europe. There are places where you should exercise caution late at night, however. These include side streets in Vesterbro, and the area around Rådhuspladsen stretching part of the way up Strøget – drunken violence is fairly common here at night. The area behind Central Station stretching up much of Istedgade is a hangout for alcoholics and junkies, but they are peaceable in the main. In the unlikely event that you are a victim of crime, contact the Danish Police immediately. In emergencies, call **112** (free of charge). Open 24 hours, the Police HQ can direct you to your nearest station. These include Central Station (33 15 38 01; map p250 P11); Halmtorvet 20, Vesterbro (33 25 14 48; map p250 Q10) and

Store Kongensgade 100 (33 93 14 48; map p249 L16).

Police headquarters
Polititorvet (33 14 14 48). **Open** 24hrs. **Map** p250 Q13.

Postal services

Most post offices open from 10am to 5.30pm Monday to Friday, and from 10am or 11am until noon or 2pm on Saturday. Larger branches have fax facilities. Copenhagen's largest post office is listed below.

Central Station Post Office
Central Station (80 20 70 30/www.postdanmark.dk). **Open** 8am-9pm Mon-Fri; 10am-4pm Sat, Sun. **Map** p250 P11.

Postal rates

In addition to the rates below, express delivery services are also available. Contact any post office for details. Letters up to 50 grammes cost 4.75kr to Denmark, 7kr to Europe and 8kr to other countries; letters up to 100 grammes cost 8kr to Denmark, 14kr to the rest of Europe and 20kr to other countries.

Poste restante

Mail can be received care of 'Poste Restante' and collected from any post office in Denmark; it will normally not be kept for a period of longer than two weeks.

If Poste Restante mail isn't addressed to a specific post office, it will be sent to the main post office at Central Station (*see above*).

Express delivery services

Budstikken is a private courier company approved by the public mail services. Call 33 26 90 00 (24 hours) for information.

Public holidays

The following are public holidays in Denmark:
New Year's Day (Nytårsdag; 1 Jan).
Maundy Thursday (Skærtorsdag; 5 Apr 2007; 20 Mar 2008).
Good Friday (Langfredag; 6 Apr 2007; 21 Mar 2008).
Easter Sunday (Påske; 8 Apr 2007; 23 Mar 2008).
Easter Monday (2.påskedag; 9 Apr 2007; 24 Mar 2008).
Common Prayer Day (Stor Bededag; 4 May 2007; 18 Apr 2008).
Ascension Day (Kristi Himmelfartsdag; 17 May 2007; 1 May 2008).
Whit Sunday (1.pinsedag; 27 May 2007; 11 May 2008).
Whit Monday (2.pinsedag; 28 May 2007; 12 May 2008).
Constitution Day (Grundlovsdag; 5 June; from noon).
Christmas (Jule; 24-26 Dec).
Most businesses and banks close on public holidays. School summer holidays in Denmark run earlier than many other countries, from about the third week in June to the second in August, and schools also take a week off in February, in mid October and over Christmas and New Year. Many Danes take their main summer holidays in the first three weeks of July.

Public toilets

You shouldn't be caught short while visiting as there is no shortage of public toilets in Copenhagen. Even better, most are clean and free to use.

Religion

There are close ties between Church and State in Denmark and the Constitution declares the Evangelical Lutheran Church to be the national church. The Danish Folkekirken (the People's Church) is funded by church members through 'Church Tax', but in spite of the fact that most Danes (87 per cent) are members, a minority of Copenhageners would call themselves religious. While

churches are often empty on Sundays, and are mainly used at Christmas, Easter, or for private arrangements such as weddings, there appears to be something of a revival of interest in the Church in Denmark. The second largest religious community in Denmark is Muslim, the third Roman Catholic. The following churches hold services in English.

Great Synagogue
Krystalgade 12 (33 12 88 68). **Services** 6.45am Mon, Thur; 7am Tue, Wed, Fri; 9am Sat; 8am Sun. **Map** p251 M13.
Orthodox Judaism.

St Alban's Church
Churchill Parken, Langelinie (39 62 77 36). **Services** *Holy Communion* 10.30am Wed; 9am, 10.30am Sun. **Map** p249 J18.
Anglican.

Sakrementskirken
Nørrebrogade 27, Nørrebro (35 35 68 25). **Services** 10am Sun (Danish); 6pm Sun (English). **Map** p246 J10.
Roman Catholic.

Sankt Annæ Kirke
Dronning Elisabeths Allé 3 (32 58 41 02). **Bus** 5A. **Services** 5pm Sat, Sun. Roman Catholic.

Smoking

Danes still can't survive without their cigarettes and smoking is permitted in nearly all cafés and restaurants. The authorities make a half-hearted attempt to outlaw it in public buildings, but many Danes stubbornly ignore the 'No Smoking' signs out of principle. The fact that there are still smoking carriages on trains should give you some idea of how determined many Danes are to resist the pressures of European bureaucracy on this issue.

Studying

Danish institutions for higher education have a friendly and open-minded policy towards international students.

Directory

Exchange programmes provide links between Danish universities and their international counterparts and in recent years exchanges have increasingly been developed through programmes such as Socrates/Erasmus, Lingua and Tempus which are all supported by the largess of the European Union and its unfortunate taxpayers. Some of the institutions also have summer schools and the largest universities and colleges have their own international offices.

For more information on courses, contact the individual institutions.

Universities/colleges

Copenhagen's universities and colleges offer a variety of qualifications over a broad spectrum of subjects. The **University of Copenhagen** (35 32 26 26, www.ku.dk) is the city's flagship establishment. Founded in 1479, it is Denmark's oldest educational institution, and, with 35,000 students, it can also lay claim to being the largest.

The city has two business schools, **Copenhagen Business School** (38 15 38 15, www.cbs.dk) and **Niels Brock College** (33 41 91 00, www.brock.dk), which combine expert tutoring with strong ties to the wider Danish business community.

Det Kongelige Danske Kunstakademi (33 74 46 00, www.kunstakademiet.dk), the Royal Academy of Fine Arts, offers a variety of fine art courses and tutoring, as well as incorporating the **School of Architecture** (32 68 60 00, www.karch.dk), the excellent **Danish Film School** (32 68 64 00, www.filmskolen.dk), the **National Drama School** (32 83 61 00, www.teater skolen.dk) and the **Rhythmic Music Conservatory** (32 68 67 00, www.rmc.dk).

Det Kongelige Danske Musikkonservatorium (33 69 22 69, www.dkdm.dk), the Royal Danish Music Conservatory, concentrates, as you might have guessed, on classical music training.

International offices

Copenhagen Business School
International Office, Porcelaenshaven 26, 2000 Frederiksberg (38 15 30 06/www.cbs.dk). Bus 29, 4A. **Open** 9am-noon, 1-3.30pm Mon-Fri.

Roskilde Universitetscenter
International Office, Bygning 4, 1, Postbox 260, 4000 Roskilde (46 74 20 58). **Open** 9.30am-12.30pm, 1.30-3pm Mon-Thur.
The international office has the overall responsibility for international activities at Roskilde University. These include programmes like ERASMUS.

University of Copenhagen
International Office, Fiolstræde 24, 1, 1010 København K (35 32 26 26/www.ku.dk/international). **Open** noon-3pm Mon-Fri. **Map** p251 M13.
Offers advice to exchange students at the University of Copenhagen on practical as well as academic matters, including admission, course registration, housing and contacts with other universities.

Other organisations

AFS Interkultur (American Field Service)
Nordre Fasanvej 111, 2000 Frederiksberg (38 34 33 00/ www.afs.dk). Bus 2A, 4A. **Open** 10am-3pm Mon-Fri.
AFS is an international, voluntary organisation that provides educational exchange programmes for people between 15 and 30 years.

STS High School & Au Pair
Larsbjornstræde 3 (33 37 71 67/www.sts.dk). **Open** 9am-4.30pm Mon-Fri. **Map** p251 N13.
STS provides personal and/or academic education at high schools, language schools or for au pairs. You have to be between ten and 26 years of age, depending on which programme you want to follow.

Language classes

AOF sprogcentret København
Gadelandet 18, 2700 Brønshøj (38 26 23 40/www.aof-sprogcenter.dk). Bus 2A, 5A. **Open** *Phone enquiries* 9am-noon, 1-2.30pm Mon-Thur; 9am-noon Fri. **No credit cards**.
Offers courses at all levels, including intensive courses in Danish.
Other locations: *Østerbro; Lyngbyvej 32F, København Ø (39 16 82 10).* **Open** *phone enquiries* 10am-3pm. *Amager; Lyongade 25, København S (32 86 03 00).* **Open** *phone enquiries* 10am-3pm.

Berlitz
Vimmelskaftet 42A, Strøget (70 21 50 10/www.berlitz.com). **Open** 8am-9pm Mon-Fri. **No credit cards**. **Map** p251 N13.
Courses are taught by native teachers; most are tailored to individual needs.

Libraries

Hovedbiblioteket
Krystalgade 15 (33 73 60 60/ www.kkb.bib.dk). **Open** *Apr-Sept* 10am-7pm Mon-Fri; 10am-2pm Sat. *Oct-Mar* 10am-7pm Mon-Fri; 10am-4pm Sat. **Map** p251 M13.
The central library has international newspapers and magazines in English, phone and fax facilities, and colour photocopying.

Det Kongelige Bibliotek
Søren Kierkegaards Plads 1 (33 47 47 47/www.kb.dk). **Open** *Information & lending department* 10am-5pm Mon-Fri; 10am-2pm Sat. *General Reading Rooms* 9am-9pm Mon-Fri; 9am-4pm Sat. *Newspapers & periodicals* 9am-9pm Mon-Fri; 9am-4pm Sat. *Research Reading Room* 9am-9pm Mon-Fri; 9am-4pm Sat. *Exhibitions* 10am-7pm Mon-Fri; 10am-5pm Sat. **Admission** free. **Map** p251 P15.
The Royal Library on Slotsholmen is Denmark's national library, but the building also serves as a general research centre, a cultural centre and a meeting place.

Telephones

Like most public services in Denmark, the phone system is efficient and simple to use. Danish phone numbers have eight digits and there are no area codes.

International codes

The international dialling code for Denmark is 45. So, to dial Copenhagen from outside Denmark, dial 00 45 and then the eight-digit number.

To call abroad from Denmark, dial 00 followed by the country access code, the area code (minus the initial 0, if there is one), and then the local number. The international code for the UK is 44; 1 for the US/Canada; 353 for Ireland; 61 for Australia.

Mobile phones

Denmark is part of the worldwide GSM network, so compatible mobile phones should work without any problems. If your phone is not GSM compatible, contact your service provider. Below are two central mobile phone shops linked to Denmark's main service providers:

Sonofon
Købmagergade 57 (72 12 44 40/ www.sonofon.dk). **Map** p251 M13.

Telia
Amagertorv 14, Strøget (80 40 44 44). **Map** p251 N14.

Operator services

For **directory enquiries**, call 118 (domestic) or 113 (international). For **operator assistance**, call 80 60 40 10. You will be charged only if you are connected.

Public phones

You'll find both card- and coin-operated phones in Denmark. **Cards** (*telekort*) come in denominations of 30, 50 and 100kr and can be used for both local and international calls; they are available from kiosks and post offices.

Telegrams

You can no longer send telegrams from Danish post offices.

Time & dates

Denmark observes Central European Time, one hour ahead of Greenwich Mean Time, and six hours ahead of Eastern Standard Time. Danes use the 24-hour clock.

When writing dates, Danes follow the day with the month, so 7 January 2008 will be written 7/1/08.

Tipping

Service is often included on restaurant and hotel bills, so any further tips should only be given for unusually good service. It's not uncommon, however, to round up a bill.

Tourist information

In addition to the resources available at the tourist offices below, the website **www.aok.dk** is an indispensable source of information on festivals, arts and entertainment in Copenhagen as well as good places to eat and drink.

Danish Tourist Board
Islands Brygge 43 (32 88 99 00/ www.visitdenmark.com).
If you plan to travel beyond the capital, check out the DTB's state-of-the-art website – it's very useful for both practical advice and news about forthcoming attractions. The DTB doesn't encourage personal callers.

UseIt
Rådhusstræde 13, 1466 Copenhagen K (33 73 06 20/fax 33 73 06 49/ www.useit.dk). **Open** Mid Sept-mid June 11am-4pm Mon-Wed; 11am-6pm Thur; 11am-2pm Fri. Mid June-mid Sept 9am-7pm daily. **Map** p251 O13.
Aimed primarily at youthful visitors to the city, UseIt is an excellent resource centre that can supply not just printed info, but can also book rooms, hold mail and store luggage. The website is also well worth a look.

Wonderful Copenhagen Tourist Information Bureau
Vesterbrogade 4A (70 22 24 42/ www.visitcopenhagen.dk). **Open** Oct-Apr 9am-4pm Mon-Fri; 9am-2pm Sat.

May, June, Sept 9am-6pm Mon-Sat. *July, Aug* 9am-8pm Mon-Sat; 10am-6pm Sun. **Map** p250 O11.
The official Copenhagen tourist office is located opposite the Radisson SAS Royal Hotel, across the road from Tivoli. It has a wealth of information on the city's attractions as well as a small souvenir shop, and offers a free accommodation booking service.

Travel advice

For up-to-date information on travel to Denmark – including the latest news on safety and security, health issues, local laws and customs – contact your home country government's department of foreign affairs. Most have useful websites.
Australia *www.dfat.gov.au/travel*
Canada *www.voyage.gc.ca*
New Zealand
www.mft.govt.nz/travel
Republic of Ireland
www.irlgov.ie/iveagh
UK *www.fco.gov.uk/travel*
USA *http://travel.state.gov*

Tax refund

Tax on goods (MOMS) in Denmark is levied at 25 per cent. Non-EU residents are entitled to claim back up to 19 per cent of the total price of any item bought in the country (providing that the purchase exceeds 300kr and that Denmark is their final EU destination before returning home). Visitors should ask shops to issue a Global Refund Cheque for each purchase. These should then be stamped by Customs (in Copenhagen Airport's Terminal 3) before you check in your luggage, and then handed in at the Global Refund desk in the Transit Hall (6.30am-10pm daily). For further information, contact Global Refund Danmark (32 52 55 66/fax 32 52 55 61/ www.globalrefund.com).

Visas/passports

Citizens of EU countries (outside Scandinavia) require a national ID card or passport valid for the duration of their stay in order to enter Denmark for tourist visits of up to three months. Tourists can stay in the country for another three months if they are working or applying for a job. For stays lasting more than six months you need a residency visa. US citizens require a passport valid only for the duration of their stay, but citizens of Canada, Australia and New Zealand require passports valid for three months beyond the last day of their visit. South African citizens need to apply for a tourist visa prior to leaving South Africa.

Weights & measures

Denmark uses the metric system. Decimal points are indicated by commas, while thousands are defined by full stops. In this guide we have listed all measurements in both metric and imperial.

When to go

Considering its northerly location, the climate in Denmark isn't particularly severe. In midsummer it hardly gets dark at all and the evening light can last well past 11pm. However, winter is cold, wet and dark and some tourist attractions are closed. Tivoli, for example, is closed for most of the winter aside from Halloween and its Christmas Market. Spring kicks off in late April, but can take a while to warm up. May and June are usually fresh and bright, with reasonable temperatures. Summer peak season is in July and August, when Copenhagen offers plenty of festivals and open-air events and the weather is probably as good as it ever gets in Scandinavia. Cruise ships bring in plenty of visitors but on the other hand July is when all of Copenhagen

migrates to the seaside for its summer holidays, so the city can seem quieter and many top restaurants and some other businesses are closed.

Women

Denmark is a country famously committed to equal opportunities for all citizens and a lot of effort has been made to achieve equal rights for women.

Women visitors to Denmark are very unlikely to encounter any harrassment problems. Copenhagen is one of the world's safest cities, even after dark, although, of course, remain vigilant.

Kvindehuset (Women's House)
Gothersgade 37 (33 14 28 04/ www.kvindehus.dk). **Open** 1-5.30pm Mon-Fri. **Map** p247 L14.
A cultural centre for women. Recycling of clothes, lesbian films, a choir, an artists' group, folk dances, social events and debates are held.

KVINFO
Christians Brygge 3 (33 13 50 88/ www.kvinfo.dk). **Open** *Sept-June* 10am-6pm Mon; 11am-5pm Tue-Thur. *July, Aug* 1-5pm Mon-Thur. **Map** p251 P15.
The Danish Centre for Information on Women and Gender has many resources relating to women's issues, including a library and information centre for gender studies.

Working in Copenhagen

Even though most people in Denmark speak English, and many companies use English as a working language, there is still a deeply ingrained prejudice in the workplace against those who are not fluent in Danish. However, the current unemployment rate is very low so there are always some vacancies open to foreigners, particularly in unskilled fields such as cleaning, catering and hotels.

EURES is a database of job vacancies throughout

the EU and contains useful information about working conditions throughout Europe.

Det Danske Kulturinstitut
Vartov, Farvergade 27L, 1463 Copenhagen K (33 13 54 48/ www.dankultur.dk). Bus 2A, 5A. **Open** 9am-5pm Mon-Thur; 9am-2pm Fri.
The Institute publishes a range of literature about the country and arranges job exchange programmes for a number of professions.

Work permits

All EU citizens can obtain a work permit in Denmark; non-EU citizens must apply for a work permit abroad and hand in the application to a Danish embassy or consular representation. The rules for obtaining work permits vary for different jobs; contact the Danish Immigration Service:

Udlændingestyrelsen
Ryesgade 53, 2100 Copenhagen Ø (35 36 66 00/fax 35 36 19 16/ www.nyidanmark.dk). **Open** 8am-3.30pm Mon-Thur; 9am-3pm Fri.

Useful addresses

The EU has a website (www.europa.eu.int/citizens rights) and helpline (00 800 6789 10 11) providing general information on your rights and useful telephone numbers and addresses in your home country. It also holds specific information on the rules for recognition of diplomas, your rights on access to employment and rights of residence and social security.

For general information about the **Danish tax system**, take a look at the Skatteministeriet (Danish Ministry of Taxation) website (www.skm.dk) or contact SKAT (Customs and tax dministration; www.skat.dk) with more specific questions.

SKAT
Sluseholmen 8B, 2450 Copenhagen SV (72 22 18 18/www.skat.dk). **Open** *Phone enquiries* 8.30am-4pm Mon-Wed; 8.30am-6pm Thur; 8.30am-2pm Fri.

Directory

Vocabulary

If, by any chance, you have a good knowledge of Swedish or Norwegian, you should be able to understand Danish well enough to get by. And if you are fluent in German, you may also recognise a fair percentage of words. For the rest of us, however, Danish is mostly impenetrable.

The problem comes not with the grammar, which is comparatively simple, but with the pronunciation, which is full of its own idiosyncrasies, particularly the seemingly endless glottal stops and swallowing of parts of words. And be warned, Copenhageners are the worst offenders in Denmark – they talk the fastest too. But do not fear, the majority of Danes have excellent English and it's tempting for visitors not to bother to try to learn any Danish at all. But an attempt to learn a few basics is always appreciated.

Here's a brief guide to pronunciation and some useful basic words and phrases.

Vowels

a	as in 'rather' or as in 'pat'
å, u(n)	as in 'or'
e(g), e(j)	as in 'shy'
e, æ	as in 'set'
i	as in 'be'
ø	a short 'er' sound
o	as in 'rot' or as in 'do'
o(v)	a short 'ow', as in 'cow'
u	as in 'bull' or as in 'do'
y	a long, hybrid of 'ee' and 'oo'

Consonants

sj	as in 'shot'
ch	as in 'shot'
c	as in 'send', but as in 'key' before a, o, u and consonants
(o)d	as the 'th' in 'those'
j	as the 'y' in 'year'
g	as in 'got', when before vowels
h	as in 'heart'
k	as in 'key'
b	as in 'bag'
r	a short guttural 'r' (less guttural after a vowel)
w	a 'v' sound

Useful words/phrases

yes	ja, jo ('yer', 'yo')
no	nej ('ny')
please	vær så god ('verser-go'), vær så venlig ('verser venlee')
thank you	tak ('tack')
hello (formal)	goddag ('godday')
hello (informal)	hej ('hi')
I understand	jeg forstår ('yie for-stor')
I don't understand	jeg forstår ikke ('yie for-stor icker')
do you speak English?	taler du engelsk ('tarler doo engelsk')?
excuse me (sorry)	undskyld ('unsgull')
go away!	forsvind! ('for-svin')

indgang	entrance
udgang	exit
åben	open
lukket	closed
toiletter	toilets (herrer: men; damer: women)
today	i dag
tonight	i aften/i nat
tomorrow	i morgen
yesterday	i går

Monday	mandag
Tuesday	tirsdag
Wednesday	onsdag
Thursday	torsdag
Friday	fredag
Saturday	lørdag
Sunday	søndag

January	januar
February	februar
March	marts
April	april
May	maj
June	juni
July	juli
August	august
September	september
October	oktober
November	november
December	december

0	nul
1	en
2	to
3	tre
4	fire
5	fem
6	seks
7	syv
8	otte
9	ni
10	ti
20	tyve
30	tredive
40	fyrre
50	halvtreds
60	tres
70	halvfjerds
80	firs
90	halvfems
100	hundrede
1,000	tusind
1,000,000	million

Food & drink glossary

æble	apple
æg	egg
ærter	peas
appelsin	orange
banan	banana
brød	bread
bønner	beans
champignon	mushroom
chokolade	chocolate
citron	lemon
dampet	steamed
eddike	vinegar
fadøl	draught beer
fisk	fish
fløde	cream
forel	trout
frisk	fresh
frugt	fruit
grilleret	grilled
gryderet	stew
grøn bønne	green bean
grøntsager	vegetables
gulerødder	carrots
hvidløg	garlic
is	ice-cream/ice
jordbær	strawberry
kaffe	coffee
kage	cake
kål	cabbage
kartoffel	potato
kød	meat
kogt	boiled
kold	cold
kylling	chicken
laks	salmon
lamme	lamb
løg	onion
marineret	marinated
mælk	milk
nødder	nuts
oksekød	beef
øl	beer
olie	oil
ost	cheese
ovnstegt	roasted
peber	pepper
pocheret	poached
pommes frites	fries/chips
pølse	hot dog
ris	rice
røget	smoked
rå	raw
sennep	mustard
sild	herring
skinke	ham
smør	butter
stegt	fried
sukker	sugar
supper	soup
svinekød	pork
te	tea
torsk	cod
vand	water
varm	warm, hot

Directory

Further Reference

Books

Non-fiction

Christianson, JR *On Tycho's Island: Tycho Brahe and His Assistants, 1570-1601.*
Biography of the famous astronomer.
Dyrbe, Helen, Steven Harris & Thomas Golzen *Xenophobe's Guide to the Danes.*
Irreverent dissection of the Danes.
Hornshøj-Møller, Stig *A Short History of Denmark.*
Authoritative summary of the country's past from the Stone Age to the present day.
Jones, Gwyn *A History of the Vikings.*
A readable account of the not-so-vicious Vikings and their world.
Levine, Ellen *Darkness over Denmark: The Danish Resistance and the Rescue of the Jews.*
The remarkable story of the exodus of Danish Jews to Sweden during the war.
Monrad, Kasper, Philip Conisbee & Bjarne Jornaes *The Golden Age of Danish Painting.*
The works of 17 painters from the first half of the 19th century.
Poole, Roger & Henrik Stangerup *A Kierkegaard Reader.*
The leading resource on Denmark's leading philosopher.
Pundik, Herbert *In Denmark It Could Not Happen: The Flight of the Jews to Sweden in 1943.*
Another account of the wartime escape of the Jews in Denmark.
Sawyer, Peter (ed) *The Oxford Illustrated History of the Vikings.*
An enjoyable survey of the Vikings.
Spangenburg, Ray & Diane K Moser *Niels Bohr: Gentle Genius of Denmark (Makers of Modern Science).*
An accessible analysis of the great Danish nuclear physicist.
Thomas, Alastair H & Stewart P Oakley *Historical Dictionary of Denmark.*
An invaluable reference book charting Denmark's cultural history.
Thoren, Victor E *The Lord of Uraniborg.*
Detailed biography of 16th-century astronomer Tycho Brahe.
Thurman, Judith *Isak Dinesen The Life of Karen Blixen.*
Authoritative biog of one of Denmark's finest prose writers, and most famous daughter.
Wullschlager, Jackie *HC Andersen: The Life of a Storyteller.*
Comprehensive biography of Denmark's top tale-teller.

Fiction

Andersen, Hans Christian *The Complete Fairy Tales.*
More than 150 of the great Dane's best-loved fairytales.
Blixen, Karen *Seven Gothic Tales.*
Blixen's darkly powerful masterpiece.
Frayn, Michael *Copenhagen.*
Extraordinary play based on the visit of the great German physicist Werner Heisenberg to his erstwhile mentor and friend Niels Bohr.
Høeg, Peter *Miss Smilla's Feeling for Snow.*
Bestselling thriller set in Copenhagen and Greenland.
Simpson, Jacqueline (ed) *Danish Legends.*
This collection comprises over 160 Danish folktales and legends.
Shakespeare, William *Hamlet.*
The bard's Danish blockbuster – possibly the greatest play ever written.
Tremain, Rose *Music and Silence.*
Beautifully written fictional account of the latter years of Christian IV.

Websites

AOK.dk
www.aok.dk/Copenhagen/ Visiting_Copenhagen
Extensive details of the major museums, galleries and sights.
Bed and Breakfast Denmark
www.bbdk.dk
While not as commonplace as it is Britain, B&Bs do exist and this is the place to start looking for them.
Copenhagen News
www.copenhagennews.com
Portal to news about Denmark appearing in the world's media.
Copenhagen Post
www.cphpost.dk
Weekly news in English from the Danish capital.
Copenhagen This Week
www.ctw.dk
Like the paper periodical it's named after this site somewhat misleadingly covers everything that's on in the city each month.
Danish Foreign Ministry
www.danmark.dk
An excellent site (Danish only) with bags of information on everything Danish.
Danish Youth Hostels Association
www.danhostel.dk
Search for a hostel and book online.
Danish Metereological Information
www.dmi.dk
Daily and long-term weather for Denmark, with an English version.

Danish Tourist Board
www.visitdenmark.dk
This beautifully presented national tourist board website has everything you could ever reasonably need to know about Denmark.
Denmark Hotels
www.danishhotels.dk
An online guide to all the star-rated hotels in Denmark.
DSB (Danish State Railways)
www.dsb.dk
Journey planner for train journeys within Denmark (in English).
Find a Grave
www.findagrave.com/country/27.html
Find out where the famous are buried in Copenhagen.
Hamlet Sommer
www.hamletsommer.dk
The website for the annual theatrical festival.
HUR
www.hur.dk
Comprehensive site on Copenhagen's efficient and excellent public transport system.
Metro
www.m.dk
The official website of Copenhagen's shiny new Underground system.
Malmö Tourist Board
www.malmo.se
Information on the sights, attractions, restaurants, festivals and accommodation in this charming city.
Øresund
www.visitoresund.info
An online guide to the strait that divides Denmark and Sweden, and the land on either side.
Rejseplanen
www.rejseplanen.dk
Useful site for journey planning within the city and country.
Skåne
www.skanetur.se
The website of the Swedish province of Skåne (Scania), now easily accessible via the Øresund Bridge.
Ungdomsinformation
www.ui.dk
Copenhagen City Council's site is full of helpful information for those planning a longer stay.
Use It
www.useit.dk
This excellent government-funded organisation offers a wealth of free information for young and budget-conscious visitors to Copenhagen.
Wonderful Copenhagen
www.visitcopenhagen.dk
The regularly updated official website of the city's efficient tourist authority offers detailed information about the city's hotels, restaurants, cafés, bars, galleries, theatres, theme parks and museums, and many useful links.

Directory

Index

Place of Interest and/or Entertainment	
Railway Station	
Park	
College/Hospital	
Pedestrian Streets	
Area Name . . . . AMAGER	
Metro Station . . . . **M**	

Maps

Copenhagen Overview

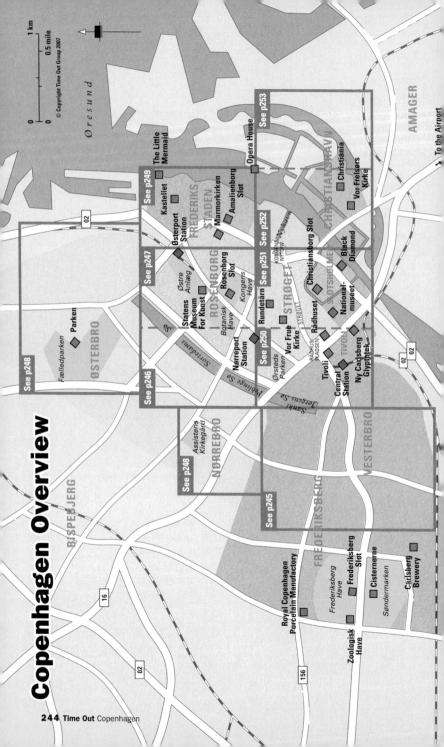

1 km
0.5 mile
© Copyright Time Out Group 2007

Øresund

AMAGER

To the Airport

See p253

Opera House

The Little Mermaid

See p249

Kastellet

Østerport Station

FREDERIKS STADEN

Marmorkirken

Amalienborg Slot

Christiania

Vor Frelsers Kirke

SLOTSHOLMEN

CHRISTIANSHAVN

Christiansborg Slot

Black Diamond

See p252

See p247

ROSENBORG

Rosenborg Slot

Kongens Have

KONGENS NYTORV

Østre Anlæg

Statens Museum For Kunst

Botanisk Have

See p251

Rundetårn

STRØGET

STRØGET

Nationalmuseet

Parken

Fælledparken

ØSTERBRO

See p248

BISPEBJERG

Sortedams Sø

See p246

Nørreport Station

See p250

Vor Frue Kirke

Rådhuset

Peblinge Sø

Ørsteds Parken

RÅDHUS PLADSEN

TIVOLI

02

02

Sankt Jørgens Sø

Tivoli

Central Station

Ny Carlsberg Glyptotek

02

Assistens Kirkegård

NØRREBRO

See p248

See p245

FREDERIKSBERG

MESTERBRO

16

02

156

Royal Copenhagen Porcelain Manufactory

Frederiksberg Have

Frederiksberg Slot

Cisternerne

Søndermarken

Zoologisk Have

Carlsberg Brewery

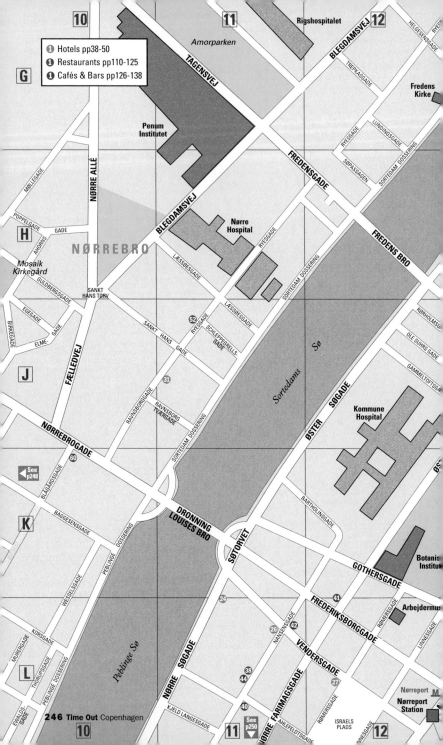

Rigshospitalet

HELGESENSGADE

RYES...

Amorparken

TAGENSVEJ

BLEGDAMSVEJ

❶ Hotels pp38-50
❶ Restaurants pp110-125
❶ Cafés & Bars pp126-138

Fredens
Kirke

TREPKASGADE

RYESGADE

LUNDINGSGADE

Penum
Institutet

FREDENSGADE

SØPASSAGEN

SORTEDAM DOSSERING

NØRRE ALLÉ

MØLLEGADE

POPPELGADE

BLEGDAMSVEJ

Nørre
Hospital

FREDENS BRO

AHORNS GADE

NØRREBRO

RYESGADE

LÆSSØESGADE

SORTEDAM DOSSERING

RØRHOLMSG...

Mosaik
Kirkegård

GULDBERGSGADE

SANKT
HANS TORV

LÆSSØESGADE

OLE SUHRS GADE

EGEGADE

52

RYESGADE

SCHLEPPEGRELLS-
GADE

GAMMELTOFTSGA...

BIRKEGADE

ELME-   GADE

SANKT   HANS   GADE

Sortedams   *Sø*

ØSTER   SØGADE

FÆLLEDVEJ

31

RAVNSBORGGADE

RAVNSBORG
TVÆRGADE

Kommune
Hospital

SORTEDAM DOSSERING

NØRREBROGADE

60

See
p248

BLÅGÅRDSGADE

BAGGESENSGADE

SORTEDAM DOSSERING

BARTHOLINSGADE

ØS...

DRONNING
LOUISES BRO

WESSELSGADE

PEBLINGE   DOSSERING

SØTORVET

GOTHERSGADE

Botanis
Institut

MURERGADE

KORSGADE

THORUPSGADE

PEBLINGE DOSSERING

Peblinge *Sø*

NØRRE   SØGADE

24

FREDERIKSBORGGADE

41

RØMERSGADE

Arbejdermus

LINNÉSGADE

EWALDS-
GADE

26

NANSENSGADE

42

VENDERSGADE

38

44

40

See
p250

NØRRE   FARIMAGSGADE

27

RØMERSGADE

Nørreport

Nørreport
Station

KJELD LANGESGADE

AHLEFELDTSGADE

ISRAELS
PLADS

NANSENSGADE

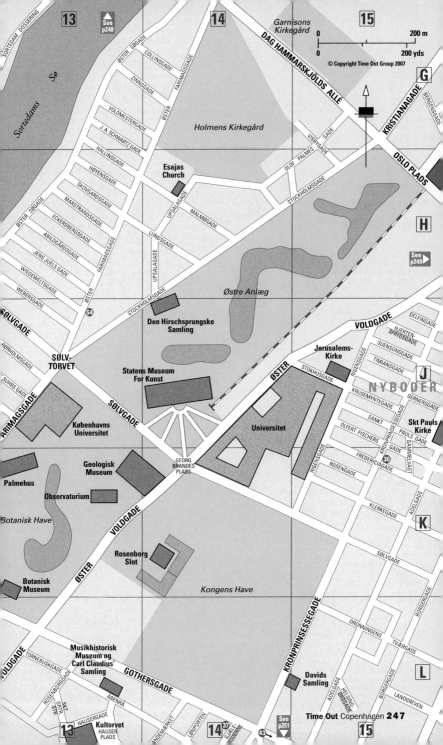

Garnisons
Kirkegård

200 m

200 yds

© Copyright Time Out Group 2007

G

SORTEDAM DOSSERING

ØSTER SØGADE

COLLINSGADE

FARIMAGSGADE

DAG HAMMARSKJÖLDS ALLE

KRISTIANAGADE

BERGENSGADE

Sortedams

Sø

ZINNSGADE

VOLDMESTERGADE

J. A. SCHWARTZ GADE

HALLINSGADE

HØYENSGADE

SKOVGAARDSGADE

MARSTRANDSGADE

ECKERSBERGSGADE

ABILDGÅRDSGADE

JENS JUELS GADE

WIEDEWELTSGADE

WEBERSGADE

ØSTER SØGADE

ØSTER

Holmens Kirkegård

VISBYGADE

OLOF PALMES GADE

STOCKHOLMSGADE

GADE

Esajas
Church

UPSALAGADE

MALMØGADE

LUNDSGADE

UPSALAGADE

OSLO PLADS

H

See
p248

See
p249

Østre Anlæg

SØLVGADE

RØRHOLMSGADE

SUHRS GADE

SØLV-
TORVET

STOCKHOLMSGADE

54

Den Hirschsprungske
Samling

VOLDGADE

Jerusalems-
Kirke

DELFINGADE

HJERTEN-
SFRYDSGADE

SUENSONSGADE

TIMIANSGADE

J

NYBODER

FARIMAGSGADE

PRIMAGSGADE

Københavns
Universitet

SØLVGADE

Statens Museum
For Kunst

ØSTER

STOKHUSGADE

RIGENSGADE

KRUSEMYNTEGADE

GERNERSGADE

KRONPRINSESSEGADE

SANKT

OLFERT FISCHERS

PAULS GADE

Skt Pauls
Kirke

GAMMELVAGT

Palmehus

Geologisk
Museum

Observatorium

Botanisk Have

VOLDGADE

Universitet

GEORG
BRANDES
PLADS

RIGENSGADE

FREDERICIAGADE

ROSENGADE

36

KLERKEGADE

ADELGADE

K

SØLVGADE

Botanisk
Museum

ØSTER

Rosenborg
Slot

Kongens Have

KRONPRINSESSEGADE

DRONNINGENS

ADELGADE

HELSINGØRSGADE

BORGERGADE

TVÆRGADE

L

VOLDGADE

TORNEBUSKGADE

Musikhistorisk
Museum og
Carl Claudius'
Samling

ROSENBORGGADE

SKT
GRTR
STR

GOTHERSGADE

ABENRÅ

Davids
Samling

LANDGREVEN

BORGERGADE

HAUSERGADE

Kultorvet

HAUSER
PLADS

LANDEMÆRKET

LINPORTEN

37
SKT.
KJ.E.
STRÆDERNE

See
p251

43

See
p251

Time Out Copenhagen **247**

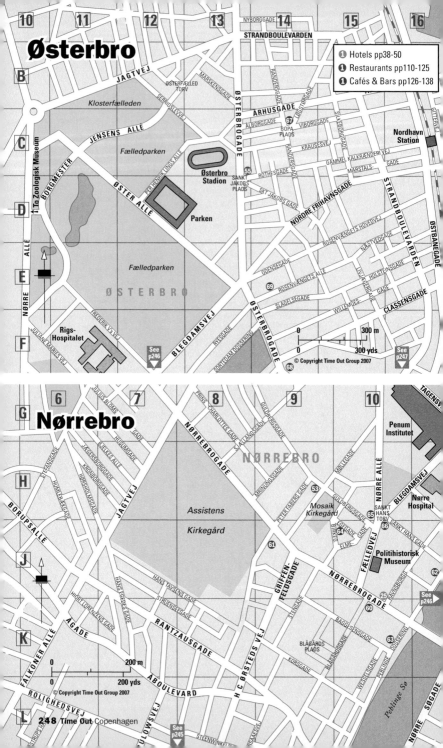

Østerbro

❶ Hotels pp38-50
❶ Restaurants pp110-125
❶ Cafés & Bars pp126-138

Klosterfælleden

JENSENS ALLE

Fælledparken

Østerbro Stadion

Parken

Fælledparken

ØSTERBRO

Rigs-Hospitalet

Nordhavn Station

Nørrebro

Nørrebro

Penum Institutet

Assistens Kirkegård

NØRREBRO

Mosaik Kirkegård

Nørre Hospital

Politihistorisk Museum

BLÅGÅRDS PLADS

Peblinge Sø

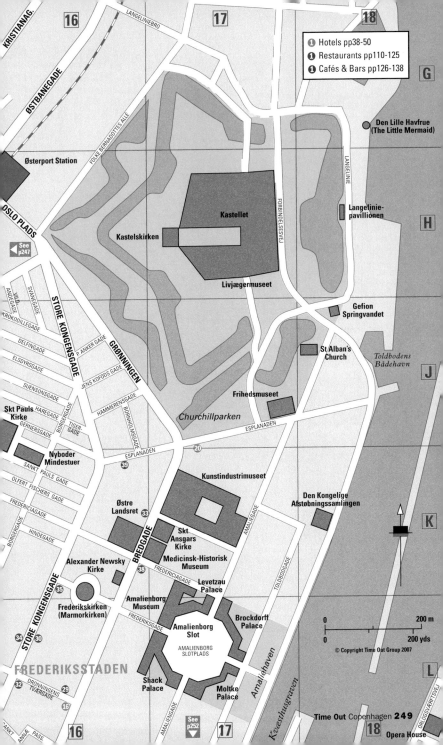

16
KRISTIANAG.
LANGELINIEBRO
17
18

ØSTBANEGADE

① Hotels pp38-50
① Restaurants pp110-125
① Cafés & Bars pp126-138

G

Den Lille Havfrue
(The Little Mermaid)

Østerport Station

FOLKE BERNADOTTES ALLÉ

OSLO PLADS

Kastellet

LANGELINIE

FORBINDELSESVEJ

Langelinie-
pavillionen

H

See
p247

Kastelskirken

VILLA
ANDEGADE

SVANEGADE

KROKODILLEGADE

P. ANKER GADE

STORE KONGENSGADE

Livjægermuseet

DELFINGADE

ELSDYRSGADE

GRØNNINGEN

JENS KOFODS GADE

SUENSONSGADE

HAREGADE

BORGERGADE

TIGER-
GADE

HAMMERENSGADE

BORNHOLMSGADE

Gefion
Springvandet

St Alban's
Church

Toldbodens
Bådehavn

J

Skt Pauls
Kirke

GERNERSGADE

Frihedsmuseet

SANKT PAULS GADE

Nyboder
Mindestuer

ESPLANADEN

Churchillparken

ESPLANADEN

OLFERT FISCHERS GADE

39

20

FREDERICIAGADE

Kunstindustrimuseet

BORGERGADE

HINDEGADE

Østre
Landsret

33

AMALIEGADE

Den Kongelige
Afstøbningssamlingen

Alexander Newsky
Kirke

BREDGADE

38

Skt
Ansgars
Kirke

Medicinsk-Historisk
Museum

FREDERICIAGADE

TOLDBODGADE

K

STORE KONGENSGADE

35

Frederikskirken
(Marmorkirken)

Amalienborg
Museum

Levetzau
Palace

34

30

FREDERIKSGADE

Amalienborg
Slot

Brockdorff
Palace

0   200 m

0   200 yds

© Copyright Time Out Group 2007

32

DRONNINGENS
TVÆRGADE

29

FREDERIKSSTADEN

AMALIENGADE

AMALIENHAVEN

AMALIEHAVEN

Kvæsthusgraven

L

SANKT
ANNÆ PASS

16

16

Shack
Palace

AMALIENBORG
SLOTSPLADS

See
p252

17

Moltke
Palace

18

Opera House

ORLOGSVÆRFTVEJ

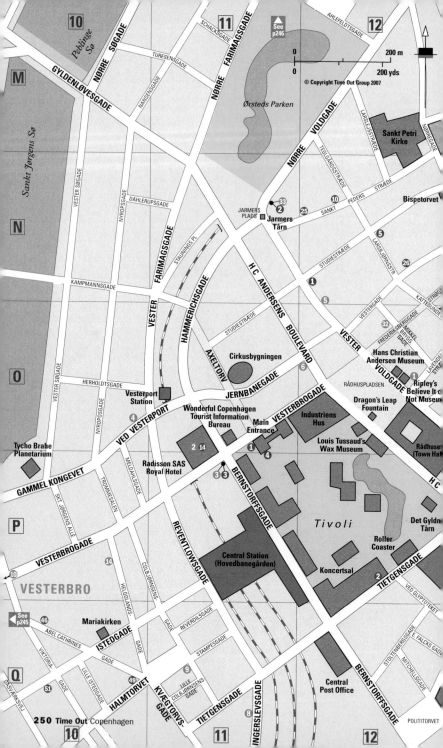

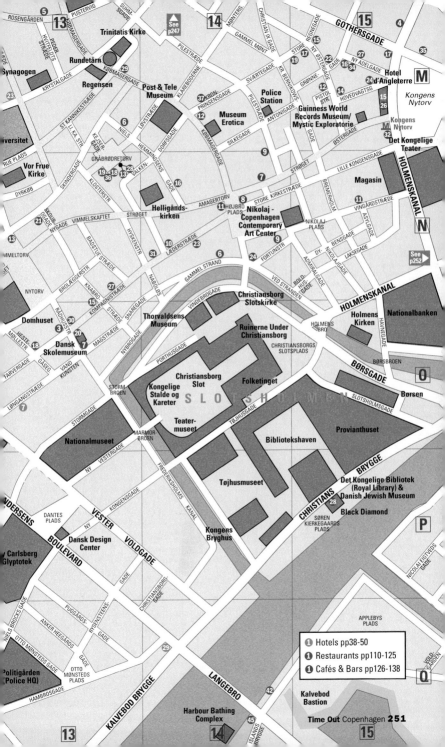

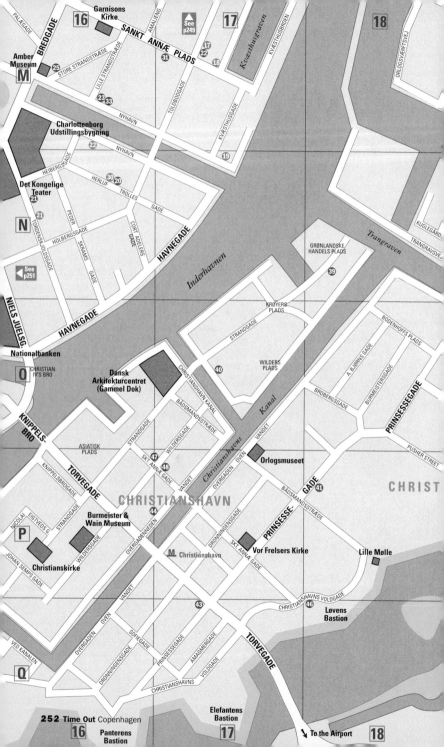

Garnisons Kirke

SANKT ANNÆ PLADS

AMALIENG

See p249

PALÆGADE

BREDGADE

Amber Museum

M

25

STORE STRANDSTRÆDE

LILLE STRANDSTRÆDE

31

17
22

18

TOLDBODGADE

Kvæsthusgraven

KVÆSTHUSBROEN

ØRLOGSVÆRFTSVEJ

23 33

NYHAVN

Charlottenborg Udstillingsbygning

22

NYHAVN

19

KVÆSTHUSGADE

HEIBERGSGADE

HERLUF

30 20

TROLLES

GADE

Det Kongelige Teater

21

21

PEDER

CORT ADELERS GADE

TORDENSKJOLDSGADE

HOLBERGSGADE

SKRAMS GADE

HAVNEGADE

Inderhavnen

Trangraven

TRANGRAVSVEJ

KUGLEGÅRD

See p251

GRØNLANDSKE HANDELS PLADS

39

BODENHOFFS PLADS

NIELS JUELSG.

HAVNEGADE

KRØYERS PLADS

STRANDGADE

A. BJØRNS GADE

BURMEISTERSGADE

Nationalbanken

Christianshavns Kanal

WILDERS PLADS

BROBERGSGADE

PRINSESSEGADE

CHRISTIAN IV'S BRO

O

Dansk Arkitekturcentret (Gammel Dok)

40

Oven

PUSHER STREET

KNIPPELS- BRO

BADSMANDSSTRÆDE

Kanal

Vandet

CHRIST

STRANDGADE

WILDERSGADE

47

SKT. ANNÆ GADE

Orlogsmuseet

BADSMANDSSTRÆDE

GADE

ASIATISK PLADS

TORVEGADE

48

OVERGADEN

PRINSESSE-

41

KNIPPELSBROGADE

CHRISTIANSHAVN

44

VANDET

Burmeister & Wain Museum

OVERGADEN NEDEN

DRONNINGENSGADE

SKT. ANNÆ GADE

Vor Frelsers Kirke

Lille Mølle

NICOLAI EIGTVEDS G.

STRANDGADE

WILDERSGADE

P

M Christianshavn

JOHAN SEMPS GADE

Christianskirke

OVEN

VANDET

43

SOFIEGADE

CHRISTIANSHAVNS VOLDGADE

46

Løvens Bastion

VED KANALEN

OVERGADEN

DRONNINGENSGADE

PRINSESSEGADE

AMAGERGADE

TORVEGADE

To the Airport

Q

CHRISTIANSHAVNS VOLDGADE

Elefantens Bastion

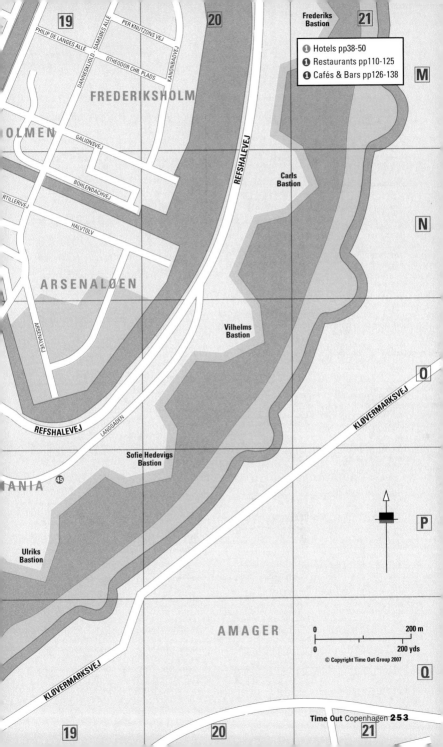

Frederiks
Bastion

❶ Hotels pp38-50
❶ Restaurants pp110-125
❶ Cafés & Bars pp126-138

M

PHILIP DE LANGES ALLÉ

PER KNUTZONS VEJ

SAMSØES ALLÉ

DANNESKIOLD.

KANONBADVEJ

OTHEODOR CHR. PLADS

FREDERIKSHOLM

OLMEN

GALIONSVEJ

BOHLENDACHVEJ

RTILLERIVEJ

HALVTOLV

REFSHALEVEJ

Carls
Bastion

N

ARSENALØEN

ARSENALVEJ

Vilhelms
Bastion

O

KLØVERMARKSVEJ

REFSHALEVEJ

LANGGADEN

Sofie Hedevigs
Bastion

ANIA   45

P

Ulriks
Bastion

AMAGER

0   200 m

0   200 yds

© Copyright Time Out Group 2007

Q

KLØVERMARKSVEJ

Street Index

Local Trains
& Metro

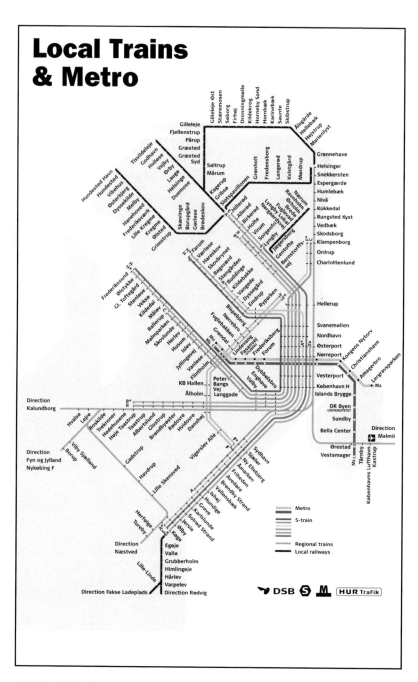